Colección Támesis

SERIE A: MONOGRAFÍAS, 264

THE SPANISH BALLAD IN THE GOLDEN AGE

Collections of traditional Spanish ballads were made in the early seventeenth century; some recorded directly from singers, others reworked by educated poets. So popular were these that Court poets composed ballads of their own. Most such poetry circulated in manuscript among a small coterie of wits and fellow poets, and it often contains references to contemporary events and people, gossip, sideswipes at institutions and individuals, and allusions to other writings of the time. The traditional popular associations of the ballad also led to many poets combining in their poems the language of the street alongside that of polite society and the schoolroom.

The purpose of this volume is to discuss some of the problems encountered by anglophone students and teachers of literature when they look at the Golden-Age ballad and to offer informed guidance on how such poems might be read.

David Pattison

THE SPANISH BALLAD IN THE GOLDEN AGE

Essays for David Pattison

Edited by

Nigel Griffin

Clive Griffin, Eric Southworth, and Colin Thompson

TAMESIS

First published 2008 by Tamesis, Woodbridge

ISBN 978-1-85566-172-1

Tamesis is an imprint of Boydell & Brewer Ltd
PO Box 9, Woodbridge, Suffolk IP12 3DF, UK
and of Boydell & Brewer Inc.
668 Mt Hope Avenue, Rochester, NY 14620, USA
website: www.boydellandbrewer.com

A CIP catalogue record for this book is available
from the British Library

This publication is printed on acid-free paper
from camera-ready copy provided by the editors

Printed in Great Britain by
CPI Antony Rowe, Chippenham, Wiltshire

CONTENTS

ABBREVIATIONS

Cov. Though the humanist Antonio de Nebrija produced a Spanish-Latin wordlist in 1495, the first substantive dictionary of Spanish was compiled by a royal chaplain, Sebastián de Covarrubias y (H)orozco (1539–1613), also famous as an emblematist. Entitled *Tesoro de la lengua castellana*, it was printed in 1611 in Madrid by Luis Sánchez. A manuscript in the writer's own hand (Biblioteca Nacional de España, MS 6159) shows that he continued to compile material for a supplement, or possibly a second edition of his dictionary, though he only got as far as the entry for Moisés. Another cleric, Benito Remigio Noydens, made some additions and a few corrections before reissuing it in 1674, again in two parts (Madrid: Melchor Sánchez). Modern editions, incorporating the 1674 changes, have been produced by Martín de Riquer (Barcelona: Horta, 1943), Felipe Maldonado (Madrid: Castalia, 1994), and Ignacio Arellano & Rafael Zafra (Pamplona: Universidad de Navarra & Vervuert, 2006). The last of these includes a CD version.

Aut. The *Diccionario de Autoridades* was the first dictionary produced by the Real Academia Española, founded in 1713. The Academy saw its role as conserving from decay and contamination the Spanish of the Siglo de Oro, which it believed represented the language at its finest. Its dictionary gives not only definitions of words but also examples of their use, many taken from writers of the period that interests us (see Candelas 2004). It was printed in six volumes (Madrid : Francisco del Hierro, 1726–39) and a three-volume facsimile was issued in 1979 by Gredos in the Biblioteca Románica Hispánica series directed by Dámaso Alonso. It is now also available online.

Abbreviations of Biblical references are to the books of the Vulgate, the Latin Bible prepared mainly by St Jerome in the late fourth century and the only version approved by the Church in Rome. Translations come from that monument to the English language, the Authorized Version of 1611.

In the chapters that follow, the poems of Góngora and Quevedo are identified by the numeration given them in the following modern editions :

G.   Luis de Góngora. *Obras completas*, 2 vols. Ed. Antonio Carreira. Biblioteca Castro. Madrid: Fundación José Antonio de Castro. I: *Poemas de autoría segura. Poemas de autenticidad probable.* 2000.

GR.   Luis de Góngora, *Romances*, 4 vols. Ed. Antonio Carreira. La Nueva Caja Negra 25. Barcelona: Quadrerns Crema. 1998.

Q.   Francisco de Quevedo, *Obra poética*. Ed. José Manuel Blecua. 4 vols. Madrid: Castalia. 1969–81.

PREFACE

Written evidence of European ballads appears from the fourteenth century onwards. Most were short, narrative poems handed down orally from generation to generation and sung at feasts, in town squares, or as repetitive chants to lighten humdrum communal tasks.[1] To this mix were added recollected or reworked fragments of heroic epic and romance originally composed by professional poets, accounts of events, past and present, and sentimental lyrics, all set to traditional tunes. Though scholarly interest in ballads has come and gone with periodic fluctuations of interest in such things as folksong, national character, and 'natural man', compositions like these continue to be sung in many parts of the world today, particularly where the conditions for oral performance have remained largely unchanged. This is popular poetry, not in the sense, as was once asserted, that it is poetry created by the people, but in the sense that it is they who have welcomed, preserved, and reworked it.[2]

Traditional Spanish ballads, or *romances viejos* as they are known ('old poems in the vernacular'), appear at much the same time as in the rest of Europe, though it has been suggested that they were being sung far earlier than that.[3] By the early sixteenth century the commercial potential of printing such ballads was widely recognized by publishers in Spain. Over the next 150 years, huge numbers of ballads, medieval and more recent, circulated in print throughout that country and its colonies in the New World, reinforcing the popularity of the tradition (Griffin 2007: 210–12).

The most common form in which these ballads were printed in the sixteenth and seventeenth centuries was the *pliego suelto*. This was normally a single sheet of paper printed on both sides, and then folded once or twice, to produce a pamphlet which could be distributed quickly and sold cheaply. Sometimes these pamphlets would be mainly in prose, with just the odd ballad included to fill up spare paper: the ballads included in the *pliegos sueltos* were flexible enough to permit truncation by the printer to fit the amount

[1] Graves gives a lively account of what he calls the 'cumulative' or repetitive nature of workplace ballads (1957: xi–xiii).
[2] The difficulties of defining the ballad and its relationship with the romance are addressed, respectively, by Nygard (1976) and Smith (1996: vi–viii). On conditions for oral performance see Menéndez Pidal (1953: II. 601). There is a good account of the sense in which ballads are, properly speaking, popular poetry in Alín (1991: 7–25).
[3] In addition to the standard essays by Menéndez Pidal (1953, 1973) and Catalán (1969, 1997–98), there are provocative accounts of ballad origins and survival by Wright (1991, 1994) and Piñero & Atero (1987).

of space he had available. On other occasions the *pliego suelto* would contain verse only: either a series of ballads or a mixture of ballads and other poetry. Although the incalculable mass of these *pliegos sueltos* were literally read to pieces and are now lost for ever, evidence survives of blind pedlars having sung their contents to advertise the printed version they then sold, a reminder of the close relation between oral and written culture in the history of the Spanish *romance*.

Ballads were also included in more expensive printed books of verse like the famous *Cancionero general*, first published in 1511. The first printed anthology exclusively dedicated to the ballad was the *Cancionero de romances* which the Antwerp publisher Martin Nuyts issued in 1547–48. This compilation gathered together poems which were already circulating in *pliegos sueltos*, and was much reprinted in Spain and the Spanish Netherlands.

The popularity of these traditional ballads with audiences both popular and learned gave rise, in the last three decades of the century, to what became known as the *romances nuevos* or *romances artificiosos*. These ballads incorporated new themes and styles which reflected the more sophisticated aesthetic tastes of the age, and they, too, were published in cheap *pliegos sueltos* and also in anthologies like Juan de Timoneda's *Rosas de romances* (Valencia 1573), the anonymous *Romancero historiado* (Alcalá de Henares 1579), and the great *Romancero general* (first edition 1600).[4]

The writers studied in this volume were brought up both hearing and reading these ballads. While elsewhere such popular song came to be disdained by learned poets (an educated contemporary in our own language inveighed against 'the frye of such wooden rythmours' who penned 'rude rythming and balducketome ballads' rather than 'applie them selves wholly ... to the true making of verse in such wise as the Greekes and Latines'), writers of Spain's Golden Age did not turn their back on the ballad tradition but, instead, adapted it to the sophisticated fashions of their day.[5] At the same time, versions of many of those same songs continued to be sung in towns and in the countryside. Ballads by poets like Góngora, Lope de Vega, and Quevedo appeared both in *pliegos sueltos* and in printed collections, although they often circulated earlier in manuscript or orally, as the ballad had always done. But these *romances*, written by educated poets, present the modern reader with difficulties that go beyond the usual problems that face us when we read works from another age.

---

[4] On sixteenth-century ballads see Piñero & Atero (1987: 13–17) and Garvin (2007).
[5] The educated writer was the Irishman Richard Stanyhurst (1583: A₄ᵇ), translator into English of the first four books of Virgil's *Aeneid*. A similar attitude can be found in Spain over a century earlier in the *Prohemio o carta* written by Íñigo López de Mendoza, Marquis of Santillana, to Pedro, Constable of Portugal ('ínfimos son aquellos que sin ningund orden, regla nin cuento fazen estos romançes e cantares de que las gentes de baxa e servil condición se alegran': López de Mendoza 2003: 649).

Lyric poetry produced in aristocratic milieux in the later Middle Ages had been dominated by the ethos and attitudes we today know as Courtly Love. The courtship behaviour codified in Andreas Capellanus's *De arte honeste amandi* (c.1185) was an updating for medieval readers of Ovid's advice to would-be lovers; it centred around the roles of the suitor as the faithful and frustrated postulant and the beloved as the beautiful but 'unkind' *belle dame sans merci* (see the texts assembled in O'Donoghue 1982). That timeless ballet was further refined in the *Canzionere* of Petrarch, the model for the European lyric throughout the Renaissance and Early Modern period. The Petrarchan idiom may strike us today as stilted or artificial, with its development of symbolic landscape, its characteristic paradoxes—ice and fire, night and day, storm and calm, and so on (Terry 1993: 18–23)—and its stock images equating lips with coral, teeth (and sometimes tears) with pearls, skin with alabaster, eyes with radiant suns, and wavy fair hair that is said to fall in golden cascades. The modern reader has to learn afresh how to read poetry like this. Helpful are Forster (1969) and Rivers (1994), who both look at European and English poetry, while Fucilla (1960) and Manero Sorolla (1987) concentrate on Spain.

As with any fashion, the attachment to Petrarchan commonplaces itself became over time the stuff of satire and ridicule. One has only to think of Shakespeare's Sonnet CXXX, 'My mistress' eyes are nothing like the sun', or Juan de Zabaleta's caricature of the typical poet in his *El día de fiesta por la mañana,* written some fifty years later (1983: 175–84). There is more than one instance, too (Quevedo's sonnet 'Sol os llamó mi lengua pecadora', Q.559, for example), of a deeper-seated disquiet about Petrarchism: this time not just with its conventionalized language, routine syntactical tricks, and hackneyed tropes for feminine beauty, but with the very woman-worship that lay at the core of the culture Petrarch's imitators had inherited from Courtly Love poetry. In verse like this, women (and, for that matter, the gods and goddesses of Classical myth) are treated as emblems of Man's fallen state. Such parodies combine a desire to outdo some of the best things found in earlier vernacular or Latin writing with a critique of the values underlying some of the most haunting and seductive examples of past literary achievement. The danger of the productions now ruthlessly mocked lay precisely in their undeniable allure. Where tales of heroism or amorous self-immolation are concerned, there lie the risks of idolatry and moral topsy-turviness, without that implying the necessary rejection of human love or human courage in all their forms. Reasonableness is all; *cordura* and *seso* (rather than uncontrolled *sexo*).[6] Mythological examples may be more teasing, since not all Classical tales were necessarily devoid of moral example, but their emphases might stand in need of correction or supplementation in the light of a

---

[6] Thus, in lines 433–34 of his *romance* 'La ciudad de Babilonia' (GR.74), Góngora berates the suicide Pyramus as 'Oh bien hideputa puto', asking '¿tan mal te olía la vida?'.

fuller Christian revelation. (In lines 185–89 of Calderón's play *El mágico prodigioso*, it is the Devil himself who remarks that tales of the pagan gods are 'falsas historias | en que las letras profanas | con los nombres de los dioses | entendieron disfrazada | la moral filosofía', 1985: 69.) The poet seeks to help us pick our way through superficially beguiling forms of attractiveness, and as part of this, to coax us into understanding just how much importance to attach to what.

The tone of the criticism on offer may not be that of the prating moralizer, but *burlas* purvey *veras*: pleasure leads to the internalization of fundamental truths. We may be charmed into better, as well as worse, moral perception and behaviour. Hearts must be moved as well as heads, and it may be more effective to meet one's fellow sinners on their own ground than to wag one's finger at them angrily from afar. Readers and listeners profit through the attention paid to their pleasure and through an avoidance of the far-fetched, as Horace had recommended: 'simul et iucunda et idonea dicere vitae', 'words at once both pleasing and helpful to life' (*Ars poetica*, lines 333–44).

Some of the pleasure offered by poetry of this type is linguistic, and this can be a problem for the modern reader. Puns, conceits, and double-entendres may provide fun, but they also make demands of readers not familiar with sixteenth and seventeenth-century Spanish. Not that all Spanish ballads of the Early Modern period are linguistically complex; some are delightfully simple, or appear so—one only has to think of Góngora's 1582 'Que se nos va la pascua, mozas' (GR.8) or Lope's 'Sale la estrella de Venus', probably written the following year (Vega 1982: 73–76). But many are, and the poets chosen for this volume revelled in playing wordgames with their readers. They developed an aesthetic of difficulty that equated intellection with beauty. Yet, in certain respects, their poems were not designed to be as difficult as we find them. Beyond the first year or two of schooling, liberal education in Early Modern Europe was conducted in Latin and focused on the analysis of Latin texts. This led writers of the time to assume that their readers or audiences would be versed in Classical learning, and that they would readily recognize stylistic devices and Classical allusions, overt as well as indirect. Most readers today are not and do not. Writers at the time felt free to use Classical allusions as a form of shorthand. The modern reader may view this parading of Classical learning as a distancing tactic, a form of obscurantism or self-aggrandisement, and it is true that for writers of the later sixteenth and early seventeenth centuries Classical allusion was a badge that identified the man of letters. But it was also an aid to communication rather than an obstacle. Much the same is true of the ways our writers use the Bible and certain Patristic writings. The former, at least in the vernacular, was forbidden to most Spaniards at the time, but educated men were familiar with it in Latin and had great chunks of it by heart; they were also

veterans of philosophical and theological debate.[7] Despite the occasional dis-
agreements between them, some of them serious, writers and readers—
setters and solvers—shared religious assumptions and a mutual competence
in orthodox discussion of them. Those assumptions and those competences
are not enjoyed by most readers today, however well educated they may be.

These *romances artificiosos* also present problems beyond the usual linguistic and cultural barriers. The period under review saw an explosion of
burlesque entertainments of all kinds, and nowhere is that more in evidence
than in Spain (Cacho 2007b). The ballad, with its traditional popular associations, proved an effective vehicle for ridicule and the grotesque, featuring
the language of the street alongside that of the schoolroom and lecture hall.
Slang is notoriously ephemeral, as those of a certain age who seek to use it
to ingratiate themselves with the young soon discover. But we have the
great good fortune that the lexicographer and emblematist Sebastián de
Covarrubias compiled the first substantive dictionary of Spanish in 1611: at
the very time, then, that is of interest to us. An even greater stroke of luck is
that, although it was put together a hundred years or so later, the *Diccionario de autoridades* uses as its base material (its *autoridades*) many of the
authors and some of the poems we shall be examining (see, for example,
Candelas 2004). Those works of reference will be the first port of call whenever we seek to discover the meanings and resonances of words and phrases
in the poems we shall be reading. Also useful are more modern compilations
of seventeenth-century idiom and slang: Alonso Hernández (1976), Hernández & Sanz (1999 and 2002), Chamorro (2002), and lists of proverbs and
sayings (Correas 1967).

Whether or not it was eventually printed, most written Golden-Age poetry
circulated in manuscript among a fairly small coterie of wits and fellow
poets. One result of this is that works often contain references, oblique as
well as overt, to contemporary events and people, frequently in the form of
sideswipes at institutions and individuals. Readers clearly found such risqué
topicality to their taste. We, as readers not living in that society, need to discover as much as we can about the people and events that are being criticized
or lampooned, if we are to understand what is being said, and, as we shall
see, a knowledge of everything from municipal bye-laws and medical practices to hairstyles and contemporary painting can prove helpful. Lope de Vega
declared one of the *romance* metre's charms to be the way it lent itself to the
treatment of a wide variety of themes and modes. These included amorous,
elegiac, heroic, and religious topics, but also satire and burlesque (see
Trueblood 1974: 48–51). Everything was grist to the balladeer's mill.

Indeed, Early Modern writers were often at their most serious when
adapting the techniques of the cartoon and the caricature, as we can see from

---

[7] On the extent to which a secular elite had emerged with direct access to the Bible
thanks to training in Latin and Greek, see Tellechea (1979).

the vast amount of comic material written about serious matters such as ill-ness or death.[8] Examples of comic material indulged in simply for the hell of it, are rare (but see pp. 80–81, below). Laughter can serve many different functions, and humorous subject matter, with its roots in the Classical writing Golden-Age authors admired, itself encompasses everything from fierce indignation and apparent frivolity to oblique irony and the gentle exposure of absurdity. Laughter was at this time generally believed at its best to be useful, and even conducive to moral and physical health. The philosophy of St Thomas Aquinas (normally known as Thomist thought) had enjoyed a revival in sixteenth-century Spain, and Aquinas had held that simply playful or humorous words, seeking nothing further than reasonable delight, have value as recreation and rest for the soul (*Summa theologica*, IIa-IIae, q.168, a.2). There is a firm sense that we should avoid being killjoys and burden-some to one another, and that we grow weary from unrelenting mental and spiritual labour as much as from physical exertion.[9] Cervantes's prologue to his *Novelas ejemplares* is of the same mind (Thompson 2005). Aquinas backed his arguments up with reference to Aristotle and Cicero, as well as to Scripture and the Church Fathers. Such thought further sees provoking laughter within reason as promoting positive moral good by showing up vice and distorted values for what they are. This laughter will be careful to avoid excessive acerbity and self-righteousness; the critic counts himself in with potential and actual other sinners, none being exempt. (If we claim that we are sinless, *nos seducimus*, 'we deceive ourselves', I John 1:8.) Thus limits are set to merriment, reasonableness being the desired measure in all things: insolence and obscenity must be avoided; a sense of balance must be main-tained; due regard is to be had for persons, time, and place. Different writers on different occasions may have different views of where the limits are to be set in particular instances, but that there are limits is generally undoubted. Boorishness will never do.

The period as a whole exhibits a tendency towards greater refinement and decorousness, even in writers who may now seem to us to offend a modern sense of decorum and also, perhaps, the decorum felt by their own contemporaries.[10] We are usually uncomfortable or downright disapproving when certain targets are attacked, such as women, blacks, gays, and Jews, even if we object less when tailors, innkeepers, or lawyers are impugned;

---

[8] See, for example, the recent survey of comic poetry on the pox by Ponce (2007).

[9] Monastics and other ascetics often took a dimmer view of merriment, though, and especially of laughing out loud. This is a firm emphasis in the Rule of St Benedict, for instance: see his Chapter 4: 'Verba risui apta non loqui' ('Not to speak words that move to laughter'), and also his Chapters 5 and 7.

[10] Close writes of 'a juvenile, robust, Aristophanic style of humour which delights in desecrating inversions, wounding derision, exuberant revelling in allusions to the body's base functions... brazenly aggressive' that the predominant ethos of the time sought to bring under civilized control. Even so, he remarks, one may find Góngora, say, 'tempera-mentally straining against' some of the controls in question (2000: 189, 236).

there are other forms of cruelty of which we disapprove as well; and the animus firing certain personal vendettas pursued in verse may likewise leave us cold. We may need to try especially hard in some cases to understand mentalities different from our own.

The passions exercise a strong pull on human beings in consequence of the Fall of Man, and vigilance must constantly be exercised against them. Those passions include pride, covetousness, lust, envy, and the other Deadly Sins; and temptation takes many forms, some crude, some subtle. The passions lead us to worship false gods like money, power, fame, sex, and worldly honour; being illusory objectives, these all offer insubstantial, impermanent mirages of happiness. Moral dangers such as these seemed especially virulent after the Spanish Court had settled at Madrid in 1561, bringing prostitutes and beggars, together with hordes of place-seekers and would-be nouveaux riches to the newly established capital; and matters looked far worse as the economic basis to an illusory later sixteenth-century boom appeared to crumble (see Elliott 1989b: Part IV).

Grafted on to pagan views about the capriciousness of fortune and Stoical responses favouring emotional detachment and self-sufficiency is a more positive Christian teaching about man's not being a slave to fortune except by choice and collusion with the Devil's wiles. An advantage pagan sages had not enjoyed was the grace made available by Christ's death. Man has a God-given capacity to exercise free will, and cardinal virtues like fortitude and prudence. Furthermore, Christians do not spurn God's creation as if it were evil in itself, but need to have a humble sense of themselves as creatures in relation to their creator, and to situate their treasure in heaven. St Ignatius Loyola, the founder of the Society of Jesus, had put the point with characteristic directness in his *Ejercicios espirituales*: 'El hombre es criado para alabar, hacer reverencia y servir a Dios nuestro Señor, y mediante esto salvar su ánima; y las otras cosas sobre la haz de la tierra son criadas para el hombre y para que le ayuden en la prosecución del fin para que es criado. De donde sigue que el hombre tanto ha de usar dellas, quanto le ayudan para su fin' (1963: 203).

Human life is ever subject to *engaño*: to the delusive perspectives and ill-ordered priorities which lead men to seek to gain the whole world, to the detriment of their souls (Matthew 16: 26–27, etc.). Yet tragic response to human error is inadequate; it is far more effective to cultivate *desengaño*. In this way, the Devil and his snares may be seen for what they are, and can be derided as follies, once wisdom is understood on God's terms, terms that make a mockery of what worldlings usually value (1 Cor. 1:20: 'stultam fecit Deus sapientiam huius mundi': 'God has made foolish the wisdom of this world'). Creative writers have a duty to help this process along, and may do so best, not by haranguing their fellow creatures, but by wooing them. Writers, to borrow Michael Hollings's phrase, are 'part of the problem trying to be part of the solution' (1977: 13). Laughter within reason may cure men of their melancholy, and either gently or with a well-timed jolt help correct distorted moral vision and the lapses that we so easily fall into through laziness or bad habit. A capacity for wholesome laughter may itself be a positive sign that *desengaño* has been activated, as opposed to a tell-tale, self-deceiving earnestness and solemnity which results in truths being mouthed rather than internalized and acted upon.

Closely related at the period with *desengaño* is the notion of *discreción*, glossed by *Cov.* (s.v. *discernir)*: 'vale vulgarmente distinguir una cosa de otra y hacer juicio dellas; de aquí se dijo discreto, el hombre cuerdo y de buen seso, que sabe ponderar las cosas y dar a cada una su lugar.' It may be remembered that St Ignatius had also written about the 'discreción de espíri-tus' (1963: 266): the word is heavy with connotations of moral and spiritual discernment. Both Lope and Quevedo were educated at the Jesuit schools that he helped to establish and which exercised an ever-increasing cultural influence during the period we are discussing (Wittkower & Jaffe 1972). *Discreción* (like *genio, ingenio,* and *agudeza*) is often also used to mean wit (especially witty wordplay), making satisfying if sometimes unpredictable and unhackneyed connections between one realm of experience and another, or coming out with a well-timed sally in company or with an apt and memorable *mot*. The underlying values of this aesthetic, as we see from Aristotle's *Nicomachean Ethics*, take in what we might call good manners in polite society, and reveal, as MacIntyre puts it (1967: 68), an unmistakable social bias, in ways that those sensitive to the evolving spirit of Golden-Age Spain could readily appreciate at the time.

*   *   *   *   *

Spanish Golden-Age ballads are normally written in the form inherited from the oral tradition of the Middle Ages and still popular today in Hispanic cultures. The traditional ballad had been chanted, and Golden-Age ballads were often sung, their regular versification facilitating their being set to music. Their versification is usually as follows:

(*a*) *The length of the line.* Each line has eight syllables, octosyllabic metre having ancient roots in Spain. To find out the length of a line of Spanish verse the syllables are counted up to, and including, the last stressed one, and then one more is added. This may at first seem odd, but it allows account to be taken of the three stress positions found in Spanish words. The position of the stress in the last word in the line is what is important when counting lines of Spanish poetry. The three stress positions are *llano* (sometimes also called *grave*), where the stress falls on the penultimate syllable (the 'e' in the word *mesa*); *agudo*, where the stress falls on the last syllable (the 'á' in the word *verás*); and *esdrújula*, where the stress falls on the antepenultimate syllable (the stressed 'á' in *tálamo*).

The following two sorts of octosyllabic line are found in poems studied in this volume:

1	2	3	4	5	6	7	(+1)	=	**8**
la	mi – tad		hue – cas	y	**cor** –	(cho)			

The word *corcho* is *llano*; the last stressed syllable (*cor–*) is therefore the seventh and, as one more (in this case, present) has to be added, the line is octosyllabic. The following line would be incorrectly counted if the convention of counting to the last stressed syllable and then adding one more were forgotten:

1	2	3	4	5	6	7	(+1)	=	**8**
y	due – los	en	que	pen –	**sar**				

This line might seem at first to contain seven syllables, but the last word, *pensar*, is *agudo*. As the last stressed syllable (*–sar*) is not followed by an unstressed one, a further syllable has to be counted in, and the line is therefore octosyllabic.

No ballad studied in this volume contains a line of verse ending with an *esdrújula* word but, if there were such a line, the rule of counting to the last stressed syllable and adding one (and only one) more would be followed, the penultimate syllable of the final word not counting for the purposes of versification.

The counting of syllables is complicated by diphthongs and elision. Diphthongs occur when two vowels join together to form a single syllable. This normally happens when two weak vowels, or a weak and a strong, come together. Weak vowels in Spanish are 'i' and 'u'; strong vowels are 'a', 'e', and 'o'. When two strong vowels are next to each other, they normally form two separate syllables, as happens for instance in the final two syllables of the word *ba|ca|la|o*. Having said that, Spanish poets sometimes give themselves licence to combine even two strong vowels into one syllable (a practice known as synalepha) or to separate two weak ones, or a weak and a strong, which would normally be expected to form a single syllable (hiatus).

Elision occurs when one word ends in a vowel sound and the next begins with another (written letters that are not pronounced do not count). The two vowels then normally combine to form one syllable, regardless of the distinction between strong and weak vowels. Thus the first line of Góngora's *romance* 'Arrojóse el mancebito' (see Chapter 3, below) is counted as follows:

1	2	3	4	5	6	7	(+1)	=	**8**
A –	rro –	jó – se	el	man – ce –	**bi** –	(to)			

This line therefore contains eight syllables, elision occurring between *–se* and *el* in the fourth.

Although the Spanish ballad is normally written in octosyllabic metre, Golden-Age poets also wrote ballads with six-syllable (hexasyllabic) lines,

these poems being known as *romancillos*. Góngora's poem 'Noble desengaño', analyzed in Chapter 2, is an example of this form:

    1   2   3   4   5   (+1) = **6**
    No – ble des – en – **ga** – (ño)

    1   2   3   4   5   (+1) = **6**
    gra – cias doy al **cie** – (lo)

(*b*) *Rhyme.* Ballads, like much Spanish poetry, employ assonance; in other
words all consonants are disregarded and rhyme involves only the last
stressed vowel and the unstressed vowel after it, if there is one. In the *romances* (and *romancillos*) assonance occurs on alternate lines (normally the
even-numbered ones), while the other lines do not rhyme at all. In the
following example, which comes from the ballad discussed in Chapter 6, the
even lines rhyme assonantally, with 'double assonance' in *ú–o*, but there is
no rhyme on the odd-numbered lines.

> Son las torres de Joray
> calavera de unos m<u>uro</u>s
> en el esqueleto informe
> de un ya castillo dif<u>unto</u>.
>
> Hoy las esconden guijarros
> y ayer coronaron n<u>ublo</u>s

'Single assonance' is found when the final words of the rhyming lines are
agudos, as is the case with Góngora's ballad (not analyzed in this volume)
'Ciego que apuntas y atinas' (GR.3):

> Ciego que apuntas y atinas,
> caduco dios, y rap<u>az</u>,
> vendado que me has vendido,
> y niño mayor de ed<u>ad</u>.

The examples in this volume show that the *romance* is a flexible form. It
has no fixed length, and the traditional ballad was not divided into stanzas,
although the *romance artificioso* tends to fall into four-line units. The ballad
therefore offers poets considerable freedom. Golden-Age writers exploited
this freedom in various ways. For example, in his 'El lastimado Belardo'
(analysed in Chapter 1) Lope de Vega includes a refrain (or *estribillo*) which
not only underscores the musicality of his *romance* and gives it shape but is
written in a different metre: the Italianate combination of seven- and eleven-
syllable lines. Quevedo goes further in his 'Son las torres de Joray' where he
slips from the *romance* into another poetic form commonly used by Golden-
Age poets: the octosyllabic *letrilla*. However, he introduces and punctuates
the *letrilla* with a refrain, again written in a combination of a seven- and an
eleven-syllable line. Here the shift from *romance* to *estribillo* and *letrilla*
calls attention to a shift in the poem's mood and meaning (see Chapter 6,

below) and provides an example of the creative manipulation of ballad versification by Golden-Age poets.[11]

*   *   *   *   *

The present volume is not a representative anthology of the Spanish ballad in the Early Modern period, nor is it meant to be. Several such anthologies are readily available, and ballads are included in many printed collections of verse from the period as well as in countless modern editions.[12] Rather, our purpose is to introduce the reader to some of the problems encountered by anglophone readers of poetry from this period, even poetry cast in a popular mode, and to offer informed guidance towards the resolution of some of them. Few, we hope, would today challenge the premiss that, before a reader can appreciate a work of art he or she must first try to understand it. This does not mean, as Helen Gardner reminded us over half a century ago (1959: 17), that the critic reads for the reader, but it does mean that one of the critic's primary functions is to assist readers to read for themselves. This is what we have had in mind both in our selection of poems and in the commentaries and line-by-line prose translations we have provided. The model for this enterprise is the excellent translation and commentary by Dámaso Alonso to one of Góngora's most difficult poems, his 'Fábula de Polifemo y Galatea' (Alonso 1994), which has served to introduce generations of readers to that work and, more widely, to the delights that lurk behind the surface difficulties of the poetry.

*   *   *   *   *

When academic life ceases to be collegial, it becomes unsustainable. That it still survives in the teeth of winds that batter from every quarter is testimony to the unremitting and largely unsung efforts of those who serve it. This volume is the result of an unusually close collaboration between colleagues; even those not named as editors have read and commented on the entire volume. It is offered as a token of our esteem and our collective affection for someone who, as Berceo has it, 'ministraba como tal servidor'. David Pattison—teacher, colleague, and friend—has taught the Spanish ballad, and much else besides, to generations of Oxford undergraduates. Though he has produced a steady stream of influential publications, much of the time which others spend promoting their careers David has devoted to helping pupils, friends, and colleagues. Twice Chairman of the Oxford Faculty of Medieval and Modern Languages, he has not only been Vice-President and Senior

---

[11] There is further help on Spanish versification at this period in Terry (1965–68).

[12] A recent example is Frenk (2004). Whole volumes are devoted to the ballads of some of the poets examined: Carreño 1979 (Lope de Vega), and Góngora (1998, 2000a).

Bursar of his college, Magdalen, but was for twenty-five years Treasurer of the Society for the Study of Mediaeval Languages and Literature and has, for over forty, been a stalwart of the Association of Hispanists of Great Britain and Ireland, which elected him as its President from 2000 to 2002.

LOPE DE VEGA

'EL LASTIMADO BELARDO' (1588–95)

with a note on Góngora's

'EN LOS PINARES DE JÚCAR' (1603)

El lastimado Belardo
con los celos de su ausencia
a la hermosísima Filis
humildemente se queja.

5 '¡Ay, dice, señora mía,
y cuán caro que me cuesta
el imaginar que un hora
he de estar sin que te vea!

¿Cómo he de vivir sin ti
10 pues vivo en ti por firmeza,
y ésta el ausencia la muda,
por mucha fe que se tenga?

Sois tan flacas las mujeres
que a cualquier viento que os llega
15 liberalmente os volvéis
como al aire la veleta.

Perdóname, hermosa Filis,
que el mucho amor me hace fuerza
a que diga desvaríos,
20 antes que mis males sienta.

¡Ay, sin ventura de mí!
¿Qué haré sin tu vista bella?
Daré mil quejas al aire
y ansina diré a las selvas:

25 *¡Ay triste mal de ausencia,*
y quién podrá decir lo que me cuestas!

No digo yo, mi señora,
que estás en aquesta prueba
quejosa de mi partida,
30 aunque sabes que es tan cierta;

yo me quejo de mi suerte,
porque es tal, y tal mi estrella,
que juntas, a mi ventura,
harán que tu fe se tuerza.

35 ¡Maldiga Dios, Filis mía,
el primero que [de ausencias]
dio luz al humano trato,
pues tantas penas aumentan!

Yo me parto, y mi partir
40 tanto aqueste pecho aprieta,
que como en bascas de muerte
el alma y cuerpo pelean.

¡Dios sabe, bella señora,
si quedarme aquí quisiera,
45 y dejar al mayoral
que solo a la aldea se fuera!

He de obedecerle, al fin,
que me obliga mi nobleza,
y aunque amor me desobliga,
50 es fuerza que el honor venza.

¡Ay triste mal de ausencia,
y quién podrá decir lo que me cuestas!'

* * * * *

It was characteristic of Siglo de Oro poets who produced *romances*, especially from the 1580s onwards, to display a sensitivity to stylistic variety and an interest in contriving, within a given poem, a stylistic interplay of elements deriving from different and even contrasting traditions. Thus one finds an intermingling and interaction of elements both 'high' and 'low' as recognized in the categories of rhetoric: elements deriving, on the one hand, from poetry of a culturally learned or emotionally refined and subtle character, and, on the other, from the poetry of the people, the *pueblo*. Among the many ways in which these elements could be brought into relation with each other, those found in *romances* belonging in one way or another to the larger world and longer traditions of pastoral literature (both verse and prose) have a distinctive interest of their own. For here, in a particularly marked fashion, it is characteristic (even if not universally the case) that the unsophisticated is adopted by the sophisticated and, in the process, is transmuted in both emotional and literary terms.

So it was that the 'pastoral myth' had entered the tradition of European poetry already in the time of Classical Greece and at the hand of Theocritus in the third century BC. In Robert Coleman's words, 'the pastoral myth is the creation of a highly civilized urban sensibility'. He comments further that:

> In his longing for a simple innocence and carefree spontaneity that he has lost, urban man looks to the country and its way of life, which he knows only as an outsider and from a distance, and creates out of it a myth embodying the ideals that he seeks.   (1977: 1)

This characterization clearly invites application, across the centuries, to the greatest pastoral poem in Spanish, Góngora's *Las soledades* (G.264), dating in the main from 1613–14. However, the interest of the *romances* relating to the pastoral tradition that we owe to both Lope de Vega and Góngora has rather more to do with the mutations and modulations of pastoral that this tradition underwent first at the hands of Virgil and subsequently in the Middle Ages and the Early Modern Period.

> **El lastimado Belardo**
> **con los celos de su ausencia**
> **a la hermosísima Filis**
> 4   **humildemente se queja.**

Belardo, wounded by the pains of jealousy that he knew his absence would bring him, humbly complains to Filis, exquisite in her beauty.

Here at the start of the poem it is relevant to note what is made clear only at its end: that Belardo is a subordinate of his *mayoral* (45), the latter defined by *Cov.* as 'el que assiste al govierno del ganado con mando, governando los demás pastores'. *Ganado*, while signifying sheep in the first place, also meant any herd that grazed in the countryside. This points us back to the start of the pastoral tradition. Theocritus called his 'First Idyll' (of fundamental importance for Virgil and so for the rest of the tradition) 'bucolic'.[1] The term comes from the Greek word for 'cowherd'. The ancient authors refer to the 'bucolica' of both Theocritus and Virgil. Indeed, the term seems to have been the original title of Virgil's *Eclogues*. The extension of 'bucolic' to anything pastoral, especially in a poetic setting, also seems to be ancient. So 'cowherds' as well as 'shepherds' had a place in the world of literary pastoral, and thus, on both scores, we see Belardo presented, by implication, in a long literary perspective.

The poem's opening lines not only establish at the outset the emotional situation for the rest of the poem but, brief as they are, evoke (or would have evoked for Lope's contemporaries) a whole literary world of complex and subtle emotional relationships. Such was the world of pastoral romance. This poem of Lope's relates at many points to that world, and its own resonance with its readers depended—and depends—to a large extent on a recognition of its connectedness to the literary world that lies behind it.

The names *Belardo* and *Filis* themselves bring to mind the poeticized pastoral world of Jorge de Montemayor's *Diana*, first published around 1560 and, in the judgement of Paul Alpers (1996: 348), the first and best of Renaissance pastoral narratives. Here we meet its shepherds Sireno, Montano, Silvano, and numerous others, and the shepherdesses Belisa, Dórida, Selvagia, and Diana herself, 'aquella en quien naturaleza sumó todas las perficiones que por muchas partes avía repartido' (Montemayor 1996: 126). These spend their youthful lives in a world of green and pleasant meadows watered by an abundant stream on whose delightful banks their shepherds' flocks feed, while those caring for them often retreat to the cool shade of nearby trees and talk and sing of the pains (mostly) of love.

Montemayor (himself Portuguese by origin) situates the pastoral scene for his work amidst the mountains of the province of León in northern Spain, along the banks of the river Esla—a part of Spain where the pastoral scene might seem to the reader to be more *verosímil*. But it is the same pastoral scene, performing the same function, as one finds in the work that, more than any other, established the taste and provided the model for pastoral literature in Early Modern Europe: Jacopo Sannazaro's *Arcadia*, first printed at Naples in 1504 but composed twenty or so years earlier. Here, too, poeticized shepherdesses and shepherds people the scene: Diana, Ofelia, Montano, Salvaggio, Serrano, and, centrally, Sincero, with his hopeless love for the fair Phyllis.

The setting here is immediately defined at the start as 'la pastorale Arcadia'. It was Virgil who turned the Arcadia of fact—an isolated part of the Greek Peloponnese—into the ideal pastoral place that so possessed the imagination of later ages. This he did in his Eclogues VII and X especially,

---

[1] The traditional designation of Theocritus's pastoral poems as 'idylls' is misleading as regards his own poems and the tradition that derived from it. The Greek word *eidyllia* means 'vignettes' and does not carry the implication of rustic languor and passivity.

composed in the later first century BC, drawing on the bucolic poems of
Theocritus. Here in Virgil already we find 'Phyllis' as the name of a country
girl of whom shepherds sing or make part of a dream of love. (The Greek
names, such as this, given to figures in Virgil's Latin eclogues, serve as a
device for integrating them into pastoral poetic fiction.) These Classical origins made fundamental contributions to the pastoral literature of the Renaissance period. Virgil's Eclogue X, which concludes the work, was especially important in this regard. Here the central figure, Gallus, is presented
as the anguished victim of his unrequited love for Lycoris, who has gone off
with another man. The poem, throughout, insists on the power of love, and
on the pain and madness that it causes: 'Love conquers all things, and we
too must yield to love' ('Omnia vincit Amor: et nos cedamus Amori', 69).
The relevance of this Virgilian background is strengthened by the fact that
Virgil was the Roman poet most often and most widely studied in the
Renaissance classroom.

   However (and this is directly relevant to Lope's *romance*), the emotional
world of Renaissance pastoral was that of pastoral profoundly modified by
the ideals and conventions of Courtly Love and subsequently by the
vernacular Italian poetry of Petrarch (Francesco Petrarca, 1304–74), whose
collected love poetry—his *Canzoniere*—can be regarded as the most
influential such collection ever to be composed.

   Courtly Love (*amour courtois*, otherwise *amour chevaleresque* or *fin'
amor*) signifies a literary codification of the values and conduct of amorous
relationships between aristocratic lovers. It is a view of love usually traced
back to the troubadour poets of Provence in the eleventh and twelfth
centuries. The love of which they sang and wrote was a spiritualization of
the erotic.[2] The lover is emotionally the vassal of his lady (the latter often
called *midons*, from the Latin *meus dominus*, 'my lord'—the *dueño mío*
applied by the Spanish soldier to his Moorish mistress in Góngora's ballad
(GR.23) 'Servía en Orán al Rey': Góngora 2000a: 180–83); it is a relationship of adoring subservience of man to woman as he idealizes and idolizes
her beauty and perfections and dwells on the emotional dependence in
which he perseveres, whatever disappointment and discouragement it brings
him. It is an essential principle of the code that conduct and address adhere
to the norms of courtesy and refinement, whatever the inner emotional
distress that they express. Hence Belardo's mode of address to Filis: *señora
mía... mi señora... bella señora*.

   This Courtly Love is basic to Petrarch's *Canzoniere*. But the latter brought
to the tradition a new complexity of emotion, a new subtlety of perception
and subsequent reflexion, both directed towards the effect produced by the
beloved on the lover, whose voice the poem presents itself as expressing.

---

[2] For a brief characterization of Courtly Love, with attached bibliography, see
Abrams (1993: 38–39).

Mood and tone range from the intense inner stress produced by the para-doxical and conflictive interpenetration of emotional pleasure and pain (the 'bitter sweetness' of love) to the sweet sadness of retrospective nostalgia. Throughout there is (in Leonard Forster's phrase) a 'hovering balance of opposites' (1969: 14): opposites that become the poles of paradox. The lady is the 'sweet enemy'; her service is felt by her lover to be bondage and ser-vitude, but at the same time he recognizes it to be his highest freedom. Loss of his lady through separation, however caused, brings him unhappiness and grief.

The central theme of this *romance* of Lope's is the enforced separation, and so *ausencia*, of the lover from his lady. This at once takes us to the core preoccupations of Renaissance pastoral literature: those of separation, absence, or loss. Such a prospect leaves Belardo in a state of *celos*: *los celos de su ausencia*. *Cov.* remarks that Spanish and Italian poets have written so much about *celos* that he will not add more of his own. He does, though, apply a Latin definition to *celoso*: 'suspiciosus in amore', 'mistrustful in love and anxious lest another enjoy what he himself loves'. The destruc-tively corrosive potentiality of *celos*, both psychological and moral, is what chiefly interested Calderón in his honour plays, and they find a memorably powerful analysis in Book III of Cervantes's first full-length work, his pastoral romance, *La Galatea*, published in 1585 (Cervantes 1995: 369–73). In Montemayor's *Diana*, Diana herself, having put Sireno behind her and married another, out of obedience to her father, evokes the obsessiveness of her husband's *celos* and their oppressive effect on her own life (1996: 281–82). Here in Lope's *romance*, *celos* signifies something less intense but still deeply preoccupying: in the words of *Aut.*, 'vale la sospecha, inquietud, y rezelo de que la persona amada haya mudado o mude su cariño o afición, poniéndola en otra'. Such *celos* remain hauntingly present to Belardo's mind throughout the poem from its very outset.

Belardo is *lastimado*. '*Lastimar* vale herir o maltratar uno a otro' (*Cov.*). This 'wounding' could as readily be emotional as physical and signify something intrinsic to the tangled relationships of the Renaissance pastoral world. So, in Montemayor's *Diana*, we read (172) that 'Sireno, un triste pastor, | recogía su ganado, | tan de veras lastimado'. Thus the very first line of Lope's *romance* 'El lastimado Belardo' serves to evoke a particular and immediately recognizable literary world; the first quatrain suffices to establish the essential elements of a situation conforming to a literary type.

The next eight lines enlarge on this as Belardo begins to address his lady directly.

> '¡Ay, dice, señora mía,
> y cuán caro que me cuesta
> el imaginar que un hora
> 8   he de estar sin que te vea!

> ¿Cómo he de vivir sin ti
> pues vivo en ti por firmeza,
> y ésta el ausencia la muda,
> 12   por mucha fe que se tenga?

'Alas, my lady,' he says, 'how dearly it costs me to imagine that I should go even one hour without seeing you! How am I to live without you when my very life rests on the constancy of my attachment to you? Yet absence changes constancy, however much faith each lover pledges (to the other).

Belardo's obsessively expressed emotional desire to be with his lady every hour runs through both quatrains; but the distress of even imagining an hour of separation modulates into a more reflective sense of the dangers of a lover's absence from his lady. One finds in these lines again, and more strongly, what has been found in the opening quatrain: that their expressiveness—and their effectiveness within the poem as a whole—largely derive from the implicit literary background to which they clearly relate. This can be illustrated by further reference to Montemayor's *Diana* and in particular to the series of exchanges (all in octosyllabic verse though not in *romance* form) between Sireno and Diana, introduced by the song of the nymph Dórida, in Book II of the work.

By the river Esla 'andava el pastor cuytado, | de ausencia muy temeroso, | repastando su ganado... Estava el triste pastor... imaginando aquel día | en qu'el falso dios de Amor | dio principio a su alegría. | Y dize viéndose tal: | "El bien qu'el amor me ha dado | imagino yo, cuytado, | porqu'este [= para que este] cercano mal | lo sienta después doblado"' (173). (The reference here is, of course, to Cupid, 'false' because of the deceptiveness, in various regards, of passionate love.)

In this context of pastoral discourse references to the working of the imagination take on a special psychological force. In general *imaginar/ imaginación* had in Lope's time a specificity and a strength of meaning deriving from a more literal understanding of the terms—'formar las especies e imágenes en la phantasía' (*Aut.*)—than is current today. In the words of Bertram Joseph (1971: 26, 255), 'for centuries before Hobbes, imagination was regarded as sensual, as distinct from rational, activity', its tendency being 'to rebel against the control of reason, by stimulating the heart into arousing the passions'. In the world of pastoral, past happiness brought back to the mind by the imagination deepens present sadness; directed towards the future, especially a future bringing absence of lover from lady, imagination can feed *celos*. Both aspects of the matter are present here in Lope's poem, though for the moment, at least, implicitly rather than explicitly so.

Firmeza and *fe* in the third quatrain are further links to the language of love. At an earlier point in the *Diana* (155), the shepherdess Ysmenia switches her affections from Alanio to Montano and does so 'con tanta firmeza que ya no avía cosa a quien más quisiesse que a él'. Alanio, in response, asks: '¿Cómo que fue possible, di, enemiga, | que siendo tú muy más que yo culpada, | con título cruel, con nueva liga | mudasses fe tan pura y estremada?' (158). Much later in the poem where, as already noted, Diana laments the unremitting *celos* of her husband, she recalls Sireno 'que la fe me tenía dada' (281).

Her account, at that late stage, of how she had come to put Sireno out of mind and marry another, is not altogether at one with what we read earlier, at the conclusion of the series of verse exchanges between her and Sireno. There they swear undying devotion to each other as now Sireno finds himself obliged to depart, and they embrace for the first and last time: 'porque los tiempos mudaron | el amor de otra manera'. 'Y aunque a Diana le dio | pena rabiosa y mortal | la ausencia de su zagal, | en ella misma [i.e. in that very absence] halló | el remedio de su mal' (183). It is fear of such a change of heart in Filis that prompts Belardo's next words:

> **Sois tan flacas las mujeres**
> **que a cualquier viento que os llega**
> **liberalmente os volvéis**
> 16   **como al aire la veleta.**

You women are so weak that, like a weathervane in the stirring air, you readily turn with any wind that comes your way.

Politically incorrect as these words will sound to modern ears, the fact remains that they express a view of womankind that prevailed from the time of Classical Antiquity down to Lope's own century. In Virgil's *Aeneid* (IV. 569–70), Aeneas is warned to flee speedily from Carthage and Queen Dido for 'woman is ever a fickle and changeable thing': 'varium et mutabile semper | femina'. His words here are clearly echoed by Petrarch in Sonnet 183 of his *Canzoniere*: 'Femina è cosa mobil per natura', so that (in the lover's words) 'I know well that a condition of love lasts but a short while in the heart of a woman': 'ond'io so ben ch'un amoroso stato | in cor di donna picciol tempo dura'. Hamlet's reproach to his rapidly remarried mother— 'Frailty, thy name is woman'—comes to mind. Or again, in Calderón's play of the 1620s *La gran Cenobia*, we read: 'Que en la fortuna [i.e. the inconstant goddess of Classical Antiquity] fuera acción contraria, | siendo muger, no ser mudable y varia' (Calderón 1636: fol. 81r). Sireno, in the *Diana*, asks Selvagia: 'Pastora... dime, ¿por qué causa sois tan movibles [las mugeres] que en un punto derribáis a un pastor de lo más alto de su ventura a lo más baxo de su miseria?' (146).

The simile of the weathervane is, of course, itself a commonplace: 'moverse a todos vientos como veleta, ser inconstante' (*Cov.*). The adverb *liberalmente*, attached to *os volvéis*, puts into Belardo's mouth a word that, in this context, is of a strikingly learned character, deriving as it does from Latin and being found regularly in standard analyses of the various virtues: *liberalis/liberaliter*, 'bountiful(ly), generous(ly)'. Corominas and Pascual give their authority to the view that this is the sense in which the corresponding Spanish word should be taken.[3] In that case, it assumes here an ironic, even sardonic, value.

However, Belardo's feelings immediately swing around, himself weather-vane like too, as he hears himself speaking these words, commonplace though they are, and he feels that he must apologize to the fair Filis for having applied them to her:

> Perdóname, hermosa Filis,
> que el mucho amor me hace fuerza
> a que diga desvaríos,
> 20   antes que mis males sienta.

Forgive me, fair Filis, for it is the intensity of my love that makes me talk this fevered nonsense rather than let myself feel the pains of my ills.

Desvariar, according to *Cov.*, is an incoherence of thought and utterance produced by a sudden onset of fever, 'con el accidente de la calentura'. It was a further commonplace that intense passionate love was a kind of madness: as Virgil's Eclogue X repeatedly says, and as Samuel Daniel, the Elizabethan poet, wrote: 'Love is a sickness full of woes, | all remedies refusing'. The fact that Belardo swings around so rapidly from reproach to apology again finds a parallel in the *Diana*. Alanio's reproach of Ysmenia has already been noted. A further two lines extend it: '¿Qué hado, Ysmenia, es éste que te obliga | a amar do no es possible ser amada?'. But at once he continues: 'Perdona, mi señora, ya esta culpa [that is, the intrinsic blame-worthiness of a reproach spoken by lover to lady], | pues la ocasión que diste, me disculpa' (158).

> ¡Ay, sin ventura de mí!
> ¿Qué haré sin tu vista bella?
> Daré mil quejas al aire
> 24   y ansina diré a las selvas:

Oh unhappy me! What shall I do without your lovely gaze? I shall speak a thousand complaints to the air and tell the woods:

Ventura, 'la buena suerte de cada uno', and thus the opposite of *desventura*, 'ruin suerte, desdicha, desgracia' (*Cov.*), is, in this line, clearly the 'good fortune' that Belardo lacks. The same phrase is applied to Sireno in *Diana* after the shepherdess Dórida has concluded her song about the unhappy outcome of the love-affair between Sireno and Diana (183): 'Pues el sin ventura Sireno... no menos lastimado estava entonces que al tiempo que por él avían passado [sus antiguas cuitas y sospiros].'

---

[3] '*Liberal*: generoso, dadivoso; este uso y el de *artes liberales* son los únicos corrientes en el Siglo de Oro'. However, the further sense given in *Aut.* would fit well here: '*Liberalmente*: significa también ligeramente, con brevedad y sin detención'.

¿ Qué haré sin tu vista bella? The ladies who inspire such love and cause such anguish in the Courtly Love, Petrarchan and Pastoral traditions are always of exquisite beauty and are beauteous in the gaze they sometimes bestow on the lover. Petrarch, in his *Canzoniere*, repeatedly writes of the beauty of the lady's eyes and their overwhelming effect. Sonnet 61 begins: 'Benedetto sia 'l giorno e 'l mese e l'anno | ... e 'l bel paese e 'l loco ov'io fui giunto | da' duo begli occhi che legato m'ànno', 'Blessed be the day and the month and the year... and the beautiful countryside and the place where I was struck by the two lovely eyes that have made me captive'. Sonnet 75, 'I begli occhi ond' i' fui percosso', 'The lovely eyes by which I was struck', ends: 'questi son que' begli occhi che mi stanno | sempre nel cor colle faville accese, | perch' io di lor parlando non mi stanco', 'these are the lovely eyes that forever dwell in my heart and kindle it with glowing sparks, so that I never tire of speaking of them'.

Daré mil quejas al aire | y ansina diré a las selvas. The many songs interspersed among the prose of *Arcadia* and *Diana* are sung by shepherds, shepherdesses, or nymphs in the open air of the pastoral scene. Diana's first song in the latter work is sung when she is alone: her audience is the valley itself, the wooded slopes, the birds and even the beasts 'de aquel espesso bosque' (136). We read later (187–88) of 'la selva de Diana, a donde habita la sabia Felicia, cuyo officio es dar remedio a passiones enamoradas', but the term seems to be less frequently applied to the pastoral place in Montemayor's *Diana* than in Sannazaro's *Arcadia*, where 'le selve' echo to birdsong, or witness the evening dancing of shepherds, or foster nascent feelings of love. *Silvae* are a regular part of landscape in Virgil's eclogues. *Ansina*, according to *Aut.*, 'es voz baxa, y antiquada', and continues to be viewed by the *Diccionario de la lengua española* of the Real Academia Española as peasant speech, that of 'habitantes rústicos'. This raises the question of what social tonality the word may have had in Lope's time and what artistic purpose he may have had in using it.

26 *¡Ay triste mal de ausencia,*
y quién podrá decir lo que me cuestas!

Oh unhappy woes of absence, who can tell just what you cost me?

The *mal de ausencia* is one of the severest afflictions suffered by the lovelorn of pastoral romances, both men and women. As Diana sorrowfully sings: 'No me diste, o crudo [cruel] amor, | el bien que tuve en presencia [the presence of her adoring lover], | sino porqu'el ['para que el'] mal d'ausencia | me parezca muy mayor' (175). At the very start of the work Sireno 'ya no llorava... el mal que la ausencia le prometía, ni los temores del olvido le importunavan, por que vía [veía] cumplidas las prophecías de su recelo' (125). So we see, here and in the course of the work at large, that the pain of separation from the loved one is intensified by fear of being forgotten and abandoned by the other, and that this fear is made more acute by *imaginaciones* which in turn feed *celos*. This is what lies behind Belardo's words *y cuán caro que me cuesta | el imaginar que un hora | he de estar sin que te vea*, words that are now transmuted into the refrain placed at the mid-point of the poem and at its conclusion, defining and confirming a predominant emotional key and giving a structure to the whole.

> **No digo yo, mi señora,**
> 28   **que estás en aquesta prueba**
> **quejosa de mi partida,**
> **aunque sabes que es tan cierta;**

I do not say, my lady, that in this moment of testing, you complain at my departure, even though you know it is so certain;

Prueba, 'time of testing, ordeal', 'es tentativa, como hazer prueva del amigo ... el ensayo de cualquier cosa' (*Cov.*). Applied to amorous relationships, the term runs back to the troubadours and French medieval Romance.

> **yo me quejo de mi suerte,**
> 32   **porque es tal, y tal mi estrella,**
> **que juntas, a mi ventura,**
> **harán que tu fe se tuerza.**

(but) I complain of my fate, because it is of such kind, and of such kind is my star, that together—to my woe—they will cause your faith (pledged to me) to be turned away (to another).

Suerte: 'Algunas vezes sinifica ventura buena y mala' (*Cov.*). *Tal mi estrella* is an allusion to the belief that the stars (and among them especially the planets) exercised either an auspicious or an inauspicious influence on human beings and their fortunes. Thus, in Spenser's *Faerie Queene* (I. VIII. 42) of the last decades of the sixteenth century: 'Ah, dearest Lord, what evill starre | On you hath froun'd, and pour'd his influence bad, | That of your selfe ye thus berobbed arre?'. *Que juntas a mi ventura*: although *ventura* most often signifies good fortune ('la buena suerte de cada uno', *Cov.*), here it clearly means ill fortune. Or, as Michael Drayton wrote in his *Endymion and Phoebe*, of 1595, 'Our lives' effects and fortunes are | As is that happy or unlucky star | Which, reigning in our frail nativity, | Seals up the secrets of our destiny' (see Joseph 1971: 261). Here, though, there is error, or near error, as well as truth—as the judgement of the age saw things. The crucial point is made (among so many others in Western Europe at large) by John Frampton, in his exactly contemporaneous *Art of Navigation*, where he discusses the influences of the seven planets: 'although they do so incline and move [human beings], they do not constrain nor bind by force, but rather as Ptolemy saith: the wise man is lord over the stars, he is wise that followeth not sensuality, but reason' (Joseph 1971: 258). A Latin maxim put the point in three words: *Sapiens dominabitur astris*. Belardo is shown as caught in the struggle between intense emotion (his feelings for Filis) and the exercise of moral reason (expressed in terms of his duty to his *mayoral*). Compare yet again Sireno addressing Diana: 'mas tú me mandas quedar | y mi ventura partir... a mi ventura | he de obedecer forçado' (179).

> **¡Maldiga Dios, Filis mía,**
> 36 **el primero que [de ausencias]**
> **dio luz al humano trato,**
> **pues tantas penas aumentan!**

The text of 36 in the Blecua edition—*el primero que la ausencia*—cannot be satisfactorily construed within the structure of this quatrain. The text given here is that of the *Romancero general* (González Palencia 1947: II. 6–7). The form of expression remains highly elliptical. According to *Cov.*, 'Dar luz a algún negocio es dar noticia dél'. Although this does not quite fit with the syntax of these lines, one may perhaps render the sense as:

> *God curse, Filis mine, the man who first made the ways of absence known to human kind in its dealings (one with another), since they bring increase to so much pain.*

In any case, José F. Montesinos (author of distinguished studies of the Siglo de Oro ballad) gives a different reading of this quatrain, following Durán:

> ¡Maldiga Dios, Filis mía,
> (36) el primero que la ausencia
> juzgó con amor posible
> y dispuso tantas penas!
>
> (Vega 1925–26: I. 64; Durán 1859–61: II. 460)

Although this makes sense in its own terms, larger questions of meaning remain.

> **Yo me parto, y mi partir**
> 40 **tanto aqueste pecho aprieta,**
> **que como en bascas de muerte**
> **el alma y cuerpo pelean.**

I am to depart, and my parting so oppresses my breast that soul and body do combat with each other (within me), as in the throes of death.

Compare Sireno, in *Diana*: 'Porque el pensar en partida | me pone tan gran pavor | que a la fuerça del dolor | no podrá esperar la vida' (174). *Bascas de muerte*: 'Las congoxas y alteraciones del pecho, quando uno está muy apassionado o de mal de coraçón o de enojo o de otro accidente' (*Cov., s.v. vascas*); for *accidente*, see above, p. 8.

The conflict of soul and body was, of course, a topic prominent in medieval and post-medieval writing, where that conflict was viewed in its various aspects, physical, moral, and spiritual.

> ¡Dios sabe, bella señora,
> 44   si quedarme aquí quisiera,
>   y dejar al mayoral
>   que solo a la aldea se fuera!

God knows, fair lady, that I should like to remain here and leave the head
shepherd to make his way to the village alone!

Mayoral is, as already noted, 'el que assiste al govierno del ganado con
mando, governando los demás pastores' (*Cov.*). These lines make explicit
for the first time the facts of the situation that has prompted Belardo's grief
and fears as he contemplates his imminent and enforced separation from
Filis. What one learns here perhaps comes as something of a surprise, in so
far as the cause of Belardo's distress may seem hardly to measure up to the
effect that it produces. Belardo's distress has been the theme of the whole
poem so far and is nowhere more dramatically expressed than in the lines
immediately preceding these (*Yo me parto... pelean*). But now one learns
that the prospect facing Belardo is no more than the obligation to go with his
master—the head shepherd—*a la aldea*, which in the nature of the case was
unlikely to be far away. Far enough away, perhaps, to prevent him, as he
thinks, from being able in the future, or at least for a time, to be with Filis.
The question, however, remains: is there a disproportion between Belardo's
distress as expressed throughout the poem down to this point and the prospect
that has occasioned this distress? If there is, how far is the emotional power
of the poem down to this point diminished in consequence?

A related question arises. Is this another point where, possibly, Lope had
at the back of his mind the lengthy verse exchange between Sireno and
Diana as recounted by the nymph Dórida in her song? Here also the
shepherd-lover, Sireno, is obliged to leave his lady by the demands of his
master: 'Mi amo, aquel gran pastor, | es quien me haze partir' (179). As the
reproachful Diana soon indicates, she understands this to mean that Sireno is
obliged to accompany his master across the seas: 'vete, pastor, a embarcar; |
passa de presto la mar' (181). This has been taken to mean that 'aquel gran
pastor' is a ruler, or one soon to rule: Prince Philip, soon to be Philip II of
Spain, who sailed to Genoa on his way to the Spanish Netherlands in 1548,
and to England (to marry Mary Tudor) in 1554. This in itself is plausible:
'shepherd' (*pastor*) was a term applied over the centuries and down to
Lope's time to rulers as 'shepherds' of their peoples. The point is made by
Cov.: 'Los reyes son pastores, y assí les dan este nombre las letras divinas y
las humanas'.

> He de obedecerle, al fin,
> 48   que me obliga mi nobleza,
>   y aunque amor me desobliga,
>   es fuerza que el honor venza.

[But] in the end I must obey him, for it is the obligation that nobility lays upon me; and although love releases from such obligations, honour still must triumph.

In the Renaissance period the nature of *nobleza,* 'true nobility', was a topic repeatedly discussed, the prevailing view being that nobility was not a matter of birth or wealth but of an individual's virtue. The words of the Roman poet Juvenal to the effect that 'the sole ground of nobility is virtue' were endlessly recalled. Here, in Lope's poem, that 'virtue' takes the form—more precisely—of personal integrity: a personal integrity that obliges one to obey the instructions of someone entitled to give them (in this case, the *mayoral*), even when they go against one's deepest and most powerful inclinations.

Honor signifies the social aspect of one's personal standing and thus relates, or properly and primarily relates, to personal *nobleza* in the sense just indicated. It thus becomes an essential element in, and precondition for, one's sense of selfhood and personal dignity, both individual and social. The depth and strength of meaning attached to the concept of *honor* in the social culture and literature of Siglo de Oro Spain will not need stressing here. It is the merest commonplace that it achieves canonic statement in the words of Pedro Crespo in Calderón's *El alcalde de Zalamea* (II. 873–76): 'Al Rey la hacienda y la vida | se ha de dar; pero el honor | es patrimonio del alma, | y el alma sólo es de Dios' (Calderón 1981: 187–88). In the present case, however, one may feel that this concluding assertion of the primacy of the honour principle raises the same kind of question as has been mentioned already in relation to the two preceding quatrains.

> *¡Ay triste mal de ausencia,*
> 52 *y quién podrá decir lo que me cuestas!'*

The refrain comes again, as it did on the first of its two appearances, after six quatrains. Now it serves to give a final structural definition to the poem as a whole. This concern with structure, articulated most obviously by means of a repeated refrain of the kind we find in the *romance* beginning '¡Ay amargas soledades' (Vega 1982: 69–70) and elsewhere, is an aspect of a sense of the poem as being, in its totality, an aesthetic artefact and evidence of Lope's care over organization and the calculation of effect.[4] Thus, seen

---

[4] As Suzanne Varga has put it (2002: 101): 'Ses multiples compositions de *romances,* bien qu'elles frappent par leur fraîcheur, leur simplicité et leur noble sobriété ne furent point le résultat d'une sorte d'engendrement spontané, mais d'une élaboration scrupuleuse, comme l'attestent les récentes découvertes de nombreuses versions précédant l'état définitif d'un même poème.' This view of the matter, shared by various modern critics, evidently runs counter to Lope de Vega's own frequently cited claim that 'estos romances, señora, | nacen al sembrar los trigos'—words which Ramón Menéndez Pidal saw as admirably catching the truth (as he saw it) that 'cuando... Lope nace a la poesía entre los versos del romancero, el romance era para todo español ejemplo de poesía natural, que brota sin cultivo' (1940a: 80).

from one point of view, it invites appreciation as a written entity. At the same time the repetition of the refrain at its conclusion places a final stress on the lyrical character of the poem: on the poem as an utterance of emotional pain in song.

In both respects it is an example of a radical, though in the last decades of the sixteenth century representative, recasting of the *romance tradicional*, which in most cases had been primarily narrative and dramatic in character. Among the nearly forty passages of verse in Montemayor's *Diana* there are only two *romances*. Of these the first is sung by a page in the street at night on behalf of his master, appealing to his lady to soften her heart towards him. He is accompanied by a quartet of musicians playing nothing more lyrical than hunting-horns and a kind of trombone. The second *romance* is the now married Diana's lament (already mentioned) over her husband's *celos* and is without musical accompaniment. All the other passages of verse, which are in a variety of metres, are presented as being sung, mostly to the accompaniment of viols (*rabeles*), flute, or pipes (*zampoñas*), or, less frequently, harps or lute or psaltery. The sweetness of the music thus produced is habitually stressed, and the lyrical character of the song is thereby much emphasized. Lope de Vega's ballad shows how thoroughly the *romance* form of verse came, towards the end of the sixteenth century, to be imbued with a similar lyrical character, conveyed here not only by the repeated refrain but also by the general flexibility of utterance, and the nuances of tone and mood, permitted and fostered by the muted patterning of assonantal rhyme in the second and concluding lines of each quatrain. All this was characteristic of the verse brought together in the numerous *Flores de romances nuevos* of the last decade or so of the sixteenth century and of their larger successors at the start of the seventeenth. The lyricism of poems such as Lope's was further heightened when set to music, mostly for accompaniment by the lute-like *vihuela*. The prevalence of this combination of voice and stringed instrument is implicitly acknowledged by Francisco López, bookseller and compiler of the 1604 edition of the *Romancero general* when he writes, in his Prologue ('Al lector'), that, having collected together 'los romances que han sido oídos y aprobados generalmente en España', he has been emboldened to 'exponerlos a la más rigorosa censura, que es la de la lección: pues ahora, escritos y desnudos del adorno de la Música, por fuerza se han de valer por sí solos, y de las fuerzas de su virtud'.

Despite this transformation of the ballad tradition represented by the *romances nuevos*, significant connexions remain. 'El lastimado Belardo', as it ends, focuses the reader's attention on a question: what will come of Belardo's attachment to Filis? The question gains in force because his emotional resistance—powerfully evoked here—to his imminent departure is countered by his ultimately firm resolution that he must nevertheless go because this is what *honor* demands. The reader is thus drawn into Belardo's dilemma and state of inner conflict as he commits himself to the uncertainties of the future. In this way the manner in which this poem ends offers an analogy to that in which *romances viejos* exhibited their technique of 'saber callar a tiempo'. In this respect, as well as in its basic *romance* form, it makes manifest its link to the ballad tradition of *poesía popular*.

On the other hand, its situational and emotional open-endedness offers a resemblance, and perhaps a connexion, to Virgil's poetic practice in bringing his eclogues to an end. Alpers characterizes this practice with the term 'suspension'. He writes: '*Suspension* is the word that best conveys how the oppositions and disparities of Virgilian pastoral are related to each other and held in the mind. As opposed to words like *resolve*, *reconcile*, or *transcend*, *suspension* implies no permanently achieved new relation, while at the same time it conveys absorption in the moment... The herdsman of pastoral poetry... is able to live with and sing out his dilemmas and pain, but he is unable to act so as to resolve or overcome them, or see them through to their end' (1996: 68–69). This critic finds such 'suspension' to be characteristic of the whole sequence of Virgil's eclogues. The first two demonstrate it clearly, though in markedly different ways. The second consists of a monologue in which Corydon, the rejected lover of Alexis, talks to him as if he were present and so conveys the varying and contrary movements of both his mind and his emotions.

Readers in Antiquity found an autobiographical significance here, seeing Corydon as speaking for Virgil. At the very start of the pastoral tradition, Theocritus used the herdsman as 'a vehicle for poetic self-expression' (Halperin 1983: 243). Alpers writes (138) that 'it is from Virgil's self-conscious handling of Theocritean representations and usages that the figure of the herdsman emerged as representative, both of the poet and of all humans'. In the case of Lope de Vega, however, there is a generally accepted direct biographical connexion between a number of his *morisco* and pastoral ballads and his passion, in his early twenties, for Elena Osorio, the daughter of a successful actor-manager of the day (for whom Lope wrote plays) and herself a married woman. In the pastoral ballads Lope refers to the lady and himself using a variety of Arcadian names, the preferred ones among them being Filis and Belardo. Elsewhere he explicitly applies the latter to himself and somewhat playfully complains that other poets, in imitation of him, have taken to using it for themselves.

The autobiographical aspect of Lope's pastoral *romances* has most recently been stressed by Antonio Sánchez Jiménez (2006: esp. 20–41), according to whom 'among the shepherds who feature in these poems Lope de Vega presents himself in the guise of a passionately enamoured Belardo seen in the various stages of his relationship [with Elena Osorio]' (33). This, in Sánchez Jiménez's view, largely explains the success of these poems with their readers, who enjoyed decoding the semi-autobiographical fiction offered. Modern readers may in turn see this approach on the part of Siglo de Oro readers as a way of dealing with the question of the 'truthfulness' or 'untruthfulness' of so obviously artificial a mode of literary expression as was the pastoral genre—an issue of some concern to Berganza in Cervantes's 'El coloquio de los perros', and of more concern to Cervantes himself, as also to many other writers of the time interested in the broad question of *verosimilitud* in fiction.

As for Lope's own pastoral *romances*, Belardo's sorrows and complaints relate, in one degree or another, to the poet's four-year-long liaison with Elena Osorio which ended with his rejection by her and her parents in 1586, whereas the seven-year period in which (as is generally held) his pastoral poems were composed began only in 1588. That was a year which he had begun in prison on charges of libelling Elena's father and uncle and in which, moreover, he began, on his release, his eight-year banishment from Madrid and acquired a wife, Isabel de Urbina. His past relationship with Elena Osorio was thus something recalled, re-lived, but also re-created in literary terms. In a recent study Felipe Pedraza Jiménez comments that, while Lope de Vega's pastoral *romances* are in the main more transparently autobiographical than his *morisco* cycle, one cannot always establish a specific relationship between real events in the poet's life and their literary 'transfiguration' in this *romance* or that one. The reason (he writes) for this uncertainly is that Lope, his friends, and his enemies turned episodes that he had lived through into poetic *motifs* re-created a considerable time after their originating situation and these were fused with other topoi and freely reelaborated. There resulted what he calls an 'extrema literaturización de las experiencias vitales [de su autor]' (2003: 40, 43).[5] Thus, as Montesinos long ago pointed out, Lope continued to write in reverent tones of 'Filis', transformed now into a poetic ideal, at a time when his feelings for the real Filis had become very different (Vega 1925–26: I. xxviii). In any case, it is as a small piece of poetic creation and recreation, combining elements and traditions drawn from high literary culture and Spanish *poesía popular*, as well as from 'life', that this poem, much appreciated in its time, possesses interest, value, and appeal. Pedraza states the central paradox found in poems such as this one: 'These disguisings and this intertwining of conventions served to refine poetic voices, lending them more purity and intimacy... Lope, through the images of himself inscribed in his *romances*, projects his voice and exaggerates his *persona* so as to give a further dimension, more intense, more capable of taking hold of us, and more brilliant, to the heartfelt outpourings of his youth.[6]

*   *   *   *   *

[5] See also 18–23 for his important comments on 'Problemas de autoría : La difícil delimitación del corpus romanceril de Lope'.
[6] 'Estos enmascaramientos y esta maraña de convenciones acendraron la voz de algunos poetas, la hicieron más pura e íntima... Lope, a través de sus trasuntos romanceriles, imposta la voz, sobreactúa... para dar una dimensión más intensa, sobrecogedora y brillante a las efusiones cordiales de su juventud' (2003: 24).

A NOTE ON GÓNGORA'S 'EN LOS PINARES DE JÚCAR' (1603)

En los pinares de Júcar
vi bailar unas serranas
al son del agua en las piedras
y al son del viento en las ramas.

5 No es blanco coro de ninfas
de las que aposenta el agua,
o las que venera el bosque,
seguidoras de Dïana:

serranas eran de Cuenca,
10 honor de aquella montaña,

cuyo pie besan dos ríos
por besar de ellas las plantas,

Alegres corros tejían,
dándose las manos blancas
15 de amistad, quizá temiendo
no la truequen las mudanzas.

¡Qué bien bailan las serranas!
¡Qué bien bailan!

In the pinewoods of Júcar I saw some mountain maidens dancing to the sound of water over stones and the sound of wind in the branches. It was not a company of nymphs in white, of those who dwell in the waters, or those whom the woods worship, followers of Diana: they were maidens of Cuenca, the honour of that mountain whose foot two rivers kiss, desiring to kiss the soles of the dancers' feet. They wove joyful rings as they went, taking each other's fair hands in amity, perhaps fearing lest their changes bring reverses to it, too. How well the maidens dance! How well they dance!

In Lope de Vega's poem we have seen various ways in which it is connected to the emotional world of pastoral, especially as that is presented in Montemayor's *Diana*. Of the pastoral scene itself, however, there is nothing (or nothing explicit) beyond the fact that Belardo is a *zagal*, a term repeatedly applied to shepherds in that work. Góngora's 'En los pinares de Júcar', in contrast, presents no pastoral-world relationships or emotions but sets its whole narrative (to call it so) against the background, or within the context, of a rural scene of maidens dancing in a pinewood. How far Góngora wished his readers (or listeners) to respond to this rural scene as a pastoral one is a question to be considered. In any case, this Note is concerned only with the issue of this poem's relationship to the literary world of pastoral and, to that end, an excerpt from this 64-line ballad (GR.52) is included here.

Colin Smith, in his still valuable study of the poem, insists that here 'Góngora was... bringing literary pastoral almost within touching distance by his seemingly direct description of rustic activity' (1973: 294). He stresses what he calls 'the bookish tradition' behind the poem: that is, the literary traditions that went into its making. Smith (288) was reacting against the view of Robert Jammes, according to whom, in this poem, 'le monde rural n'est vu ni en réaction contre le monde des Cours, ni à travers des souvenirs littéraires, mais directement'. Smith could usefully have questioned more closely than he does Jammes's use of the term *folklorique*:

'Cette apparition enthousiaste de la vie rurale et provinciale dans ce qu'elle a de plus authentiquement folklorique' (1967: 445–46), since the word, of nineteenth-century coinage, relates to the revaluation of *lo popular*, the culture of 'the people', 'Das Volk' (that is, the people of the land rather than the urban masses), which was so important an element in European Romanticism and in consequence carries associations and implies evaluations of questionable relevance to a seventeenth-century poem. Nevertheless, Smith's basic contention stands: Góngora's triumph here 'is a triumph of art rather than of realism' (294)—that is, of rural realism.

The art that Smith so highly praises is manifested most fundamentally in the fabric and functioning of the poem in itself, but also includes Góngora's appropriation and refashioning of his literary sources. So Smith writes that the poem's form 'is that of the traditional and native *romance*, daringly married towards the end to the native *romancillo*; but in these ancient forms are expressed what is surely a very Renaissance sensibility, learned allusions to mythology and to architecture, to the classical gold of Arabia, and so on' (285). As for the dancing maidens, 'there is all that *vocabulario suntuario*, which charmingly assimilates these particular dancers to the generality of Renaissance art' (290). (One might think in particular of the dancing of the Three Graces in Botticelli's *Primavera*.) It is thus, in summary, that Smith sees Góngora's art of combining together *lo popular* and *lo culto*, the ballad tradition and Renaissance literary culture. While one would certainly not wish to contest this in broad terms, there are some further points of a more particular kind that seem to merit consideration.

For Smith it is evidence of Góngora's debt here to the ballad tradition that this poem begins as it does. Its description of the scene, he writes, 'has begun with two native ballad elements: the place names at the start (compare 'En Santa Gadea de Burgos' and 'A Calatrava la Vieja'), and in the second line the emergence of the poet as eye-witness (compare 'caballeros vi asomar') (286). It is of course the case that many ballads of the traditional type begin by placing their narrative in a specific location. Another example would be: 'Allá en Garganta la Olla — en la vera de Plasencia, | salteóme una serrana — blanca, rubia, ojimorena' (Díaz Roig 1985: 267–68). This ballad, telling of an encounter between a traveller and a sexually predatory *serrana* who carries him off to her cave, points us back, however, in a perhaps unexpected way to kinds of late medieval poetry other than the ballad that are of interest for readers of a poem such as 'En los pinares'.

In the *Libro de buen amor* of Juan Ruiz, Archpriest of Hita—a work of the earlier fourteenth century—one section is made up of four poems telling of a traveller, fearful of the mountains around him and the icy weather, who has encounters with monstrous and aggressive *serranas*. This basic situation parodies that of the *pastourelle*, where the poet, passing through springtime meadows, meets a fair shepherdess and pays elegantly expressed court to her. In one of these poems, the fictive poet takes an amorous initiative in a pinewood:

> Por el pinar ayuso [abajo] fallé una vaquera,
> que guardava sus vacas en aquesa rribera.
> 'Omillo me' [me humillo], dixe yo, 'serrana fallaguera [halagüeña];
> o morar me he con vusco [con vos] o mostradme la carrera.'
>
> (Ruiz 1989: 312, stanza 975)

There is an echo here of the Courtly Love style in the self-humbling of the poet before the lady, but this serves a parodic, comic function within the quatrain taken as a whole, which otherwise is emphatically down-to-earth.

For small, elegant, and non-parodic poems about *serranas* in *pinares* one moves forward a century to the *serranillas* of the Marqués de Santillana, Íñigo López de Mendoza. One of these begins:

> Por todos estos pinares
> nin en Val de la Gamella
> non vi serrana más bella
> que Menga de Mançanares.
>
> Desçendiendo'l Yelmo ayuso,
> contra Bóvalo tirando,
> en esse valle de suso [de arriba]
> vi serrana entrar cantando.　　　　(López de Mendoza 2003: 93)

The setting here (as of the *serrana* poems of the *Libro de buen amor*) is the Sierra de Guadarrama, north of Madrid ('Val de la Gamella' may well be Navalagamella, near El Escorial). So it is for another of these *serranillas*, beginning:

> De Loçoya a Navafría,
> açerca de un colmenar,
> topé serrana que amar
> tod' ombre codiçia avría.　　　　　　　　　　　　　　　　(99)

While no pinewood is explicitly mentioned here, the poem's recent editors point out that the place names mentioned mean that the action of the poem develops in the 'famoso pinar' of Navafría (99). It is in any case clear from these *serranillas* of the Marqués de Santillana that neither the initial naming of a precise location for what follows, nor, within a line or two, the emergence of the poet as eye-witness (as Smith puts it) was a poetic procedure limited to *romances viejos*. A wider view of poetic precedents for Góngora's poem seems to be called for.

This is not to imply that Góngora can be taken to have known, or even known of, the *Libro de buen amor*, or that we can be confident that he had knowledge of the Marqués de Santillana's *serranillas*. The Marqués, for his part, did have some knowledge of the *Libro de buen amor* : indeed, he

possessed a manuscript copy of it (it was not printed until 1790) and refers
to it in a work of his own of the late 1440s. However, as Ian Michael has
recently pointed out, 'he was probably the last near-contemporary to have
had a reasonably clear picture of the full range of medieval poetry in Spain',
and, 'when we turn to the sixteenth century, we find almost complete ignor-
ance of that early literature': that is, vernacular literature in prose as well as
verse dating from before the mid-fifteenth century.[7] On the other hand, the
editors of Santillana's *Poesías completas*, writing of his *serranillas*, comment
that this type of poem fully established itself in Santillana's lifetime (1398–
1458), being appreciated by those who enjoyed the playful elegance of its
lyricism: 'gracias a esta esencia, se comprende mejor la abundancia de
serranillas o canciones de serrana escritas por varios poetas' (2003: 25).
Furthermore, these poems were most often written in a strophic form that
included a repeated refrain.

Robert Jammes writes of the interest in rustic life that found such
powerful and abundant expression in Spanish literature at the start of the
seventeenth century.[8] Góngora's poem witnesses to that interest, and in his
case, whatever the nature of the links (including manuscript transmission
and tradition) between the fifteenth-century *serranilla* poets and himself, it
would seem that there was a significant connexion here, even though it was
one among others.

There is, perhaps, one other literary connexion which takes us in an
entirely different direction but deserves notice. This brings us back to
Theocritus, the founder of the pastoral tradition in European literature, as we
have seen. Again one is concerned only with the first few lines of Góngora's
poem, but nevertheless with the field of poetic reference in which Góngora
is implicitly inviting us to place it. Richard Hunter, in his annotations to
Anthony Verity's recent translation of Theocritus, writes of 'Idyll I' that
'this poem, with its beautiful, musical opening... seems always to have been
placed first in ancient collections of Theocritus's poetry, and came to
symbolize the essence of the bucolic genre' (Theocritus 2002: 85). It was, in
consequence, placed first in editions of Theocritus brought out in the age of
printing. One did not need to have knowledge of Greek in order to read him.
There were numerous Latin editions of his poems which thus put them
within reach of the larger educated literary public. Commentators of Garcilaso's *oeuvre* cite them in Latin. So also did Lope de Vega in his *Introducción a la justa poética de San Isidro en las fiestas de su beatificación*
(1872a: 146). Góngora, who clearly had an excellent knowledge of Latin
but not, it seems, of Greek, will have known him in this way.

Idyll I begins thus:

---

[7] Michael (2005: 261, 263). Together with this essay, two earlier studies of the 1960s
remain helpful: Whinnom (1967) and Rodríguez-Moñino (1968).

[8] Jammes (1967: 445). See also the broad examination of this issue in Salomon
(1965: 171–96).

THYRSIS: There is sweet music in that pine tree's whisper, goatherd,
            There by the spring. Sweet too is the music of your pipe;
            You would win the second prize to Pan...

GOATHERD: Shepherd, your song sounds sweeter than the water
            tumbling over there from the high rock.[9]

The sequence of correspondences between these lines and the opening
quatrain of Góngora's *romance* is striking: the pine(s), the sound of the
breeze in the branches and that of the water falling from or over rocks: in
each case a musical sound, as explicitly stated by Theocritus and implicitly
suggested by Góngora as his *serranas* dance to its accompaniment. Later,
one of these dancing maidens sings, accompanying herself with castanet-
like clicking of pebbles in her hands. Thus the opening quatrain of the
romance establishes a situation and mood that extend right through the
poem, while in both poems—that of Theocritus as well as Góngora's—this
continuity of key and mood is sustained by repeated refrains. If there is a
degree of indebtedness to Theocritus here, it is a significant one and gives
some further precision to the contribution of 'the bookish world' which
Smith stresses, while acknowledging that it is combined with elements
derived from Góngora's first-hand knowledge of Cuenca and its situation,
with its two rivers and deep ravine—knowledge acquired when he went
there in the spring of 1603 in furtherance of the business of the Cathedral
Chapter of Córdoba, of which he was a member. The bringing together of
locations and scenes of the 'real' world and scenes and associations of a
highly poeticized nature is, as we have seen in examining Lope de Vega's
poem, a feature of pastoral that runs throughout the tradition from Classical
Antiquity to Montemayor's *Diana*, and indeed later. There is a notable
example of this, relating to the Sierra de Cuenca, in Garcilaso's Eclogue I.

The flowing musicality of Góngora's poem is its most striking aspect. As
one manuscript comment put it: 'No tiene otro assumpto [= asunto] más que
la imaginativa, para cantarlo en vihuela' (Góngora 1998: II.109). Góngora
had acknowledged his delight in music on an important occasion a full fifteen years earlier, when he was called upon by the new Bishop of Córdoba to
answer a series of charges alleging insufficient diligence and propriety as
one of the cathedral clergy. The concluding charge was that 'Vive—en fin—

---

[9] Latinists may find interest in the following renderings of these opening lines: (*i*)
[THYRSIS:] 'Dulcis est susurrus, & pinus, o caprarie, illa | Quae ad fontes canit: dulce
autem & tu | Fistula canis: post Pana secundum praemium auferes.' ... [CAPRARIUS:]
'Dulcior, o pastor, tuus cantus quam quae resonans | Illa a petra distillat superne aqua'
(1579: 3) (*ii*) [THYRSIS:] 'Dulcem susurrum & pinus ista, o pastor caprarie, | Quae est
iuxta fontes, resonat: suaviter vero & tu | Fistula canis: secundum Pana proximum
praemium feres' ... [CAPRARIUS:] 'Dulcius, o pastor, tuum carmen est, quam effusa | Illa
quae de rupe ex alto defluit unda' (1604: 5).

como muy mozo [he was twenty-seven] y anda de día y de noche en cosas
ligeras; trata representantes de comedias, y escribe coplas profanas'. To this
Góngora replied—clearly not much crestfallen—that 'ni mi vida es tan escan-
dalosa ni yo tan viejo que se me pueda acusar de vivir como mozo'. As to his
consorting with actors, he conceded that they did come to his house, as they
did to the houses of other 'hombres honrados y caballeros', but indeed 'más
a la mía por ser [yo] tan aficionado a la música' (Artigas 1925: 62–63).

Describing, in his poem, the flowing movement of the dancing of the
serranas, he writes:

> **Alegres corros tejían,**
> **dándose las manos blancas**
> **de amistad, quizá temiendo**
> 16 **no la truequen las mudanzas.**

They wove joyful rings as they went, taking each other's fair hands in amity,
perhaps fearing lest their changes bring reverses to it, too.

Smith (285) comments on the final word here: 'the complicated Renaissance conceit of the *mudanzas* (both 'the changing figures of the dance' and
'fickleness')'. *Cov.* gives a larger account of the term: '(*i*) 'Cierto número
de movimientos que se hacen a compás en los bailes y danzas'; (*ii*)
'Inconstancia o variedad de los afectos o de los dictámenes'; (*iii*) 'Cambio
de parecer o de variedad'; (*iv*) 'Fragilidad, inconsistencia'. All these meanings
come together in different degrees in Góngora here; but *fragilidad* seems to
deserve special emphasis, for the reason that, in this sense, *mudanzas* was
likely to bring to the mind of a seventeenth-century Spanish reader of poetry
the argument and conclusion of one of Garcilaso de la Vega's finest and
most famous sonnets, Sonnet XXIII:

> En tanto que de rosa y d'açucena
> se muestra la color en vuestro gesto [rostro],
> y que vuestro mirar ardiente, honesto,
> con clara luz la tempestad serena;
> 5   y en tanto que'l cabello, que'n la vena
> del oro s'escogió, con buelo presto
> por el hermoso cuello blanco, enhiesto,
> el viento mueve, esparze y desordena:
> coged de vuestra alegre primavera
> 10   el dulce fruto, antes que'l tiempo ayrado
> cubra de nieve la hermosa cumbre.
> Marchitará la rosa el viento elado,
> todo lo mudará la edad ligera
> por no hazer mudança en su costumbre.   (Garcilaso 1981: 125–28)

The happy springtime of youth soon passes: grasp its sweet fruit while you
have it, for fleeting time will not change its ways. Góngora, in the flower of

youth at the start of his twenties, reworked Garcilaso's sonnet in a superb sonnet of his own (G.24): 'Mientras por competir con tu cabello' (Góngora 1976: 230). Now, however, the conclusion is not merely the grey chill of old age but death and dissolution: 'tierra... humo... polvo... sombra... nada'. *Las mudanzas* in 'En los pinares de Júcar' carry only a hint of the unstoppable mutability of human existence behind the beauty and gaiety of youth, but it is there, starting echoes, for Góngora's readers and hearers, of other poems (in a way that was characteristic of Siglo de Oro poets and poetry) and thus, with a touch, brings to mind one of the abiding preoccupations of pastoral literature, the fragility of happiness, and gives a moment of emotional depth to a delightfully lyrical poem.

LUIS DE GÓNGORA

'NOBLE DESENGAÑO' (1584)

Noble desengaño,
gracias doy al cielo,
que rompiste el lazo
que me tenía preso.

5 Por tan gran milagro
colgaré en tu templo
las graves cadenas
de mis graves yerros.

Las fuertes coyundas
10 del yugo de acero,
que con tu favor
sacudí del cuello,

las húmidas velas
y los rotos remos,
15 que escapé del mar
y ofrecí en tu puerto,

ya de tus paredes
serán ornamento,
gloria de tu nombre
20 y de Amor descuento.

Y así, pues que triunfas
del rapaz arquero,
tiren de tu carro
y sean tu trofeo

25 locas esperanzas,
vanos pensamientos,
pasos esparcidos,
livianos deseos,

rabiosos cuidados,
30 ponzoñosos celos,
infernales glorias,
gloriosos infiernos.

Compóngante himnos,
y digan sus versos

35 que libras captivos
y das vista a ciegos.

Ante tu Deidad,
hónrense mil fuegos
del sudor precioso
40 del árbol sabeo.

Pero ¿quién me mete
en cosas de seso,
y en hablar de veras
en aquestos tiempos,

45 donde el que más trata
de burlas y juegos,
ése es quien se viste
más a lo moderno?

Ingrata señora
50 de tus aposentos,
más dulce y sabrosa
que nabo en adviento,

aplícame un rato
el oído atento,
55 que quiero hacer auto
de mis devaneos.

¡Qué de noches frías
que me tuvo el hielo
tal, que por esquina
60 me juzgó tu perro,

y alzando la pierna,
con gentil denuedo
me argentó de plata
los zapatos negros!

65 ¡Qué de noches destas,
señora, me acuerdo
que andando a buscar
chinas por el suelo

para hacer la seña
70 por el agujero,
al tomar la china,
me ensucié los dedos!

¡Qué de días anduve
cargado de acero
75 con harto trabajo,
porque estaba enfermo!

Como estaba flaco,
parecía cencerro:
hierro por de fuera,
80 por de dentro hueso.

¡Qué de meses y años
que viví muriendo
en la Peña Pobre,
sin ser Beltenebros;

85 donde me acaeció
mil días enteros
no comer sino uñas,
haciendo sonetos!

¡Qué de necedades
90 escribí en mil pliegos,

que las ríes tú ahora
y yo las confieso,

aunque las tuvimos
ambos, en un tiempo,
95 yo por discreciones
y tú por requiebros!

¡Qué de medias noches
canté en mi instrumento:
'Socorred, señora,
100 con agua mi fuego!'

donde aunque tú no
socorriste luego,
socorrió el vecino
con un gran caldero!

105 Adiós, mi señora,
porque me es tu gesto
chimenea en verano
y nieve en invierno,

y el bazo me tienes
110 de guijarros lleno,
porque creo que bastan
seis años de necio.

*   *   *   *   *

This poem (GR.14) appears to be a relatively early work by Góngora: its date of composition is generally agreed to be 1584. It is a six-syllable *romancillo*, rhyming in *é–a,* a choice of metre indicative of 'genre'.

Arguably the most remarkable thing about the text is an, at first sight, abrupt shift of tone from 49 onwards, preceded by a brief, ironic, transitional passage (41–48). What up to this point had predominantly seemed to be a moral, even religiously inspired, reflection on the dangers of earthly loves, cast in suitably elevated language, gives way to a sequence of scabrous, not to say scatological anecdotes about the speaker's amorous follies, where we find down-to-earth, plain statement still occasionally interspersed with *culto* language, now used to quite unequivocally burlesque effect. We come to see that the poem's first-person speaker is heartily tired of being an unrequited lover; but what is puzzling is his apparently inconsistent attitude towards his conversion. Has he really taken it to heart? Has it all been 'a bit of a joke'? Does the speaker's coarse humour from 49 onwards suggest that, with talk of this kind, more authentic sentiments are breaking out, whereas there had been an element of emotional pretence in the more conventionally 'proper' moral language that went before? Does the speaker's shifting tone and focus suggest that he may in fact be less *desengañado* than he might have seemed to be before, less truly detached from earthly vanities like *loco amor*? On the other hand, perhaps the speaker really is a new man in a profounder moral/religious sense, one who has learnt that key Golden-Age lesson of *desengaño*? It is hard to be sure, and that fact draws us into the poem's drama. Rather like an accomplished playwright, Góngora places on stage a soliloquizing character and invites us to make of him such sense as we can.

I take it, in short, that Góngora's play here is not so much with the moral commonplace of the folly of lovers, as with what might be called the problematic authenticity of the sense of sin, the fitfulness of our moral insight ('insight' is the word that I have used to translate *desengaño*). He problematizes our capacity to analyse our experiences without the distortions introduced by *amour-propre*, and to translate our findings into effective moral action and reaction for the future. When will men ever learn? And he asks whether such perversity, such a propensity to self-deception and posturing, such a lack of fortitude, should more appropriately draw from us tears or laughter. *Desengaño* can, after all, be experienced at different levels. It may involve no more than a transitory 'disappointment', as when we have misplaced our hopes, and suffer a temporary upset. Or the term can have a deeper, Christian/Stoic value: it can relate to how we might arrive at a radical critique of the way in which humans clutch at pleasures that will not endure, the way in which they try to dodge the facts of mortality and moral weakness. *Engaño* lies with the overweening world of human desires; a world that, for the Christian, denies or ignores the message of the Cross, which was the price that had to be paid for our redemption and the outpouring of that grace without which we are as nothing. As John Newton, the later hymn-writer, put it, drawing on the language of the Sermon on the Mount, 'Fading is the worldling's pleasure, all his boasted pomp and show; solid joys and lasting treasure none but Sion's children know' ('Sion's children' being those who hope to get to Heaven, the 'Jerusalem on high'). To pass from *engaño* to *desengaño* may be more easily said than done; the road to Hell is paved with good intentions. Can a poet help the dullness of our blinded sight?

This much granted, it would be wrong to give the impression that everything about 1–40 is equally solemn. Early readers of the poem would have been 'warned' about genre in advance, by meeting this text among others that the manuscripts unanimously classed among Góngora's *romances burlescos* (on the bottom step of the ladder of seriousness, that is to say, down a level from *romances satíricos*). In the text itself, as well, there is at least one overt clue to the poet's humorous intentions, and it is the way in which Cupid is referred to, in a rather cheeky periphrasis, as 'the lad with the bow and arrows', *el rapaz arquero* (22). Beyond that, we are likely to notice a jarring effect between the normal expectations aroused by the choice of *romancillo* metre, and a rhetorical style which gets increasingly over-the-top, especially from 23 onwards: in 25–32, and in the context of other classicizing allusions in 1–32 as a whole, we find an extensive list of lovers' emotional torments; there are Biblical allusions in 33–36, culminating in the extravagant *culto* writing of 37–40—all this, before we are brought down with a sharp bump in 41 onwards. (I shall return to each of these features later on.) Before leaving this general point, it might be remarked, in the context of discussing what is new about the *romancero nuevo* more widely, that this poem is not an isolated example of a burlesque manner among Góngora's early *romances*. It is now claimed indeed that the '*romancero nuevo* revolution' was begun by Góngora himself in 1580, with the composition and dissemination of his *romancillo burlesco* 'Hermana Marica' (GR.4; see Góngora 2000b: I. xii–xiii).

In the opening forty lines of 'Noble desengaño', the *culto* Góngora draws on a number of learned intertexts, ones so familiar to educated readers of his time as to have become commonplaces. This is a type of poetry that offers its readers the chance to recognize allusions to important Classical writers, in both Latin and Italian. Góngora implies by this that his modern poem has venerable roots, and that there is very little new under the sun. His literary references work on a principle of expressive economy, filling out a later poem's context if its reader is sufficiently well read to catch the clues on offer. In this *romancillo*, we find allusion to such learned topoi as love likened to sailing in dangerous waters, and the lover's state resembling one of captivity. When it comes to love as a form of captivity, the reference, involving Petrarch, might either be to the God of Love dragging his prisoners along in a triumphal procession such as Roman generals staged, or nearer still to the historical conditions of Góngora's own day, it may involve allusion to being in love as resembling being captured by Moorish pirates in the Mediterranean.[1]

To start with the references to love and seafaring, principal, although far from unique among the Latin intertexts on offer here, is Horace.[2] For the Latin poet, seafaring and the attendant exposure to sudden storms, and loss of life and possessions, had stood for a wide gamut of disorderly passions. He characteristically concluded that adventurousness may be closer to temerity than real courage; that it is better to stay at home than risk dangers that no amount of rational activity can conjure. There is one great Horatian ode, though, that uses seafaring imagery not of a wide range of passions, but specifically to explore the threat to which erotic obsession lays people open;

[1] For Petrarchism generally, see the excellent Forster (1969), especially Chapters 1 and 2. For another facet of the motif of freedom from fetters, see Sumption (1975: 109–13).

[2] For Horace, see Odes I.3, I.14, I.28, II.10, 3.29; Epode II. Compare Catullus, IV, and the lines against seafaring in Ovid, *Metamorphoses,* I. Lope is plainly drawing on this tradition, and later Italian and Spanish Petrarchan elaborations of it, when he comes to compose his *barquillas* in the early 1630s, as does Góngora himself in his grand *Soledad segunda*. Joseph Fucilla (1960: 255) is more inclined to think that Góngora is drawing primarily on a sonnet by Tansillo, 'Qual huom che trasse il grave remo e spinse'. It should be remembered too that, from a Christian perspective, the vanity of seafaring receives its ultimate condemnation in Apoc. 18: 10–20.

it is his famous Ode, I.5, 'Quis multa gracilis te puer in rosa', which is given
here in the translation by John Milton (1971: 96–97):

> What slender youth, bedewed with liquid odours,
> Courts thee on roses in some pleasant cave,
> Pyrrha, for whom bind'st thou
> in wreaths thy golden hair,
> plain in thy neatness; O how oft shall he
> on faith and changed Gods complain: and seas
> rough with black winds and storms
> unwonted shall admire [*cause to be astonished*]:
> who now enjoys thee credulous, all gold,
> who always vacant [*available*], always amiable,
> hopes thee; of flattering gales
> unmindful? Hapless they
> to whom thou, untried, seem'st fair. Me in my vowed
> picture the sacred wall declares t'have hung
> my dank and dropping weeds [*clothing*]
> to the stern god of the sea.

Góngora's indebtedness to this Classical poem with its rueful, even bitter,
ironies, is obvious, and it is what 13–20 plainly refer to. For readers who
know their basic Latin literature, therefore, the hint is given here already,
before the anecdotes of 49 onwards, that the *lazo*, *cadenas*, and so forth that
have held the speaker prisoner have been specifically those of erotic obsession. The idea that sailors saved from shipwreck should hang votive offerings
in Neptune's temple is found in Virgil too (*Aen.*, XII.766–69), as Góngora's
older contemporary Herrera noted when he commented on the earlier
sixteenth-century master Garcilaso's Sonnet VII, 'No pierda más quien ha
tanto perdido'. Among the Spanish modern classics, Góngora and his readers
also knew well another poem by Garcilaso that draws on the same Horatian
original, his Sonnet XXXIV, 'Gracias al cielo doy que ya del cuello'.

References to being held prisoner by Love come either side of those to
seafaring; or rather, in the opening twelve lines or so of the poem, the two
strands seem to run together, and Góngora appears to have in mind those
people captured by Turkish or North African pirates, condemned to row in
the enemy's galleys if not to incarceration in Algiers, as had happened to
Cervantes. Góngora's *romance* 'Amarrado al duro banco' (GR.11) refers to
Christians made to row in Islamic galleys in this way. The Christians at
home made sometimes considerable efforts to rescue or ransom such
unfortunates, on whose return their former chains were hung as a thank-
offering, if not inside, on the external walls of churches. (One recalls, for
example, those that festoon the flanks of San Juan de los Reyes in Toledo.)

We find in 21–32 references to the victory parade of a Roman general,
with the victor mounted in his chariot (*carro*, 23), and his prisoners and the

material spoils of war following behind. In Britain one may view Mantegna's glorious painting *The Triumphs of Caesar* in Hampton Court as one great representation of the theme. Most immediately in Góngora's thoughts, I dare say, though, is the poet Petrarch, who in the mid-fourteenth century had composed his *Trionfi*, that recount a number of symbolic dreams. The first of these, *Trionfo d'Amore,* pictures Love as a conquering hero, leading a string of famous lovers, some in chains, as Petrarch's spirit guide explains: 'qual con più gravi | leggi mena sua vita aspra ed acerba | sotto mille catene e mille chiavi', 'some, obedient to more onerous laws, lead a tough and bitter life, secured by a thousand chains and a thousand keys'.

The opening section of Góngora's *romancillo,* therefore, offers us a number of complementary takes on the lover's state: some Classical; some more Christian (see below); some more distanced in time; some, however conventionalized, a good deal closer to contemporary experience. (Although the Christians had quite recently struck what at the time seemed a knockout blow against the infidels' naval power in the Battle of Lepanto in 1571, Spanish fears of the Muslim danger from the sea remained real enough.) The effect of such a plethora of cultural references in the opening of Góngora's poem is, I think, somewhat indeterminate. Its style might be no more than the sort of *culto* writing that mainly adopts a rhetorical elevation in keeping with its moral subject-matter, but when we begin to wonder about the speaker's true emotional state, things get more teasingly interesting. Are this speaker's words perhaps not (yet) maturely pondered? Perhaps what is being presented here is the hyperbole of one in the first flush of deliverance, but still exasperated, hurt, and angry. Perhaps his is the language of one who actually protests just a bit too much? It is important to grasp that the poem presents us not with the Reverend Luis de Góngora writing in an uncomplicated *propia persona,* but with a little dramatic monologue, that proves the more fascinating the more carefully we attend to it. Luis Cernuda described Robert Browning's 'dramatic monologues' in the following terms: 'lo típico y constante en su obra no es expresar su propia experiencia del mundo, sino aquella de otros, animando con pasiones dramáticas seres distintos del propio autor, a quienes éste da voz en soliloquios o monólogos' (1993–95: III. 238). To make an, I hope, obvious point, such procedures were not Browning's own invention. We find them in our Spanish Golden-Age non-dramatic poets, who themselves drew on Classical antecedents—Ovid's *Heroides* spring to mind. Nor, on a slightly different but related track, should we overlook the importance of Horace's ironic, self-conscious, poetic self-projection. David Armstrong has written about his Odes, 'the perpetual challenge in every apparently simple word to consider why it is the right word here; the endless forcing of the reader to stop and ask, Why this change of thought? Why this sudden intrusion of something grand into a very simple passage, or vice versa?—all these demand reflection at every line' (1989: 73).

*   *   *   *   *

> **Noble desengaño,**
> **gracias doy al cielo,**
> **que rompiste el lazo**
> 4   **que me tenía preso.**

Noble Insight, I give thanks to Heaven for breaking the bonds that held me
prisoner.

As so often in balladry, traditional as well as 'nuevo', we find here an *in*
medias res opening. Someone is talking out loud, and we can overhear him.
This is a dramatic device. Our curiosity is aroused. Who is this? What is he
talking about? To what extent may we take his words at face value? What
emotional state is he in, and to what extent does that colour his utterances?

Insight (*desengaño*) is addressed directly and called *noble*. There is
nothing here as yet (the choice of metre to one side) to suggest that anything
other than elevated sentiments are being voiced, an impression that the
following lines apparently do nothing to diminish:

> **Por tan gran milagro**
> **colgaré en tu templo**
> **las graves cadenas**
> 8   **de mis graves yerros.**

For such a great miracle, I shall hang up the heavy shackles of my weighty
errors as a thank-offering in your shrine.

There is some wordplay here: *templo* may be a pagan temple or a Christian
church; and Góngora plays on related meanings of *grave* (Latin, *gravis*)
'weighty', and literally heavy; burdensome, either in the literal or the metaphorical sense. The chains of galley-slaves freed from enemy hands were, as
mentioned earlier, customarily hung in Christian churches as ex-votos (offerings made in fulfilment of a religious vow). Doubt about the exact nature of
a *templo* plays a creative role in Góngora's Sonnet LIII, 'De pura honestidad
tempo sagrado' (G.13; Góngora 1976: 118). He also puns on *yerro* | [*h*]*ierro*.
This lover's mistaken erotic obsession has kept him prisoner and rendered
him impotent for anything else; this has been a grave error, one that may
now weigh heavily on his conscience too. Has he really seen the light? Or is
he just rather embarrassed and angry, whilst venting his spleen in the late-
found language of moral rectitude and spiritual realignment? On a comparable tack, one might ask whether *yerros* is best translated as 'mistakes', or
as something more morally serious than that? *Cov.* does not clear our doubts
on this point, as his dictionary glosses *errar* as 'pecar, no acertar'.

> **Las fuertes coyundas**
> **del yugo de acero,**
> **que con tu favor**
> 12   **sacudí del cuello,**

> las húmidas velas
> y los rotos remos,
> que escapé del mar
> 16 y ofrecí en tu puerto,
>
> ya de tus paredes
> serán ornamento,
> gloria de tu nombre
> 20 y de Amor descuento.

The powerful steel yoke from which, thanks to you, I shook my neck free, the still damp sails and shattered oars that I rescued from the sea and offered up on my return to port, will from now on adorn your shrine-walls, to the glory of your name and as a black mark to Cupid.

This language very much suggests the condition of a galley-slave. Although it is a personified *Desengaño* that is being addressed here rather than God directly, the word *gloria* and the phrase *con tu favor* invoke a religious sensibility that is conscious of its own weakness and reliance on divine help. A chiasmus in 19–20 points a contrast between *gloria* and *descuento* that is not quite as pointed as one might have expected: *descuento* sounds gently ironic and euphemistic. (*Cov.* confirms that this word meant a discount, 'something off the bill', in Góngora's time also; Jones (1966: 153) translates the word as 'depreciation'.) The transitive use of *escapar* is no longer current; *húmidas*, rather than *húmedas*, reflects Golden-Age pronunciation.

> Y así, pues que triunfas
> del rapaz arquero,
> tiren de tu carro
> 24 y sean tu trofeo
>
> locas esperanzas,
> vanos pensamientos,
> pasos esparcidos,
> 28 livianos deseos,
>
> rabiosos cuidados,
> ponzoñosos celos,
> infernales glorias,
> 32 gloriosos infiernos.

So, since you have triumphed over that lad with the bow and arrows, your chariot should be drawn by, and your trophies should be crazy hopes, pointless brooding, distant wanderings, fickle desires, rabid cares, poisonous jealousy, hellish pleasures, glorious torments.

I have already commented (p. 26) on the import of calling Cupid *el rapaz arquero*, with its mischievously disrespectful implications, that rather stand out against a more straightfaced background. (*Cov.*, though, interestingly and relevantly for our present purposes, links this word for a lad, *rapaz*, with the notion of rapacity, an etymology which Corominas supports.) The imagery inspired by Roman triumphs and the symbolic use of them by Petrarch have already been mentioned. Indeed, the strong paradoxes of 31–32 very much recall the Petrarchan analysis of love's torments. It is also relevant to recall that *gloria* is a well-attested euphemism for orgasm, as in Act XIV of *Celestina* (Rojas 1991: 501; see also Alzieu 1975, nos. 11, 14, 31) : lovers' lusts may lead to Hell, just as the pursuit of sexual pleasure may itself involve emotional pain. The speaker's dogged enumeration of the lover's sufferings wittily suggests a degree of exasperation on his part, together with the way in which lovers pass rapidly 'from one damned thing to another', from torment to torment in giddy succession. Note as well that Love and its effects are personified, but featuring as they do as elements in a somewhat protracted list, there is a hint of something inauthentic about the feelings involved, as if they are not truly or deeply felt at all.

> **Compóngante himnos,**
> **y digan sus versos**
> **que libras captivos**
> 36   **y das vista a ciegos.**

They should compose hymns in your honour, the lines of which will proclaim that you set at liberty those that are captive and give sight to the blind.

The speaker's rhetoric now extends to include allusions, not just to Classical poetry, but to Holy Scripture, to the words from the prophet Isaiah (61: 1) that got Jesus into trouble when he applied them to himself in the synagogue at Nazareth (Luke 4: 18–19): 'Spiritus Domini super me proper quod unxit me evangelizare pauperibus misit me praedicare captivis remissionem et caecis visum' ('The Spirit of the Lord God is upon me, because he has anointed me to preach good news to the poor. He has sent me to proclaim release to the captives, and the recovery of sight to the blind'). This allusion keeps in play the notion that being in love is like being held prisoner in a foreign land, and it also alludes to the common saying 'Love is blind'. But if we take its Biblical origins seriously, such language suggests that the *desengaño* to which Góngora's character is laying claim is of the most serious sort, namely a God-given gift that comes by inspiration of the Holy Spirit. Is the speaker being entirely serious here? Perhaps he is still sounding off, flying off the handle, rather than speaking with due consideration. Perhaps he is trying to put the best available gloss on feelings of embarrassment and hurt, borrowing from contemporary cant? Or has he learnt a lasting lesson? Whatever the case with the invented character, the poet's own take on things is more genuinely comic and detached, whilst pointing to a real truth, however hard to come by, hard to make 'flesh of one's flesh', and hard to sustain. (Góngora, like certain other writers of his time, was deeply suspicious of moralizing, both from the point of view of its efficacy and as regards the motivations and self-awareness of those who indulge in it.)

> **Ante tu Deidad,**
> **hónrense mil fuegos**
> **del sudor precioso**
> 40 **del árbol sabeo.**

A thousand censers should honour your God-like nature, burning incense from the precious gum (sweat) of the Sheban tree.

This is a complicated, extremely *culto* way of extending the speaker's references to religious cult. (*Deidad* was capitalized in the Chacón manuscript completed in the 1620s.)[3] The speaker tells us people should not only sing hymns to Insight, but burn incense too. If *templos* and ex-voto offerings belong in either Roman or Christian culture, the language here refers us away from an exclusively pagan domain: the exotic and opulent Queen of Sheba, whose gifts to King Solomon included pungent-smelling things (*aromata*), is the Queen of Saba in the Latin Bible (III Regum = I Kings 10: 1–2; compare Psalm 71(72): 10). What, too, could be more refined than the speaker's learned hyperbole and circumlocution? We are about to be brought down with a very disconcerting bump in what follows, in such a way as to make us wonder further to what extent the speaker has really been emotionally, spiritually, committed to his hyperbolic praise of *desengaño*:

> **Pero ¿quién me mete**
> **en cosas de seso,**
> **y en hablar de veras**
> 44 **en aquestos tiempos,**
>
> **donde el que más trata**
> **de burlas y juegos,**
> **ése es quien se viste**
> 48 **más a lo moderno?**

But why am I getting into all this heavy talk and brain-teasing stuff (at least, I think it's my brain that's being teased), when if you want to be supercool these days you need to lighten up, and use more jokes than anybody else?

Our speaker's flow of thought and feeling seems unpredictable; this switch is dramatic. One wonders, too, what contemporary satirical reference might be in play here. Who are the successful jokers among Góngora's peers, who render the efforts of more serious moral writers relatively ineffectual? The fact is, in any case, that, as we have noted already, Góngora was already himself an established writer of burlesque pieces. (I keep up the insistence that Góngora and the speaker of this poem should not necessarily be fused,

---

[3] There is a the modern facsimile of this: Góngora (1991).

or at least, not thoroughgoingly so.) The basic opposition here is between that well established pair, *burlas* and *veras*, often at this period presented as antithetical terms: in the contrast between tragedy and comedy; between the philosopher who weeps (Heraclitus) and the philosopher who laughs (Democritus); between the wise man (*sapiens*, *sabio*) who has learnt the lesson of *desengaño* in Stoic or in Christian terms, and the fool (*stultus*, *necio*) who has not learnt, or will not. At the same time, a classic apology for comedy was that it might make learning easier: the bitter pill of wisdom might be more readily swallowed if pleasantly coated. Góngora might seem to be teasing us here, as to where he stands—as to whether he is having fun and just being frivolous and facetious, or whether there is more method in his procedure, involving charming or amusing us into a sharper moral awareness. (I believe the latter is the case, a claim I shall return to later.)

Note that the speaker uses the metaphor of *vestirse*: this makes satirical fun of people who always want to dress in the latest fashions, be those never so ridiculous (see below, pp. 149–52), but it also refers to the commonplace idea that rhetoric 'clothes' thought. In consequence, Góngora's point would be that naked truth may be found beneath the fancy comic dress that decks it out. Another possibility is that he, the poet, is getting back at contemporary critics of the *culto* manner: his suggestion is that his critics are incapable of any elevation of feeling and expression, whereas he can do that, and outstrip them in the 'lower' forms of burlesque as well—as we are about to see.

In 42, the poet puns on *sexo/seso*—in some moralists' view, a radically antithetical pair, since lovers are all mad, incapable of rational thought about their obsessions or about anything else. (Corominas shows that the word *sexo* was current at this period, even if *Cov.* does not carry it.) The double-take here further reveals that all the weighty talk about *desengaño* up to this point in the poem may in fact have had sexual urges at its root; it is sex that has led to at least temporary disappointment, if not to a more durable form of repentance. It also suggests that, as the latter part of the text dwells anecdotally on all the sexual humiliations that the speaker has endured over a six-year period, this may perhaps speak to the reader's intelligence, and lead to corrective reactions on our part (if not the speaker's). One appalling anecdote after another illustrates the full extent to which lovers may persist in their folly:

> **Ingrata señora**
> **de tus aposentos,**
> **más dulce y sabrosa**
> 52   **que nabo en adviento,**
>
> **Aplícame un rato**
> **el oído atento,**
> **que quiero hacer auto**
> 56   **de mis devaneos.**

Ungrateful mistress—of your own establishment—, sweeter and tastier than turnips in Advent, listen carefully to me for a bit, because I want to make confession of my past mental wanderings.

Góngora's speaker now goes in for deflationary humour: the lady is no longer mistress of his heart; merely of her own home, with the extra suggestion, I think, that she lets out rooms or keeps a boarding-house (in terms of social station, no lady, therefore, she). The joke about turnips in 52 is more complex. It refers to a proverbial phrase recorded by Correas: 'Cada cosa en su tiempo, y nabos en Adviento'. (Advent comes in winter, and is a semi-penitential season in the Church's calendar.)[4] We can gloss that in a number of ways, not least as praise of a regular if plain existence, hardly the lover's usual state! But one wonders also if the speaker is not delivering a backhanded compliment to the former *dama*, damning her with faint praise and with an outlandishly ungallant comparison. It needs to be remembered as well that *nabo* has an obscene sense ('knob') that was current in Góngora's day as well as our own. To describe his past follies as *devaneos* sounds comic-euphemistic, rather than the voice of true repentance, since, says *Cov.*, *devaneos* may be caused by a blow to the head.

> **¡Qué de noches frías**
> **que me tuvo el hielo**
> **tal, que por esquina**
> 60 **me juzgó tu perro,**
>
> **y alzando la pierna,**
> **con gentil denuedo**
> **me argentó de plata**
> 64 **los zapatos negros!**

When I think of the number of cold nights I spent, so frozen stiff that your dog thought I was a street corner, and cocking its leg on an aristocratic impulse, plated my black shoes with a silvery shower!

The comedy here springs from the contrast between the scatological action and its extravagantly *culto* linguistic wrapping. (*Argentó de plata* is pleonastic, in fact, and Góngora would later use it, without any irony, in his *Polifemo*.) *Argentar* is a *cultismo*, although one with thirteenth-century roots, being used to mean 'to plate with silver': 'plating' conveys that this dog pees copiously, or perhaps—another suggestion—we should think of the dog's pee standing in for the silver buckles this man is too poor to have on his shoes. It is in any case a further 'poetic' observation that the dog's urine appears silver in the moonlight. To this is added the delicious phrase *con gentil denuedo*, further bringing the scene to life, by capturing the animal's carefree aristocratic disdain for its (very differently placed) victim. A little

---

[4] Correas (1967), a modern edition of the 1627 original.

later, Cervantes would put the same animals to use, to comment on human silliness and vice, in the 'cynical (= 'doggy') philosophy' of his wonderful *Coloquio de los perros*. In Góngora we find an overall gist that lovers will poeticize and glory in any humiliation, when suffered for the beloved's sake. Anything is to be preferred by them to being ignored; love being blind, they just cannot see the awfulness of their situation for what it is. Góngora ridicules the elegant diction of Petrarchism and other Courtly Love poetry, as a rhetoric that glosses over and prettifies things that when judged by stricter moral standards, have very little beautiful about them.

> **¡Qué de noches destas,**
> **señora, me acuerdo**
> **que andando a buscar**
> 68 **chinas por el suelo**
>
> **para hacer la seña**
> **por el agujero,**
> **al tomar la china,**
> 72 **me ensucié los dedos!**

When I think of the number of nights I can remember grubbing about in search of pebbles to throw in through your window to attract your attention by the agreed signal, and when I picked one up, I got my fingers dirty!

Despite the euphemism of 72, the speaker means that the dog that pissed on his shoes, or one of its friends, had been busy in the area already, so that when he picks up what in the dark he takes to be a pebble, it turns out to be something different... The contrast between fantasy and reality could hardly be more marked.

> **¡Qué de días anduve**
> **cargado de acero**
> **con harto trabajo,**
> 76 **porque estaba enfermo!**
>
> **Como estaba flaco,**
> **parecía cencerro:**
> **hierro por de fuera,**
> 80 **por de dentro hueso.**

When I think of the number of days that I put on armour, to feign a courage I didn't feel; this was no mean feat, because I was weak through illness, so thin that I looked like the bells they hang round mules' necks: iron on the outside, and on the inside a clapper of bone!

A key to these lines is supplied by Carreira (Góngora 1998: I.299), who picks up a reference to another proverb recorded by Correas: 'cargado de hierro, ca[r]gado de miedo', which carries the gloss 'por los que se cargan de armas por salir de noche'. I interpret this as meaning that cowards try to cover up and put on a brave show. As we can see from the following quatrain also, the speaker now fantasizes that he is an enamoured knight from the world of chivalric romance, a world that Góngora had mocked in another burlesque *romance* of two years earlier, 1582, 'Diez años vivió Belerma' (GR.10: 106–14). Merging with this is another commonplace image of the lover, also here made subject to mockery, that of love as a sickness, and of the lover whose watching and waiting has made him ill. The stress remains on the contrast between outward appearance and inner reality. This lover is *flaco*, weak, both physically (which he did and does recognize) and morally (which he did not realize at the time, but now at least claims to grasp). The ridiculous conceit (also in Quevedo) of a knight in armour so thin through lovesickness that his bones rattle around inside his steel casing and make a sound like a bell (you can hear him rattle: *cencerro, hierro*), is reinforced when we realize that *cencerros* both adorn the necks of mules (which are stubborn and sterile) and are used in *cencerradas*, those popular charivaris embarked upon by villagers to show displeasure at social deviance, especially when involving people who have in some way made themselves sexually ridiculous or reprehensible—adulterers, say, or old men marrying a young wife. It may also be relevant to note that in Góngora's day, *hueso*, like *nabo*, was slang for the penis: this, after all, has been at the root of the protagonist's troubles.

> ¡Qué de meses y años
> que viví muriendo
> en la Peña Pobre,
> 84 sin ser Beltenebros;
>
> de me acaeció
> mil días enteros
> no comer sino uñas,
> 88 haciendo sonetos!

When I think of the months and years together that I faced a living death in the Peña Pobre, although I was no Beltenebros; I spent a thousand days on end biting nothing but my nails, writing sonnets!

Góngora here still ridicules the lovers of chivalric romance (whom Cervantes also had in his gunsights in *Don Quixote*). *Vivir muriendo* belongs to the world of Petrarchan paradox; Beltenebros was the name that Amadís de Gaula adopted for his lover's penance in the bare mountains of the Peña Pobre (an episode brilliantly ridiculed in *Don Quixote*, I. XXV–XXVI). But superimposed on this is a more mundane, or demeaning, truth: Góngora's speaker is no knight errant—not even able to live off a private income—and so he has to have recourse to another sort of *peña*, the pawnbroker's shop. He is too lovesick to eat, but perhaps too impoverished as well: all he has to eat are the fingernails he bites, as he tries to compose love poems to his

ungrateful 'lady'. The poet's tone is humorous, but he once more remorse-
lessly exposes the sordid moral and physical realities beneath a lover's
fantasies. In the next two quatrains, he continues his attack on the verses
lovers write (Amadís had done this on the Peña Pobre, and Don Quixote
imitated him in his *locuras* in the Sierra Morena):

> **¡Qué de necedades**
> **escribí en mil pliegos,**
> **que las ríes tú ahora**
> 92 **y yo las confieso,**
>
> **aunque las tuvimos**
> **ambos, en un tiempo,**
> **yo por discreciones**
> 96 **y tú por requiebros!**

*When I think of the number of stupid things I wrote on thousands of sheets
of paper. You laugh at them now, and I admit to having written them. But
both of us once thought differently: to me, they were feats of delicate wit; to
you, they were the authentic language of love!*[5]

It is hard not to suspect that Góngora is gently self-ironizing at this point,
since he had already in the earlier 1580s himself—his burlesque verses to
one side—written a good deal of serious love poetry. But to return to the
poem's speaker, it is worth noting that, according to him, his loving service
had not been systematically disparaged. However ungallant it may be on his
part to turn on his former mistress and involve her in blame for what has
happened, it now emerges that, according to him, she has not faultlessly and
simply played the role of the *belle dame sans merci*, the courtly lady of
Petrarchan convention, who refuses to requite her captive lover's attentions
to the smallest degree. Also, the import of the word *necedades* in 89 should
not be missed, since in the serious *desengaño* language of [neo-]Stoicism,
the *necio* is the *stultus*, the person whose values and behaviour are upside-
down, since he lives in the *engaño* of one who ignores human frailty. We
shall find the word *necio* right at the end of the poem... The word
discreción, on the other hand, has complex and varied semantics, ranging
from the paying of light, witty compliments, through Wit, to the serious moral
virtue akin to prudence. *Cov.* says that the *discreto* is 'el hombre cuerdo y de
buen seso, que sabe ponderar las cosas y dar a cada una su lugar'.

> **¡Qué de medias noches**
> **canté en mi instrumento:**
> **'Socorred, señora,**
> 100 **con agua mi fuego!'**

---

[5] *Cov.* defines *dezir requiebros* as follows: 'es sinificarle [a la dama] sus pasiones, loar
su hermosura y condenar su crueldad. Desto han dicho harto los poetas, y para mí basta.'

> donde aunque tú no
> socorriste luego,
> socorrió el vecino
> 104 con un gran caldero!

When I think of the number of midnight hours that I played my musical instru-
ment and sang, 'Quench, my lady, with water my fire', although you didn't
do so in the end, while one of the neighbours did, using a large bucket!

It appears that in 99–100, the poem quotes from an earlier anonymous text,
surviving from a *pliego suelto* of 1576: 'Socorred con agua al fuego, | ojos,
apriesa llorando, | que se está el alma abrasando' (Góngora 1998: I. 302). It
is plain in any case that what is being mocked here are still the convention-
alities of Petrarchan love poetry. On a former occasion the speaker's cries
have been wilfully or accidentally misunderstood with brutal literalism, and
instead of his lady's tears, finally moved to pity by her paramour's plight, he
has been solaced by a well deserved bucketful. With respect to 102, might
socorrer not have the sense of 'to confer sexual favours'? Other *double-*
entendres in the text make this seem likely. If so, raw sexual urges may once
more be seen to lurk beneath Petrarchan elevation of sentiment—an insight,
after all, already extremely familiar to readers of one of Spain's greatest late
medieval classics, *Celestina* (the attitude of which towards the moral equivo-
cations it unmasks being, similarly, endlessly fascinating).

> Adiós, mi señora,
> porque me es tu gesto
> chimenea en verano
> 108 y nieve en invierno,
>
> Y el bazo me tienes
> de guijarros lleno,
> porque creo que bastan
> 112 seis años de necio.

Lady, farewell: your behaviour makes what is already bad, worse: like light-
ing a fire in summer or snowing in winter. I'm sick to death and very angry,
because I reckon six years is quite enough time to have been so stupid.

Carreira points out (Góngora 1998: I. 302) that Góngora's speaker is, accidentally or deliberately, inverting a contemporary commonplace: in a text of
1636 we read, 'la apacible conversación que es chimenea de invierno y
cantimplora de verano'. But the phrasing also builds on the Petrarchan topos
of love as an 'icy fire'. Lines 109–10 literally refer to stones in the gall-
bladder, an extremely painful condition, but also in play is a popular saying
recorded by Correas: 'No me cague el bazo: *cagar el bazo* se dice por enfadar
y amohinar'; medicine at this time thought that the spleen was the seat of
anger and of melancholy.

The sharpest point is reserved for the final word, as the key [neo-]Stoic notion of *necedad* returns. It is bad enough that it should have taken six years for this lover to take 'no' for an answer, but now at least he convicts himself of having been a *necio*. Better late than never. But does he really know what he is saying, and will the effects of this setback last? We will never know for sure what level of insight is entertained by him—whether he has learnt a serious moral lesson that will stick and 'change his life', or whether, rather, what we have here is a case of late-acquired hurt pride that uses Christian and Classical references and assertions of a change of heart as a kind of sticking-plaster. But—to come to what is perhaps my main point— I believe that Góngora's strategy is not just teasing but also coherent: he seeks to amuse us into entertaining an awareness that may or may not escape the speaker he has invented and placed on stage. His sense of human sinfulness is such that he takes life *por lo cómico* here, rather than *por lo trágico;* his medium is *burlas* rather than 'in your face' *veras;* he is a philosopher who laughs, rather than one who weeps; like Rabelais, and Cervantes, he believes in therapeutic laughter; one guesses that he might have sympathized with Erasmus's *Praise of Folly* (1509), as he would no doubt have relished the Archpriest of Hita's *Libro de buen amor.* The Christian gospel has laughed tragedy out of court. A light, carefree comedy, neither acerbic nor cynically unconcerned, might be taken to be proof that some important degree of *desengaño* has been reached, one consistent with the teaching of the Sermon on the Mount, neither world-hating, nor yet in hock to worldly things.[6] Human sinfulness remains a fact, none the less. 'Held, we fall to rise', Browning wrote in the 'Epilogue' to his late poetic collection *Asolando*, and the Christian hope is to rise. Góngora, I expect, hoped to help us in our ascent. His text might actually help in this regard or it might not; but it is unlikely to do us harm.

[6] For a fuller treatment of this topic, see Screech (1997).

LUIS DE GÓNGORA

'ARROJÓSE EL MANCEBITO' (1589)

Arrojóse el mancebito
al charco de los atunes,
como si fuera el estrecho
poco más que medio azumbre.

5 Ya se va dejando atrás
las pedorreras azules
con que enamoró en Abido
mil mozuelas agridulces.

Del estrecho la mitad
10 pasaba sin pesadumbre,
los ojos en el candil,
que del fin temblando luce,

cuando el enemigo cielo
disparó sus arcabuces,
15 se desatacó la noche,
y se orinaron las nubes.

Los vientos desenfrenados
parece que entonces huyen
del odre donde los tuvo
20 el griego de los embustes.

El fiero mar alterado,
que ya sufrió como yunque
el ejército de Jerjes,
hoy a un mozuelo no sufre.

25 Mas el animoso joven,
con los ojos cuando sube,
con el alma cuando baja,
siempre su gloria descubre.

No hay ninfa de Vesta alguna
30 que así de su fuego cuide
como la dama de Sesto
cuida de guardar su lumbre.

Con las almenas la ampara,
porque ve lo que le cumple;
35 con las manos la defiende
y con las ropas la cubre.

Pero poco le aprovecha,
por más remedios que use,
que el viento con su esperanza
40 y con la llama concluye.

Ella entonces derramando
dos mil perlas de ambas luces,
a Venus y Amor promete
sacrificios y perfumes.

45 Pero Amor, como llovía
y estaba en cueros, no acude,
ni Venus, que con Marte
está cenando unas ubres.

El amador, en perdiendo
50 el farol que le conduce,
menos nada y más trabaja,
más teme y menos presume.

Ya tiene menos vigor,
ya más veces se zambulle,
55 ya ve en el agua la muerte,
ya se acaba, ya se hunde.

Apenas espiró, cuando
bien fuera de su costumbre,
cuatro palanquines vientos
60 a la orilla le sacuden.

Al pie de la amada torre
donde Hero se consume,
no deja estrella en el cielo
que no maldiga y acuse.

65   Y viendo el difunto cuerpo,
      la vez que se lo descubren
      de los relámpagos grandes
      las temerosas vislumbres,

      desde la alta torre envía
70   el cuerpo a su amante dulce,
      y la alma donde se queman
      pastillas de piedra azufre.

      Apenas del mar salía
      el Sol a rayar las cumbres
75   cuando la doncella de Hero,
      temiendo el suceso, acude;

      y viendo hecha pedazos
      aquella flor de virtudes,
      de cada ojo derrama
80   de lágrimas dos almudes.

      Juntando los mal logrados,
      con un punzón de un estuche
      hizo que estas tristes letras
      una blanca piedra ocupen:

85   'Hero somos y Leandro,
      no menos necios que ilustres,
      en amores y firmezas
      al mundo ejemplos comunes.

      El Amor, como dos huevos
90   quebrantó nuestras saludes;
      él fue pasado por agua,
      yo estrellada mi fin tuve.

      Rogamos a nuestros padres
      que no se pongan capuces;
95   sino, pues un fin tuvimos,
      que una tierra nos sepulte.'

* * * * *

The bare bones of the narrative may be quickly rehearsed. Leander was a young man from Abydos, who met Hero the priestess of Aphrodite (Venus) at a religious ceremony in Sestos, on the other side of the Hellespont (or Dardanelles), the stretch of water dividing Europe from Asia, that varies from just under one, to just over four miles in width. Hero's father was governor of the fortress of Sestos, in charge of the tower from which she ultimately jumps to her death. Leander and Hero's was a *coup de foudre* romance, and in order to continue with their meetings, it was agreed between them that he would swim across the water to meet her. This, according to Ovid, he did a number of times, until storms at sea impeded the continuation of their secret pleasures. But after a brief period, he could bear separation (and Hero's taunts) no longer, and one night he rashly took the plunge, guided by a lantern that she held, only for the storm to extinguish both her light and his life.

In this *romance* (GR.28), Góngora is returning to an old and very familiar story from Classical times, that had been taken up again in the Renaissance. Among the Romans, Ovid had drawn on the tale, by including verse letters from Leander to Hero and from Hero to Leander in his *Heroides*, XVIII and XIX. Virgil had introduced a brief mention of the lovers in his *Georgics* (III. 258–63), in the context of comment on the irresistible strength, but short-livedness, of the breeding instinct, as it affects both men and beasts.[1] Góngora himself claims particularly to have had in mind the version

---

[1] 'Omne adeo genus in terris hominumque ferarumque | et genus aequoreum, pecudes pictaeque volucres, | in furias ignemque ruunt: amor omnibus idem' (*Georgics*, III. 242–45), translated by Dryden (1944: 409–10) as: 'Thus every creature, and of every kind, | the

of the story told by the late Greek poet Musaeus, in the fifth century AD. Among Spanish poets of the Renaissance, he also drew on, but was not at all impressed by, Boscán's near-2800-line retelling of the tale (1999: 245–324). Where Góngora stands out from what until his time had been the standard presentations of the young lovers is in his utterly disrespectful treatment of what had generally before then been considered a predominantly tragic tale. The basic Classical story was well known, but our poet's handling of it is highly unconventional; what we get from him is rumbustious burlesque.

Góngora lambasts the couple because they are both *necios*, as Hero's servant says (86); both have been carried away by powerful sexual feelings, and this has led Leander in particular to be guilty of rashness (52). The storm that blows out the light and causes the young man's death by drowning can indeed be taken to represent the stormy nature of the pair's erotic urges and the way in which their passion extinguishes the light of reason in them both, thereby earning Góngora's scathing, but still comically expressed, disapproval. As to the fundamentals of such an analysis, Ovid is in the background: the Roman poet himself draws the parallels between the storms at sea and the sexual turmoil in Leander's heart (*Heroides*, XVIII. 129, 171–72), but more importantly still, he insists that both Leander's and Hero's passions lead to rash behaviour: 'Either I do not know how rash I am, or an incautious love will send me out into the sea. If it remains swollen for a few nights more, I shall try to cross, despite the waves; and either happy daring shall leave me safe on the opposite shore, or death will bring an end to my anxious love!' (*Heroides*, XVIII. 189, 193–96).[2] Ovid's handling of the lovers' plight is not burlesque, however, even if he was often accused elsewhere of displaying a 'wit out of season', or inappropriate rhetorical display and inappropriate humour.

'Arrojóse el mancebito' was composed in 1589, and so in chronological terms, Góngora's attack is of an early date, if, say, we compare it with the very different, but far more traditional and tragic treatment of the tale by Marlowe, probably written in the same decade. On the other hand, by the time that in his 'Sueño de la muerte' of 1621, Quevedo numbers Hero and Leander, and Pyramus and Thisbe, among lovers with upside-down priorities, such a critique was well established, Góngora himself having returned to the story of the former pair at greater length in his romance of 1610, 'Aunque entiendo poco griego' (GR.63), and dealt with the latter pair in his astonishing ballad 'La ciudad de Babilonia' of 1618 (GR.74). 'Aunque entiendo poco griego'

---

secret joys of sweet coition find. | Not only man's imperial race, but they | that wing the liquid air, or swim the sea, | or haunt the desert, rush into the flame: | For Love is lord of all, and is in all the same.'

[2] 'aut ego non novi, quam sim temerarius, aut me | in freta non cautus tum quoque mittet amor; | ... | sit tumidum paucis etiamnunc noctibus aequor, | ire per invitas experiemur aquas; | aut mihi continget felix audacia salvo, | aut mors solliciti finis amoris erit!' Compare Hero's admissions later, 'non patienter amo' (XIX.4), and that she once upbraided Leander as *temerarius* (XIX. 87–88).

was, we are told, specifically written in order to supply a Part I, which the already written 'Arrojóse el mancebito' could then directly follow on from as Part II. The two parts are entirely of a piece in tonal terms, although written 'back to front' and at a distance in time from one another. Part I tells how the lovers, children of poverty-stricken parents, first meet. The couple's courting precedes an initial sexual encounter, which in turn leads to an anxious resolve to meet again for further adventures when the religious rites are over and they have to separate. Both of them in fact are so 'up for it' (Góngora's vulgarity and anachronisms perhaps authorize our own) that all prudence is literally cast to the winds. (Ovid's poem stresses the strength of Hero's sexual desire, every bit as much as Leander's: he has her show no 'ladylike' demureness.) This later-composed Part I, 'Aunque entiendo poco griego', is, like this Part II, full of joking wordplay; and in it Leander is presented as a *virote*, a strutting Andalusian *macho*, 'grande orinador de esquinas'; she, as decked out in borrowed finery. Their courtship dance is presented as a mating display, in which she is likened to a bird of prey, and he, successively, to a sparrow, cockerel, pigeon, and peacock. It is in the later text that Góngora lays claim to his awareness of Musaeus's (very different) treatment of the story, and makes his carping references to Boscán's lengthy and serious version.

$$* \quad * \quad * \quad * \quad *$$

Arrojóse el mancebito
al charco de los atunes,
como si fuera el estrecho
4   **poco más que medio azumbre.**

The lad threw himself into the puddle of tuna, as if the straits had only a couple of pints of water in them.

Góngora's disrespectful treatment of his protagonist is in evidence from the very first line of the poem, where Leander is called, in the diminutive form, a *mancebo* (according to *Cov.*, an adolescent still subject to his father's authority—whereas in this burlesque *romance* Leander has no time for filial sentiment or duty). Opening this line with the verb *arrojóse*, what is more, focuses on the basic questions the poet asks about the youth's behaviour, since, in *Aut.*, *arrojado* is glossed as follows: 'resuelto, inconsiderado, intrépido, y que pica en temerario y atrevido'. Those adjectives are not synonyms, you notice, but point to a range of meanings opening out the moral implications of the lad's physical action, in such a way as to authorize the *romance*'s burlesque manner. It will soon become plain that the adjective *temerario* fits the case quite well (remember note 2, above). It might be noticed, too, that the verb *arrojarse* is also glossed by *Aut.* as 'metafóricamente atreverse a decir a uno alguna claridad o desengaño'. That is very much Góngora's business in the poem as a whole, as is confirmed by his use of assonance in *ú–e*, frequent in comic contexts. Reference to the Hellespont as 'el charco de los atunes' is plainly also intended to be disrespectful and belittling. It appears to have been used by a number of Góngora's contemporaries and followers. *Charco*, certainly, conveys that the swaggering young Leander is blind to danger, and considers this considerable stretch of water as little more than a puddle, a point elaborated on in 3–4 (a *medio azumbre* is about a litre). In Ovid, Hero eggs Leander on, despite the storm, taunting him that the Hellespont is only a pond (XIX. 145–46).

An initially puzzling reference to tuna fish is cleared for us once we remember that these fish make an annual journey through the Pillars of Hercules and across the Mediterranean to spawn in the Black Sea. In addition, Pliny's *Natural History* (IX. 20, 50) discusses tuna at some length, not least the kind found in Pontus—the Black Sea and the area around it, including the Hellespont, the Sea of Marmara and the Bosphorus. This more learned source is an additional reason why Góngora may have linked the scene of his poem with such fish, but at one point, whilst on the subject of the fishes' eyesight—better on the right than on the left—Pliny comments that tuna are in any case, 'natura hebete'. In its immediate context, this means that 'neither eye is all that good', but *hebes* in Latin more generally means stupid or obtuse, which is certainly in tune with Góngora's judgement on Leander in his poem as a whole. A comparable reference to bear in mind is in Horace's *Satires* (II. 5). There (line 3) we find the wily Ulysses down on his luck (*dolosus*; compare *el griego de los embustes*, 20). He consults Tiresias about how to repair his fortunes and get rich. Tiresias recommends legacy-hunting—finding some wealthy old man to flatter, with a view to obtaining an inheritance—summing up as follows: 'plures adnabunt thynni et cetaria crescent', 'More tuna will swim up, and fill your fishponds for you' (44). The great seventeenth-century commentator Dacier, for example, explains here that the tuna represent rich fools who can be caught when needed, and he provides a parallel passage in the same sense from the Greek satirical writer Lucian (Horace 1733: III. 270). In other words, what we find in the *culto* Góngora is a recondite reference or two to Classical literature, transposed to a very different context. His learned but humorous allusions are relevant, though: they link a Leander, who prides himself on his strength as a swimmer, with the sort of 'big fish' who actually are not at all clever, and are easily caught.

> **Ya se va dejando atrás**
> **las pedorreras azules**
> **con que enamoró en Abido**
> 8 **mil mozuelas agridulces.**

He now gradually leaves behind his tight blue breeches, which he'd worn to conquer the hearts of a thousand bitter-sweet girls from Abydos.

We find humorous bathos in this quatrain: reading across the line-endings disconcerts our conventional expectations of meaning. Where we might have expected the banks of the Hellespont to be left behind, what are left behind instead are Leander's tight blue trousers. (Ovid too had made a good deal of play with Leander's stripping off, leaving his clothes on shore, and swimming naked to meet his mistress: *Heroides*, XVIII. 33–34, 57–58.) It was, we gather from Góngora, the lad's alluring physique as emphasized by these breeches that had turned the girls on, rather than any moral qualities in him. The girls themselves are then belittled as manipulative harridans (*agridulces*), and note as well the hyperbole of *mil*. Leander's vanity as a *macho* seducer is part of the total unattractive picture of him that Góngora paints. This is anything but an idealized account of the relations between the sexes, and it evinces scant sympathy for any of those involved.

> **Del estrecho la mitad**
> **pasaba sin pesadumbre,**
> **los ojos en el candil**
> 12   **que del fin temblando luce,**
>
> **cuando el enemigo cielo**

He swam halfway across the straits with no difficulty, his eyes on the trembling lamp, that lights his goal, when the hostile heavens…

The mood of 9–13 reverts to a more apparently serious rhetoric, as may be observed from the syntactic inversion of 9, and the alliteration of 10. We also spot a double-take on *temblando* in 12, conveying the literal flickering of Hero's light, together with the dramatic irony—possibly humorously intended, possibly not—that it is as if the flickering flame of Hero's lantern that was trembling both with lust and in anticipation of the danger lying in wait for this rash youth; *fin* in the same line punningly refers simultaneously to Leander's intentions or ends, and to the end that in fact awaits him.

> **disparó sus arcabuces,**
> **se desatacó la noche,**
> 16   **y se orinaron las nubes.**

… fired their blunderbusses, night undid its trousers and the clouds started pissing.

An explicit note of bathos soon returns, in the comic anachronism of *arcabuces* in 14, and in what follows. The heavens are imagined as not just figuratively, but literally, hostile: they are *hostes*, an enemy army, armed with distinctly modern blunderbusses, in the form of lightning and claps of thunder. (The first documented use of the word *arcabuz* is shortly before 1559, according to Corominas.) The lowering sky then becomes a personified night that lets down his trousers (literally, undoing the 'points', or laces that used to be used to attach one's breeches to one's upper garments; compare

p. 152, below), both (one imagines) farting (thunder once more), and then crapping on the boy below. The scatological humour continues in 16, as, following the thunder, it begins to piss down with rain. (Note as well, however, how in 15–16, Góngora retains the syntactic parallelism, together with the alliteration—*noche*, *nubes*—sometimes employed in the *romances viejos*: in context, such stylistic allusions to a more solemn poetic mode reinforce the effect of bathos, rather than complicate our responses to the lovers, so firmly are their inadequacies exposed elsewhere.)

> **Los vientos desenfrenados**
> **parece que entonces huyen**
> **del odre donde los tuvo**
> 20 **el griego de los embustes.**

At this point it seemed as if the unleashed winds were escaping from the wineskin in which the wily Greek (Ulysses) had been keeping them.

Lines 17–20 refer to the story told near the beginning of Book X of Homer's *Odyssey*, where as Ulysses and his men leave the island of Aeolus, the Sea God Poseidon imprisons the adverse winds in a leather bag or wineskin, in order to favour the Greeks, although later in the same book they will be entrapped by the enchantress Circe who (appropriately enough for Góngora's purposes, if we catch the allusion) stands for the sensual pleasures that militate against duty, and turn men into swine. It is tempting to think, too, that mention of the winds keeps in play the allusion to farting that we met just now. Still the poet's tone is disrespectful, as the Classical hero's wiliness and resourcefulness are bluntly referred to in the circumlocution *el griego de los embustes* (20). The word *desenfrenados* (17) has a double meaning: the winds are both unleashed from their confinement, and are furiously out of control (as is Leander himself, however 'cool' he likes to play things). *Cov.* glosses *desenfrenado* as 'el caballo sin freno y el hombre que no pone freno... a sus apetitos y desórdenes'.

> **El fiero mar alterado,**
> **que ya sufrió como yunque**
> **el ejército de Jerjes,**
> 24 **hoy a un mozuelo no sufre.**

The fierce and angry sea which had put up with Xerxes's army (hammering on it) like an anvil is not today prepared to put up with a mere lad.

In this quatrain, we find more wordplay, conveying that the sky and sea rebel since they will not tolerate something that so offends the natural order as Leander's *necedad*. The sea is *alterado* both in the literal sense of now being different from before, and in the sense of being angry. *Sufrir* is used in two slightly different senses also—the literal and more figurative senses of 'to put up with'. (Góngora here, I think, is recalling Hero's taunt to Leander that surely he is not cowed by the god of the sea: *Heroides*, XIX. 145–46). Together with this, we find a reference to the famous happening in Classical history, when during the Persian Wars of the late fifth century BC, the bulk of Xerxes's forces had crossed the Hellespont on a bridge built of ships lashed together. When this bridge was destroyed by a storm, Xerxes famously had the sea whipped, and fetters thrown into it to symbolize his ultimate mastery. We note the appropriately 'noisy' alliteration of the sounds, presumably all [š], represented by the graph <j> in 23. This anecdote feeds the allusion in 22 to a sound like that of hammers beating on an anvil. Góngora is also playing with a proverb recorded by his contemporary Gonzalo Correas, 'cuando fueres yunque, sufres', meaning that if it is your allotted task or destiny to suffer, you should do so uncomplainingly. His implication is that the sea found Leander's incursion a step too far, however much it had been prepared to 'suffer' in the case of the great Persian monarch, who was playing out a truly heroic, morally well founded destiny. In the fourth century BC, Alexander the Great too had crossed here to begin his mighty campaigns of Asian conquest: how very different such prowess is from Leander's lack of it. The gods who understandably had favoured the great Macedonian and Persian leaders could not tolerate the trivial, self-gratifying behaviour of this rash youth. Leander's callow inexperience is underscored: mockingly called a *mancebito* before, now he is spoken of as a *mozuelo*, a 'mere lad'.

> **Mas el animoso joven,**
> **con los ojos cuando sube,**
> **con el alma cuando baja,**
> 28 **siempre su gloria descubre.**

But the plucky youth, with his eyes when he's above the waves and with his soul when he goes under, always keeps his end in view.

Despite a reference in 25 to the wording of the opening line of Garcilaso's wholly serious Sonnet XXIX, 'Passando el mar Leandro el animoso', the quatrain of 25–28 keeps up the deflationary humour in the parallelistic syntax of 26–27. Leander now sometimes sinks below the angry waves: he has his sights literally set upon his goal when his head is above water, but only figuratively so when he goes under. Things have started to go wrong in earnest. It may be well to remember also that *gloria* can have a sexual connotation (see above, p. 32). It is no religious quest that drives Leander on but, rather, lust.

> **No hay ninfa de Vesta alguna**
> **que así de su fuego cuide**
> **como la dama de Sesto**
> 32 **cuida de guardar su lumbre.**

No Vestal virgin watches over the (sacred) flame as carefully as the lady from Sestos takes pains to guard her lamp (fire).

The poet's attention now, after twenty-eight lines, finally switches to Hero, 'la dama de Sesto' ('Sesti puella', 'the girl from Sestos', Ovid had called her), and she, with heavy irony, is compared to one of those Classical paragons of chastity, a Vestal virgin (or actually, to make matters even worse, as it were, 'una ninfa de Vesta'), in either case, one of those entrusted with guardianship of that goddess's sacred flame. Vesta was also goddess of the domestic hearth, but domestic virtues are hardly in play here, either. Góngora's chiasmus, 'de su fuego cuide... cuida de... su lumbre', involves more than an elegant lexical variation on synonyms (*fuego/lumbre*), since of the two words, *fuego* additionally connotes the fire of sexual passion, spoken of by the Roman poets. There is still more in play here, too, in the way that we find an accumulation of synonyms (*cuide, guardar, ampara, defiende, cubre*) that recall the lexicon of Courtly Love, and the way in which the *damas* of that literary world so carefully defend their chastity. It is too late, in Hero's case, of course. Rather than the shining jewel of her virginity, it is a real lamp that she is trying to protect, as part of the plan to satisfy her physical desire. And comically but aptly, she appears to lift her skirts in her efforts to save the light (with the rakish implications that such a picture cannot fail to have):

> Con las almenas la ampara,
> porque ve lo que le cumple;
> con las manos la defiende
> 36 y con las ropas la cubre.

She shields it behind the battlements, because she understands where her interests lie; she protects it with her hands, and covers it with her clothes.

In 33–36, parallelistic syntax is used once more, but at 34, Góngora inserts a mischievous but ironic comment. Hero, he implies, thinks she knows on which side her bread is buttered, that being the prospect of her sexual encounter with Leander; but his moral point is precisely that she does not know where her true interests lie.

> Pero poco le aprovecha,
> por más remedios que use,
> que el viento con su esperanza
> 40 y con la llama concluye.

But it does her little good, for all the resources she can summon, because the wind puts paid to her hopes, her waiting, and to the flame, all in one go.

Line 37 shows, in any case, that Hero's attempts at protecting the guiding flame are of no avail. Góngora drives his point home with a cruel zeugma (here employing a single verb with two objects, one a thing, *llama*, the other a moral quality, *esperanza*): the flame of hope is literally extinguished. I say 'a moral quality', but it must be remembered too that *esperanza* may also be translated as 'waiting' (or here, teeth-grinding sexual frustration):

> **Ella entonces derramando**
> **dos mil perlas de ambas luces,**
> **a Venus y Amor promete**
> 44　**sacrificios y perfumes.**
>
> **Pero Amor, como llovía**
> **y estaba en cueros, no acude,**
> **ni Venus, que con Marte**
> 48　**está cenando unas ubres.**

She then, pouring out two thousand pearls from each of her bright lights, promises sacrifice and incense to Venus and Cupid. But Cupid, since it's raining and he's naked, doesn't come, and nor does Venus, because she's supping udders with Mars.

Next for sarcastic treatment, in 41–44, are the conventional hyperboles of Petrarchism (*mil*; plus *perlas* for tears and *luces* for eyes). Góngora's basic point is that what is actually going on is distinctly unheroic and by no means admirable. He subverts the language of the *romances viejos* and of the Petrarchan lyric, since both, he believes, as previous sentimental treatments of the tale of Hero and Leander have done, misrepresent the moral reality of the story: this pair are not beautiful losers; they are losers pure and simple. In 41–42, we find a humorous muddling of the terms of Petrarchan convention, thereby producing a mixed metaphor: Petrarch's *perlas* are usually teeth, not tears. (Góngora sometimes follows that Petrarchan convention, as in the second line of his sonnet 'La dulce boca que a gustar convida', G.41: Góngora 1976: 135; but we also find him equating pearls and tears in serious contexts, as in the *romances* 'Amarrado al duro banco', GR.11, line 24, and 'Las flores del romero', GR.58, line 24: Góngora 1998, I. 274, II. 175.) His sarcastic intent in the present instance is compounded by a ludicrous mixture of hyperbole and precision, by specifying *dos mil*, although we find the equation between pearls and tears in other Gongorine poems. In 43–48, Hero promises incense and sacrifice to Venus and Cupid, since she was a priestess of the former. (Ovid too, but in a very different key, has Hero beseeching Venus's favour: *Heroides,* XIX. 159–60.) But if the human lovers are handled in knockabout style, so also in Góngora are the gods themselves. Lines 45–46 make a joke based on the conventional depiction of Cupid as a naked baby, whereas 47–48 involves a belittling multiple hit: 'cenando unas ubres' represents the gods eating the coarsest rustic fare (cows' udders), with an additional scabrous hint that the udders in question are those of the bare-breasted goddess (compare p. 183, below). The loves of Mars and Venus belong to Classical idyll—we may recall

Botticelli's beautiful treatment of it in the painting that now hangs in the National Gallery in London—and this reference to their adultery also shows how sexual love distracts men from their martial duties. I think that this allusion here, along with the one to Xerxes earlier, invites us to consider another sense in which love has turned Leander away from the proper pursuits of a young man. However humans dress things up, they are prone to the selfish satisfaction of all manner of base physical urges.

> El amador, en perdiendo
> el farol que le conduce,
> menos nada y más trabaja,
> 52 más teme y menos presume.
>
> Ya tiene menos vigor,
> ya más veces se zambulle,
> ya ve en el agua la muerte,
> 56 ya se acaba, ya se hunde.
>
> Apenas espiró, cuando
> bien fuera de su costumbre,
> cuatro palanquines vientos
> 60 a la orilla le sacuden.
>
> Al pie de la amada torre
> donde Hero se consume,
> no deja estrella en el cielo
> 64 que no maldiga y acuse.

The lover, on losing sight of the lamp that guides him, swims less and struggles more, is more afraid and less presumptuous. Now he has less strength, now he sinks beneath the waves more often, now he sees that the water will be his death, now he's had it, now he's drowning. He's hardly expired when, quite contrary to their normal custom, four litter-bearer winds throw him up on to the shore with a jolt. At the foot of the beloved tower where Hero is consumed with anguish, he leaves no star in the sky that he does not curse and blame.

Another joke follows in 51, since *nada* is used both as part of the verb *nadar*, 'to swim', and as the noun, meaning 'nothing' (in which case we have a sequence, from *menos* through *nada* to *más*). Line 52 sums up what is wrong with the lovers' behaviour: they are both, he especially, guilty of *presunción*, which is a manifestation of *necedad*; they lack the cardinal virtue of prudence, that steers the right course between excessive and insufficient caution. Góngora enjoys play with *más* and *menos* here in a kind of double chiasmus (*menos, más, más, menos, menos, más*); then there are the repeated *yas*, as the phrases become shorter breathed, and Leander sinks to his death—but not, we gather from 57–60, quite beneath the waves. Any

remaining possibility of pathos is cancelled by a 'low', anachronistic reference to late sixteenth-century taxi-drivers: the stormy winds are personified
as litter-bearers, who in their usual way (I take it that *bien fuera de su
costumbre* is meant ironically) 'deliver' their customer not quite where he
was intending to go, and do so with a nasty jolt! The young man dies
cursing his fate, blaming the stars, rather than his own folly, blind to the last
(63–64). The motif of fate will be taken up again in a burlesque key, in 92.

In 61–62, Hero appears to be at the top of her tower still, since in 69–70,
that is where she is going to jump from, to her death. Leander, then, is
thrown up on shore at the foot of his mistress's tower, and there, on the
beach below, uses his last breath to rail against fate. Important here is what,
in 57, is meant by 'apenas espiró': is it 'no sooner had he breathed his last'
or rather, 'breathing with great difficulty'? For *apenas*, *Cov.* gives 'lo que
con mucha pena y dificultad se haze', and for *espirar*, says that the verb
normally means to die; however, *Cov.* continues, 'en la lengua latina tiene
otras diversas sinificaciones, de que nosotros no usamos (but this is
Góngora!) como *spirare*' ('to breathe, or be alive'). It is only proper to
point out, however, that this reading of the passage is not generally agreed
upon. Golden-Age texts are not so strict as more modern usage when it
comes to the referents of pronouns, and ambiguities can result from this
(see, for example, pp.150 and 167, below). For some, Leander dies in 57,
and Hero is the subject of all the verbs in 62–65, so that we might alter-
natively translate the whole as follows: 'At the foot of the beloved tower
where Hero is consumed with anguish, she leaves no star in the sky that she
does not curse and blame.' On this latter interpretation, *se consume* could be
triple-edged: not just 'consumed with anguish', but also, consumed with the
sort of unbecoming fury which gives rise to Hero's imprecations and which
results from her previously having been consumed with sexual desire. It is
this frustrated desire that prompts her despairing suicide.[3]

Y viendo el difunto cuerpo,
la vez que se lo descubren

---

[3] It is conceivable that Góngora might have had in mind also a comparable scene in
Aeneid IV where from a tower Dido views Aeneas's preparations for departure. To draw
on *Aen.* IV was risqué in at least the Jesuits' opinion, since, taken as a whole, it was
deemed too strong for students of Humanities (Pavur 2005:166). If such an allusion is in
play here, Dido's own self-immolation on a funeral pyre enters Góngora's poem at 71–
72. Virgil's lines 408–12 are specially pertinent: 'quis tibi tum, Dido, cernenti talia
sensus, | quoque dabas gemitus, cum litora feruere late | prospiceres arce ex summa,
totumque uideres | misceri ante oculos tantis clamoribus aequor! | improbe Amor, quid
non mortalia pectora cogis!': 'What pangs the tender breast of Dido tore, | When, from
the tower, she saw the covered shore, | And heard the shouts of sailors from afar, | Mixed
with the murmurs of the watery war! | All-powerful Love! What changes canst thou
cause | In human hearts, subjected to thy laws!' (Dryden 1944: 97). In 1588, the year
before Góngora's text was written, his rival Lope had referred to Dido atop her tower in
his *romance* 'De pechos sobre una torre' (1982: 84–85, no. 12).

de los relámpagos grandes
68   las temerosas vislumbres,

desde la alta torre envía
el cuerpo a su amante dulce,
y la alma donde se queman
72   pastillas de piedra azufre.

And seeing the dead body when the fearsome glimpses permitted by great flashes of lightning reveal it to her, from her high tower she sends her body to join her sweet lover and her soul to a place where they burn sulphur pastilles.

Leander's death is quickly followed by his *dama*'s suicide, accompanied by mock-melodramatic lightning (65–68), and with an elevated statement, that is immediately qualified by a brutal joke: as she jumps from her tower, her body joins her lover's (69–70)—whilst since she is a suicide, her soul goes straight to Hell, a point conveyed by comic periphrasis. The line-ending at 71 adds to the humour, since one thinks at first that what will burn will be both Hero's body and soul, or those of both her and her lover. (Previously they had burned with lust, and this now leads them to burn in Hell.) But Góngora's reference to Hell is altogether jokey in tone. Hell and the Devil are popularly associated with the smell of sulphur, but here, and with more bathos still, the sulphur is burnt in the form of pastilles, such as might be burnt in a sick-room, to ward off contagion. Hero is spiritually sick; and however much the Pagan Stoics might have admired, even recommended, suicide in certain circumstances, for the Christian conscience such action betokens the sin of despair, the failure to trust in God's grace and to order one's priorities accordingly, something quite properly deserving of Hell.

Apenas del mar salía
el Sol a rayar las cumbres
cuando la doncella de Hero,
76   temiendo el suceso, acude;

y viendo hecha pedazos
aquella flor de virtudes,
de cada ojo derrama
80   de lágrimas dos almudes.

Juntando los mal logrados,
con un punzón de un estuche
hizo que estas tristes letras
84   una blanca piedra ocupen:

The Sun had scarcely risen from the sea to gild the mountain tops when Hero's maid, fearing what might happen, comes on the scene, and seeing that flower of all the virtues smashed to pieces, she sheds a couple of

gallons of tears from each eye (1 almud = 11.25 litres). Joining the unhappy
pair together, and taking a bodkin from its case, she used it so that these sad
letters should occupy a white stone tablet:

It is left to Hero's maid to provide the couple's epitaph. In 73–74, this girl
(who features a certain amount in Ovid) is introduced through a most *culto*
periphrasis for dawn, in an Italianate idiom similar to that of 41–42, but
Góngora's elevated manner here is once more introduced, only the better to
be shot down by what follows after: *hecha pedazos* (77) might normally be
taken in a figurative sense, except that here its reference is grotesquely
literal; there is sarcasm too in calling Hero *aquella flor de virtudes* (78), in a
way that is comparable to the import earlier of reference to the Vestal
virgins; and we find the bathetic hyperbole of *dos almudes* (80), a measure
that both belongs to the marketplace and is a gross exaggeration to boot.[4]
Similar bathos proceeding from mention of inappropriately banal or everyday objects then comes when the servant is described getting a bodkin out of
its case to scratch her mistress's and Leander's epitaphs which, even so, and
according to Classical custom, she inscribes on white stone. (Bodkins might
additionally suggest to certain readers familiar with *Celestina*, say—see
below—, an instrument such as might be used by bawds to 'repair' the
maidenheads of fallen women—see for example Rojas 1991: 233–34, and
compare p.149, below.)

> **'Hero somos y Leandro,**
> **no menos necios que ilustres,**
> **en amores y firmezas**
> 88   **al mundo ejemplos comunes.**

'We are Hero and Leander, no less foolish than we are famous, common
enough examples to the world of fidelity and loving sentiments.

This epitaph comically states what is yet an uncompromising verdict on the
couple; its somewhat gross directness may, as it were, be that of a comic
servant who writes it, one who has no taste for or understanding of her
masters' *mores*, but one suspects that her critique of their *necedad* is very
much shared by Góngora also (86) and has motivated his handling of them
from first to last. *Necedad* in neo-Stoic terms is the name given to impru-
dence (see above, p.38), the lack of the cardinal virtue that involves the
exercise of good judgement, particularly with respect to what lies in humans'
power to effect and what does not; *necedad* is the overweening pride that
would ignore human frailty, that would deny the need for grace, and neglect
treasure in Heaven for earth's all-too-transitory, unreliable, sensual pleasures.
This couple's mutual 'fidelity' as they might idealize it (*firmeza*) has actually,

---

[4] To make matters still worse, *Aut.* tells us the *almud* is a 'medida de cosas secas,
como son trigo, cebada, garbanzos… avellanas, bellotas y castañas'. We heard earlier in
the poem that Hero's tears, if not merchandise of this sort, at least were pearls.

in this poem's opinion, been a purblindness and stubbornness that makes them an all-too-common example of more widespread human behaviour: they are *ejemplos comunes*, both in the sense of being in plentiful supply and in the sense of being not noble or tragic but, rather, cheap and vulgar. It is this awareness that in Góngora's eyes makes the lovers deserving of all they get: their fates, and the sort of poetic treatment that subjects conventional and unthinking moral appreciations to more radical criticism.

> El Amor, como dos huevos
> quebrantó nuestras saludes;
> él fue pasado por agua,
> 92   yo estrellada mi fin tuve.

Love, has broken our health, like two eggs: he was boiled and I was scrambled.

This quatrain jokily drives the poem's message home still further, in a series of naughty puns revolving around the word *huevos*: these mean, both obviously but oddly, eggs, and, perhaps less obviously but entirely aptly, testicles. As might be said these days, it is an excess of testosterone that has led the lovers—Leander, every bit as much as his *dama*—to neglect their own fragility and throw their lives away. The verb *quebrantar* goes both with breaking eggs and with having one's health broken; also in play is the saying 'parecerse como un huevo a otro huevo'—in English 'to be as like as two peas in a pod', with the implication here that both lover and mistress have been equally mistaken and perverse. Then come the jokes about two ways of cooking eggs, jokes that seem well to predate Góngora's adoption of them (they are found in the mid-sixteenth-century writer Melchor de Santa Cruz): Leander was boiled/ drowned, Hero was scrambled/shattered. On top of this latter jest, *estrellada* also refers us back to 63, and makes fun of the pair as 'star-crossed lovers'. It is an aspect of Leander's (or perhaps Hero's) self-dramatization that the stars have conspired against them, which is a view of matters that the poem itself simply does not endorse.

> Rogamos a nuestros padres
> que no se pongan capuces;
> sino, pues un fin tuvimos,
> 96   que una tierra nos sepulte.'

We ask our parents not to put on mourning, but since we shared a common fate, may we be buried in a common grave.'

After all this bravura punning, the poem ends rather quietly, even non-committally. On the surface anyway, 94 means that the parents should not adopt the dress of public mourning. (Conceivably also in Góngora's mind is *Cov.*'s additional gloss that 'antiguamente era el hábito de los españoles honrados en la paz', which would imply that these parents are anything but *honrados* by their offspring's reckless behaviour.) Although reference to the couple's parentage is included at some length in the later-composed 'Part I' of the story, here the final quatrain introduces the first mention of them. Perhaps (I can offer nothing stronger than a possibility) there is a line of thought in play here that offers analogies to, if not actually draws upon, the ending of *Celestina*, in which we read the highly rhetorical lament pronounced by Pleberio, Melibea's father, after his daughter has despairingly flung herself to her death, also from a tower, following the accidental and very messy demise of her lover Calisto. Pleberio's *planctus* (Rojas 1991: 81–85) is now generally thought to raise more questions than it answers: about the girl's parents' social standing, their degree of responsibility for her suicide, and more generally, about what, in so far as Pleberio's is concerned, might be an emotionally and morally appropriate stance to take when faced with such disaster, to some indeterminate degree self-inflicted. Góngora here takes a different path, by making Hero's servant recommend that the parents abstain from public displays of grief, but he may also, in his own way, be keeping in play some of the questions that Pleberio's speech had raised in the earlier masterpiece.

*   *   *   *   *

The poem is brutally, uncompromisingly, funny, but in a most self-conscious way. What is more, we know too much about the poet's subtlety of approach in other texts to take the judgements that are so strongly implicit here quite simply at face value. The lovers are roundly condemned for their upside-down values, but arguably the unfeeling jokes the poet offers as a harsh corrective to a conventional sentimental treatment of them are not quite his last word.

A further point to consider is the extent to which 'Arrojóse el mancebito' is a particularly misogynistic text. We get a silly and impetuous Leander at the start, whereas Hero's appearance is dramatically withheld. She dominates the second half of the poem: she is an active if ineffectual accomplice; she is the deliberate suicide... To this extent Góngora has an antecedent in Ovid's own *Heroides*, where Hero's letter follows on from Leander's, and modifies one's understanding of the whole; in it the woman's own lustful feelings and shared responsibility for the disaster are very much insisted upon. Even so, both he and she are ridiculed and both equally condemned as *necios*.

For all that, our poet rather seems to enjoy his testy stance towards the pair. Perhaps once more we should be wary of identifying an implicit narrator's stance too simply with Góngora's own, particularly as regards such wilful exclusion of all sympathy for the young pair. The poet seems so much to relish playing the role of an intolerant curmudgeon, indulging a cruel but very funny brand of humour, that we should be on our guard. The narrator's one-sidedness, however vivacious, might better still be taken as an invitation to be amused, but then to enter some correctives of our own, based on a recognition that a significant part of Leander's trouble had been to think that he could buck more general truths about the vulnerability of human beings in the face of larger forces and greater powers: truths that affect ourselves as much as him.

LUIS DE GÓNGORA

'EN UN PASTORAL ALBERGUE' (1602)

En un pastoral albergue,
que la guerra entre unos robles
lo dejó por escondido
o lo perdonó por pobre

5 do la paz viste pellico
y conduce entre pastores
ovejas del monte al llano
y cabras del llano al monte,

mal herido y bien curado,
10 se alberga un dichoso joven,
que sin clavarle amor flecha,
le coronó de favores.

Las venas con poca sangre,
los ojos con mucha noche,
15 le halló en el campo aquella
vida y muerte de los hombres.

Del palafrén se derriba,
no porque al moro conoce,
sino por ver que la hierba
20 tanta sangre paga en flores.

Límpiale el rostro, y la mano
siente al Amor que se esconde
tras las rosas, que la muerte
va violando sus colores.

25 Escondióse tras las rosas,
porque labren sus arpones
el diamante del Catay
con aquella sangre noble.

Ya le regala los ojos,
30 ya le entra, sin ver por dónde,
una piedad mal nacida
entre dulces escorpiones.

Ya es herido el pedernal,
ya despide el primer golpe
35 centellas de agua. ¡Oh, piedad,
hija de padres traidores!

Hierbas aplica a sus llagas,
que si no sanan entonces,
en virtud de tales manos
40 lisonjean los dolores.

Amor le ofrece su venda,
mas ella sus velos rompe
para ligar sus heridas:
los rayos del Sol perdonen.

45 Los últimos nudos daba
cuando el cielo la socorre
de un villano en una yegua
que iba penetrando el bosque.

Enfrénanlo de la bella
50 las tristes piadosas voces,
que los firmes troncos mueven
y las sordas piedras oyen;

y la que mejor se halla
en las selvas que en la Corte
55 simple bondad, al pío ruego
cortésmente corresponde.

Humilde se apea el villano
y sobre la yegua pone
un cuerpo con poca sangre,
60 pero con dos corazones;

a su cabaña los guía,
que el Sol deja su horizonte,
y el humo de su cabaña
les va sirviendo de Norte.

65 Llegaron temprano a ella,
     do una labradora acoge
     un mal vivo con dos almas,
     y una ciega con dos soles.

     Blando heno en vez de pluma
70 para lecho les compone,
     que será tálamo luego
     do el garzón sus dichas logre.

     Las manos, pues, cuyos dedos
     desta vida fueron dioses,
75 restituyen a Medoro
     salud nueva, fuerzas dobles;

     y le entregan, cuando menos,
     su beldad y un reino en dote,
     segunda envidia de Marte,
80 primera dicha de Adonis.

     Corona en lascivo enjambre
     de Cupidillos menores
     la choza, bien como abejas,
     hueco tronco de alcornoque.

85 ¡Qué de nudos le está dando
     a un áspid la invidia torpe,
     contando de las palomas
     los arrullos gemidores!

     ¡Qué bien la destierra Amor,
90 haciendo la cuerda azote,
     porque el caso no se infame
     y el lugar no se inficione!

     Todo es gala el Africano,
     su vestido espira olores,
95 el lunado arco suspende,
     y el corvo alfange depone.

     Tórtolas enamoradas
     son sus roncos atambores,
     y los volantes de Venus
100 sus bien seguidos pendones.

     Desnuda el pecho anda ella,
     vuela el cabello sin orden;
     si le abrocha, es con claveles,
     con jazmines si lo coge.

105 El pie calza en lazos de oro,
     porque la nieve se goce,
     y no se vaya por pies
     la hermosura del orbe.

     Todo sirve a los amantes;
110 plumas les baten, veloces,
     airecillos lisonjeros,
     si no son murmuradores.

     Los campos les dan alfombras,
     los árboles pabellones,
115 la apacible fuente sueño,
     música los ruiseñores.

     Los troncos les dan cortezas
     en que se guarden sus nombres,
     mejor que en tablas de mármol
120 o que en láminas de bronce.

     No hay verde fresno sin letra,
     ni blanco chopo sin mote;
     si un valle 'Angélica' suena,
     otro 'Angélica' responde.

125 Cuevas do el silencio apenas
     deja que sombras las moren
     profanan con sus abrazos
     a pesar de sus horrores.

     Choza, pues, tálamo y lecho,
130 cortesanos labradores,
     aires, campos, fuentes, vegas,
     cuevas, troncos, aves, flores,

     fresnos, chopos, montes, valles,
     contestes de estos amores,
135 el cielo os guarde, si puede,
     de las locuras del Conde.

*   *   *   *   *

The Latin poet Horace (65–8 BC) famously remarked in his *Ars Poetica* (*The art of poetry*) that a poem was like a painting. In explaining what he meant, he distinguished between pictures which please the viewer only once, and those which have the power to please, however often they are looked at.[1] This ballad is a good example of a poem which is like the second kind of painting. It may be enjoyed on a first reading, though difficulties of interpretation will become apparent. But further readings will enable the reader to resolve some of these, and will heighten appreciation of the ballad's subtlety, depth, and grace. In fact, this was also a popular subject with artists, not least for its delicate eroticism (Lee 1977: 20–26, 34, 36–47, 50–51). The scenes most commonly painted were Angelica's tending of Medoro's wounds, and the lovers' carving of their names on tree trunks.

The story of the love of Angelica, princess of Cathay (an old name for China, and occasionally for India) for the Moorish soldier Medoro, whom she encounters while fleeing from the unwelcome attentions of her would-be suitor Orlando, is based on a short episode (Canto XIX, stanzas 16–31) in the immensely long epic poem *Orlando furioso*, by the Italian Renaissance poet Ludovico Ariosto.[2] Ariosto's poem was well known and highly regarded throughout the Golden Age; it is, for example, one of the few books praised in the scrutiny of books in Don Quixote's library (I. VI). This episode was a popular subject in the ballad tradition: the *Romancero general* of 1600–05 contains four ballads which deal with parts of the story Góngora tells here (González Palencia 1947: I. 205, 600, 755, 778).[3]

Despite the fact that Ariosto's epic is written in the heroic metre of the *ottava reale*, Góngora retains a regular *romance* form for his version (GR.50), with assonance in *é–o* throughout. His use of language and imagery, however, is much more complex and sophisticated than that of these ballads in the *Romancero general*.[4] While Ariosto adopts a predominantly narrative tone, Góngora's poem is a work of intense lyricism. He omits Ariosto's long account of how Medoro came to be badly wounded as he and a companion loyally sought to bury the body of his slain king, and replaces this with a generic reference to *la guerra*. He shows a particular interest in the metamorphosis of the once hard-hearted Angélica into a sensual and passionate lover, something which clearly appealed to his poetic imagination, since he was to

[1] 'Ut pictura poesis... haec placuit semel, haec deciens repetita placebit': 'A poem is like a picture... This pleased but once; that, though ten times called for, will always please' (*Ars Poetica*, lines 361, 365; see Horace 1929: 480–81).
[2] For an English translation, see Ariosto (1975–77: I. 588–91). For sixteeth-century Spanish versions see Alonso (1962: 14). For an analysis of the relationship between Ariosto and Góngora's poem, see Edwards (1972: 75–78) and Alonso (1962: 9–13, 56–70). On Cathay, see Góngora (1998: II. 91).
[3] Alonso (1962: 14–15) notes three others, on other aspects of the episode which are omitted by Góngora.
[4] 'Toda la poesía no es más que una sucesión de ingeniosidades, conceptos, antítesis, hipérboles, alusiones a adagios, alusiones mitológicas, cultismos, notas de humor, etc., y toda ella está expresada en un lenguaje casi exclusivamente metafórico' (Alonso 1935: 21). Alonso used the poem as a prime example in his demolition of the once fashionable critical view that distinguished between the early Góngora who wrote with clarity and the obscure poet of his later works, notably the *Polifemo* (G.225) and the *Soledades* (G.264).

trace a similar process in one of his most famous and controversial poems, the *Polifemo* of 1613–14 (see Alonso 1962: 36). There, the sea-nymph Galatea, who has spurned all offers of love, encounters the handsome young Acis, and the poem charts the change in her emotions, from initial fear to total surrender to love. In both poems, too, Góngora connects the lovers with the mythological archetypes of Venus and Adonis, the goddess of love and the youth she adored, endowing them with a more universal frame of reference, as the particular lovers of his verses become the archetypes of lovers more generally. He would have been familiar with Ovid's account of the tragic ending of the affair of Venus and Adonis in the *Metamorphoses* (x. 519–739), which is replicated in the *Polifemo*. But despite a hint of menace at the very end of this ballad, Góngora is faithful to Ariosto's episode, which celebrates love's fulfilment in an idealized setting.

> **En un pastoral albergue,**
> **que la guerra entre unos robles**
> **lo dejó por escondido**
> 4 **o lo perdonó por pobre**
>
> **do la paz viste pellico**
> **y conduce entre pastores**
> **ovejas del monte al llano**
> 8 **y cabras del llano al monte,**
>
> **mal herido y bien curado,**
> **se alberga un dichoso joven,**
> **que sin clavarle amor flecha,**
> 12 **le coronó de favores.**

In a pastoral retreat, which among some oaks was left alone because it was hidden [because the place was hidden away in the woods] or pardoned [ignored] because it was poor, where peace wears a shepherd's jerkin, and amid shepherds leads sheep from the high ground to the low, and goats from the low ground to the high, badly wounded and well cared for there shelters a happy youth, who was crowned with favours, without love having hit him with an arrow.

Cov. indicates that a *pellico* is a garment made of soft animal skin, usually worn by shepherds, while *monte* refers to rough high ground that is uninhabited.

The idealized pastoral setting is established from the start, with a brief evocation of a *locus amoenus*, a 'pleasant place', which became a commonplace of lyrical poetry of this kind, and which included features such as a shady retreat from the sun, cooling breezes, green meadows, flowers, birdsong, and water.[5] War is raging around this oasis of peace and calm. Góngora

---

[5] See the essay 'The ideal landscape', in Curtius (1953: 183–202).

personifies both war and peace: war has left this spot alone because it is too remote and hidden away for soldiers to have discovered it, or because it is too poor to be worth fighting over. He draws attention to the idyllic nature of the place and of the simple and natural life the shepherds lead by turning the peacefulness they embody into the subject of the action: peace substitutes for them as the agent which leads the shepherds' sheep and goats to the appropriate pasture for the season. He further underlines this by the careful balances he establishes: the parallel constructions of 3–4 and 7–8, *entre unos robles* and *entre pastores*, and polyptoton, the use of the same stem word in different grammatical constructions: here *albergue* and *se alberga*. But just as importantly, another kind of 'war' will take place, the battle of love, the weapons of which are Cupid's bow and arrow, shot at unsuspecting victims, the wounds of which go deep but can be healed if love is recipro- cated, as it will be here. Love as a kind of war is a conventional metaphor with roots in Classical Antiquity and best known, perhaps, to Góngora through line 8 of Petrarch's Sonnet CCXXVI, 'e duro campo di battaglia il letto' (Petrarca 1964: 288) and line 8 of Garcilaso's version of this in his Sonnet XVII, 'y duro campo de batalla el lecho' (Garcilaso 1995: 34).

For most of the poem the lovers are further removed from individuality by Góngora's preference for periphrastic allusions to them over direct naming. Medoro's name is not referred to until 75, while Angélica's has to wait until almost the very end (123–24), when it echoes through the surround- ing countryside. The first character we meet is a simply a *dichoso joven*; we do not know who he is or why he is *dichoso*, but he is clearly a well- favoured young man. The desciption of the *joven* as *dichoso* when he has been badly wounded, and the equally paradoxical statement that an apparently dying man is *bien curado*, are both puzzling. In fact, Góngora is playing with the temporal frame, linking events which have taken place before the ballad opens with those which are yet to come: Medoro was wounded and is found *mal herido*, and Angélica will nurse him back to life (*bien curado*) in the lines which follow. Conversely, in the war of love which is about to take place, it is she who will be wounded by love for him, and both lovers who will find fulfilment in its consummation.

> **Las venas con poca sangre,**
> **los ojos con mucha noche,**
> **le halló en el campo aquella**
> 16   **vida y muerte de los hombres.**

His veins with little blood, his eyes with much night [full of the darkness of death], that life and death of men found him in the countryside [or on the battlefield].

Picking up from the *mal herido* of 9, the poet now tells us through peri- phrasis and metaphor that the *dichoso joven* is badly wounded and close to death. He has lost a lot of blood, and his eyes see nothing; they are full of *noche*, either closed, or lost in the gathering darkness of death. This may be a pastoral paradise protected from warfare, but it is not immune to pain and suffering: such juxtapositions are common in the pastoral poetry of the Golden Age, and nowhere more so than in the *Polifemo*, in which young Acis will be crushed to death by the jealous Cyclops, as the young lovers are disturbed in their hiding-place after their lovemaking.[6] But a further contrast now appears: the youth is found by what is periphrastically and paradoxically described as *aquella vida y muerte de los hombres*. The paradox of life and death co-existing in a single person is rooted in the traditions of Petrarchan love poetry and refers to the contradictory emotional states engendered by falling in love—its life-enhancing pleasures and its death-like pains. These paradoxical states are personified in the as yet unnamed Angélica, their very embodiment: men see her beauty and fall in love with her, but she coldly disdains them. She finds the wounded soldier *en el campo*, a place of ambivalent meaning. As 'countryside' it is a reminder of the natural setting of the scene and of the way in which love can flourish naturally in an environment far removed from the artificiality and the hypocrisy of the city or the Court. Its other meaning, 'battlefield', is also doubly appropriate, as the locus of the literal *guerra* in which Medoro nearly lost his life, and of the metaphorical 'battle' of love which is about to begin. What could have been a chance encounter amid the beauties of nature thus becomes the opening skirmish in the war of love.

> **Del palafrén se derriba,**
> **no porque al moro conoce,**
> **sino por ver que la hierba**
> 20 **tanta sangre paga en flores.**

She dismounts from her palfrey [a small saddle horse for a woman], not because she knows [or recognizes] the Moor, but because she sees the grass repaying so much blood with flowers.

Angélica's dismounting represents the first sign that her heart is capable of tenderness and compassion. Góngora makes it clear that it is the sight of Medoro's wounds which causes her to stop, not because she has any idea of who he is or what will happen. The plainness of 17–18 then gives way to more elaborate metaphor, a pattern similar to the previous quatrain, in which Medoro's veins were described literally as containing *poca sangre*, and his eyes, metaphorically and antithetically, as *con mucha noche*. She stops at the sight of Medoro's blood flowing out from his wounds on to the grass, blood which is transformed into red flowers blooming there. This is the first connection Góngora makes in the ballad between the protagonists and the myth of Venus and Adonis. In the *Metamorphoses*, Adonis is gored to death

---

[6] See also three of the four tapestries woven in an idyllic spot by the nymphs in Garcilaso's Eclogue III, especially the fourth, which depict the loss of love through violence and death.

by a wild boar, and grieving Venus turns his blood into the anemone, 'a flower... of blood-red hue' (*flos de sanguine concolor*: X.735), clearly alluded to here (Ovid 1984: 116–17).

The fact that Angélica sees metaphorical *flores* rather than literal *sangre* mirrors the emotional change which is just beginning to affect her: a scene of horror becomes one of beauty to which she is attracted. This constant shifting between literal and metaphorical planes of discourse, and the way in which one metaphor begets others, is characteristic of Góngora's poetic diction, and we need to sense the intellectual connections between the images he uses for the fundamental meanings to emerge. This will become clearer as the poem proceeds.

> **Límpiale el rostro, y la mano**
> **siente al Amor que se esconde**
> **tras las rosas, que la muerte**
> 24 **va violando sus colores.**

She cleans his face, and her hand feels Love hiding behind the roses, for death is violating their colours.

Once more, a literal action—Angélica's washing away of the blood on Medoro's face (which allows her to see it properly)—is followed by allusion and metaphor. It is the touch of her hand, marking the first physical contact, which, though she does not realize this yet, awakens the love which will quickly turn to passion for the wounded youth. The way in which her actions are made to run across the line endings suggests the rapidity with which love is effecting change in her. Love, in the figure of Cupid, is so tiny that he can hide behind the roses, which themselves represent the colour of his cheeks, a metaphor derived from a commonplace Petrarchan simile, though one rarely applied to male beauty. Roses are also flowers associated with the pleasures of love. But his face is whiter than it should be, because his blood is draining away and death is close. The *rosas* of Medoro's complexion continue the metaphorical connexions between the youth and flowers begun with his blood blooming as *flores* in the grass (19–20).

The verb *violar* is a strong one. In Golden-Age usage its primary meaning is 'to rape' (*Cov.*). Death is portrayed as 'raping' the colour of Medoro's cheeks, by turning them a different hue. The verb may also conceal some wordplay, since it resembles another Classical flower associated with love, the *vïola*, probably the *culto* version of *violeta*, 'violet' (compare *Polifemo*, 42). But the metaphor conceals a further allusion to a well-known topos derived from Classical poetry, specifically a passage in Eclogue III of the Roman poet Virgil.[7] Góngora uses the same allusion in one of his early love sonnets, 'La dulce boca que a gustar convida' (1584), in which he warns

[7] 'Qui legitis flores et humi nascentia fraga, | frigidus, o pueri, fugite hinc, latet anguis in herba': 'You lads who cull flowers and strawberries that grow so low, begone from here; a chill snake lurks in the grass' (Virgil 1999: 46–47).

lovers not to touch the inviting lips of their beloved, 'porque entre un labio y otro colorado | Amor está, de su veneno armado, | cual entre flor y flor sierpe escondida' (G.41: 6–8), and, more extensively, in the *Polifemo* (281–88).

> **Escondióse tras las rosas,**
> **porque labren sus arpones**
> **el diamante del Catay**
> 28 **con aquella sangre noble.**

It [Love] hid behind the roses so that their harpoons could meld the diamond of Cathay [Angélica] with that noble blood [Medoro's].

The poetic text becomes denser with allusion, periphrasis and metaphor. Angélica is a princess of Cathay but also a *diamante*, the hardest known substance, because of the hardness of her heart: she has hitherto been entirely resistant to the charms of any man. Góngora is emphatic about the process. Love, as we have just seen, *se esconde*, is hiding like the proverbial serpent *tras las rosas* for a suitable victim, not among the flowers but behind the young man's ruddy complexion, and Angélica has begun to be moved as she wipes clean the young man's face. He now repeats the same sequence of words but shifts it into the past to emphasize the reason for Love's hiding in this way: *Escondióse tras las rosas | porque...* This quatrain describes in more detail—but also in a highly condensed manner—how she begins to fall in love with him. Roses, especially metaphorical ones (that is, Medoro's cheeks), do not have harpoons or arrows, but they do have thorns which can wound: Góngora means that the sight of his face (*rosas*) is the cause of love's piercing her defences with its traditional weapons. According to ancient belief, the only substance capable of softening a diamond was blood (*Cov.*: 'con ningún instrumento se labra, si no es con otro diamante y con la sangre del cabrón caliente'). So here love's weapons are being forged as the hard-hearted princess tends to the noble young man's bleeding wounds, which soften her hardness through compassion, and engender love. Góngora's mastery of metaphor can be seen in the way in which the imagery of blood and flowers, introduced in 20, unites the separate elements of the story: Medoro's blood, red like flowers in the grass; his cheeks, like *rosas*; the effect of the scene on the hitherto hard-hearted princess. This is matched only by his ability to allude concisely at the same time to the Classical topoi of Venus and Adonis and the serpent lurking in the grass, and to an ancient belief about blood having the power to soften diamonds.

> **Ya le regala los ojos,**
> **ya le entra, sin ver por dónde,**
> **una piedad mal nacida**
> 32 **entre dulces escorpiones.**

Ya es herido el pedernal,
ya despide el primer golpe
centellas de agua. ¡Oh, piedad,
36   **hija de padres traidores!**

Now she gives him her eyes; now there enters into her, without her seeing
from where, a [sense of] mercy/compassion ill-born among sweet scor-
pions. Now the flint is struck, now the first blow emits sparks of water. Oh
compassion, daughter of traitorous parents!

The process of Angélica's falling in love with Medoro accelerates, with the
repeated conjunction *ya* (anaphora; see p. 85, below). Having touched him
with her hand, she now likes what she sees and dwells longingly on his
features. This is one possible sense of *ya le regala los ojos*. But *Cov.* defines
regalarse as *derritirse*, 'to melt', as of snow. This meaning creates a tighter
linkage with the other images in this part of the poem, which focus on the
process of the softening of the hard-hearted princess at the sight of the
young man's wounds. A sense of mercy or compassion grows within her,
though she cannot see (continuing the imagery of *los ojos*) where it has
come from. This *piedad* is described as *mal nacida* and *hija de padres trai-*
dores because it has breached her hitherto impregnable defences. The image
of the *dulces escorpiones* is a good example of how Góngora creatively re-
works and reinvigorates a traditional Petrarchan paradox, to which he has
already alluded in the more conventional terms of life and death in 16. Now
he takes the contradictory, bitter-sweet experience of being in love, and
connects it to other images in the poem. Love is painful (*escorpiones* sting)
and pleasurable (and hence *dulces*). But the metaphorical scorpions also
connect with earlier images. In 21–23 we noted an implied reference to the
'snake in the grass', to the dangers which await lovers when they reach out
to pluck the flowers of love, where poisonous creatures lurk in the under-
growth. The scorpion is such a creature, and may suddenly strike someone
unawares. Moreover, its sting, like Cupid's arrows of love, has a sharp point
and is intended to pierce and wound the flesh, just as Cupid's arrows are let
fly at the unsuspecting victim, whose heart is pierced by them. The consequence is the paradoxical state of being in love, simultaneously painful and
pleasurable. Góngora does not choose his images haphazardly, and to follow
the ways in which he creates a richly patterned texture of metaphor and
allusion across the poem enhances our understanding and appreciation of his
artistic skill.

A similar process can be seen in the image of the flint and the paradoxical *centellas de agua* it emits when struck. We need to recall Angélica's
hardness of heart. She has already been described as *el diamante del Catay*.
The flint is another hard stone, which, like the diamond, represents her
indifference to men. The result of the compassion and love she is now
experiencing is the oxymoron of *centellas de agua*. The two nouns cannot

properly coexist, as water extinguishes its contrary element, fire. Her tears are indicative of the fire of love which is beginning to burn within her, and, just as flints emit sparks when struck, so Angélica sheds hot tears when her flinty heart is wounded and her defences are breached. But there is also a correspondence between tears and *centellas*, since sparks bear a similar relation to fire as droplets or tears do to water. Connexions of this kind between apparently incompatible elements, which require intellectual elucidation in order to be grasped, are characteristic not so much of the *culteranismo* often associated with Góngora but with the verbal wit which defines *conceptismo*. Baltasar Gracián, the greatest exponent and theorist of *conceptismo*, praised him on both accounts: 'Fue este culto poeta cisne en los concentos ['harmonious songs'], águila en los conceptos; en toda especie de agudeza eminente' (1969: I. 79).

> **Hierbas aplica a sus llagas,**
> **que si no sanan entonces,**
> **en virtud de tales manos**
> 40 **lisonjean los dolores.**

She applies herbs to his wounds which, if they do not at once heal them, flatter pain by virtue of such hands as hers.

The first three lines are straightforward enough: Angélica uses the skills she has acquired to dress his wounds with healing herbs. These skills are given a more prominent place in Ariosto's poem (Alonso 1962: 11, 37), but Góngora prefers to concentrate on the hands which administer them and the physical effects they produce on the wounded soldier and the princess. They do not work an immediate cure, but the power of her hands (*virtud* means 'power' as well as 'virtue' in Golden-Age Spanish, as in the English phrase 'by virtue of') 'flatters' the pain Medoro is experiencing from his wounds, that is, makes it seem more bearable. *Cov.* notes (*s.v. lisonjero*) that *lisonja* is traditionally portrayed as 'una maceta hermosa de olorosas flores que encubre una vívora enroscada y ésta: *latet anguis*'. Thus, flattery's symbol picks up images and allusions we have already encountered, especially the snake (or viper) coiled among the flowers and waiting to strike the unwary hand. It is impossible to know if Góngora had this connection in mind, but it is quite likely. Thus, his choice of the verb *lisonjear* is doubly appropriate: its metaphorical sense suggests that Angélica's ministrations are beginning to provide some relief for Medoro, and its pictorial emblem engages with the connections we have already looked at between love, arrows, stings, and flowers. Gracián cites these lines as an example of understatement, in which the poet 'dice mucho, pero no todo lo que iba a decir' (1969: I. 214): in other words, they contain more meaning that a cursory reading could ever reveal.

> **Amor le ofrece su venda,**
> **mas ella sus velos rompe**

> **para ligar sus heridas:**
> 44 **los rayos del Sol perdonen.**

Love offers her his bandage [or blindfold], but she tears her veils to bind up his wounds: may the Sun's rays spare her.

Cupid is traditionally portrayed as blindfolded and therefore shoots his arrows at random (hence the saying 'love is blind'). Here, he offers her his blindfold so that she can bandage Medoro's wounds. Instead, she removes the veils covering her head and hair, and tears them into strips for this purpose. *Venda* and *velos* are linked both by meaning and by sound. Both share the common quality of being made of cloth, while the paronomasia (the rhetorical term for the use in close proximity of similar-sounding words) brings the blindfold of Cupid into close relationship with the bandages she makes (as she binds up Medoro's wounds, so she falls in love with him). The last line calls on the sun not to burn her fair skin now that her head is unprotected, but it also has echoes of traditional Petrarchan hyperbole: the blonde hair of a beautiful woman is commonly said to outshine the sun, so that when Angélica removes what covers her head the poet expresses the wish that the sun will forgive her for replacing it as the brightest object that can be seen.

> **Los últimos nudos daba**
> **cuando el cielo la socorre**
> **de un villano en una yegua**
> 48 **que iba penetrando el bosque.**
>
> **Enfrénanlo de la bella**
> **las tristes piadosas voces,**
> **que los firmes troncos mueven**
> 52 **y las sordas piedras oyen;**
>
> **y la que mejor se halla**
> **en las selvas que en la Corte**
> **simple bondad, al pío ruego**
> 56 **cortésmente corresponde.**

She was tying the last knots when heaven helps her in the form of a peasant on a mare who was riding through the wood. The sad and compassionate cries of the beautiful woman stopped him, cries which move solid tree-trunks and which deaf stones hear; and simple goodness, better found in the woods than at Court, courteously responds to the plea for mercy.

At this point the narrative resumes. Lines 45–50 are relatively straightforward (though see 85–86 for a very different tying of *nudos*): the cries of the beautiful young woman cause a passing peasant to dismount. Lines 51–52, however, contain a further allusion to Classical mythology: the power of the sweet singer Orpheus to make inanimate objects like rocks, and natural objects like trees, respond to his music (see the beginning of Book XI of

Ovid's *Metamorphoses*, as well as the account of his descent into the underworld to rescue his dead bride Eurydice, in X. 1–185). But Angélica's cries are likened to the music of Orpheus in an unusual way. Whereas he was credited with the power to charm rocks and trees to follow him as he moved, her cries have the opposite effect: they cause a human being to stop. There is a further, more hidden allusion to the myth which connects it with the metaphor of the snake in the grass or among the flowers (22–23). Eurydice died because she was bitten on the ankle by a serpent lurking in the grass as she fled from the attentions of an unwanted suitor (Virgil, *Georgics*, IV. 458–59; Ovid, *Metamorphoses*, X. 10). In Ariosto's poem, Angelica has been fleeing from the crazed attentions of Orlando when she chances upon Medoro. She too will be bitten, stung, pierced by Love in the metaphorical guise of the unseen serpent, the sweet scorpions, and the arrows of Cupid. But the consequence will be a celebration of love and life, not death. Stylistically, the simple isocolon (parallelism) of 51–52 is followed in 53–56 by one of the most famous hyperbatons in Góngora's poetry. Hyperbaton inverts the logical or expected word order, often for the sake of emphasis, and is one of the most characteristic ways in which Góngora's sentence structure imitates the flexible order of words in Latin poetry. Here, *la* belongs to *simple bondad*, but the definite article is separated from its noun by the eleven words of the relative clause which qualifies it, in a violent syntactical disruption which goes beyond anything his predecessors practised.

Two other points should be noted. First, as with *la paz* (5–6), an abstract moral quality substitutes for the person who embodies it: the *villano* becomes *la simple bondad*, because his innate goodness has answered Angélica's cries and has courteously responded to her *pío ruego*. Second, the way in which Góngora attributes simple goodness to a countryman picks up on the commonplace Golden-Age theme known as 'menosprecio de corte y alabanza de aldea', so named from a work of that title of 1539 by a prolific and very popular writer, Fray Antonio de Guevara (1481–1545), Bishop of Mondoñedo. In this tradition, the moral goodness to be found in the simple life of country folk is favourably contrasted with the vanity, ambition and deceit found at Court (compare Chapter 7, below). Góngora underlines the point with more verbal play, combining polyptoton with alliteration: *Corte, cortésmente, corresponde.* The peasant responds *cortésmente,* behaving like the naturally noble man he is, whereas *en la Corte* all is corrupt, self-seeking, and hypocritical.

> Humilde se apea el villano
> y sobre la yegua pone
> un cuerpo con poca sangre,
> 60 pero con dos corazones;
>
> a su cabaña los guía,
> que el Sol deja su horizonte,

y el humo de su cabaña
64   les va sirviendo de Norte.

Llegaron temprano a ella,
do una labradora acoge
un mal vivo con dos almas,
68   y una ciega con dos soles.

Humbly the peasant dismounts, and places on the mare a body with little blood but with two hearts; he guides them to his cottage, for the sun is sinking below the horizon, and the smoke of his cottage serves them as a compass [literally, 'as north']. They soon arrive there, where a peasant woman welcomes a man scarcely alive but with two souls and a blind woman with two suns.

The peasant takes the physically wounded Medoro and Angélica, wounded by love, back to his home (a *cabaña* is defined by *Cov.* as 'albergue de pastores, choça o casa pagiza en el campo, donde se recogen de noche con su ganado'). The play between literal and metaphorical senses continues: Medoro may literally have little blood in his body, but metaphorically he has two hearts, because he possesses Angélica's as well as his own. The sun is setting, and through the gathering darkness the smoke from the cottage chimney guides them to their destination as if it were the north star, by which sailors navigate by night. The image is inspired by the last lines of Virgil's Eclogue I, but the turning of the smoke into a metaphorical north star, because it is fulfilling a similar guiding function, is Góngora's own invention.

The simple kindness of the peasant is underlined by that of his wife, who welcomes the couple. The way the couple are described continues the series of metaphorical and allusive periphrases, based on the paradox of one individual apparently being endowed with two hearts, souls, and suns. Medoro is *mal vivo* because he is literally very ill, but he has *dos almas*, his own and now also Angélica's (see the progression in 9, 13–14, 59–60). She is *ciega* with love for him, as befits someone struck by blind Cupid's arrows, despite possessing *dos soles*: the characteristically Petrarchan hyperbole which boasts that a beautiful woman's eyes outshine the sun is condensed into metaphor by Góngora, so that her bright eyes become *soles*. This image marks the culmination of a further progression within the poem, as the sun moves from being a metaphor for Angélica's uncovered hair (44), through the literal meaning of sunset (62), to this second metaphorical incarnation for her eyes (68).

Blando heno en vez de pluma
para lecho les compone,
que será tálamo luego
72   do el garzón sus dichas logre.

Soft hay instead of feathers makes up their bed, which in due course will be the marriage-bed where the youth attains his pleasure.

In keeping with the pastoral simplicity of the place, the couple are given a mattress of hay, rather than the soft feathers enjoyed by the rich and powerful at Court. But such simplicity is irrelevant when it comes to love, for on it their love will be consummated. Whereas *lecho* is a normal Golden-Age word for 'bed', the word *tálamo* is of Greek origin, and adds a *culto* touch to the text (Góngora's evocations of the simple pastoral idyll are often expressed, paradoxically, in highly elaborate language, most notably in his most controversial poem, the *Soledades*). *Cov.* defines it as 'el lugar eminente, en el aposento donde los novios celebran sus bodas y reciben las visitas y parabienes; sinifica algunas vezes la cama de los mesmos novios'. He also tells us that *garzón* means the same as *mancebo* and the Latin *adolescens*, a young man between the ages of fifteen and thirty. *Do* is an archaic form for 'donde'. But the lovemaking still lies in the future, *luego*; for the moment, it is their courtship we are beginning to witness. As the next verses make clear, once Medoro regains his strength, events move fast.

> **Las manos, pues, cuyos dedos**
> **desta vida fueron dioses,**
> **restituyen a Medoro**
> 76 **salud nueva, fuerzas dobles;**
>
> **y le entregan, cuando menos,**
> **su beldad y un reino en dote,**
> **segunda envidia de Marte,**
> 80 **primera dicha de Adonis.**

Her hands, then, the fingers of which were gods in respect of this life [Medoro's], restore new health and double strength to Medoro; and they bestow on him, at the least, her beauty and a kingdom as a dowry, the second [cause of] envy for Mars, and the first [cause of] bliss for Adonis.

Earlier, in 21 and 36–40, physical touch first awakened love in Angélica, as with her hands she wiped Medoro's face clean and then applied medicinal herbs to his wounds. Now those same instruments of her compassion bring about the fulfilment of love, as she gives herself to him. Through their healing power they have restored Medoro to life when he had been close to death, as if they had the power of gods, and they have made him even stronger than before. They likewise yield to him her beauty and her dowry as a princess of Cathay. Delicately, Góngora indicates that they have consummated their love in this idyllic, peaceful place. The indirect allusion to the myth of Venus and Adonis in 19–20 becomes explicit in 79–80, which follow on from the reference to Angélica's hands as life-giving *dioses* (74). In Classical mythology, Mars, the god of war, who loved Venus, the goddess of love, becomes jealous when he discovers her being unfaithful to him with handsome young Adonis, whom she loved. Now the event is being replayed, with Angélica playing the part of Venus/Aphrodite, Medoro that of Adonis, and the absent

and unnamed Orlando that of Mars—though, ironically, since he is not
Angélica's husband and she despises him, Mars thus has a new or second
reason to be envious (first Adonis, now Medoro), while Medoro/Adonis
experiences the bliss of union with Angélica/Venus, his first love. The allusion is characteristically condensed in meaning; readers are not told why Mars
should feel envy (or jealousy) for a second time, but are expected to work
this out for themselves. But it is expressed in the apparent simplicity of a
perfect parallelism, with both lines constructed out of the same elements:
ordinal number, noun, conjunction, and name. Poetic licence allows for the
fact that the assonance of *Adonis* is slightly irregular (*ó–i* rather than *ó–e*).

> **Corona en lascivo enjambre**
> **de Cupidillos menores**
> **la choza, bien como abejas,**
> 84 **hueco tronco de alcornoque.**

A playful swarm of baby Cupids is flying above [literally, 'crowns'] the cot-
tage, like bees around the hollow trunk of a cork oak.

Góngora continues his delicate and allusive description of the couple's
lovemaking. The simplicity of the natural world, represented by the cottage
and by the poem's only simile, *bien como* bees swarming around the hollow
cork tree, is linked with the more *culto* world of Cupid. The *Cupidillos* may
reflect the *putti* of Classical and Renaissance art, who are usually depicted
as winged babies flying above lovers; they may equally be a poetic way of
imagining doves (the birds of Venus, and therefore of love) over the house.
The word *lascivo* is certainly *culto*, and its meaning here is probably
'playful', as in Góngora's *Soledades,* I. 281 (in other contexts in that work it
approximates to 'sensual, lustful': I. 293, II. 83).

> **¡Qué de nudos le está dando**
> **a un áspid la invidia torpe,**
> **contando de las palomas**
> 88 **los arrullos gemidores!**
>
> **¡Qué bien la destierra Amor,**
> **haciendo la cuerda azote,**
> **porque el caso no se infame**
> 92 **y el lugar no se inficione!**

What a great number of knots base envy is tying in her asp (viper), as she
counts the sighing and the cooing of the doves! How effectively Love exiles
her, making a whip out of his bowstring, so that the event should not be
censured and the place not be infected/corrupted [by envy or ill-repute].

Envy was traditionally portrayed as a woman accompanied by an asp (a
snake). Here, then, faced with the love of these two well-matched young
people, she is having a hard time of it: each time the doves coo (a sound

intimately associated with lovemaking) she ties a knot in the snake, as if to count how often they do this. The sound of the doves also functions as a metaphor for the lovemaking of the couple themselves.[8] We have already been introduced to poisonous creatures in 32, to envy in 79, and to the doves, possibly, in 81–82. The knots of envy are here a negative sign, of frustration, against which we may set their positive counterpart, the *últimos nudos* Angélica *daba* to the bandages she was preparing for Medoro's wounds when help arrived in the form of a *villano* (45). Now Love chases envy away: this love, unlike the love, say, of Hero and Leander in the ballad 'Arrojóse el mancebito' (see Chapter 3, above), is appropriate and pure, and envy can have no place here. The instrument he chooses is the string of his bow, from which the arrows of love are shot, but which now becomes the whip which drives envy away.

> Todo es gala el Africano,
> su vestido espira olores,
> el lunado arco suspende,
> 96   y el corvo alfange depone.
>
> Tórtolas enamoradas
> son sus roncos atambores,
> y los volantes de Venus
> 100   sus bien seguidos pendones.

The African is all finery. His clothes give off perfumes; he hangs up his crescent bow and puts down his curved cutlass. His sounding war-drums are turtle-doves in love; and the banners he follows so well are the head-scarves of Venus.

These lines complete the transformation from the wounded Moorish (hence *el Africano*) soldier we encountered at the start to the ecstatic lover. He lays aside his armour for the battle of love, and is all finery and fragrance. The doves mentioned in 86–87 are more precisely named as turtle doves, traditional exemplars of marital fidelity (White 1984: 145–46), so their presence here suggests a connubial atmosphere, even though marriage as such is not mentioned. Their cooing replaces the sound of the drums of war. The head-scarves worn by Angélica/Venus become the banners he follows (*volantes* are defined by *Aut.* as a 'género de adorno pendiente que usaban las mujeres para la cabeza, hecho de tela delicada'). Góngora makes a poetic correspondence between the drums and the doves (through their common property of sound, represented by the paronomasia of *tórtolas* and *atambores*) and between banners and scarves (through their common properties of fabric and shape). Like the *pastoral albergue* at the start of the ballad, the scene represents the complete antithesis of war, yet at the same time the battles of love have been

---

[8] The association of doves with lovers is commonplace; for an extended example see *Polifemo*, 318–30.

fought and won. Having shown us Medoro as a soldier in the war of love, Góngora now switches his attention to Angélica.

> **Desnuda el pecho anda ella,**
> **vuela el cabello sin orden;**
> **si le abrocha, es con claveles,**
> 104 **con jazmines si lo coge.**
>
> **El pie calza en lazos de oro,**
> **porque la nieve se goce,**
> **y no se vaya por pies**
> 108 **la hermosura del orbe.**

Bare-breasted she goes, her hair flies in disorder: if she binds it, it is with carnations; if she ties it, with jasmine. Her feet are [literally, 'her foot is'] shod with golden cords so that the snow may rejoice and so that the beauty of the globe may not run away.

Line 100 contains a famous example of the so-called 'Greek accusative', a learned poetic device found only in Latin poets, in which the adjective (*desnuda*) agrees with the subject of the verb (*Angélica*) and not the noun it qualifies (*pecho*). A rough translation would be 'bare as to the breast'. It is a highly *culto* usage, though by no means confined to Góngora in Golden-Age literature.[9] Angélica, once so cold and hard-hearted, has now given herself over to love, her abandonment of constraints symbolized by her partial nudity and the letting down of her hair. There is a playful contrast in the two stanzas between abandonment and confinement. If Angélica's hair is bound, it is only with perfumed flowers, carnations and jasmine alike being associated with the pleasures of love as well as human beauty in Petrarchan poetry. She is, in other words, 'bound', but only by nature. The final two lines of this section are very difficult, but seem to mean something like this: she walks virtually barefooted so that the whiteness of the skin of her feet (depicted by the Petrarchan metaphor of *nieve*) can be appreciated; she has wrapped some golden *lazos* around her feet, and because these are in some sense an impediment, they prevent Angélica (periphrastically and hyperbolically described as *la hermosura del orbe*) from running away (one of the meanings of *irse por pies*). *Cov.* gives the relevant meaning of *lazo* as 'Zapato de lazo, calçado de villano', suggesting conformity with the simple peasant world in which the lovers find themselves. Wilson paraphrases these lines as 'She shoes her feet in golden hobbles so as to set off the snow of her skin and so that the beauty of the world personified in her cannot take to its heels'. He also suggests that the lines contain an allusion to the peacock (1953: 90–91; see also Góngora 1998: II. 99). The beauty of the peacock's fanned tail,

---

[9] For example, lines 18–19 and 76 of Garcilaso's Canción v (Garcilaso 1995: 85, 89), and lines 14–15 of Fray Luis de León's ode 'Al licenciado Juan de Grial', which probably imitate Garcilaso (León 1988: 133).

with its eyes (represented by *orbe*) was contrasted from Classical times onwards with the ugliness of its feet (*pies*); see White (1984: 149). So perhaps Angélica's beauty outshines that of the peacock, as earlier it did the sun's (44), because, unlike the bird's, her feet also are beautiful.

> Todo sirve a los amantes;
> plumas les baten, veloces,
> airecillos lisonjeros,
> 112   si no son murmuradores.
>
> Los campos les dan alfombras,
> los árboles pabellones,
> la apacible fuente sueño,
> 116   música los ruiseñores.
>
> Los troncos les dan cortezas
> en que se guarden sus nombres,
> mejor que en tablas de mármol
> 120   o que en láminas de bronce.
>
> No hay verde fresno sin letra,
> ni blanco chopo sin mote;
> si un valle 'Angélica' suena,
> 124   otro 'Angélica' responde.
>
> Cuevas do el silencio apenas
> deja que sombras las moren
> profanan con sus abrazos
> 128   a pesar de sus horrores.

Everything serves the lovers. Feathers fan them, swiftly, [and] caressing [literally, 'flattering'] breezes, if not slanderous ones. The meadows provide carpets for them; the trees pavilions; the peaceful fountain, sleep; the nightingales, music. Tree-trunks provide bark for them, on which their names are better preserved than on marble tablets or bronze plaques. There is no green ash without its text, no white poplar without its sayings; if one valley resounds [with the name] Angelica, another valley replies 'Angelica'. With their embraces, they profane caves where the silence scarcely allows shadows to dwell, in spite of the horror of such places.

The world of nature, which has provided so many metaphors for the protagonists as they fall in love, is now drawn into the couple's lovemaking. The *plumas* are likely to belong to the doves we encountered in 87–88. Wordplay dominates the description of the light breezes: they 'caress' the ardent lovers with their coolness, but *lisonjear* usually means 'to flatter' (see above, p. 67), and is associated with the kind of behaviour one finds at the Court, as courtiers jostle for position. *Murmurar*, defined by *Cov.* as 'dezir mal de alguno, medio entre dientes', also characterizes Court life, for similar reasons. Here, if the breezes 'flatter', they do so in an innocent and gentle manner. They do not carry the sound of behind-the-back criticism and have no negative associations, as *murmurar* has.

There is an element present, too, of the myth of the Golden Age, as expressed by Ovid at the start of the *Metamorphoses*. The lovers do not need the rich and costly trappings of luxury, but are content with the gifts of nature: meadows for carpets, trees for shelter, the sound of water for peaceful sleep, birdsong for music. In each of these cases nature is contrasted positively with art, as a sign that this love is idyllic and pure, uncorrupted by greed or possessiveness. In Ariosto's original, the two lovers carve their names on tree-trunks as they pass through the countryside; Góngora contrasts this with the way rich and powerful people try to perpetuate their names in monuments of marble or bronze, to defy the passage of time. *Mejor* does not mean that the lovers' names last longer but that they are more appropriately commemorated in this natural way. This moment was often depicted in paintings, and Antonio Machado echoes this scene in his 'Campos de Soria'; even today, if one walks along the River Duero from San Polo to San Saturio in Soria, one can still see trees carved with the names of lovers. Nature too seems animated, endowed with the power of speech as Angelica's name echoes across the valleys.

The argument of the last four lines of this section is more complex. In the original, the lovers make love inside dark caves; indeed, Orlando's madness will increase when he discovers their names carved on the walls of such a place. Ariosto may well have been remembering the cave where Dido, Queen of Carthage, sheltered from a storm with Aeneas, whom she loved (*Aeneid*, IV. 165–66), the beginning of a process which will lead to her suicide after the hero abandons her. These caves are so silent it is as if even shadows feared to inhabit them. The grammatical sense of the unexpressed subjects and the possessives needs to be grasped: the lovers are the subject of *profanan* and *sus abrazos* are theirs, whereas *sombras* are the subject of *moren* and *sus horrores* refers to the fearful gloom of the *cuevas* and the *sombras*. But the caves where Angélica and Medoro embrace are not like the cave of Dido and Aeneas. They bring light and life to places where darkness dwells, and only in that positive sense can be said to be profaning them, through failing to respect their essential nature. This is, paradoxically, a good kind of profanity, in which the power of love, not fear, is celebrated in such dark and dangerous places.

> **Choza, pues, tálamo y lecho,**
> **cortesanos labradores,**
> **aires, campos, fuentes, vegas,**
> 132   **cuevas, troncos, aves, flores,**
>
> **fresnos, chopos, montes, valles,**
> **contestes de estos amores,**

el cielo os guarde, si puede,
136 **de las locuras del Conde.**

So: may heaven protect you, if it can—cottage, marriage-bed, bed, courteous peasants, breezes, fields, fountains, riverbanks, caves, tree-trunks, birds, flowers, ash trees, poplars, mountains, valleys, [all of you] witnesses to this love—[protect you] from the madness of the Count.

The poem ends with an invocation to the human and natural elements which have together contributed to the celebration of this love. It recapitulates them in no particular order, and only the *vega* is added: *choza, cabaña* (61); *lecho, tálamo* (70–71); *cortesanos labradores* (47, 56–57, 66); *aires* (111); *campos* (15, 113); *fuentes* (115); *cuevas* (125); *troncos* (117); *aves* (132); *palomas* (87); *tórtolas* (97); *ruiseñores* (116); *flores* (20, 132); *rosas* (23, 25); *jazmines* (104); *fresnos* (121); *chopos* (122); *montes* (7–8); *valles* (123–24). They are to be *contestes*, 'witnesses', of *estos amores*: Cov. defines *contestes* as 'los testigos que dizen una misma cosa en sustancia', and that is precisely their function here. The only note of menace and mystery comes in the last two lines, with the wish that they may be kept safe from *las locuras del Conde*. The sudden appearance of new character, and the implication that the story does not really end at this point, is characteristic of the often unresolved endings of the *romances viejos*. But readers of the poem, familiar with the story from Ariosto, would have known that for once it had a happy ending. Mad Count Orlando discovers traces of the lovers, but never finds them, and they disappear from Ariosto's poem to live happily ever after. On the other hand, the addition of the words *se puede* to the desire that heaven should protect the lovers strikes an odd note. A *cielo* so circumscribed in its power cannot surely represent the omnipotent Christian God, who acts as he pleases. It seems to suggest something more like fate, which is perhaps appropriate for lovers who (unlike Orlando) presumably do not belong to the Christian world.

Góngora signals his poem's kinship with the traditions of the *romancero viejo* through the regularity of the octosyllabic *romance* metre, the lack of any contextual explanation for Medoro's wounds or Angélica's presence at the beginning, and the unexpected and unexplained ending. But in virtually every other respect it is a quite different kind of work. By detaching the episode from Ariosto's epic Góngora turns it into a virtually self-contained poem with a strong erotic charge. There is a narrative, but of the barest kind. Instead, Góngora creates an intensely lyrical and sensual world in which humans act in harmony with the predominant powers of nature, peaceful and restorative. At its heart lie two transformations, that of Medoro from a state bordering on death to physical health and vigour, and that of Angélica from a cold-hearted princess to a passionate woman. It is she who takes the initiative to set that process into motion, even though she does not realize that love will gain entry to her heart through her compassion. Medoro's role is understandably passive, especially at the start, and the only action attributed to him alone is his laying aside of the weapons of war (95–96). Once their transformations are complete the two consummate their love, and nature, even in its dark places, witnesses their coupling.

These transformations are achieved through a sustained play of literal and metaphorical meanings, in which physical realities are themselves transformed into metaphor. Images evolve across the poem, often changing their sense as they do, are reinforced by allusions to Classical myths and commonplaces, and create interlinked series of ideas: a battlefield becomes the place where a different and life-giving kind of war is waged; Medoro's blood turns to red flowers blooming in the grass, like that of Adonis, and his cheeks become roses behind which love, in the form of Cupid with his bow and arrow, lurks like the proverbial snake in the grass. The Classical allusions to Venus and Adonis and to Orpheus are more than decorative or stylistic features intended to contribute towards the *culto* aesthetic Góngora espouses; they are appropriate because they engage in different ways with the situation in which the ballad's protagonists find themselves—rejected suitors, the triumph of love over death. Petrarchan similes, like roses and suns, become freestanding metaphors, and Petrarchan commonplaces are given new life as Góngora follows the poetic logic of his images and creates memorable oxymorons like sweet scorpions and sparks of water. Alongside such *conceptista* reworkings of the traditions he inherits, he deploys the full range of *culto* armoury, in the use of stylistic devices such as hyperbaton, parallelism, antithesis, paradox, oxymoron, and Classical allusion. This is a carefully crafted poem, full of artifice, which nevertheless evokes a world of natural beauty and simplicity. The more one reads it, the more one sees in it, and the greater one's sense of *admiratio*, pleasurable wonder, at what the poet has achieved.

FRANCISCO DE QUEVEDO

'TESTAMENTO DE DON QUIJOTE' (1606–14?)

De un molimiento de güesos,
a puros palos y piedras,
don Quijote de la Mancha
yace doliente y sin fuerzas.

5 Tendido sobre un pavés,
cubierto con su rodela,
sacando como tortuga
de entre conchas la cabeza;

con voz roída y chillando,
10 viendo el escribano cerca,
ansí, por falta de dientes,
habló con él entre muelas:

'Escribid, buen caballero,
que Dios en quietud mantenga,
15 el testamento que fago
por voluntad postrimera.

Y en lo de "su entero juicio",
que ponéis a usanza vuesa,
basta poner "decentado",
20 cuando entero no lo tenga.

A la tierra mando el cuerpo;
coma mi cuerpo la tierra;
que según está de flaco
hay para un bocado apenas.

25 En la vaina de mi espada
mando que llevado sea
mi cuerpo, que es ataúd
capaz para su flaqueza.

Que embalsamado me lleven
30 a reposar a la iglesia,
y que sobre mi sepulcro
escriban esto en la piedra:

"Aquí yace Don Quijote,
el que en provincias diversas
35 los tuertos vengó, y los bizcos,
a puro vivir a ciegas."

A Sancho mando las islas
que gané con tanta guerra:
con que, si no queda rico,
40 aislado, a lo menos, queda.

Ítem, al buen Rocinante
(dejo los prados y selvas
que crió el Señor del cielo
para alimentar las bestias)

45 mándole mala ventura,
y mala vejez con ella,
y duelos en que pensar,
en vez de piensos y yerba.

Mando que al moro encantado
50 que me maltrató en la venta
los puñetes que me dio
al momento se le vuelvan.

Mando a los mozos de mulas
volver las coces soberbias
55 que me dieron, por descargo
de espaldas y de conciencia.

De los palos que me han dado,
a mi linda Dulcinea,
para que gaste el invierno,
60 mando cien cargas de leña.

Mi espada mando a una escarpia,
pero desnuda la tenga,
sin que a vestirla otro alguno,
si no es el orín, se atreva.

65   Mi lanza mando a una escoba,
      para que puedan con ella
      echar arañas del techo,
      cual si San Jorge fuera.

      Peto, gola y espaldar,
70   manopla y media visera,
      los vinculo en Quijotico,
      mayorazgo de mi hacienda.

      Y lo demás de los bienes
      que en este mundo se quedan,
75   lo dejo para obras pías
      de rescate de princesas.

      Mando que, en lugar de misas,
      justas, batallas y guerras
      me digan, pues saben todos
80   que son mis misas aquestas.

      Dejo por testamentarios
      a don Belianis de Grecia,
      al Caballero del Febo,
      a Esplandián el de las Xergas.'

85   Allí fabló Sancho Panza,
      bien oiréis lo que dijera,
      con tono duro y de espacio,
      y la voz de cuatro suelas:

      'No es razón, buen señor mío,
90   que, cuando vais a dar cuenta
      al Señor que vos crió,
      digáis sandeces tan fieras.

      Sancho es, señor, quien vos fabla,
      que está a vuestra cabecera,
95   llorando a cántaros, triste,
      un turbión de lluvia y piedra.

      Dejad por testamentarios
      al cura que vos confiesa,
      al regidor Per Antón
100   y al cabrero Gil Panzueca.

      Y dejaos de Esplandiones
      pues tanta inquietud nos cuestan,
      y llamad a un religioso
      que os ayude en esta brega.'

105   'Bien dices (le respondió
      Don Quijote con voz tierna):
      ve a Peña Pobre, y dile
      a Beltenebros que venga.'

      En esto la Extremaunción
110   asomó ya por la puerta;
      pero él, que no vio al sacerdote
      con sobrepelliz y vela,

      dijo que era el sabio proprio
      del encanto de Niquea;
115   y levantó el buen hidalgo
      por hablarle la cabeza.

      Mas, viendo que le faltan
      juicio, vida, vista y lengua,
      el escribano se fue
120   y el cura se salió fuera.

*   *   *   *   *

Part I of Miguel de Cervantes Saavedra's *El ingenioso hidalgo don Quijote de la Mancha* was published in 1605, and Part II in 1615 with the title intriguingly changed and the protagonist moved up the social ladder to *El ingenioso caballero don Quijote de la Mancha* (see Cervantes 2005). Francisco de Quevedo's *romance* 'Testamento de don Quijote' makes fun of Cervantes's novel shortly after its publication by parodying it. It is in the usual *romance* form of octosyllabic lines with assonance (here in *é–a*) in alternate lines. It typifies the early reception of Cervantes's novel, which was seen as a straightforward piece of burlesque, a parody of the once popular chivalric romances (fictional prose tales of medieval knights errant who defeat wicked enemies and rescue damsels in distress), without any of the tragic elements or deep and hidden meanings that readers and critics from the eighteenth century onwards have found in it. Quevedo's ballad is a piece of fun for fun's sake, and for the sake of attacking Cervantes by mercilessly mocking his creation: those were times of intense professional rivalry among writers. In others of Quevedo's writings, laughter is used to teach a moral lesson, but not here.

This ballad illustrates the huge difference between the sense of fun of the early seventeenth century and that of the early twenty-first: it is not so easy to laugh nowadays at madness, violence, suffering, or death. But for seventeenth-century readers, steeped in the inexorable logic of the Roman Catholic doctrine of free will, Don Quixote's predicament is ridiculous and laughable because he has brought it all on himself by his own foolish choice of behaviour, spending too much time reading pulp fiction and too little time sleeping; he therefore deserves no sympathy, only mockery. We can laugh at the suffering of our fellow human beings so long as pity or fear do not intervene.

Cervantes's novel is much funnier than Quevedo's ballad makes it seem (Russell 1969). Can a parody of a parody ever be successful? And the need in a commentary to explain the jokes does not enhance the poem's comicality.

> **De un molimiento de güesos,**
> **a puros palos y piedras,**
> **don Quijote de la Mancha**
> 4   **yace doliente y sin fuerzas.**

With his bones smashed to smithereens by blows from sticks and stones, Don Quixote de la Mancha lies in pain and without strength.

Most of the adventures caused by Don Quixote's delusions end with severe beatings for him, particularly in Part I. These beatings are presented as funny events, since they are appropriate punishments for his stupidity. Quevedo makes it clear from the outset that his treatment of Don Quixote's death is going to be comical, too, in his offhand use to refer to the beatings of the colloquial terms *molimiento* (literally 'grinding', 'milling') and *a puros palos y piedras*, whose alliteration on a plosive sound both mimics the noise of the blows and draws attention to the expression's jokiness.

> **Tendido sobre un pavés,**
> **cubierto con su rodela,**
> **sacando como tortuga**
> 8   **de entre conchas la cabeza;**

Stretched out on a long wooden shield, covered by his little round infantry-man's shield, poking his head out like a tortoise between its shells,

One of the reasons why Don Quixote is laughable in the novel is his inappropriate dress: not only is it stupid for a man to ride about seventeenth-century Spain in armour, but his armour itself is a mixture of ill-matching pieces, including a *rodela*, the round shield used by foot-soldiers that he carries from I. VII to I. XXXVII in place of the more appropriate *adarga* (oval leather shield) which he uses in the rest of Part I and the *escudo* (metal shield with the classic shape) which he has throughout Part II. The strange idea of Don Quixote having a shield for bedclothes came to Quevedo from the beginning of I. XVI, where his wretched bed at a roadside inn has sheets made of shield-leather. The *rodela*, small and inflexible, is an even less effective, warm, or comfortable cover for him as he lies, according to the *romance*, on a *pavés*, a long wooden shield that protected the whole body: the picture conjured up is that of a tortoise lying helplessly on its back, with the larger top shell underneath, the smaller, more rounded under-shell exposed, and the four legs waving in the air. These are strange lines, because—apart from the shield-leather sheets—Don Quixote is never portrayed like this in Cervantes's novel, whereas nearly all the other references in Quevedo's ballad are to clearly identifiable scenes in Part I. Sancho Panza, however, at the end of his period as governor of the 'island' of Barataria, is tied by his subjects, in the face of a feigned invasion, between two *paveses* because he has no armour, and he falls to the ground where he 'quedó como galápago encerrado y cubierto con sus conchas' (II. LIII).

> con voz roída y chillando,
> viendo el escribano cerca,
> ansí, por falta de dientes,
> 12   habló con él entre muelas:

in a gnawed voice, and squealing, seeing the notary close to him, he spoke to him as follows, muttering through his molars because of his lack of front teeth:

Don Quixote loses most of his teeth when he attacks a flock of sheep believing it to be a great army and the shepherds repel him with stones from their slings (I. XVIII). Quevedo plays with the common expression *hablar entre dientes*, 'to speak through one's front teeth', 'to mutter', and produces the absurd notion of speaking through one's back teeth, with the words presumably trickling out of the corners of the mouth. Playing with set expressions was a frequent comic device of the period. The startling concept of a *voz roída* is another comical reference to *muelas*: if one speaks through them, then one does indeed gnaw what one says. It also suggests that Don Quixote's voice is weak and that he has reduced himself to such poverty that the only thing he has available to gnaw (like a rat or a mouse) is not any kind of food but his own voice; *chillando* also associates Don Quixote with rodents. The notary has been summoned so that the dying man can dictate his will to him, the first step that the Christian should take in order to die a good death: he must put the things of this world in order, as a preliminary to attending to the things of the other world.

> 'Escribid, buen caballero,
> que Dios en quietud mantenga,
> el testamento que fago
> 16   por voluntad postrimera.

'*Write, good gentleman —and may God keep you in quiescence— the testament that I make as my last will.*

The addition of *en quietud* to the stock expression *que Dios mantenga* is a reference to Don Quixote's restless life as a knight errant (see 102). *Fago*, instead of *hago*, reminds us of Don Quixote's habit of lapsing into the archaic language of his beloved chivalric romances. Part I of *Don Quixote* ends with a reference to his death; Part II ends with him making his will on his death-bed, but in a way quite unlike that described in this ballad.

> **Y en lo de "su entero juicio",**
> **que ponéis a usanza vuesa,**
> **basta poner "decentado",**
> 20 **cuando entero no lo tenga.**

And as regards "of sound mind", which it is your custom to write, it will be sufficient to put "a little the worse for wear", if my mind is not sound.

Here there is yet more fun at the expense of a set expression. *Decentado* means 'incomplete' as a result of having been nibbled at, or having had a slice cut off, or having been affected by illness: Don Quixote suggests a euphemism so as not to admit that he is mad, which would have the disastrous effects of both invalidating his will and, even worse, making it impossible for him to receive the last rites and thus obtain salvation and secure a place in heaven. At the end of Part II of Cervantes's novel, however, Don Quixote does regain his sanity before making his will and receiving the last rites.

> **A la tierra mando el cuerpo;**
> **coma mi cuerpo la tierra;**
> **que según está de flaco**
> 24 **hay para un bocado apenas.**
>
> **En la vaina de mi espada**
> **mando que llevado sea**
> **mi cuerpo, que es ataúd**
> 28 **capaz para su flaqueza.**

I bequeath my body to the earth; may the earth eat my body; it is so thin that it will hardly provide a single mouthful. I order my body to be carried away in the scabbard of my sword, a coffin that is adequate for its thinness.

Quevedo uses rhetorical figures to make yet more fun with a set expression, the one in 22: first the chiasmus—*tierra... cuerpo... cuerpo... tierra*—draws our attention to it, and then Don Quixote takes this commonplace prosopopeia and metaphor literally and creates the joke by a process of *reductio ad absurdum* (showing the absurdity of some proposition by taking it to its logical extreme). The notion of Don Quixote being buried in his own scabbard is a comic conceit, and like all conceits it gives us two surprises: first presenting us with an apparently absurd and unjustifiable metaphor (a scabbard is a coffin), and then providing a perfect justification for it (Don Quixote is so very emaciated that he will fit inside his scabbard). What is more, a knight's sword is the symbol of his worth and is thus identified with his person: he is his sword. Immense comic exaggeration, often using the device of *reductio ad absurdum*, is one of Quevedo's specialities.

> **Que embalsamado me lleven**
> **a reposar a la iglesia,**
> **y que sobre mi sepulcro**
> 32   **escriban esto en la piedra:**
>
> **"Aquí yace Don Quijote,**
> **el que en provincias diversas**
> **los tuertos vengó, y los bizcos,**
> 36   **a puro vivir a ciegas."**

Let them carry me, embalmed, to rest in the church, and let them write this on the stone over my grave: "Here lies Don Quixote, he who in diverse provinces avenged wrongs/one-eyed people, and cross-eyed people too, by living so very blindly."

The assumption that he will be embalmed and taken to lie in state or be interred (*reposar* could mean either, or both) inside a church is an expression of Don Quixote's comical delusions of grandeur: these things only happened to the great and the good when they died, not to petty and impoverished country gentlemen like him. Part I of *Don Quixote* ends with a number of spoof epitaphs in the style of this one. Here the punning joke depends on the two meanings of *tuerto* indicated in the translation: it was one of the duties of knights errant to avenge wrongs, but Don Quixote acts blindly in believing that this behaviour is appropriate for the times in which he lives.

> **A Sancho mando las islas**
> **que gané con tanta guerra:**
> **con que, si no queda rico,**
> 40   **aislado, a lo menos, queda.**

To Sancho I bequeath the islands that I won by making so much war: with which, if he is not left rich, he is at least left isolated.

Sancho Panza, the humble villager whom Don Quixote takes as his squire, longs to be made the powerful and wealthy governor of one of the islands he believes his master is bound to conquer (I. VII) but which, of course, he never does conquer. The pun here is on the noun *isla* and the verb *aislar*, etymologically 'to put on an island': Quevedo's Don Quixote implies that Sancho is such a menace that he needs to be kept away from the rest of humanity. The chiasmus —*queda rico, aislado… queda*— foregrounds the joke's key word, *aislado*. In the novel the word always used by Don Quixote is not *isla* but the pretentious Latinism *ínsula*, but Quevedo sacrifices it to the wordplay.

Ítem, al buen Rocinante
(dejo los prados y selvas
que crió el Señor del cielo
44   para alimentar las bestias)

mándole mala ventura,
y mala vejez con ella,
y duelos en que pensar,
48   en vez de piensos y yerba.

Moreover, to good Rocinante (I leave aside the meadows and woods that the Lord of Heaven created to feed beasts/horses) I bequeath bad fortune and with it a bad old age, and duels/griefs/bad food on which to graze/ponder, instead of fodder/thoughts and grass.

Ítem is legal language, the word used to introduce each entry in a will. *Rocinante* is Don Quixote's 'steed', in reality a wretched nag responsible for one of the worst beatings, at the hands of some muleteers, when it tries to force its amorous attentions on their pony-mares after its master has stopped in a lush meadow at the edge of a wood so that it can graze there (I. XV). The ambiguity of *bestia*, meaning both 'horse' and 'beast', reinforces the fun. As the translation indicates, 47 and 48 contain yet another of those multiple puns of which Quevedo, that lover of verbal fireworks, was so fond: Don Quixote fought many duels, experienced much grief, and ate plenty of bad food. A still unresolved textual enigma is the exact nature of the *duelos y quebrantos* that, according to the novel's second sentence, were what Don Quixote ate on Saturdays, days of semi-abstinence (Cervantes 2005: I. 38); but what is clear is that this was not good food.

Mando que al moro encantado
que me maltrató en la venta
los puñetes que me dio
52   al momento se le vuelvan.

Mando a los mozos de mulas
volver las coces soberbias
que me dieron, por descargo
56   de espaldas y de conciencia.

I order that the punches given me by the enchanted Moor who maltreated me at the wayside inn be returned to him forthwith. I order that the tremendous kicks given me by the footmen be returned, for the relief of my shoulders and my conscience.

The insistent repetition of the word *mando* is yet another rhetorical device, called anaphora when, as here, it comes at the beginning of successive clauses or sentences: it serves to tie this part of Don Quixote's discourse together. People making death-bed wills were most anxious to ensure that all the property they had borrowed be returned to its owners, to avoid the possibility of theft being included in their list of sins when they went to meet their Maker. A jealous muleteer thrashes Don Quixote by night at a wayside inn and is assumed by the latter to be an enchanted Moor, since he is convinced that no ordinary human being could defeat him (I. XVI–XVII). Lines 53–56 refer to I. IV, in which Don Quixote is beaten and kicked by the servants of some merchants whose coach he stops to demand they recognize that his lady-love Dulcinea is the most beautiful woman in the world. In 55–56, two nouns that are not normally associated (*espaldas*, *conciencia*) are coupled by each being separately related to a third word (*descargo*); this rhetorical device is known as syllepsis or zeugma and is often found in elegant comic and humorous writing (see, for example, Alexander Pope's 'to stain her honour or her new brocade', and lines 2–3 of Quevedo's 'A la Corte vas, Perico', discussed below. p. 118). The fun usually derives, as it does here, from one of the nouns being abstract and with lofty connotations, and the other being concrete and prosaic, producing a witty effect of incongruity and bathos.

> **De los palos que me han dado,**
> **a mi linda Dulcinea,**
> **para que gaste el invierno,**
> 60 **mando cien cargas de leña.**

From the blows/sticks that I have been given, I bequeath a hundred loads of firewood to my splendid Dulcinea, so that she can see the winter out.

Every knight errant has his lady-love, a beautiful aristocrat for whose sake he performs his gallant deeds. Don Quixote makes a robust peasant-girl, Aldonza Lorenzo, from a local village called El Toboso, into his imagined lady, and rechristens her Dulcinea del Toboso. The reference to firewood emphasizes the ridiculous mistake that Don Quixote has made concerning the social class of the lady-love: a humble peasant would indeed be grateful for such a gift to help her survive the winter, but not a lofty aristocrat! There is more punning here, this time on the two meanings of *palo*; and the *cien cargas* remind us again of the very many beatings that Don Quixote suffers in Part I.

> **Mi espada mando a una escarpia,**
> **pero desnuda la tenga,**
> **sin que a vestirla otro alguno,**
> 64 **si no es el orín, se atreva.**

I bequeath my sword to a hook, but it must keep my sword bare, and not allow anyone or anything else, except rust, to dare to clothe/wear it.

A knight's armour, and in particular his sword, was such a precious symbol of his status, power, and virtue that it was never to be used by any other man: Don Quixote's sword is to be hung on a hook, and only rust is to be allowed to touch it. There is a pun here on the two meanings of *vestir*: nobody else must wear it, only rust must clothe it. At the end of Part II of Cervantes's novel, Don

Quixote's chronicler Cide Hamete Benengeli performs a similar action, hanging his pen on a rack and saying that no other chronicler must pick it up.

> **Mi lanza mando a una escoba,**
> **para que puedan con ella**
> **echar arañas del techo,**
> 68   **cual si San Jorge fuera.**

I bequeath my lance to a broom-head, so that it can be used to brush spiders from the ceiling, as if it were St George.

This is a comically absurd contradiction of the insistence in the previous stanza on the untransferability of a knight's armour, and another example of bathos. To reinforce this, an isocolon links 61 and 65. It was customary to invoke St George when killing a spider, with the words 'San Jorge, ¡mata la araña!', no doubt a humorously ironical reference to his well-known slaying of the dragon. Here, then, there is still more comical bathos.

> **Peto, gola y espaldar,**
> **manopla y media visera,**
> **los vinculo en Quijotico,**
> 72   **mayorazgo de mi hacienda.**

I entail my breast-plate, gorget, back-plate, gauntlet and half-visor on my little Quixote, the heir to my estate.

This is a strange variation from the novel, in which Don Quixote is unmarried and childless. Perhaps Quevedo is insinuating that Don Quixote's relationships with Dulcinea or the other female protagonists are less chaste than he claims. A passage in the first chapter of Part I lists his pieces of armour and narrates how he cannot find a visor, and makes a half-visor out of cardboard.

> **Y lo demás de los bienes**
> **que en este mundo se quedan,**
> **lo dejo para obras pías**
> 76   **de rescate de princesas.**

And I leave the rest of my property remaining in this world for the charitable work of rescuing princesses.

Rescuing ladies in distress was another of the tasks of a knight errant: I. xxIX–XLVI narrate Don Quixote's attempts to help 'Princess Micomicona' in her plight. The expression *obras pías* normally refers not to rescuing fine ladies but to succouring the poor.

> **Mando que, en lugar de misas,**
> **justas, batallas y guerras**
> **me digan, pues saben todos**
> 80   **que son mis misas aquestas.**

I order that jousts, battles and wars be said for me instead of masses, because everyone knows that those are my masses.

Quevedo here uses the method of *reductio ad absurdum* to mock the fact that the knight errant regarded his adoration of his lady as his religion, and fighting as his practice of that religion.

> **Dejo por testamentarios**
> **a don Belianis de Grecia,**
> **al Caballero del Febo,**
> 84 **a Esplandián el de las Xergas.'**

I appoint as executors Don Belianis of Greece, the Knight of Phoebus, and Esplandian, the hero of The Exploits.

These are heroes of well-known chivalric romances, listed in I. VI of Cervantes's novel, in which the village priest and barber scrutinize Don Quixote's library. Esplandián was the hero of *Las xergas de Esplandián* (*The Exploits of Esplandian*). Don Quixote's madness continues unabated.

> **Allí fabló Sancho Panza,**
> **bien oiréis lo que dijera,**
> **con tono duro y de espacio,**
> 88 **y la voz de cuatro suelas:**

Then spake Sancho Panza; you will all hear what he said, in a hard tone, slowly, and in a four-square voice:

Fabló is archaic, and was archaic when Cervantes wrote, like *fago* in 15 (see also *fabla* in 93). Line 86 is a formula used in Spanish epics and ballads to emphasize the importance of the speech that follows (see, for example, *Poema de mio Cid*, lines 70, 188, etc.); so there is more bathos and mock heroism here, where it introduces the speech of a common peasant. *Zapatos de cuatro suelas* were stout shoes with four layers of leather on the soles, and this adjectival phrase was extended metaphorically to mean 'strong', 'firm', and also used with emphatic meaning in expressions like *pícaro de cuatro suelas* and *tonto de cuatro suelas,* echoes of which are also present here. Once more, Quevedo plays with a set expression for comic effect.

> **'No es razón, buen señor mío,**
> **que, cuando vais a dar cuenta**
> **al Señor que vos crió,**
> 92 **digáis sandeces tan fieras.**
>
> **Sancho es, señor, quien vos fabla,**
> **que está a vuestra cabecera,**
> **llorando a cántaros, triste,**
> 96 **un turbión de lluvia y piedra.**

> **Dejad por testamentarios**
> **al cura que vos confiesa,**
> **al regidor Per Antón**
> 100 **y al cabrero Gil Panzueca.**
>
> **Y dejaos de Esplandiones**
> **pues tanta inquietud nos cuestan,**
> **y llamad a un religioso**
> 104 **que os ayude en esta brega.'**

'It isn't right, good master, just when you're about to give an account of yourself to the Lord who created you, for you to say such terrible stupid things. It's Sancho, sir, here talking to you, at the head of your bed, sadly weeping in buckets a squall of rain and hail. Appoint as executors the priest who confesses you, the alderman Per Antón, and the goatherd Gil Panzueca. And forget all about Esplandions, because they give us so much bother, and call for a holy father to help you out of this fix.'

At the end of Part II of the novel Sancho Panza does the opposite, begging his master not to stop being a knight errant, because their adventures together have been such fun, and it is Don Quixote himself who decides that now he is about to meet his Maker it is high time to renounce his foolish ways: the salvation of his soul depends on it. Per Antón and Gil Panzueca (a relative of Sancho Panza's?) do not appear in the novel. Their rustic names contrast with the fanciful names of the chivalresque heroes. Sancho is a specialist in malapropisms, and he mispronounces *Esplandián* as *Esplandión*, bringing this exotic name down to earth by giving it a comical augmentative suffix and creating yet more bathos.

> **'Bien dices (le respondió**
> **Don Quijote con voz tierna):**
> **ve a Peña Pobre, y dile**
> 108 **a Beltenebros que venga.'**

You are right,' Don Quixote replied in a weak voice, 'go to Peña Pobre, and tell Beltenebros to come.'

The eponymous hero of the most famous of the chivalric romances, *Amadis of Gaul*, renames himself Beltenebros and goes to do penance on a desolate island called Peña Pobre, 'Poor Rock', after an argument with his lady-love Oriana (see above, p. 37). There he meets a hermit who helps him with his devotions: Quevedo (or his Don Quixote, as his mind fades away) has confused the two men. In the novel, Don Quixote imitates Amadis's action by isolating himself in the range of hills known as the Sierra Morena in I. XXV–XXX.

> **En esto la Extremaunción**
> **asomó ya por la puerta;**
> **pero él, que no vio al sacerdote**
> 112 **con sobrepelliz y vela,**

dijo que era el sabio proprio
del encanto de Niquea;
y levantó el buen hidalgo
116   **por hablarle la cabeza.**

Mas, viendo que le faltan
juicio, vida, vista y lengua,
el escribano se fue
120   **y el cura se salió fuera.**

At this point Extreme Unction appeared at the door; but he, who did not see the priest with his surplice and candle, said that it was the very same sage who had been involved in the enchantment of Niquea; and the good hidalgo raised his head to talk to him. But, seeing that he lacked sanity, life, sight, and speech, the notary went away and the priest left the room.

Lines 109–110, with their striking metonymy (it is the priest who appears at the door, not his attribute the sacrament, which is abstract and invisible), are another example of the use of rhetoric for comic effect—here somewhat eery and ghostly. Yet Don Quixote continues raving about *Amadis of Gaul*: Niquea is the heroine of this work, enchanted by a witch, not a sage. So he dies mad, without making a will and unconfessed, and with the consequential threat to the eternal life of his soul: the opposite of what happens at the end of the novel. Quevedo has treated Don Quixote throughout the ballad with sadistic contempt, also implied in this anticlimactic ending, whereas Cervantes's attitude changed as he wrote: at the beginning of his novel Quixote was just an old fool who deserved all the disasters he brought upon himself, but by the end the author had warmed to his creation and gave him a model Christian death.

*   *   *   *   *

It is noteworthy that every one of the very many lines in the Quevedo ballad that show a detailed knowledge of Cervantes's novel refer to Part I. This cannot be a coincidence. I believe that critics are wrong to assume, as they do, that Quevedo must have written his ballad sometime after 1615, when Part II was first published, as a parody of Cervantes's account of his protagonist's death. No, it was the other way round: Quevedo wrote the ballad sometime after 1605 but before Part II was published, seizing on the fact that Don Quixote's death is mentioned at the end of Part I but not narrated, and being all too ready to fill this gap. After all, Cervantes had invited such participation by quoting *Orlando furioso*, XXX. 16 at the very end of Part I: 'Forse altro canterà con miglior plectro' ('Perhaps someone else will sing with a better plectrum'). So the last pages of Part II are a refutation of Quevedo's ballad, just as its last chapters are a refutation of the spurious sequel by Alonso Fernández de Avellaneda: *Segundo tomo del ingenioso hidalgo don Quijote de la Mancha*, published in Tarragona in 1614. There are, however, three loose similarities between Quevedo's ballad and Part II of Cervantes's *Quixote*, all involving events that come towards the end of the novel: Don Quixote making a will, Don Quixote or Sancho Panza lying between shields and looking like tortoises, and the hanging up by Don Quixote or by Cide Hamete of the sword or pen. These are to be explained by supposing that Quevedo's ballad, like Avellaneda's sequel, came to Cervantes's attention as he reached the end of his great effort, and that he adapted these ideas of Quevedo's to his own purposes, taking good care to change them so as to put Quevedo in the wrong, just as he did with some of Avellaneda's ideas. With both Quevedo and Avellaneda, Cervantes felt the need to defend against cruel scoffers a fictional creation of whom, maybe despite himself, he had become very fond. As he makes the chronicler Cide Hamete Benengeli's pen say after being hung up in its rack: 'Para mí sola nació don Quijote, y yo para él' (II. LXXIV).

So this little-known ballad deserves to be better known as the direct cause and source of the much-discussed last scene of the novel, the protagonist's recovery of sanity on his death bed.

FRANCISCO DE QUEVEDO

'SON LAS TORRES DE JORAY' (1621?)

FUNERAL A LOS HUESOS DE UNA FORTALEZA QUE GRITAN MUDOS DESENGAÑOS

Son las torres de Joray
calavera de unos muros
en el esqueleto informe
de un ya castillo difunto.

5 Hoy las esconden guijarros,
y ayer coronaron nublos.
Si dieron temor armadas,
precipitadas dan susto.

Sobre ellas, opaco, un monte
10 pálido amanece y turbio
al día, porque las sombras
vistan su tumba de luto.

Las dentelladas del año,
grande comedor de mundos,
15 almorzaron sus almenas
y cenaron sus trabucos.

Donde admiró su homenaje,
hoy amenaza su bulto :
fue fábrica y es cadaver ;
20 tuvo alcaides, tiene búhos.

Certificóme un cimiento
que está enfadando unos surcos,
que al que hoy desprecia un arado,
era del fuerte un reducto.

25 Sobre un alcázar en pena,
un balüarte desnudo
mortaja pide a las yerbas,
al cerro pide sepulcro.

Como herederos monteses,
30 pájaros le hacen nocturnos

las exequias, y los grajos
le endechan los contrapuntos.

Quedaron por albaceas
un chaparro y un saúco,
35 fantasmas que a primavera
espantan flores y fruto.

Guadalén, que los juanetes
del pie del escollo duro
sabe los puntos que calzan,
40 dobla por él, importuno.

Este cimenterio verde,
este monumento bruto
me señalaron por cárcel :
yo le tomé por estudio.

45 Aquí, en cátedra de muertos,
atento le oí discursos
del bachiller Desengaño
contra sofísticos gustos.

Yo, que mis ojos tenía,
50 Floris taimada, en los tuyos,
presumiendo eternidades
entre cielos y coluros ;

en tu boca hallando perlas
y en tu aliento calambucos,
55 aprendiendo en tus claveles
a despreciar los carbunclos ;

en donde una primavera
mostró mil abriles juntos,
gastando en sólo guedejas
60 más soles que doce lustros,

con tono clamoreado,   75   *Las glorias de este mundo*
que la ausencia me compuso,   *llaman con luz para pagar con humo.*
lloré mis versos siguientes,
más renegados que cultos :   Este mundo engañabobos,
                                        engaitador de sentidos,
65   *Las glorias de este mundo*   en muy corderos validos
     llaman con luz para pagar con humo. 80 anda disfrazando lobos.
                                          Sus patrimonios son robos,
     Tú, que te das a entender   su caudal insultos fieros ;
     la eternidad que imaginas,   y en trampas de lisonjeros
     aprende de estas rüinas,   cae después su imperio sumo.
70   si no a vivir, a caer.
     El mandar y enriquecer   85   *Las glorias de este mundo*
     dos encantadores son   *llaman con luz para pagar con humo.*
     que te turban la razón,
     sagrado de que presumo.

*   *   *   *   *

Most men of letters in Quevedo's day were dependent for their livelihood upon patronage. This gave them experience of the vagaries of fate as their own fortunes rose and declined alongside those of their patrons. For many writers the intrigue and rivalries of the Court, in particular, were the stuff of their everyday experience. Quevedo was not only intimately acquainted with Court life but, as a protégé of the Duke of Osuna, Viceroy of Naples, had navigated the murky waters surrounding Philip III. He would later have to trim and tack in those of Philip IV and his favourite the Count-Duke of Olivares. In this ballad he uses the description of a ruined building to symbolize the precarious nature of life at Court and, indeed, of all human life.

There was a long tradition in Classical poetry, and in its sixteenth- and seventeenth-century descendants, of contemplating the ruins of once-famous cities like Rome and Carthage, and drawing conclusions from that contemplation. These varied from warnings (that power and glory are ephemeral and that fortune is mutable) to consolation (that time lessens pain just as it erodes ruins) (Lara 1983: 223–33). One facet of this tradition in Spain was a poetry that focused upon Spanish ruins more specifically as an emblem of national decline (Vranich 1980). Quevedo writes within this tradition, echoing motifs and even details from earlier Spanish poems (e.g. fallen towers that had once competed with the clouds, birds being the only inhabitants of ruined buildings). However, he adapts inherited material to his own purposes. From the outset, he takes as his subject the ruins of a humble Spanish fortress in the back of beyond rather than those of a great city of Antiquity.[1] His choice of a ruined Spanish castle may well be more than a nod to the ballad 'Castillo de San Cervantes' (1591) by Luis de Góngora (GR.36; Góngora 2000a: 326–31); 'Son las torres de Joray' (Q.766) not only contains

---

[1] Quevedo would later refer to the area round Joray as 'estos desiertos' (Q.131: 1).

echoes of that earlier poem, but provides Quevedo with an opportunity to outshine the wit of his rival Góngora and implicitly to criticize the frivolity of the earlier ballad which had treated the ruins of San Cervantes with comic disdain as a place for illicit sexual encounters. The castle of Joray, nowadays known as the Castillo de Eznavejor, lies near the small town of La Torre de Juan Abad (province of Ciudad Real) of which Quevedo had acquired the *señorío*. He spent a good deal of time in that town, sometimes when banished from Madrid as a consequence of falling out of favour with successive monarchs and their advisers. 'Son las torres de Joray' was probably written in 1621 when Quevedo was suffering one such period of banishment as a consequence of his association with Osuna and the duke's disgrace.[2]

We should resist the temptation of automatically identifying the 'voice' of a poem with the poet himself (see above, p. 16). In some poems, such as Góngora's ballad 'Noble desengaño' (see Chapter 2, above), a 'poetic voice' is created through whom the poem is narrated, Góngora maintaining all the while an ironic distance between himself and this 'voice', as he mocks, criticizes, judges, or is more complexly ambivalent about it. In 'Son las torres de Joray', however, there appears to be little ironic distance between the 'poetic voice' and Quevedo. The ballad is neo-Stoic: it advocates indifference to concerns over which the individual has little control, like human love and political fortune, such matters being transient, arbitrary, and of little consequence when implicitly compared to the Christian's inner life in the context of inevitable death.[3] As a victim of the slippery business of politics, Quevedo had good reason to cultivate such Stoicism as a response to adversity and disappointment.

Wit, or *agudeza* as it was called in Spain, was a feature of much poetry of the seventeenth century, and Quevedo was a brilliant practitioner of it. Wit was a particularly appropriate vehicle for a neo-Stoic view of the world in which superficial appearances (*parecer*) are pithily contrasted with the underlying truths (*ser*) that readers are forced to recognize as they peel away the layers of meaning in the poet's conceits. With its apparently incongruous yet apt metaphors and its trenchant assertions, 'Son las torres de Joray' not only employs this pedagogical method, but also, as we realize towards the end of the poem, is wittily structured. Just as the ruined castle of Joray silently

---

[2] It was in the summer of 1621, when he became *señor* of La Torre de Juan Abad, that Quevedo was permitted to leave Uclés, to which he had been banished, and to serve the remainder of his exile in his *señorío*. He was sent there again the following year. Another possible date of composition of 'Son las torres de Joray' would be 1628, when Quevedo was again banished to the countryside. However, one of the manuscript copies of the poem contains the note 'Quevedo, estando preso por los negocios del [duque] de Osuna en Joray', which makes the earlier date more likely. See Quevedo (1969–81: III. 64), and Jauralde (1998a: 419, 426, 551).

[3] This neo-Stoic opposition between the outward (*lo ajeno*) and the inner life (*lo propio*) is epitomized in the title of Quevedo's *La cuna y la sepultura para el conocimiento propio y desengaño de las cosas ajenas* (1634). He had long been attracted to this philosophy.

teaches the poet, so does the structure of the ballad tacitly educate readers when it dawns upon them in a flash of enlightenment where the poem has been leading all along.

*   *   *   *   *

FUNERAL A LOS HUESOS DE UNA FORTALEZA QUE GRITAN MUDOS DESENGAÑOS

Funeral of [or funeral poem to] the bones of a castle which silently yell out 'desengaños'.

The title of the ballad introduces some of its principal motifs: the mocking comparison of the castle to human remains, its ruins being described as bones, a skull, and a skeleton; the observation that time is destructive, with the obvious conclusions we should draw from this; and the lesson in *desengaño* that the ruins teach us. The verb *desengañar* is defined by Quevedo's contemporary, Sebastián de Covarrubias, as: 'Sacar del engaño al que está en él. Hablar claro, porque no conciban una cosa por otra. Desengañarse, caer en la cuenta de que era engaño lo que tenía por cierto' (see above, p. 26).[4] The title also introduces the conceit that the ruins shout out a moral to the onlooker, yet are mute: the lesson they teach is so obvious that it comes over loud and clear, but the ruins can communicate only through images interpreted by the spectator.[5] An implicit contrast will be drawn in the poem between the ruins' honest, eloquent silence and language's potential for deceit exemplified by the posturing of academic wordsmiths, by lovers' vacuous formulas, and by courtiers' flattering tongues. Quevedo implies that words lend themselves to duplicity and frivolity, while what is in front of one's eyes does not, if properly interpreted, mislead.

In 1621 Quevedo was optimistic that the death of Philip III (which occurred in March of that year) and the advent of the new regime of Philip IV would lead to the restoration in Spain of what Elliott (1989a: 191) calls 'the ancient Castilian virtues that had been eroded by the long reign of self-interest, luxury and sloth' during the reign of the late monarch. It is fitting that the ruins of a Castilian castle, with their suggestion of an earlier and more austere age (Alfonso VIII had finally captured Joray from the Moors in the thirteenth century and had given it to the Military Order of Santiago), as well as of the military muscle which Quevedo believed had become slack under Philip III's regime, should provide the lessons which, in this poem, he will pass on to a self-serving courtier and thus to his readers.

---

[4] Where *Cov.* provides no guidance to contemporary meanings, I turn to *Aut.*, which, although published a century after the composition of 'Son las torres de Joray', frequently draws upon this ballad to illustrate its definitions.

[5] This conceit of the silent speech of ruins had appeared in Góngora's 'Castillo de San Cervantes': 'Háblale mudo mil cosas, | que las oirá, pues sabemos | que a palabras de edificios | orejas los ojos fueron' (Góngora 2000a: 329).

> **Son las torres de Joray**
> **calavera de unos muros**
> **en el esqueleto informe**
> 4   **de un ya castillo difunto.**

The towers of Joray are the skull of walls [standing] on the formless skeleton of a now deceased castle.

Being the highest point of the castle, the ruined towers are likened to a skull, the uppermost part of the skeleton constituted by its broken walls; the skeleton is *informe* because the ruins are a shapeless pile of debris.

> **Hoy las esconden guijarros,**
> 6   **y ayer coronaron nublos.**

They are today buried underneath pebbles whereas yesterday they were in the clouds.

Quevedo contrasts the present state of the towers with their former glory; the speed with which this fall took place—the rapidity with which the works of men are brought low—is emphasized by the contrast between *hoy* and *ayer*. Line 6 is ambiguous: it could mean either that the clouds capped the towers or that the towers were once so high that they projected from the clouds, appearing like crowns above them. The choice of the word *coronar* suggests the shape of the towers' turrets or crenellations, which recall the decorations on a crown, while the clouds upon which the metaphorical crown sits suggest its wearer's white or grey hair. Only when we reach the end of the poem shall we realise that this evocation of a crown has more sinister implications. The second suggested meaning of 6 would convey grammatically the impotence of the once-powerful towers by means of the contrast between their once having been the subject of the verb *coronar*, while they are now the mere object of *esconder* because humble pebbles cover them.

> **Si dieron temor armadas,**
> 8   **precipitadas dan susto.**

If they were awesome when standing, they are terrifying now they have collapsed.

Quevedo draws upon a commonplace of previous poetry: ruins lead to contemplation of power undone. Characteristically, however, he revitalizes this topos by using a conceit: the towers once inspired fear in potential foes, but their collapse provokes even greater terror. We are at first surprised and intrigued that a heap of rubble can be more awesome than a towering castle, but realise that Joray's decrepitude is terrifying because it teaches us that if the strongest and seemingly most durable of buildings cannot withstand the onslaught of time, our own lives must be brief and hang by a thread. The contrast goes further: the attackers' fear for their physical safety in this life is as nothing compared with the poet's (and our) fear for the soul in the next. The word *precipitadas* emphasizes the suddenness and violence of the towers' collapse, providing a warning of other calamities for which the unwary are not prepared such as death or the loss of political power.

> **Sobre ellas, opaco, un monte**
> **pálido amanece y turbio**
> **al día, porque las sombras**
> 12 **vistan su tumba de luto.**

Above them a dark hill [or wilderness] appears in the weak and murky dawn so the shadows can dress the castle's tomb in mourning.

It is unclear which of the two nouns, *monte* and *día*, is qualified by the adjectives *opaco*, *pálido* and *turbio*, but the context suggests that *opaco* describes *monte*, while *pálido* and *turbio* qualify *día*, although all three could as easily qualify *monte*. The once proud castle which used to dominate from a height the area under its control—arable land (22), pastures (27), trees (34), and river (37)—is now itself dominated by a mere hill. Although dawn normally brings brightness, here it is pale and the sun does not shine clearly; surprisingly, daylight is a reminder of death as it casts dark shadows over the dead castle, clothing its ruins in mourning. The mention of mourning picks up the *difunto* of 4, continuing the image of the castle as a person who has died. *Monte* was used to mean hill or uncultivated land covered by scrub and trees (see above, p. 61), the latter sense also referring familiarly to tousled hair. If this is a secondary meaning here, Quevedo would be pursuing the comic image of the ruins as a skeleton, the skull's being capped by vegetation which looks like its wild hair.

> **Las dentelladas del año,**
> **grande comedor de mundos,**
> **almorzaron sus almenas**
> 16 **y cenaron sus trabucos.**

That great gobbler up of worlds, time ['el año'], has taken out great bites, lunching on the castle's battlements and dining on its catapults.

The ruined walls have irregular gaps in them; they look as if a giant has taken great bites out of them. Quevedo echoes here a famous passage of Ovid's *Metamorphoses* (XV. 234–36): 'tempus edax rerum, tuque, invidiosa vetustas, | omnia destruitis vitiataque dentibus aevi | paulatim lenta consumitis omnia morte', 'Oh Time, you great destroyer, and you, envious Age, together you wipe out everything. Slowly gnawing away, you devour all things in lingering death'. But the poet gives these chilling lines a macabre and comic twist by specifying that the battlements provided time's lunch and the catapults its dinner. And it is ironic that siege machines designed to demolish castle walls are themselves destroyed, along with the walls, by ravenous time.

> **Donde admiró su homenaje,**
> **hoy amenaza su bulto:**
> **fue fábrica y es cadaver;**
> 20   **tuvo alcaides, tiene búhos.**

Where its tallest tower once inspired awe, now the formless ruins serve as a warning; it was once a sumptuous edifice, but is now a corpse; it was once inhabited by castle governors, but now owls live in it.

Quevedo elaborates on the contrast, introduced in 5–6, between a glorious past and a decrepit present. The *homenaje* was the principal tower of a castle where, as *Cov.* explains, governors customarily swore fealty to their lord. Perhaps the cry of the owl recalls the sound of solemn oaths being sworn in a deep voice by the long-dead governors. A further contrast is between day and night, the owl being associated with the dark, and therefore death. Indeed, the owl was thought to be a bird of ill omen, and was associated with lustful hypocrites who took advantage of darkness to cloak their nefarious activities, the word also being used colloquially to refer to prostitutes. By contrasting *alcaides* (see p. 165, below) with *búhos* Quevedo may again be suggesting that the austere military values of the past have degenerated into what he perceived as the decadence of Philip III's reign. The typical Golden-Age idea of *admiratio*, or awe, was once provoked by the loftiest of the castle towers; now, echoing 7 and 8, a different sort of dread is felt by the poet as he ponders the ruins of the once splendid tower.

> **Certificóme un cimiento**
> **que está enfadando unos surcos,**
> **que al que hoy desprecia un arado,**
> 24   **era del fuerte un reducto.**

Foundations, which are obstructing some furrows, testified to me that what the plough nowadays despises was once a redoubt of the fortress.

With the word *certificóme* Quevedo introduces the language of last wills and testaments (compare above, Chapter 5), foreshadowing references to *herederos* (29) and *albaceas* (33), and elaborating on the motif of the castle as a deceased person. Joray's foundations obstruct the furrows because a farmer ploughing the land where the castle once stood strikes the buried stones with his plough, pushing them aside with disdain. The poet pursues the theme of the mighty brought low by time: a powerful redoubt—a secondary fortification which has resisted the onslaughts of Moorish and Christian armies over the centuries—now lies in ruins and is half buried, serving merely to impede the plough. As we have seen, Quevedo believed that Spain under Philip III had forsaken military virtue; here it is suggested that a castle that had once resisted the sword is now defenceless even against ploughshares. *Reducto* clinches this criticism with a pun: the word not only refers to a piece of military architecture, but suggests something 'reduced', in other words something which has degenerated.

> **Sobre un alcázar en pena,**
> **un balüarte desnudo**
> **mortaja pide a las yerbas,**
> 28   **al cerro pide sepulcro.**

Protruding from a suffering castle, a bare section of fortification begs the grass for a winding sheet and beseeches the hill to bury it.

The fortress of Joray stood on an outcrop, or *peña*; it was an *alcázar en [una] peña*. Quevedo punningly transforms this into an *alcázar en pena*, suggesting *ánimas en pena*, and so comparing the castle to a soul in purgatory. At first the idea of something as immobile as a fortress wandering like a lost spirit (*ánimas en pena* were thought to wander if they had not received a proper burial) seems a preposterous image but, as always happens with a successful conceit, we are forced to concede that there is a certain aptness in the image while remaining conscious of its incongruity. This is because 26–28 confirm that the castle's ruins, which had previously been likened to a skeleton, are still partly unburied. The bastion is *desnudo*, or bare, because it will stick out of the ground like scattered bones until vegetation grows over it, providing it with a shroud, or until the hill collapses and inters it just as the pile of earth alongside a freshly dug grave is shovelled on top of the coffin.

> **Como herederos monteses,**
> **pájaros le hacen nocturnos**
> **las exequias, y los grajos**
> 32   **le endechan los contrapuntos.**

Like wild heirs, night birds perform the castle's funeral rites, while rooks chant contrapuntal laments for it.

Herederos picks up the idea that the castle is a dead person, so it would have left heirs. By describing wild nocturnal birds officiating at the castle's funeral, Quevedo not only recalls its lack of a proper burial, but may also be evoking, through the birds' screeching, age-old funerary rituals—in particular keening during the night before committal of the body—which survived in rural Spain where this poem is set. The Golden-Age Church considered such practices to be pagan or Jewish, and tried to impose what it considered more appropriate ways of mourning (e.g. *contrapuntos*, or singing in counterpoint).[6] However, even the performers of this music are birds, and particularly raucous ones at that, their cawing being a mockery of such a sophisticated

---

[6] Amelang (2005: 20–27) describes rural funerary ritual in early modern Spain.

compositional technique. With their black plumage and their indifference to
the castle's 'death', the cawing rooks may even recall the custom—much
criticized at the time—of employing professional mourners, who would here
be a further example of the hypocrisy which is castigated throughout the
ballad. The mighty castle is brought so low that there is no proper accompaniment at its funeral, just squawking.[7]

> **Quedaron por albaceas**
> **un chaparro y un saúco,**
> **fantasmas que a primavera**
> 36   **espantan flores y fruto.**

Its executors were a stunted oak and an elder bush; ghosts that in spring
astonish by producing flowers and fruit.

Executors are the people named in a last will and testament as those responsible for carrying out a dead person's wishes, normally concerning his funeral,
and the division of his estate. The *chaparro* is a stunted oak which grows on
the poor soil associated with the *monte* of 9; the elder was a source of
medicinal remedies and therefore appropriately associated with the new life
of spring. Both are very common trees in Spain, emphasizing the humbling
of the castle. Lines 35–36 could be construed either as 'fantasmas que espantan a [la] primavera con flores y fruto', or as 'fantasmas que en primavera
espantan con [sus] flores y fruto'. The meaning seems to be that these bushes
or stunted trees give us (or spring) a shock by producing blossom and fruit
because they had looked so dead in winter that one cannot credit that they
have sprung into life; rather, they are like ghosts which remain dead although
they can move. The conceit lies in our being shocked by signs of life, when
it is normally apparitions that frighten us and death that catches us unawares.
Quevedo's choice of *chaparro* and *saúco* is particularly appropriate: despite
its straggly appearance in winter, the elder tree flowers in Spain when spring
has hardly arrived, producing large, perfumed blossoms; the *chaparro* similarly fruits early. For a further reason why the *saúco* might shock us, see
below p. 216.

> **Guadalén, que los juanetes**
> **del pie del escollo duro**
> **sabe los puntos que calzan,**
> 40   **dobla por él, importuno.**

The River Guadalén, which knows what size of shoe the bunions on the hard
crag's foot take, bends round it because the crag obstructs its course.

---

[7] I suggest that Quevedo may have had in mind Góngora's ballad 'Castillo de San
Cervantes' when writing 'Son las torres de Joray'. Lines 5–32 of the latter seem to develop
a series of ideas contained in Góngora's lines: 'Las que ya fueron corona | son alcándara de
cuervos, | almenas que, como dientes, | dicen la edad de los viejos' (Góngora 2000a: 327).

As the castle's ruins have been portrayed as a human body, the outcrop on which they stand is described as a foot. Lumps on the crag are therefore imagined to be bunions swelling its toes. It is at first an absurdly comical image but, again, we have to concede its strange appropriateness. This is because bunions come with old age, and so pick up the idea of time's depredations, as well as the ugliness and decrepitude that they bring. *Doblar* not only means to bend round but also to toll (of a death knell), so the poet here pursues the funeral motif though the sound of the flowing water. The juxtaposition of the River Guadalén and the ruins near which it runs contributes to the poem's theme of *desengaño*: the castle was haughty and, being built of stone, was designed to stand for ever; the river, on the other hand, is merely water which, as it constantly passes by, might seem transient. However, the apparently immovable works of men have crumbled into ruins while the accommodating river, which forms a bend round the castle's crag rather than striking it head-on, is still flowing. It enjoys permanence in its apparent transience, and Man's works are shown to be ephemeral while God's are everlasting.[8]

> **Este cimenterio verde,**
> **este monumento bruto**
> **me señalaron por cárcel:**
> 44 **yo le tomé por estudio.**

This green cemetery, this rough tomb, was selected as my prison; I used it as a place [or subject] of study.

The motif of Joray's funeral has run through the first half of the ballad: death (4), mourning (12), shroud and grave (27–28), funerary rites (29–32), last will and testament (21, 29, 33), and tolling bell (40). This motif is now rounded off in 41–42 with references to graveyard and tomb. The ruins among the grass make for a green cemetery, something unremarkable to an English reader, given our tradition of burying the dead in grassy graveyards surrounding churches, but which could well have struck a Spanish Golden-Age reader as startlingly oxymoronic. Similarly, *monumento bruto* is surprising: while death is ugly and crude, tombs are elaborately carved from stone; however, this one is rough-and-ready because it is mere rubble, emphasizing Joray's ignominious end and, perhaps, the barbarous nature of the wilds to which Quevedo has been banished. He may be playing with similar-sounding words, *cimiento* (21) and *cimenterio* (41, *cementerio* in modern Spanish): if so, the association of the two words emphasizes that the step from the building of the castle to its demise—or, given its presentation as a person, from birth to death—has been a matter of just a few lines. (On a possible Golden-Age pronunciation here, see also above, p. 31.) It is characteristic of writing on

---

[8] This is the theme of Quevedo's sonnet about the ruins of Rome, 'Buscas en Roma a Roma, ¡oh peregrino!' (Q.213), where the River Tiber is all that remains intact of the ancient city and similarly mourns its passing.

the theme of *desengaño* that objects are imbued with significance. Quevedo was educated by the Jesuits and remained close to them all his life, letters written by highly placed members of the Society during his fourth and last period of imprisonment (December 1639–July 1643) not only doing much to keep him abreast of developments at Court but also indicating that there were Jesuits lobbying for his release (Crosby 2005). The Jesuits employed emblems as a pedagogical method: the viewer was trained to interpret these pictures, employing wit to discover their covert meanings and associations (Porteman 2000). Here the poet will depict himself undergoing this educative process, while he teaches his reader to do the same with the images he creates. He also points out the irony of his situation. He has been banished from Court, and the ruins which lie near where he is 'imprisoned' are intended to be a place of punishment and isolation for him; yet he has turned this isolation to good effect by transforming these ruins into a place and object of study. Moreover, they provide a solitary, metaphorical university where he learns crucial lessons, not the superficial ones taught in a real university located in the sort of city from which he has been banned.[9]

> Aquí, en cátedra de muertos,
> atento le oí discursos
> del bachiller Desengaño
> 48   contra sofísticos gustos.

Here, I listened carefully to lectures from the graduate Desengaño, who holds the Chair of the Dead, in which he attacked subtle deceit.

Quevedo picks up the word *estudio* and develops a new line of thought in which he depicts the ruins as a place of learning, drawing for his description upon language borrowed from the world of academia. Among the ruins he is not subjected to what he considered the pointless subtleties of university disputations (*sofísticos gustos*, referring to sophists' arguments—in other words, complicated but fallacious ones) but, rather, he learns important lessons for life. The silent ruins are implicitly, and favourably, compared with lecture halls and those who lecture in them.[10] Quevedo thus rehearses one of his favourite themes: the austere virtues of arms, symbolized by the castle, are to be prized above intellectual frivolity or posturing.

Cátedra de muertos presumably means that either Bachiller Desengão holds a Chair in Death, or that the poet claims to have heard him teach in the Department of Death Studies. The death of the castle has been the principal subject of the poem up to this point; now Bachiller Desengaño will point out its implications for the poet, allowing him both to reject frivolous activity and to instruct others in his turn. A *bachiller* could lecture in a seventeenth-

---

[9] An institution of higher learning could be termed *estudio, universidad*, or *colegio*.

[10] Quevedo would later criticize the formulaic nature of contemporary education which, in his view, taught pupils to engage in futile intellectual exercises; see Jauralde (1998a: 61).

century university if he was a Bachelor of Divinity, and so a man of some learning. However, despite the positive comparison of Bachiller Desengāno to those who hold forth in real universities, Quevedo may be introducing a note of warning here. This is because the word *bachiller* could also mean a slick but empty talker, an idler who, like the Devil, was an inveterate questioner (*Cov. s.vv. bachiller* and *curioso*). If Quevedo wrote this ballad in the early 1620s, as was suggested above, its composition would have coincided with that of his 'Sueño de la muerte' in which he criticized what he saw as a plague of law graduates feeding off Spain: 'Hay plaga de letrados... y todos se gradúan de dotores y bachilleres, licenciados y maestros.'[11] Elsewhere he would inveigh, albeit through the mouths of fictional characters, against *bachilleres*.[12] If Quevedo is exploiting the negative connotations of the term *bachiller*, he would here be introducing the warning elaborated in 73–74 against excessive reliance upon our ability to use reason. In this case we would be alerted to the dangers of assimilating unthinkingly the lessons of *desengaño*.

I have interpreted *sofísticos gustos* as the empty arguments of sophists. However, it may also allude to an elaborate but meretricious style of speech and writing. The phrase would therefore form a bridge between the instruction the poet received in the university of the ruins and what he will go on to say to Floris (49–64) where he parodies this style.

> **Yo, que mis ojos tenía,**
> **Floris taimada, en los tuyos,**
> **presumiendo eternidades**
> 52 **entre cielos y coluros;**

I had my eyes fixed on yours, sly Floris, assuming that life would go on for ever in a heaven with celestial spheres [of our love];

Interplay between the general and the particular is a common feature of Golden-Age thinking. Writing of the period frequently applies general truths to particular cases. Thus the seemingly universal, eternal verities enshrined in the Classics or in mythology are drawn upon to indicate how one should interpret a particular situation, or to provide consolation for a particular ill. Conversely, general truths are extrapolated from particular examples, as happens in the present ballad when the poet draws general conclusions from his contemplation of the castle's ruins.

In 45–48 the poetic voice implies that he was taught a general truth by Joray; he now applies it to a particular situation, that of his love for a real or

---

[11] Quevedo dated the dedication to this 'Sueño', 'En la prisión y en la Torre [de Juan Abad], a 6 de abril 1622'; see Quevedo (1991: 308, 353).

[12] e.g. 'las monarquías [...] siempre las han adquirido capitanes, siempre las han corrompido bachilleres', cited from *La hora de todos y la Fortuna con seso* in Jauralde (1998a: 722).

imagined woman. The switch from a depiction of the castle to his affair with Floris is not, then, as arbitrary as it might at first seem.[13] The poet has been trained by the ruins to see through appearances, and he now uses this know-ledge to free himself from a foolish infatuation. Quevedo here contrasts two ways of looking: one where the eyes rest only on surfaces, and the other where *desengaño* allows a deeper truth to be perceived. Before learning the lesson taught by looking at the ruins, his eyes had fixed upon those of his lady (49–50). In writings influenced by Neoplatonic theories the lover would look into his mistress's eyes and be transported through them to a higher realm; this was another way of seeing beyond surface appearances, but there is no indication that this is what had happened between the poet and his Floris. Indeed, quite the contrary: it is hinted that their relationship was superficial and based upon self-interest, because she is unflatteringly described as *taimada*. *Cov.* defines this adjective as follows: 'Vale tanto como bellaco, astuto y señalado, que passa los ojos por todo y lo advierte calladamente; puede venir de la palabra griega *thauma*... que en lengua dórica vale tanto como espectáculo.' By choosing this particular word to describe Floris, Quevedo insinuates that their relationship had been based upon the wrong way of looking: her superficial beauty in his eyes, and his financial potential in hers (see 59–60, below). Seduced by her eyes and made oblivious of the havoc caused by the passing of time, the poet had naively assumed that the heavenly (*cielos, coluros*) bliss of his passion would go on for ever. This is ironic: a contemplation of the heavens should have alerted him to eternal truths but, in his stupidity, he had merely taken them to represent an impossibly everlasting love. The word *presumiendo* in this context has strongly negative connotations of presumption and over-confidence. Quevedo uses it twice in this ballad (in 51 and 74), both times critically. A recherché term like *coluros*, which refers to two meridians on the celestial sphere, is typical of the language found in the highly-wrought love poetry of the period; here Quevedo mocks the use of such a highfalutin term of learned Greek origin. It not only suggests insincerity but also an inappropriate abstraction and idealization of what was a materialistic relationship.

> **en tu boca hallando perlas**
> **y en tu aliento calambucos,**
> **aprendiendo en tus claveles**
> 56   **a despreciar los carbunclos;**

I found pearls in your mouth and perfume on your breath, and learnt to despise rubies in comparison with the carnations [of your lips];

---

[13] Earlier in his career Quevedo had addressed love poems to 'Floris' and 'Filis', but, as is the case with most Petrarchan love poetry, it is impossible to identify these muses with individual women (compare the comments on Lope de Vega's use of Arcadian names, above p. 15).

Now he has shaken off the delusions of love, the poet can mock the clichés of Petrarchan love poetry which, it is later implied (63–64), he had used in the *culto* poetry he had written in Floris's honour (her lips are red carnations, her teeth are pearls). Earlier in the ballad he educated us by depicting himself undergoing an educative process; here he is similarly self-conscious, parodying what he imagines having written to his lady. Through that parody he makes a serious point: precious stones like rubies are durable and have lasting value. Floris's attractions, which he at least said he preferred, will— like all things human—soon vanish, just as a flower's beauty and blossom's scent fade.[14] Indeed, the lady's very name, Floris —which comes from the Latin word for flower—encapsulates this warning. When he was besotted by Floris's appearance the poet had 'learnt' (*aprendiendo*, 55) that gems were inferior to her ephemeral charms (he may not only have learnt this by gazing at her lips, but also from the words those lips formed). This was false learning. Now that he has seen how time ravages even the strongest of buildings and has attended Bachiller Desengaño's lectures, he has learnt the truth and can break free from the thrall in which she has held him. In 69 he will use the verb *aprender* again and return to the idea of how true learning can teach one to see through appearances.

> en donde una primavera
> mostró mil abriles juntos,
> gastando en sólo guedejas
> 60 más soles que doce lustros,

where spring showed a thousand Aprils together, I lavished more that twelve lustres' worth of suns just on the ringlets on your brow,

The mention of *abril* recalls Spanish sayings in which that spring month denotes beauty (e.g. 'María está hecha un abril'); however, as April is associated with flowers, its use cruelly underlines the transience of female beauty. The Petrarchan commonplaces the poet had mouthed when praising Floris (the lady as spring, her hair as golden as the sun, etc.) are again mocked, but fun is particularly poked at the exaggeration used in Courtly Love poetry; so we have a thousand Aprils, while Floris's tresses are brighter than sixty years' worth of sunshine (*lustro* means a period of five years; there may even be a play on *lustro/lustre*, *lustre* meaning 'shine', which could describe Floris's golden locks). Presumably *gastando* means 'I (the poet) lavished', just as he is the subject of *presumiendo* (51), *hallando* (53) and *aprendiendo* (55). If so, the poet, in his Petrarchan nonsense, had lavished so many metaphors on his lady's tresses, comparing them to the sun, that he can now say that he spent a whole lifetime of suns on them or, rather, on just a few ringlets. De-

---

[14] *Calambucos* refers to the white blossom of a strongly scented Latin American tree (*Calophyllum brasiliense*). It was exotic in Quevedo's day, but by at least 1659 it had been acclimatized to Andalusia (see Wagner 2001: 37).

scribing her hair as the sun perhaps implies that she was the centre of the poet's cosmos around which he orbited.[15] The word *gastar* can imply waste, suggesting that the poet squandered many years as Floris's suitor. This brings an edge to Quevedo's parody of the sort of exaggeration employed in love poetry of the period: the mention of a thousand Aprils and twelve lustres portrays a lover wasting his life on trivialities and oblivious to time's hustling him towards death. On the other hand, *gastar* can also refer to the spending of money. The round, golden sun may even suggest the shining disc of a coin, insinuating that the poet spent a great deal on Floris's hair, with the implication that it was artificial (or artificially blond; see p. 217, below). All that glistens in her appearance would then be fool's gold financed with real gold.

> **con tono clamoreado,**
> **que la ausencia me compuso,**
> **lloré mis versos siguientes,**
> 64   **más renegados que cultos:**

pitifully pleading in a loud voice inspired by [your] absence, I wept the following lines [which are] more like blasphemies than elaborate poetry:

He talks of his forced absence from his ladylove, who is presumably still at Court. However, rather than the lover's lament we are led to expect from his tears, his words come out as a curse which is in stark contrast to the *culto* love poetry he had previously addressed to her. Indeed, while the ballad has up to this point contained several *cultismos* derived from Latin or Greek (e.g. *coluros*, *lustros*), the urgent lesson contained in 65–66 will be written in the plainest Castilian. The poet reveals that the punishment of exile has again worked to his benefit. It enabled him to learn from the ruins of Joray; this, coupled with his separation from his lady, has then made him appreciate how hollow was their relationship, reflected in the hollowness of the language he had previously used to express his admiration for her. This may be a further critique of 'Castillo de San Cervantes' and therefore of Góngora: the *culto* style cultivated by the latter and parodied by Quevedo in this ballad in the verses he suggests he had addressed to Floris is shallow and artificial.

Quevedo puns on the verb *clamorear*: it could mean to toll, suggesting the demise of the poet's love as well as reminding us of the River Guadalén's tolling for the dead castle. *Clamorear* could also mean 'to shout out', and was used to refer to Man's entreaties to God.[16] Here it suggests that

---

[15] Heliocentrism—the acknowledgement that the sun is at the centre of our planetary system—was, however, a delicate subject at this period. Galileo would be forced to recant his support for Copernicus in 1633, and Quevedo appears to have been prudently ambivalent before that date; see Tato (2000–01).

[16] Under *clamar/clamorear*, *Cov.* refers to Psalm 101 (102): 'Domine audi orationem meam et clamor meus ad te veniat', 'Hear my prayer, O Lord, and let my cry come unto thee'. Similarly, the Vulgate text of Psalm 129 (130), 'De profundis clamavi ad te Domine', 'Out of the depths have I cried unto thee, O Lord', uses the same word for 'cry' (*clamavi*);

the lover cried out to his lady as if she were his god. However, *renegar* (64) could refer in Quevedo's day to the backsliding of Jews or Moslems who had officially embraced Christianity but had then returned to their old beliefs, or to a Christian who abandoned his faith. So the poet presents himself as a double apostate: firstly because he worshipped Floris rather than God, and secondly because he now rejects her and the blasphemous 'religion' of which she is the deity. *Aut.* defines a *renegado* as a man who is 'desesperado de condición, y maldiciente'; Quevedo's choice of vocabulary thus couples apostasy with the vilifying of the woman who was formerly the object of his devotion (and of his devotions). Although the primary meaning of the adjective *culto* (64) refers to the sort of elaborate language that the poet mocked in 52–60, it can also mean 'learned', while, as a noun, *culto* is both the homage paid to an object of love and a rite or religion. Rather than treating his lady with reverence, the poet now rejects what he realizes was his idolatrous cult of her. At the same time, the assertion of 65–66, which 61–64 introduce, not only eschews any *culto* rhetoric, but also the sort of futile academic learning he had rejected earlier in the poem at Joray.

The dense, punning implications of these lines suggests that words here begin to have real meaning in contrast to the fatuous clichés of 52–60. The break with this former love poetry is emphasized by an unexpected break in the pattern of versification. Up to this point the poem has been a ballad, following the pattern of octosyllabic lines rhyming assonantally on even lines which we associate with that predominantly narrative form in Spanish poetry. However the refrain, or *estribillo* (65–66), is written in *silva* metre— a combination of 7- and 11-syllable lines:

> *Las glorias de este mundo*
> 66 *llaman con luz para pagar con humo.*

The glories of this world seduce us with promises but they all vanish into thin air.

This pedagogical refrain makes Quevedo's disillusioned message clear. It is further emphasized both by being repeated twice and by the binary structure of its second line in which we are attracted by something bright (*luz*) but ungraspable, only to be rewarded with something equally impalpable, but unattractive (*humo*), with all its associations of death, destruction, and disappearance. The *estribillo*, which at first appears simple, is charged with meaning. *Gloria* associated with *mundo* recalls the Latin phrase 'sic transit gloria mundi' or 'so the world's glory passes away', often repeated by moralists in the Golden Age and traditionally pronounced at the installation of popes to remind them that, despite the lavish ceremony in their honour, their position and power are transient. *Gloria* was also used in a less elevated

a reference to this latter psalm would be particularly appropriate in Quevedo's ballad because it is one of the seven penitential psalms, and is also associated with funeral liturgies.

context to refer to sexual pleasure (see pp.32 and 48, above), which is appropriate here because it recalls the poet's desire for Floris which is recounted
immediately before this refrain. Such ephemeral and insubstantial glories
beckon (*llaman*, which derives from the same Latin word as *clamar*, but here
seduces the *engañado* rather than referring to the cries of 61). They do so
like a candle flame (*llamar* may even suggest *llamear*, 'to blaze', while
candlelight evokes, again appropriately, the flames to which Petrarchan
lovers were attracted, only to be burnt by them). The refrain makes it clear
that the light or fire is quickly extinguished leaving us with nothing but
smoke; the flames are a bonfire of the vanities. *Pagar* can mean to pay or to
please, but here it is used ironically: the reward of being duped by a
beguiling light is mere *humo*; this is how we are paid back for being
engañados and, in turn, we pay a high price for our foolishness. *Humo* is
particularly rich in resonances. The phrase *vender humos* was applied to the
lies of confidence-tricksters who promised access to the monarch's inner
circle and the benefits flowing from such access. In the light of Quevedo's
portrait of favourites later in this ballad, this would be tantamount to one
impostor's pretending to have the ear of others in a world of venal smoke
and mirrors. *Tener muchos humos* means to give oneself airs, which would
again be appropriate in the context of the parvenu favourites we are about to
encounter in the poem. *Irse todo en humo* was applied to something which
had promised a great deal but proved to be empty. This is an apt description
the poet's love affair.[17] *Humo* also recalls the biblical Wisdom of Solomon,
2: 2–4, which is imbued with Stoic philosophy and where the image of
smoke expresses the transitory nature of human life.[18] This Book of the
Bible is known as 'Sapientia' in the Vulgate, the Latin Bible of the Roman
Catholic Church, but is found in the Apocrypha in the Authorized Version.

---

[17] *Humo* was also the name of a black silk from which mourning apparel was made; this
would be particularly apposite in this death-laden context. I have not, however, been able to
ascertain whether the word was already being used in that sense as early as the 1620s.
Anastasio Rojo Vega kindly informs me that he has found evidence of the cloth known as
humo in the Valladolid archives by at least 1651.

[18] 'Quia ex nihilo nati sumus et post hoc erimus tamquam non fuerimus quoniam fumus
afflatus est in naribus nostris et sermo scintillae ad commovendum cor nostrum quia
extincta cinis erit corpus et spiritus diffundetur tamquam mollis aer et transiet vita nostra
tamquam vestigium nubis et sicut nebula dissolvetur quae fugata est a radiis solis et a calore
illius adgravata et nomen nostrum oblivionem accipiet per tempus et nemo memoriam
habebit operum nostrorum', marvellously rendered in the 1611 Authorized Version of the
Bible as: 'For we are born at all adventure: and we shall be hereafter as though we had
never been: for the breath in our nostrils is as smoke, and a little spark in the moving of our
heart: Which being extinguished, our body shall be turned into ashes, and our spirit shall
vanish as the soft air. And our name shall be forgotten in time, and no man shall have our
works in remembrance, and our life shall pass away as the trace of a cloud, and shall be
dispersed as a mist, that is driven away with the beams of the sun, and overcome with the
heat thereof.' The Wisdom of Solomon puts these words into the mouths of the ungodly,
but they nevertheless seem to have resonated with Spanish poets of the Golden Age.

We have seen that the refrain carries a clear message and is written in *silva* metre; it introduces a shift in both content and form in the rest of the ballad. Much of the poem up to this point has been funny; indeed, assonance in *ú–o* often seems to have been associated with humour: the poem has been comically macabre and grotesque. It will now become deadly serious. This altered tone is reflected by a change in versification. Lines 67–74, and 77–84 consist of two *letrillas*, each followed by the repeated refrain. Instead of the assonantal rhyme on alternate lines typical of the ballad, they have full rhyme following the pattern ABBAACCD and EFFEEGGD respectively, with the second line of the refrain rhyming fully with D, and the first line rhyming assonantally with it. The introduction of *letrillas* at this stage is surprising, for they are traditionally associated with comic verse. These changes in tone and versification indicate that we have come to the crux of the poem. The poet casts himself in the role of a teacher passing on what he himself had learnt by contemplating the castle of Joray. We also realize with a jolt that 65–86 are addressed not to Floris, as we had at first assumed, but to a corrupt and complacent favourite. In them Quevedo systematically picks up points he has made earlier in the poem and which may not until now have seemed to be directed to any coherent end. We begin to realize that they were, and the whole poem is thus revealed to be witty in its structure: at first it seemed to consist of a series of independent elements (the ruined castle, an unsatisfactory love affair, the poet's fulminating against favourites), but we now realize that it is a carefully integrated whole. As we have seen, conceits require readers to relate apparently unconnected elements by a leap of the intelligence. In a similar process, we now connect the seemingly disparate sections of the poem, appreciating not only its logical progress from past (the castle's glory years, the poet's former infatuation with Floris), through the present (the state of the ruins and his enlightenment) to the future (the warning to the courtier of what will befall him), but, more importantly, its unity of purpose.

> **Tú, que te das a entender**
> **la eternidad que imaginas,**
> **aprende de estas rüinas,**
> 70 **si no a vivir, a caer.**
> **El mandar y enriquecer**
> **dos encantadores son**
> **que te turban la razón,**
> 74 **sagrado de que presumo.**
>
> *Las glorias de este mundo*
> *llaman con luz para pagar con humo.*

You who make yourself imagine that your power is eternal, learn from these ruins, if not to live, at least to fall. The urge to command and the craving to pile up riches are two sorcerers who cloud your reason, which I count on as a sure place of refuge. The glories of this world seduce us with promises but they all vanish into thin air.

While the poet's *yo* has been central up to this point, he now addresses *tú*—an unnamed courtier—instructing him to open his eyes. The poet warns him to prepare stoically for his inevitable fall from power by learning the lesson of Joray. He urges the courtier to use his reason in order to avoid being duped by his imagination and by the seduction of power and wealth, described as sorcerers (defined in *Aut.* as dazzlers of one's faculty of reason).

However, the word *presumo*, with its negative charge we have already seen in 51, may well be double-edged here. The poet assumes reason to be a sure place of refuge, but this confidence is misplaced. Quevedo is a neo-Stoic in his awareness of the limits of human reason, being suspicious of the strand in pagan Stoicism that leads to the sin of pride through overconfidence in Man's unaided efforts. He is conscious that we can never deserve salvation through our own puny efforts, but are saved through divine grace and the sacrifice Christ made for us. On the one hand reason is vital to enable us see through the deceit of the world, and in this sense it is one of the real *glorias del mundo*. On the other, it can also be one of those *glorias* which end up in *humo* unless we remain aware of its limitations. The poet implies that he has himself been a miscreant (the *sagrado* to which he looks for refuge meant a safe-haven for those on the run from justice) and a dupe (he had allowed himself to be fooled by sly Floris). Just as the Preface to this volume points out (p. xii), 'the critic counts himself in with potential and actual other sinners'. Here, having had his eyes opened by Joray, the poet is, as a fellow reprobate, in an ideal position to teach the courtier and us. The lesson will be to open our own eyes and apply our reason, yet bearing in mind its limitations.

Like a good teacher, the poet is careful to take us back through earlier sections of the poem in order to trace the process of his own enlightenment: the description of the castle (*estas ruinas*), and the ruins as his place of learning (*aprende*), while *la eternidad que imaginas* recalls *presumiendo eternidades* (51) and his affair with Floris. In this way he draws upon his own experience to provide a lesson for the courtier. He himself had once confidently assumed that time was infinite; Joray had taught him that death is imminent and that Floris, with her ephemeral charms, had distracted his attention from that reality. The courtier, he suggests, is similarly fooled by the assumption that his power will last for ever, but the allusion to Floris suggests not only that the delights of power are transient but that power itself is as superficial as mortal beauty and, perhaps, that it is possible to be infatuated with power just as a man can be infatuated with a woman. Floris's charms had bewitched the poet; the courtier is bewitched by authority and the chance to enrich himself, failing to use his reason to discover how superficial are both power and wealth.

This is doubly ironic. First, the poet may seem to be in a worse position than the favourite because he is a suffering banishment from Court; he is really at an advantage because his banishment had led him to *desengaño*, while the favourite is in peril because he is still the victim of seductive appearances. Second, the poet lectures the courtier just as Bachiller Desengaño had lectured him, but we have seen how double-edged the word *bachiller* can be. The poet is therefore also in a precarious position if he presumes that human reason alone can provide a safe-haven. The Christian connotations of the word *sagrado* (sanctuary or, as an adjective, sacred) further emphasize this point.

> **Este mundo engañabobos,**
> **engaitador de sentidos,**
> **en muy corderos validos**
> 80 **anda disfrazando lobos.**

This world which deceives fools, beguiling their senses, disguises wolves as bleating Court favourites.

Engañabobos means both 'trickster' and 'nightjar'. The latter flies soundlessly at dusk and at night, pouncing on its unsuspecting prey. It was also erroneously believed to suck milk from goats and ewes, hence its common Spanish name of *chotacabras*. Quevedo transforms *engañabobos* into an adjective to suggest that the world is lethal, deceptive, and full of opportunists looking to suck others dry. Indeed, in his *Natural History* (X. LVI), Pliny had maintained—appropriately in this context—that the bird's stealing of milk also had the effect of blinding its victims (1936–62: II. 366). Bachiller Desengaño has taught the poet not to be *engañado* by the world; he is therefore no longer the *bobo*, or the *necio* castigated by Góngora in his 'Arrojóse el mancebito' (see above, Chapter 3). This picks up the earlier reference to reason which can expose the duping of one's senses (the world is referred to as an *engaitador de sentidos*). In *engaitador* Quevedo chooses a word which refers specifically to the bamboozling of others with empty promises and honeyed words. This in turn relates to another supposed attribute of the nightjar, its ability to imitate the human voice, and reinforces one of this ballad's central concerns: its distrust of language.

The poet puns on the word *validos*: they are those powerful favourites who, with a word insinuated into the king's ear, can put an end to careers, fortunes, or even lives. However, they pretend to be as meek as lambs (*corderos*) whose *balidos*, or bleating, would have been pronounced, and even written, the same as *validos* in seventeenth-century Castilian. By using the phrase *corderos validos* Quevedo produces brilliant grammatical ambiguity: if *corderos* acts as an adjective qualifying the noun *validos*, the favourites are lamb-like; if, on the other hand, *validos* acts as an adjective qualifying the noun *corderos*, those lambs are esteemed or trusted (*valido* as the past participle of the verb *valer*). A kaleidoscope of possible meanings results from this play on words: for instance, trust is wrongly placed in favourites who speak with apparent mildness—the deceptiveness of language again being suggested—or they all repeat the same platitudes sycophantically like bleating sheep (quite the opposite of the *cordura*, or wisdom, favourites should possess). Yet behind this disguise they are really the proverbial wolves in sheep's clothing (80), which is another example of the difference between *ser* and *parecer*.[19]

The mention of lambs may also call to mind the saying *tan presto va el cordero como el carnero*: whatever our age, death may carry us off at any moment. This chimes in with one of the ballad's central themes and ironically warns the favourite that he may well present himself as a lamb but he should remember that nobody, however high and mighty, should consider himself exempt from the inexorable law that time destroys.

> **Sus patrimonios son robos,**
> **su caudal insultos fieros;**
> **y en trampas de lisonjeros**
> 84 **cae después su imperio sumo.**
>
> *Las glorias de este mundo*
> *llaman con luz para pagar con humo.*

Their inherited fortune is robbery, their wealth consists of cruel assaults, but their supreme authority eventually crumbles thanks to the traps laid for them by flatterers. The glories of this world seduce us with promises but they all vanish into thin air.

Lines 81–82 contain multiple meanings. On the one hand, favourites are metaphorically rich only in thefts from, and attacks on, those unfortunate to be in a weaker position (*insulto* meant 'assault', not 'insult', at this period). On the other hand, the poet suggests that their wealth is not just metaphorical: the material prosperity they enjoy is the product of robbery because they are voracious in enriching themselves rather than serving the monarch disinterestedly. Furthermore, the word *robo* is used in Navarre as a measure of land, so Quevedo may also be implying that they increased their estates by stealing land. He could even be voicing his frequent complaint that the Spain of his day allowed upstarts to enrich themselves at the expense of the old aristocracy whose wealth was vested in their estates. Indeed, *Cov.* defines *patrimonio* as inheritance while *caudal* is liquid capital available for investment in trade, so Quevedo may be insinuating that nouveau riche favourites' lack of inherited wealth (they have no aristocratic forebears) and their illegitimate acquisition of property contrast with what he considered the legitimacy of nobles' landed inheritances. *Caudal* was also used to refer to intellectual capacity, suggesting here that principal courtiers employ their talents in attacking others rather than for the common

---

[19] Matthew 7:15, 'adtendite a falsis prophetis qui veniunt ad vos in vestimentis ovium intrinsecus autem sunt lupi rapaces', 'Beware of false prophets, which come to you in sheep's clothing, but inwardly they are ravening wolves.'

good. Their wealth not only puts them in a position to do this with impunity; that wealth itself constitutes an assault on decency. The description of their attacks on others as *fieros*—cruel and also terrifying like those of wild beasts (*fieras*)—reinforces the criticism in 80 that favourites are in reality ravening wolves.

However, 83–84 imply that the biter will be bit: the courtier abuses others, but soon he will fall victim to his rival's snares. Behind the word *trampas* the reader may glimpse the popular saying *Dios ve las trampas*, which implies both that deceivers eventually have the tables turned on them, and that those preoccupied with superficial worldly achievements will not escape divine punishment. The power of Quevedo's courtier is described as *imperio sumo*, or the highest authority. This phrase, coming at the very end of the poem before the final repetition of the refrain, takes us back to the ballad's first lines, demonstrating its artistic and moral coherence. This is for two reasons. First, the Court favourite is tacitly likened to the loftiest tower of the castle at Joray. We now realise why, in 17, the *homenaje* was mentioned, because the more elevated his position, the greater will be his fall (see also 70). The tops of those towers had been likened in 6 to crowns, a comparison which we now appreciate contained the acerbic subtext of favourites usurping the authority which rightly rested with the royal master they should have been serving.[20] Second, the word *imperio* is frequently encountered in poetry about ruins where it refers to the lost sway of what was once a mighty or imperial city.[21] Here it is used in its meaning of the authority wielded by an individual; this not only equates favourite with potential ruin, in both senses of the word, but also explains why Quevedo chose from the outset to describe the remains of a fortress as a person, albeit deceased. What might at first have seemed a humorous comparison is now seen to have deadly serious intent.

The message in these closing lines, as throughout the whole ballad, is characteristically neo-Stoic: we should pay no heed to worldly concerns for they are a snare and delusion which distract us from the important truth that death awaits us all. But we may glimpse hubris of a more blasphemous sort behind the favourite's *imperio sumo*, for the highest authority he has appropriated does not even rest with his master, the monarch, but with God.

*   *   *   *   *

[20] In the year when this ballad was probably composed, 1621, Quevedo sent the Count-Duke of Olivares his treatise *Política de Dios* in which he insisted upon the theme of bad kings being ruled by their favourites.

[21] For example, the Cordoban artist and poet Pablo de Céspedes (1540?–1608) wrote of a ruined Carthage: 'El ancho imperio de la gran Cartago | tuvo su fin con los soberbios techos, | sus fuertes muros de espantoso estrago | sepultados encierra en sí' (cited by Lara 1983: 227).

Quevedo had fallen victim of the Court and the disgrace of his patron in the dying days of Philip III's reign. If this ballad was written in 1621 at the time of his banishment, it is only natural that he should have found solace in the conviction that those he believed responsible for his fall from grace should, in turn, fall themselves; and he casts himself in the superior role of the righteously indignant teacher able to warn them of their impending fate. Such instruction assumes that its recipient might take the lesson to heart. Quevedo's criticism of the regime of Philip III, who was governed by his *validos*, could here be coupled with the hope, which he certainly harboured at that time, that the new regime of Philip IV and Olivares would learn from the failures of the recent past and restore standards of integrity and good government. 'Son las torres de Joray' thus contains a rather different sort of interplay between the general and the particular from the one mentioned above: despite his general recommendation of Stoic indifference to the world, Quevedo reveals his intense concern with contemporary political developments. Indeed, his scarcely concealed fury at the machinations of favourites and sycophants suggests that he could not himself take to heart the lesson of Stoic detachment which he professed.

FRANCISCO DE QUEVEDO

'A LA CORTE VAS, PERICO' (date unknown)

INSTRUCCIÓN Y DOCUMENTOS PARA EL NOVICIADO DE LA CORTE

A la Corte vas, Perico;
niño, a la Corte te llevan
tu mocedad y tus pies;
Dios de su mano te tenga.

5   Fiado vas en tu talle,
caudal haces de tus piernas,
dientes muestras, manos das,
dulce miras, tieso huellas;

mas si allá quieres holgarte,
10   hazme merced que en la venta
primera trueques tus gracias
por cantidad de moneda.

No han menester ellas lindos,
que harto lindas se son ellas;
15   la mejor facción de un hombre
es la bolsa grande y llena.

Tus dientes, para comer
te dirán que te los tengas,
pues otros tienen mejores
20   para mascar tus meriendas.

Tendrás muy hermosas manos,
si dieres mucho con ellas:
blancas son las que dan blancas,
largas las que nada niegan.

25   Alabaránte el andar,
si anduvieres por las tiendas
y el mirar, si no mirares
en dar todo cuanto quieran.

Las mujeres de la Corte
30   son, si bien lo consideras,

todas de Santo Tomé,
aunque no son todas negras.

Y si en todo el mundo hay caras,
solas son caras de veras
35   las de Madrid, por lo hermoso
y por lo mucho que cuestan.

No hallarás nada de balde,
aunque persigas las viejas,
que ellas venden lo que fueron,
40   y su donaire las feas.

Mientras tuvieres qué dar,
hallarás quien te entretenga;
y en expirando la bolsa,
oirás el *Requiem aeternam*.

45   Cuando te abracen, advierte
que segadores semejan;
con una mano te abrazan,
con otra te desjarretan.

Besaránte, como al jarro
50   borracho bebedor besa,
que en consumiendo le arrima
o en algún rincón le cuelga.

Tienen mil cosas de nuncios,
pues todas quieren que sean
55   los que están, abreviadores,
y datarios, los que entran.

Toman acero en verano,
que ningún metal desprecian;
Dios ayuda al que madruga,
60   mas no, si es a andar con ellas.

Pensóse escapar el Sol,
por tener lejos su esfera,
y el invierno, por tomarle,
ocupan llanos y cuestas.

65 A ninguna parte irás
que de ellas libre te veas,
que se entrarán en tu casa
por resquicios, si te cierras.

Cuantas tú no conocieres,
70 tantas hallarás doncellas,
que los Virgos y los Dones
son de una misma manera.

Altas mujeres verás,
pero son como colmenas:
75 la mitad huecas y corcho,
y lo demás miel y cera.

Casamiento pedirán,
si es que te huelen hacienda.
Guárdate de ser marido,
80 no te corran una fiesta.

Para prometer, te doy
una general licencia,
pues es todo el mundo tuyo,
como sólo le prometas.

85 Ofrecimientos te sobren,
no haya cosa que no ofrezcas,
que el prometer no empobrece,
y el cumplir echa por puertas.

La víspera de tu Santo
90 por ningún modo parezcas,

pues con tu bolsón te ahorcan,
cuando dicen que te cuelgan.

Estarás malo en la cama
los días todos de feria.
95 Por las ventanas, si hay toros,
meteráste en una iglesia.

Antes entres en un fuego
que en casa de una joyera,
y antes que a la platería
100 vayas, irás a las galeras.

Si entrar en alguna casa
quieres, primero a la puerta
oye si pregona alguno;
no te peguen con la deuda.

105 Y si por cuerdo y guardoso
no tuvieres quien te quiera,
bien hechas y mal vestidas
hallarás mil irlandesas.

Con un cuarto de turrón
110 y con agua y gragea
goza un Píramo barato
cualquiera Tisbe gallega.

Si tomares mis consejos,
Perico, que Dios mantenga,
115 vivirás contento y rico
sobre la haz de la tierra.

Si no, veráste comido
de tías, madres y suegras,
sin narices y con parches,
120 con unciones y sin cejas.

*   *   *   *   *

The Court was the seat of power. Ambitious young men would go there in search of advancement, fame, and fortune, hoping to attract the attention and patronage of the powerful, and also to take full advantage of the many pleasures life at Court offered. The figure of the exemplary courtier, skilled in both arms and letters and schooled in virtue, as depicted in *Il libro del cortegiano* (1528) of Baldassare Castiglione, attracted many Renaissance writers, including Garcilaso de la Vega and Juan Boscán, who translated it into Spanish (1534). At the same time, across the substantial corpus of Golden-Age moral and satirical literature, the Court was commonly depicted as constructed upon hypocrisy, flattery, deceit, and corruption, in contrast with the truthfulness, simplicity, and virtue of life in the countryside. The first significant representation of this tradition comes in Fray Antonio de Guevara's *Menos-precio de corte y alabanza de aldea* (1539), while satirical representations of Court life remain powerfully present for over a century: see, for example 'Crisi undézima' of the 'Primera parte' (1651) of Baltasar Gracián's allegor-ical novel *El criticón*, entitled 'El golfo cortesano' (1984: 225–45). Serious neo-Stoical writing of the same period sought to educate the reader against the deceptive lures of fame, riches, and power, on the grounds that they were ephemeral, beyond one's ability to control, a source of endless worry and stress, and unable to deliver the happiness they appeared to promise. In many ways, a ballad like this one (Q.726) implies the same lesson, but does so through the weapons of laughter, scorn, and derision.

Quevedo himself wrote both seriously and satirically about the Court. His 'Epístola satírica y censoria contra las costumbres presentes de los castellanos', addressed in the 1620s to the Count-Duke of Olivares, the chief minister of Philip IV, contains a sustained attack on the love of luxury and idleness of the present, financed by huge government debts to foreign ban-kers, in contrast to the simple virtues which had once made Castile great. Part III, chapter VI of Quevedo's picaresque novel *El Buscón* covers similar material to this poem, as do several of his other ballads, and passages from his satirical vision of Spanish society, *Los sueños* (1990 and 1971).

Quevedo is an inveterate practitioner of punning and word-play, and this ballad is a prime example. Even the word *corte* may not be immune: *cortar* (from which comes the noun *el corte*) is what pickpockets and cutpurses do, rob people of the money they are carrying by dexterous use of a sharp knife to cut open their clothes without their being aware of it (the name of the second of the eponymous protagonists of Cervantes's exemplary novella 'Rinconete y Cortadillo' carries this sense, since that it his 'profession'). It is impossible to follow the twists and turns of this ballad unless one is aware of the multiple meanings of many of the words Quevedo uses and the ways in which he plays them off against each other (which makes full and accurate translation well nigh impossible). Many have meanings which link them to *germanía*, or criminal slang, and in particular with the underworld of theft, prostitution, and imprisonment. Quevedo was very familiar with its jargon and uses it in many of his comic and satirical works.

The central point of the ballad is that any young man who wishes to go to Court in search of his fortune should beware of the women he will find there, because their sole intent will be to milk him dry of all his money. Quevedo provides many variations on this theme. The verbal play produces the wit, *ingenio*, of the poem, but the laughter it produces has, as so often in his writing, a bitter side to it. Nevertheless, for all the misogyny of this and many other ballads and other verses by Quevedo, one should remember that he is also the author of some of the finest love sonnets ever written in Spanish, which strike a quite different tone. One should therefore be cautious about too autobiographical a reading of Quevedo's poetry. The success of this ballad is not to be measured by asking whether or not he was a misogynist, but by coming to appreciate the vigour, verve, and wit which he applies to a series of commonplace observations on women's rapacity, many of which go back at least as far as the satirical poetry of the Latin poets Martial, whose verse Quevedo translated into Spanish, and Juvenal (see below, pp. 136 and 146).

The ballad follows an entirely regular form, written out in quatrains and with an *é–a* assonance throughout. Quevedo's first editor, his friend Josef Antonio González de Salas, was responsible for the titles of all the poems: 'Los títulos... que preceden a cada poesía... [son] míos, pues siendo ellos muy breves, dan grande luz para la noticia del argumento que contiene cada una' (Quevedo 1981: 11). Here, the word *documentos* means 'advice'; *noviciado* refers both to the period of time spent as a novice in a religious Order and to the place where novices lived, and is here applied ironically to a novice at the Court. Cervantes similarly subverts the term when he has his arch-villain Monipodio excuse Rinconete y Cortadillo their term of novitiate for entry into his criminal gang, on the grounds that they are already experienced thieves (1986: I. 216).

INSTRUCCIÓN Y DOCUMENTOS PARA EL NOVICIADO DE LA CORTE

A la Corte vas, Perico;
niño, a la Corte te llevan
tu mocedad y tus pies;
4   **Dios de su mano te tenga.**

You're off to the Court, Perico; your youth and your feet are carrying you to the Court, lad; may God hold you in his hand.

Perico is a diminutive of Pero, itself a familiar version of Pedro. In the poem it stands for any young man intent on seeking his fortune at Court, but the name has other resonances, of worthlessness, foolishness, and immorality: *Cov.* cites *no lo estimo en el baile del rey don Perico* and *Perico el de los palotes, un bobo que tañía con dos palotes* (*palotes* are 'drumsticks'). Both these characters appear in *Los sueños* ('El sueño de la muerte'), where *en tiempo del rey Perico* is an expression which means 'in the good old days', 'in the distant past', while *Perico de los Palotes* appears alongside some other idiots (Quevedo 1972: 205, 234). More importantly, *Pericón* or *Perico* could mean an 'hombre o mujer de vida libre y desarreglada', while *ser un perico* meant 'ser una prostituta, una mujer despreciable' (Alonso 1976: 603). Perico is being taken to Court by his youth and his feet, the zeugmatic double subject of *llevan* (compare above p. 86): one, *mocedad*, abstract, the other, *pies*, concrete, indicating his chief asset, more fully explored in the next few lines. It is, of course, ambition which is driving him. The pious wish in the fourth line is in reality an ironic warning: Perico will need all the help he can get if he is to survive, let alone prosper.

> Fiado vas en tu talle,
> caudal haces de tus piernas,
> dientes muestras, manos das,
> 8 dulce miras, tieso huellas;
>
> mas si allá quieres holgarte,
> hazme merced que en la venta
> primera trueques tus gracias
> 12 por cantidad de moneda.

You place your faith in your figure, your legs are your capital, you show your teeth, shake hands, look sweetly, walk upright; but if you want to have a good time there, please exchange your graceful features at the first inn for a pile of cash.

This young man is sure he will attract attention, because he is good-looking, charming, and personable; the emphasis on his physical features and comportment drives this home. The use of the adjectives *dulce* and *tieso* (8) in place of adverbs is a Latinate construction. However, what he will need most of all is money. The imagery of guarantee and investment cements the relationship between his fine appearance and attractive manners, and their earning potential. *Caudal* can mean both what a prostitute earns and, by metonymy, her body which brings in her income (Alonso 1976: 191; compare pp. 112–13, above). *Holgarse* sometimes has a sexual meaning in this period, and the ballad now gravitates towards that subject. Inns were often used as places of trade and commerce, as well as prostitution; hence the suggestion that Perico exchange his physical assets, in which he places such confidence, for monetary gain, which is the indispensable requirement for success at Court. He cannot, of course, literally cash in his looks for money; the request to do so contains a veiled warning which the rest of the ballad will explicate.

> No han menester ellas lindos,
> que harto lindas se son ellas;
> la mejor facción de un hombre
> 16 es la bolsa grande y llena.

They don't need pretty boys, they are pretty enough to themselves; a man's best feature is a big, full moneybag.

Quevedo depersonalizes women, simply referring to them as *ellas*. They are not interested in young men, however good-looking, because they are so taken up with their own appearance (an element of narcissism is here suggested by the reflexive use of *se*). A *lindo* was a young man who paid great attention to his looks and dress, with a hint of effeminacy about him (not in the sense of being homosexual, but more in the sense of the modern 'metrosexual', perhaps). What really turns women at Court on is a man who will lavish money on them, not the physical features which Quevedo implies

Perico is so confident of possessing. *Bolsa* can also have a sexual meaning, in which case Quevedo is punning again: the line means 'a big, full scrotal sac', a metonymy for the size and potency of the male member, as well as Perico's bank balance. Given that the link between sex and money in the world of the Court is one of the major themes of the ballad, this seems probable (see *Cov.*, *s.v. potra*). Quevedo will now drive home the link between Perico's teeth, hands, and legs, in which he has placed such trust, and how these women view them as a means towards getting their way.

> **Tus dientes, para comer**
> **te dirán que te los tengas,**
> **pues otros tienen mejores**
> 20   **para mascar tus meriendas.**

They will tell you your teeth are good enough to eat with; well, they've got better ones for munching the meals you'll give them.

The wordplay continues and increases. These ladies, it seems, will praise Perico's teeth, already mentioned as one of the features he shows off: 'they're good enough to eat'. But in fact they do no such thing, because they are more interested in their own than in his: their teeth will work their way through as much food as he will offer them at his expense. Further criticism of their behaviour is implied because it was considered vulgar to show one's teeth, which at the period were quite likely to be in a poor condition. The physicality of the verse is increased by the alliterations on [t] in 17–18, and [m], in 19–20, imitating the action of the lips and teeth as they masticate the freebies. *Mascar* is a vulgar term for eating at this period (*Cov.*), and can also carry slang overtones of drinking: *beber, sobre todo beber vino* (Alonso 1976: 518).

> **Tendrás muy hermosas manos,**
> **si dieres mucho con ellas:**
> **blancas son las que dan blancas,**
> 24   **largas las que nada niegan.**

You'll have very beautiful hands if you give a great deal with them: white hands are those that give money, long/generous hands, those that refuse nothing.

Hands, like teeth in the previous quatrain, are part of the repertoire of the Petrarchan lady's idealized beauty, but these qualities are undermined by being applied to the dashing young man for what they can do, not for what they are. His hands will be beautiful to the ladies who seek him out as long as they are generous in giving them what they want in terms of meals and gifts. They are *blancas*, 'white', a sign of aristocratic beauty, hands untouched by the coarseness of manual labour or working in the fields in the heat of the sun, when they give *blancas*, 'coins of low value' (*Cov.*: 'moneda menuda').

They are *largas*, because long hands were thought beautiful and because the adjective means not only 'long' but also 'noble', 'generous': that is, such hands refuse no request for money to be spent on those who ask. Thus, traditional images for female beauty, transferred to the young man, are subverted by punning to become images of female greed and rapacity. *Dieres*, like *anduvieres* and *mirares* in the following quatrain, is in the future subjunctive, a virtually obsolete tense in modern Spanish.

> **Alabaránte el andar,**
> **si anduvieres por las tiendas**
> **y el mirar, si no mirares**
> 28 **en dar todo cuanto quieran.**

They'll praise the way you walk as long as you walk by the shops, and the way you look, as long as you're unconcerned about giving them whatever they want.

Both the way Perico walks and the way he looks will be praised for similar reasons. As long as his legs carry him to shops, where he will spend money on the ladies he has met, they will praise his carriage: Quevedo is playing on the different meanings of *andar*, 'to walk', and *andar por*, 'to go by way of'. *Tienda* was also a slang term for a house where a prostitute worked (Alonso 1976: 735). Quevedo then contrasts Perico's *mirar*, 'look, appearance', with his *no mirar en*, 'not being concerned about', pandering to their every whim for possessions. The power of a woman's glance was a frequent theme in Petrarchan love poetry, but it could also be mercilessly satirized, as in Quevedo's ballad 'Los médicos con que miras' where he writes of *los delitos de tu cara*, 'the crimes of your face' (Q.706: 20), in another attack on women's use of their sexual allure to entrap men into lavishing every last penny on them.

> **Las mujeres de la Corte**
> **son, si bien lo consideras,**
> **todas de Santo Tomé,**
> 32 **aunque no son todas negras.**

If you think about it, the women of the Court all come from Santo Tomé, though they are not all black.

The punning and word-play intensify. São Tomé and Príncipe are islands in the Gulf of Guinea, off the coast of West Africa, which straddle the Equator. They were Portuguese colonies from the late fifteenth century until they achieved independence in 1975. The Spanish Crown ruled Portugal from 1580 to 1640, so that Quevedo probably considered them part of the Spanish Empire. The indigenous inhabitants of the islands were black. Why, then, does Quevedo make a link between the ladies of the Court and these distant islanders? Because *Tomé* also means 'I took', and that is what Court ladies do; they take whatever their young suitor may offer them. *Tomé* was also often used in the period as a typical name for a black slave (see Quevedo's famous ballad 'Boda de negros', Q.698: 33, 'Él se llamaba Tomé'). It was insulting, as was the term *perro*, sometimes applied to them (it seems to have derived from the Spanish expression '*to, to*', used to summon dogs). The irony here, surely, is that it is the young white buck who will, if he is not extremely careful, become the slave to the material appetites of these women. They are not literally black, obviously, because they are white (or at least that is what they would be if you could see beneath the layers of make-up, lines 73–76). But all of them are in the business of taking whatever they can get. *Santo Tomé*, no doubt for the same punning reason, was also the patron saint of rogues and swindlers, which adds insult to injury (Alonso 1976: 741, citing this ballad). *Negro* could mean 'crafty' and 'cunning' (*ibid.*: 554; compare p. 155, below), and may also carry overtones of moral evil.

> **Y si en todo el mundo hay caras,**
> **solas son caras de veras**
> **las de Madrid, por lo hermoso**
> 36   **y por lo mucho que cuestan.**

And if there are faces everywhere, the only real/expensive ones are those of Madrid, on account of their beauty and of the great amount that they cost.

The quatrain turns on a common enough pun, *caras*, the plural noun meaning 'faces', and *caras*, the feminine plural adjective agreeing with *las [mujeres]*, meaning 'expensive'. The most beautiful women are found at Court, but also the most expensive (Madrid became the capital of Spain only in 1561, when Philip II moved his Court there). The phrase *de veras* is ironic, because there is nothing true either about their outward appearance (73–76) or their inward disposition. The only true thing about them is that they are expensive to maintain. According to some writers, from Classical Antiquity onwards, the face revealed the true person (*Cov.* quotes the view that 'Es la cara por donde una persona se conoce'), in which case the ladies of Madrid have the only 'true' faces because those who appreciate their beauty must be made aware of their cost.

> **No hallarás nada de balde,**
> **aunque persigas las viejas,**
> **que ellas venden lo que fueron,**
> 40   **y su donaire las feas.**

You'll find nothing free even if you pursue old women, because they sell what they were, and ugly women sell their wit.

Not all the women at Court are beauties, but regardless of this, old women and ugly women still cannot be had for nothing. Old women 'sell what they were', that is, the fact that once they were young and perhaps attractive;

they might also be bawds, like Celestina in the work usually known by her name. Unattractive women were often famed for their spirit and humour, and that is what they offer in exchange for money. Quevedo's ballad 'Muy discretas y muy feas' (Q.740) takes up this theme more fully: ugly women may be intelligent, but the poet is looking for something rather more physically appealing. A similar point is made by the protagonist of Quevedo's *El Buscón*, when he says that he only wants women to sleep with, and you might as well sleep with Aristotle, Seneca, or a book as with a clever and plain one (III. VII; Quevedo 1990: 223). *Cov.* comments: 'muchas mugeres moças son feýssimas y a algunas viejas les queda el rastro de aver sido hermosas'.

> **Mientras tuvieres qué dar,**
> **hallarás quien te entretenga;**
> **y en expirando la bolsa,**
> 44 **oirás el *Requiem aeternam*.**

As long as you've got something to give you'll find someone to keep you company, and when your purse pegs out, you'll hear the 'Eternal rest grant them, O Lord'.

Requiem aeternam are the first two words of the last part of the funeral Mass: 'requiem aeternam dona illis Domine, et lux perpetua luceat eis', 'Eternal rest grant them, o Lord, and let light perpetual shine upon them.' Here the allusion is comic and ironical. As long as Perico has money to lavish on these ladies, he will never be short of their company. But as soon as his money gives out—his purse expires—he will be given the push and that will be the end of his sexual adventures with them. The requiem will be pronounced over his 'dead' purse as a sign that any such relationship is finished. Equally, if his *bolsa* in the sexual sense fails to produce the goods, that is, if he becomes impotent (perhaps as a result of contracting syphilis from them), they will abandon him. The ability of women to shop until, in this case, the male provider of the cash drops is portrayed hyperbolically in 'Sueño del Infierno', where the narrator sees a 'gran tropa de casados' and comments that 'la mujer era ayuno del marido, pues por darla la perdiz y el capón, no comía; y que era su desnudez, pues por darla galas demasiadas y joyas impertinentes iba en cueros' (Quevedo 1972: 113; the reference to *capón* also implies impotence): husbands must fast because their wives are gluttons and eat splendidly, and they must go naked, because all their money is spent on jewels and finery to please them.

> **Cuando te abracen, advierte**
> **que segadores semejan;**
> **con una mano te abrazan,**
> 48 **con otra te desjarretan.**

When they embrace you, be warned, they're like reapers. They embrace you with one hand and hamstring you with the other.

The simile in this quatrain depends on understanding pre-mechanical ways of bringing in the harvest. Reapers would go out into the fields, gather in their arms a bundle of ears, then cut them off near the base. It is this image to which women are likened when they embrace their prey. *Abrazar* implies putting both arms around Perico, just as reapers gather up the golden ears in their arms; the colour of the corn creates a link with the golden coins such women prize so highly. The reapers then literally sever the stalks and bundle up the armful of corn. These women metaphorically do the same, but with their *manos*. A *segador* was also a slang term for anyone who earned their living by crime (Alonso 1976: 701), so that the overall effect of the verse is to treat women as criminals, fleecing the vulnerable and the naive. *Desjarretar* has both a literal and a metaphorical meaning. The *jarrete* is the hamstring, and the verb literally means 'to cut the leg of an animal off at that point in order to immobilize it' (it belongs to the vocabulary of the slaughterhouse). Metaphorically, *desjarretado* means 'lacking in strength'. So these women deprive you of your money as if they were cutting it off from you as reapers cut the corn. It may also imply that they are expert pickpockets (again, metaphorically): they remove your wallet with the very hand which is entwined around you. By doing this, they leave you powerless.

> **Besaránte, como al jarro**
> **borracho bebedor besa,**
> **que en consumiendo le arrima**
> 52 **o en algún rincón le cuelga.**

They will kiss you in the same way as the sozzled drinker kisses the jar; once he's finished, he sets it to one side or hangs it in some corner.

This is a particularly difficult verse. *Cov.* defines *arrimar a uno* as 'destruyrle y dexarle como muerto y desmayado, pegado a la pared', which seems more in tune with the sense than the normal meaning of *arrimar* in the period as 'llegar una cosa a otra'. *Arrimarse*, the reflexive form, has the slang meaning of practising illicit love, while *vivir arrimado* can mean to live with someone to whom you are not married (Alonso 1976: 66). The metaphor has changed from corn and livestock to drink, with the strong and comic alliteration in [b] mimicking perhaps the action of the lips as they drink from the vessel. But the meaning is the same. Perico will find plenty of women who will pay him attention, but they will lose interest in him as soon as they have drunk their fill of him, that is, when he has no more cash to spend on them. Then, as the boozer loses interest in the vessel and puts it down, so will they with him. *Besar el jarro* means 'beber un trago de vino' (Alonso 1976: 110); a well known example of the expression comes in the first 'tratado' of the mid-sixteenth-century picaresque tale *Lazarillo de Tormes*, where Lazarillo's first master, the blind man, is shown giving the jar 'un par de besos callados'. (*Cov.* tells us that only vulgar people drink like this.) *Colgar a uno* may also have a secondary meaning beyond its usual sense of 'to hang up'. There was a widespread custom that on someone's birthday gifts would be hung around their neck. The only gift these women give you, once they have drunk you dry, is, ironically, to discard you. *Colgar* is also slang for 'to hang', in the sense of to execute (Alonso 1976: 212; see below p. 130). In that sense, these women will be the death of Perico.

> **Tienen mil cosas de nuncios,**
> **pues todas quieren que sean**
> **los que están, abreviadores,**
> 56 **y datarios, los que entran.**

They're just like Papal nuncios, because they all want those who are present to be issuers of Papal briefs in their visits and those arriving to be givers of benefices.

This is perhaps the most difficult part of the poem to unravel. The imagery switches again, abruptly, to the legal language of the Papal Court. A *nuncio* is the official representative or ambassador of the Pope in another country. A Papal brief is a written mandate from the Pope concerning a less serious matter than a Papal bull, and an *abreviador* was an official who worked in the office which issues them. Quevedo, however, is playing on the same double meaning that English can have, on the etymological meaning of *breve* as 'short'. These ladies do not wish the men they are entertaining to stay around for long, but they do want those about to visit them to be *datarios*. These were officials in a tribunal of the Roman Curia which dealt with the benefices and other ecclesiastical offices which could be sold. Again, Quevedo is playing the term off against its root, *dar*, meaning that anyone intending to visit one of them will be welcomed as long as he brings some kind of gift. As usual, though, there is another level of meaning. Alonso cites this text as an example of *datarios* having its slang meaning of 'payments made to swindlers and prostitutes' (1976: 256). Just as the Papal nuncio presides over a Court to which lesser officials come on business of various kinds, these ladies receive visitors whose stay must be brief so that others can be fitted in, and they expect to be given gifts by their suitors, or paid for the sexual services they offer.

> **Toman acero en verano,**
> **que ningún metal desprecian;**
> **Dios ayuda al que madruga,**
> 60 **mas no, si es a andar con ellas.**

They take steel in summer, because they despise no metal. 'God helps the early riser', but not if it's to hang around with them.

Water was drunk with a heated steel object in it in order, it was believed, to ease bodily obstructions, which were particularly acute in the summer. *Cov.* explains that *vino azerado* or *agua azerada* would have 'un pedaço de azero, muy encendido' placed in it and be used for 'ciertos remedios medicinales'. He gives the commentary on the Greek physician Dioscorides by the Spanish doctor Andrés de Laguna as his source. Such obstructions might be constipation, or (as more likely here) obstructions in the menstrual flow (see also, pp. 157–58, below). Quevedo, however, does not attribute this custom to a medical need, but to these women's love of metal, a metonymy for coins, money. Grotesquely, then, their love of money becomes the reason for their having recourse to this (to us) strange remedy. The second part of the quatrain refers to a well known proverb, 'A quien madruga, Dios le ayuda', a more religious version of our 'The early bird catches the worm'. This may be true in many cases, but God cannot help any man foolish enough to rise early simply so that he can visit one of these ladies, because she will fleece him. The emphasis on seasons and times of day will continue into the next three quatrains and provides the loose kind of connection typical of the way the ballad is constructed.

> **Pensóse escapar el Sol,**
> **por tener lejos su esfera,**
> **y el invierno, por tomarle,**
> 64   **ocupan llanos y cuestas.**

The sun thought he was safe from them because his sphere is far distant, and in winter, in order to take/catch him, they occupy level ground and slopes.

The sun is golden and round, so it is like a gold coin, and therefore an object of desire on the part of the ladies of the Court. It moves in its own *esfera*, one of the concentric celestial spheres of the pre-Copernican universe. Its motion across the heavens is therefore entirely independent of them, but by comic hyperbole Quevedo personifies the sun and makes it vainly imagine itself free from their grasping greed because it is at a safe distance. These women are everywhere, as their occupation of *llanos* and *cuestas* suggests, plying their trade (Quevedo may well be alluding specifically to the prostitutes of Madrid) to gain metaphorical sun, that is, gold. He turns the way in which they fill the streets as they *toman*, 'take', the winter sunshine into an expression of their desire to *tomar*, or 'steal' him. In fact, they are out and about in fine weather in order to get suitable young men into their clutches. The sun's distance and movement, its colour and shape, and their parading the streets on the prowl for men's riches are thus brought into close relationship with each other by personification (the sun) and double meaning (*tomar*).

> **A ninguna parte irás**
> **que de ellas libre te veas,**
> **que se entrarán en tu casa**
> 68   **por resquicios, si te cierras.**

You can go nowhere where you will be free of them; they will get into your house through the cracks if you shut the door.

The picture of voracious hordes of women extends from the outdoors in winter to everywhere, even to the security of one's own home behind bolted doors. But the reference to their getting in through the cracks (*resquicio* is the gap between the door and the doorpost, or a crack in the wall) is more pointed than it might seem. This was an ability commonly believed to be possessed by witches, who were reputed to enter and to leave houses through the smallest of cracks, and is much discussed by writers on witchcraft of this period. Quevedo makes reference to this in order to paint them as evil and to exaggerate their persistence: however hard Perico tries to keep them at bay, they will always find a way into his wallet.

> **Cuantas tú no conocieres,**
> **tantas hallarás doncellas,**
> **que los Virgos y los Dones**
> 72 **son de una misma manera.**

You will find as many virgins as the women you haven't met/had sex with, because Virgos and Dons are all of a kind.

Conocer has the meaning of 'to know in person' and 'to know carnally', and Quevedo plays with both. All the women Perico has *not* yet met will claim, when he does, that they are virgins, and therefore the more desirable, because they will be pure and undefiled by carnal sin, respectable enough to be sought in marriage. They will not be, of course, but the claim of virginity will enhance their appeal and their value (see also p. 166, below). *Virgo*, the Latin for 'virgin', is also one of the twelve signs of the zodiac, and therefore has a place in astrology. Quevedo regards all these women who claim to be virgins as liars, just as astrology deceives, and so too do titles like *don*, which were freely assumed by those with no right to them, as an indication of noble status. He often pokes fun at people with pretensions to the title and who use it without being entitled to it, to pass themselves off as aristocrats (just as these women pass themselves off as virgins when they are no better than whores). Quevedo makes the same joke in 'Sueño del Infierno' ('aunque las mujeres pienso que han trocado ya los virgos por los dones, y así todas tienen don y ninguna virgo', Quevedo 1972: 117).

> **Altas mujeres verás,**
> **pero son como colmenas:**
> **la mitad huecas y corcho,**
> 76 **y lo demás miel y cera.**

You'll see tall/noble women, but they're like beehives: they're half hollow and cork, and the rest is honey and wax.

Here Quevedo uses the slightly insulting term *mujeres*, in place of the more respectful *señoras* or *damas*. Likening them to beehives seems extravagant and ridiculous, almost surreal, but he is the master of such conceits (though

technically this is a simile). If one looks at paintings of female members of
the royal family, such as those Velázquez painted of Queen Mariana of Aus-
tria and the princesses María Teresa and Margarita in 1652–53 one can see
the kind of extravagance which Quevedo had in mind (even though the paintings postdate the ballad by a decade or two). These tent-like dresses were
supported by a framework, perhaps made of cork because of its lightness,
but largely hollow inside; though *corcho* also refers to the *chapines*, a kind
of overshoe with a cork platform worn to raise ladies' shoes above the mud
and to increase the wearer's stature: *Cov.* again cites Laguna, who wrote
that the Greeks called women 'cortezas de árboles, por ir empinadas en cor-
chos'. *Altas* has a secondary meaning here, too: 'noble'. That, at least, is what
these ladies would like Perico to believe that they are. *Cov.* also tells us that
chapines were originally hollow so that women could bear their weight, and
that in many places only married women wear them, which would make an
ironical connection with the previous stanza, concerning the lack of virgins.
Hollowness, too, suggests the emptiness and the vanity of those who spend
so much time and money on such forms of dress. Quevedo associates these
women with beehives because these too are constructed of very light material
and are hollow inside (*Cov.*: 'la caxa de corcho o pino hueco en que las
abejas labran su miel'). Moreover, honey and wax, both products of the beehive, formed the basis of much of the make-up used in the period. In that
sense, then, the simile is remarkably apposite (compare, perhaps, the name
'beehive' given to a certain hairstyle of the 1950s and '60s). Quevedo takes
the constituent elements of the beehive—hollowness, cork, honey and
wax—and applies each of them humorously to the extravagant clothes these
ladies wear and the make-up they use to hide their defects. There is a further
suggestion of falseness and vanity in their wishing to appear taller than they
actually are. He paints a memorable picture of the effects of make-up in
'Sueño del Infierno' (Quevedo 1972: 132–33), contrasting the features with
which women were born with the entirely artificial beings they become
when they cover themselves in this way. Their resemblance to beehives may
also hint at other characteristics: the noise of female gossip, like the buzzing
of bees; and the fact that if Perico puts in his hand in the hope of finding
sweet honey, he will get badly stung.

> **Casamiento pedirán,**
> **si es que te huelen hacienda.**
> **Guárdate de ser marido,**
> 80   **no te corran una fiesta.**

They'll ask for marriage, that is, if there's a sniff of property about you.
Beware of being a husband; don't let them play tricks on you.

Just in case Perico is flattered to be in receipt of proposals of marriage (normally the man would propose to the woman, but here, in the upside-down
world of the Court, the roles are reversed), he should know that the only

reason such women would make them would be for their own personal gain. They will be trying to work out how much he is worth, and if they think he has got plenty behind him they will try to hook him. So he should beware of becoming a husband and be wary of their guiles. *Correr una fiesta* means 'to play a joke on someone', but *correr* has two other slang meanings, 'to steal' and 'to fuck' (Alonso 1976: 231–32). Quevedo probably has all these meanings in mind.

> **Para prometer, te doy**
> **una general licencia,**
> **pues es todo el mundo tuyo,**
> 84   **como sólo le prometas.**
>
> **Ofrecimientos te sobren,**
> **no haya cosa que no ofrezcas,**
> **que el prometer no empobrece,**
> 88   **y el cumplir echa por puertas.**

I give you general permission to make promises, because the whole world is yours, as long as you only promise it. Be generous in offering, let there be nothing you don't offer, because making promises doesn't impoverish you. It's keeping them that gets you kicked out.

You can offer and promise as much as you like, as long as you never actually give what you promise. Promises cost nothing, whereas keeping them will ruin Perico. The speaker adopts a semi-legal tone with the word *licencia*, which was often used to express some kind of formal permission (e.g. for the printing of books). The use of polyptoton across these lines (*prometer/ prometas/prometer* and *ofrecimientos/ofrezcas*) emphasizes the advice, as does the alliteration in [**p**], [**pr**], [**m**], and [**c**].

> **La víspera de tu Santo**
> **por ningún modo parezcas,**
> **pues con tu bolsón te ahorcan,**
> 92   **cuando dicen que te cuelgan.**
>
> **Estarás malo en la cama**
> **los días todos de feria.**
> **Por las ventanas, si hay toros,**
> 96   **meteráste en una iglesia.**

Do not appear at all on the eve of your birthday, because they hang you with your wallet when they tell you they're giving you a present. You are to be ill in bed on all feast days, and when bullfights are on; to avoid window-seats you will hide yourself away inside a church.

People celebrated their saint's day more than their birthday: the day on which the saint after which they were named was honoured in the Church's calendar. Normally, one might expect to be given presents and to throw a party in celebration, but the speaker's advice is to shun all public appearances on such a day. As noted above (52), the custom in Spain at this time was for gifts to be hung around the neck of the person whose day it was, hence *cuando te cuelgan*. Instead of this being a sign of affection and generosity, it is the exact reverse. They will make you pay time and time again for any gift they give you and will not be satisfied until your resources are exhausted. Hence, grotesquely, they are depicted as putting Perico to death by being hanged, the slang meaning of *colgar*, by his wallet, whenever they hang a present round his neck, because they will spend every last penny of his. Similarly, the speaker warns against being out and about among the crowds at festivals; better to pretend to be ill in bed, because there will be so many women on the look-out and so much potentially to buy for them, not to mention the pickpockets and other criminals who frequent such gatherings. *Feria* also has the slang meaning of 'negocio de las prostitutas con sus clientes o con su rufián ['pimp']' (Alonso 1976: 357). Bullfights were another great draw, and the most expensive seats were window-seats, which ladies of this kind would naturally demand. Churches, on the other hand, make good hiding-places, and were places of sanctuary, where thieves and other criminals could seek refuge from the law. *Toro* could also be applied metonymically, through its horns, to a cuckold (Alonso 1976: 743). If Perico were to become involved with married ladies, he would be wise to keep it as secret as possible, hide it away rather than show it off.

> **Antes entres en un fuego**
> **que en casa de una joyera,**
> **y antes que a la platería**
> 100 **vayas, irás a las galeras.**

Rather go into a fire than a jeweller's shop, and you'll be off to the galleys before you enter the silversmiths' quarter.

The hyperbolic warnings continue, with further variations on the theme of where to go and where not to go. The normal word for jeweller is *joyero*; Quevedo makes her a female, compounding the problem. The ladies of the Court love to be taken to jewellers' shops and be bought things. Such shops, *Cov.* tells us, contained 'cosas delicadas de oro y seda, tocas, guantes', among other things (a *joyera* may also denote any woman with a taste for trinkets). A *platería* was a street or district in which silversmiths plied their trade, and would be extremely bad news for Perico's bank balance. Jewellers were a common target for Quevedo (see 'Sueño del Infierno', and 'Sueño de la muerte': Quevedo 1972: 108, 122, 218–19). By recommending that Perico prefer two things which threaten death—a burning house, and being sentenced as a galley slave, which was tantamount to a death sentence—to the loss of all his income in such places, Quevedo is hinting, as he does elsewhere, that being enslaved to such women is a fate worse than death.

Si entrar en alguna casa
quieres, primero a la puerta
oye si pregona alguno;
104 no te peguen con la deuda.

If you want to enter a house, listen at the door first, to see if anyone's calling out; don't get stuck with the debt.

When a property was transferred from one owner to another, any outstanding debts on the property became the responsibility of the new owner (this remains the case in Spain, as would-be British buyers there are often warned). It was therefore vital to ensure that it was debt-free. The normal way of signalling such debts was by employing a *pregonero*, a 'crier', to announce them outside the property. Quevedo takes this legal point and humorously applies it to Perico's merely entering a house to pay a visit to a lady. Her demands will be such that it will be the equivalent to being saddled with such a debt.

Y si por cuerdo y guardoso
no tuvieres quien te quiera,
bien hechas y mal vestidas
108 hallarás mil irlandesas.

Con un cuarto de turrón
y con agua y gragea
goza un Píramo barato
112 cualquiera Tisbe gallega.

And if through being sensible and careful you've no one to love you, you will find plenty of Irish girls, well built and badly dressed. With a pennyworth of turrón and with water and hundreds and thousands, a cheapskate Pyramus can enjoy any Galician Thisbe.

If all the advice so far is taken, there is a real risk that Perico will still be single. The narrator therefore proposes an inexpensive solution. Irish girls had the reputation for being easy catches and cheap. The line *bien hechas y mal vestidas* is a joke at the expense of Góngora, whose poetry Quevedo disliked; Góngora was especially fond of this antithetical formula (see, for example, *mal herido y bien curado*, in 'En un pastoral albergue', above, p. 62). Equally, girls from Galicia were said at the time to be very ugly and dirty, and easily impressed by the smallest favours, coming as they did from poor peasant communities, the term *gallega* being used to denote a bargain-basement prostitute (see p. 139). *Turrón* remains a traditional Spanish delicacy, made of nuts (usually almonds) and honey. The *cuarto* was a low denomination coin, worth four *maravedíes*. Such girls would be happy with water rather than expensive drinks, and *gragea*, defined by *Cov.* as 'una especie de confitura muy menuda... de granitos redondos', instead of more refined delicacies. The reference to Pyramus and Thisbe is to two ill-fated lovers of Classical legend (see, for example, Ovid's *Metamorphoses*, IV). In likening these sordid transactions to two faithful lovers of Classical Antiquity who were united only in death, Quevedo is being deliberately subversive.

> **Si tomares mis consejos,**
> **Perico, que Dios mantenga,**
> **vivirás contento y rico**
> 116 **sobre la haz de la tierra.**
>
> **Si no, veráste comido**
> **de tías, madres y suegras,**
> **sin narices y con parches,**
> 120 **con unciones y sin cejas.**

If you were to take my advice, Perico, whom God preserve, you will live happy and rich on the face of the earth. If not, you will be eaten up by aunts, mothers and mothers-in-law, with no noses but with plasters, with ointments but without eyebrows.

The poem ends with a warning about the consequences of ignoring the advice it has given Perico. The polite formula *Dios te mantenga* repeats with slight variation the wish expressed in the fourth line of the poem, *Dios de su mano te tenga*. The expression *sobre la haz de la tierra* is originally biblical, a Hebrew idiom found, for example, from Genesis 1:2 onwards, with the simple meaning of 'on earth'. But by the Golden Age it had acquired two meanings: 'living at one's ease', in the proverbial saying *Vivir sobre la haz de la tierra*, and 'living as a coward'. Failure to heed the advice leads to an apparently puzzling and bathetic conclusion. The armies of aunts, mothers and mothers-in-law are apparently self-explanatory: they are the ladies at Court who want to marry off their daughters and nieces, or who have succeeded in so doing, to eligible young men (that is, young men with a large income). However, the slang meaning of *tía* is 'whore' and of *madre* 'go-between', a figure immortalized in the character of Celestina. She can be the Madame of a brothel or a woman too old to work as a prostitute who devotes herself to procuring girls for men who pay her for her services. Syphilis, an incurable disease until the twentieth century, caused the structure of the nose to collapse, and the eyebrows to fall out (see also pp. 199 and 217, below). It is unclear whether the last two lines refer to the women or to Perico; perhaps they are intentionally ambiguous and include both. Women who had the disease would cover the sores and pustules it caused with plasters. *Unciones*, according to Alonso (1976: 765), formed 'el remedio y ungüento que se aplica para curar el mal gálico', that is, syphilis. If these lines refer to Perico, the words *veráste comido* represent the inevitable consequence of his ignoring the earlier warning about women's appetite for meals at his expense (17–20). If he falls for their ploys, not only will all his wealth be devoured by their greed, but the very physical charms he possessed at the beginning and which he was advised to exchange for money (11–12) will have vanished. The collapse of his nose, a common metaphor for the male member, would also signal his sexual impotence. Either way, the ballad ends on a bitter note. For all the metaphorical deaths it has promised Perico if he is not careful, the threat of syphilis will literally be the end of him and all his dreams of success and riches.

FRANCISCO DE QUEVEDO

'LOS BORRACHOS' (1627–28?)

Gobernando están el mundo,
cogidos con queso añejo
en la trampa de lo caro,
tres gabachos y un gallego.

5   Mojadas tienen las voces,
los labios tienen de hierro,
y por ser hechos de yesca,
tienen los gaznates secos.

Pierres, sentado en arpón,
10   el vino estaba meciendo,
que en un sudor remostado
se cierne por el cabello.

Hecho verga de ballesta,
retortijado el pescuezo,
15   Jaques, medio desmayado,
a vómito estaba puesto.

Roque, los puños cerrados,
más entero y más atento,
suspirando saca el aire,
20   por no avinagrar el cuero.

Maroto, buen español,
hecho faja el ferreruelo,
vueltos lágrimas los brindis
y bebido el ojo izquierdo,

25   con palabras rocïadas
y con el tono algo crespo,
después que toda la calle
sahumó con un regüeldo,

dijo, mirando a los tres
30   con vinoso sentimiento:
'¿En qué ha de parar el mundo?
¿Qué fin tendrán estos tiempos?

Lo que hoy es ración de un paje
de un capitán era sueldo
35   cuando eran los hombres más
y habían menester menos.

Cuatro mil maravedís
que le dan a un escudero
era dádiva de un rey
40   para rico casamiento.

Apreciábase el ajuar
que a Jimena Gómez dieron
en menos que agora cuesta
remendar unos greguescos.

45   Andaba entonces el Cid
más galán que Gerineldos,
con botarga colorada
en figura de pimiento:

y hoy, si alguno ha de vestirse,
50   le desnudan dos primero:
el mercader de quien compra
y el sastre que ha de coserlo.

Ya no gastan los vestidos
las personas con traerlos:
55   que el inventor de otro traje
hace lo flamante viejo.

Sin duda inventó las calzas
algún diablo del infierno,
pues un cristiano atacado
60   ya no queda de provecho.

¡Qué es ver tantas cuchilladas
agora en un caballero;
tanta pendencia en las calzas,
y tanta paz en el dueño!

65 Todo se ha trocado ya;
todo al revés está vuelto;
las mujeres son soldados,
y los hombres son doncellos.

Los mozos traen cadenitas;
70 las niñas toman acero:
que de las antiguas armas
sólo conservan los petos.

De arrepentidos de barba
hay infinitos conventos,
75 donde se vuelven lampiños
por gracia de los barberos.

No hay barba cana ninguna,
porque aun los castillos pienso
que han teñido ya las suyas,
80 a persuasión de los viejos.

Pues, ¿quién sufrirá el lenguaje,
la soberbia y los enredos
de una mujer pretendida,
de éstas que se dan a peso?

85 Han hecho mercadería
sus favores y sus cuerpos,
introduciendo por ley
que reciban y que demos.

¡Que si pecamos los dos,
90 yo he de pagar al momento,
y que sólo para mí
sea interesable el infierno!

¿Que a la mujer no le cueste
el condenarse un cabello,
95 y que por llevarme el diablo,
me lleve lo que no tengo?

¡Vive Dios, que no es razón,
y que es muy ruinmente hecho,
y se lo diré al demonio,
100 si me topa o si le encuentro!

Si yo reinara ocho días,
pusiera en todo remedio,
y anduvieran tras nosotros
y nos dijeran requiebros.

105 Yo conocí los maridos
gobernándose ellos mesmos,

sin sostitutos ni alcaides,
sin comisiones ni enredos;

y agora los más maridos
110 (nadie bastará a entenderlos)
tienen por lugarteniente
la mitad de todo el pueblo.

No se les daba de antes
por comisiones un cuerno,
115 y agora por comisiones
se les dan más de quinientos.

Solían usarse doncellas:
cuéntanlo ansí mis agüelos;
debiéronse de gastar,
120 por ser muy pocas, muy presto.

Bien hayan los ermitaños
que viven por esos cerros,
que si son buenos, se salvan,
y si no, los queman presto;

125 y no vosotros, lacayos
de tres hidalgos hambrientos,
alguaciles de unas ancas
con la vara y el cabestro.

Y yo, que en diez y seis años
130 que tengo de despensero,
aun no he podido ser Judas,
y vender a mi maestro.'

En esto Pierres, que estaba
con mareta en el asiento,
135 dormido cayó de hocicos,
y devoto besó el suelo.

Jaques, desembarazado
el estómago y el lecho,
daba mis tiernos abrazos
140 a un banco y a un paramento.

Sirviéronle de orinales
al buen Roque sus greguescos:
que no se halló bien el vino,
y ansí se salió tan presto.

145 Maroto, que vio el estrago
y el auditorio de cestos,
bostezando con temblores,
dio con su vino en el suelo.

*　　*　　*　　*　　*

Peppered as it is with innuendo and wordplay, much of it salacious, this ballad (Q.697) is representative of the satirical works on which Quevedo's reputation rests. In the standard *romance* form of octosyllabic lines and with assonance in *é–o* in alternate lines, it seems at first sight a simple burlesque: an example of a poet at the height of his powers and having fun.[1] As Arthur Terry puts it, 'Time and again, the mercurial quality of Quevedo's imagination—his ability to seize on the slightest hint of an alternative meaning—creates the kind of verbal effect which seems to detach itself from the apparent subject of the poem' (1993: 156). Yet the close proximity in the very first quatrain of *cogidos*, *queso*, and a costly *trampa* triggers thoughts of the tale of the Fox and the Crow, memorably treated by both Juan Ruiz and Don Juan Manuel (see also the notes on 8 and 148, below); a further implication of *trampa*, discussed in Chapter 6, may well be in play, too.[2] By alluding to a traditional morality tale right at the outset, Quevedo signals that—chortles, sniggers, and guffaws notwithstanding—this poem, like so many others from the same stable, will have lessons to impart. Similarities of tone and matter between this poem and certain writings of the Roman satirist Juvenal, a poet Quevedo knew well and cited often, also serve to reinforce the reader's sense that here, in an openly comic context, he is giving vent to real outrage at the ways fashion and change have overturned the divine scheme of things.[3]

Quevedo's poems, like those of many of his contemporaries, circulated in manuscript among a small coterie of wits and practising poets; editions of his works were eventually printed in large numbers and sold out quickly, and the author himself and others often revised them both before and after publication. The result of this process is that many variant versions survive (Quevedo 1932: lvi; Cacho 2004). The earliest known version of the ballad we are reading here comes in the Zaragoza MS *Cancionero de 1628* (Blecua 1945; Quevedo 1969–81: II. 305; Jauralde 1998a: 611), the variants listed by Blecua probably being of a later date. Six of these (1969–81: II. 305–20, Q.697: texts *C–H*) locate the action in a particular tavern, the Taberna del Toro. That could, of course, be a generic allusion; quite a few Spanish towns and cities could boast a Calle or a Taberna del Toro. But we know from the *Buscón* and elsewhere that Quevedo was not averse to using real locations for his tavern scenes and, if the ballad was written soon after his return to Madrid in 1627 (Jauralde 1998a: 515, 517), then he almost certainly had in

---

* An early version of this paper was given in November 2006 at University College Cork. I am grateful to all those who commented helpfully at the time and, in particular, to our hosts on that occasion Stephen Boyd and Terence O'Reilly.

[1] For introductions to the burlesque, see Jump (1972) and, for Spain, Cacho (2007b).

[2] *Libro de buen amor*, st.1437–44 (Ruiz 1989: 611–13); *El Conde Lucanor, enxiemplo* v (Don Juan Manuel 1969: 77–81); see Devoto (1972: 369–72). Also above, p. 113.

[3] See Juvenal, *Satires* VI. 9–20, 112, 246, 342, 366–78, etc.; also below, pp. 146, 166. Codoñer (1982) identifies direct influences of Juvenal on two Quevedo sonnets: Q.120, '¿Miras la faz que al orbe fue segunda', and Q.122, 'En la heredad del pobre, las espigas'.

mind the Mesón or Taberna del Toro in the Calle de los Oliveros (the modern Calle Alcalá). From 1620 onwards, he had been acquiring a number of properties in the fashionable Comediantes quarter of the capital (the actors' guild would from 1631 be based there, in the church of San Sebastián where Lope de Vega is buried); those properties, in the Calle de Cantarranas and the Calle de Francos (the modern-day Calle de Lope de Vega and Calle de Cervantes), were just a few hundred metres from the Mesón del Toro, a vast drinking den on a site opposite the entrance to the modern Gran Vía and straight across the road from the Convento de San Hermenegildo, where Lope celebrated his first Mass in 1614. The tavern site is today occupied in part by the Círculo de Bellas Artes.[4] In the 1620s the owner had enlarged and improved it, obtaining exemption in 1624 from the tax levied on establishments offering accommodation (*regalía de huésped de asiento*) in return for an annual rent of 10,000 maravedís and a further annual sum (or *servicio*) of 300 *ducados*, both payable to the Crown (Huarte 1930). Quevedo's apparently generalized comments that we find in the version we have here concerning scams involving adulterated wine acquire, in those later versions of the ballad, a specific and topical edge.[5]

*   *   *   *   *

**Gobernando están el mundo,
cogidos con queso añejo
en la trampa de lo caro,
4   tres gabachos y un gallego.**

Three gabachos and a gallego are putting the world to rights, ensnared by stale cheese into paying over the odds.

The first word of the poem, *gobernando*, establishes a tone of irony. As 16, 24, and then the last four strophes of the ballad make all too clear, *gobernando*, 'steering a steady course', and *gobernándose*, 'behaving properly, walking in a straight line', are not skills at which these four drinkers excel.

Cogidos con (queso añejo), which can be construed as both 'trapped by (cheese, cheese in a mousetrap)' and 'trapped along with (stale cheese, cheese that has been there for an age)', also introduces a feature of many satirical and burlesque compositions by our poet: a penchant for picking up on another meaning for a word or phrase and then producing, almost as a riff, a

[4] Quevedo's purchases were intended solely as speculative investments; when in Madrid, he normally lodged in a *posada* (Crosby 2005: 285).

[5] I owe this information to the kindness of Valentín Gallego Moreno and the good offices of María Luisa López-Vidriero. The inns along the Calle de los Oliveros were eventually closed in 1641 as the whole area, close to the new Buen Retiro palace, was transformed into a preserve of Church and nobility, and the street itself into the preferred route for major religious processions (Deleito 1942: 58–60, 155).

stream of further words associated with that other sense (a proceeding Gracián refers to slightingly as 'acumular las semejanzas', though, as we shall see, Quevedo on occasion 'las va aplicando': Gracián 1969: I.118). *Cogidos*, 'trapped', also means 'caught, arrested', and is followed by *trampa*, 'trick, falsehood' but also 'animal trap, mousetrap, snare', *mojadas* (5) both 'wet' and 'subjected to the water torture', *hierro* (6) 'iron, rust' and 'leg iron, shackle', *yesca* (7) both 'tinder, flint' and 'galley fodder', *retortijado* (14) 'twisted' as well as 'tortured, racked', *(tener a alguien en) jaque* (15) '(to have someone) at a disadvantage' [originally from the term at chess 'to have/put an opponent in check'] but also 'to (have/put someone on the) rack', *puesto a vómito* (16) 'throwing up' and 'singing under torture', *aire* (19) 'air, breeze, rumour' but also 'informant, grass', *suspirando* (19) 'exhaling, inhaling, sighing' and 'turning informant', and *faja* (22) meaning both 'sash, girdle' and 'whip, lash'. Later on, we will have gentle reminders of this lexical subset, with *desnudan* (50) 'they strip (prior to torture on the rack)', *calzas* (57) 'leggings, stockings, breeches' and 'leg irons', *mozos* (69) 'lads, servants' and 'hooks (on a chain)', *cadenitas* (69) 'necklaces, bracelets' and 'chains', and the whole of 135–40. The sources I have consulted are silent on the subject of *(sentado en) arpón*, '(seated on a) harpoon' (9), yet it, too, clearly should belong to this set of words to do with crime and punishment, perhaps as a synonym for *potro*, 'rack', or a slang term for the Judas Chair (compare *(h)arpar*, 'to lacerate, to tear').

A note to Part II, chapter XXIIII in a recent edition of *Don Quijote* makes it clear that *lo caro* had a specific meaning in the wine world of the day: '*vino de calidad*: eran vinos caros los de San Martín, Ciudad Real, La Membrilla, Alaejos y Medina del Campo; ordinarios los de otras procedencias' (Cervantes 2005: I.908; compare Quevedo 2003: I.459). As the name suggests, inns could charge more for *lo caro*, though those offering it were obliged to advertise their prices at the street-entrance to their premises (Alvar 1989: 164). Here, *trampa de lo caro* suggests that the four drinkers are ensnared not by fine wine but, more appropriately, by both cheese and rotgut (the *vinos bellacos* sometimes dubbed in the slang of the day *lo pío*). The adjective *añejo* used to qualify *queso* may also be have the sense of 'age-old', 'as in the traditional tale', with wine, rather than cheese, being the prize treasured by these drinkers. That interpretation would give specific weight to the final line of the poem (see below, p. 171).

Before citing the opening four lines from our *romance, Aut.* defines *gabacho* as 'soez, asqueroso, sucio, puerco y ruín', and explains that 'es voz de desprecio con que se moteja a los naturales de los Pueblos que están a las faldas de los Pyreneos, entre el río llamado Gaba, porque en ciertos tiempos del año vienen al Reino de Aragón, y otras partes, donde se ocupan y exercitan en los ministerios más baxos y humildes'. Quevedo uses the term in other poems of the 1620s, among them two *romances*: 'Enero, mes de coroza' (Q.685: 30, accusing a cat of being *gabacho* as its mewing mimics the cry of a street pedlar) and 'Tomando estaba sudores' (Q.694: 23, where French accents are subjected to mockery). The names he gives his three *gabachos*—Pierre(s), Ja(c)ques, and Roque (Roch)—confirm this French or Pyrenean connection.

Gallego, 'Galician', was synonymous with *lacayo*, 'servant', and Quevedo uses it in this sense in the mid-1630s in *La hora de todos y la Fortuna con seso* (1987: 291–92); our poem later confirms that this *gallego* is indeed a *despensero*, or steward (130) and that the three *gabachos* are *lacayos* (125). *Gallegos* are frequently depicted by Quevedo and his contemporaries as stupid, unwashed, lower-class servants: e.g. 'Floris, la fiesta pasada' (Q.673: 16) and 'Canto los disparates, las locuras' (possibly also written in the late 1620s), where among those attending a burlesque joust staged in Paris are (Q.875: 157–60) 'los gallegos | mal espulgados, llenos de catarros, | matándose a docenas y a palmadas | moscas, en las pernazas afelpadas' (compare the remarks on Galicia in the *romance* 'Cansado estoy de la Corte', Q.749 : 113ff.). *Gallegas* figure in works of this period as low-class prostitutes: in Quevedo's famous *romance* 'A la corte vas, Perico' (Q.726: 109–12; see above, p. 131); in his burlesque 'Señor don Leandro' (early 1610s?, Q.771: 30); and in Chapter IV of Alonso Fernández de Avellaneda's 1614 sequel to Cervantes's *Don Quijote*, Part I, where the innkeeper offers Don Quijote a bed for the night with the words 'Si quiere posada, entre, que le daremos buena cena y mejor cama; y aun, si fuere menester, no faltará una moza gallega que le quite los zapatos; que, aunque tiene las tetas grandes, es ya cerrada de años; y como vuesa merced no cierre la bolsa, no haya miedo que ella cierre los brazos ni deje de recebirle en ellos' (Fernández de Avellaneda 1971: 101).[6]

> Mojadas tienen las voces,
> los labios tienen de hierro,
> y por ser hechos de yesca,
> 8   tienen los gaznates secos.

Their voices were well oiled, their lips were like iron [rust coloured] and, since they were constructed of tinder, their gullets were parched.

Though it indicates the way that, when they are into their cups, the speech of these drinkers becomes slurred (*voces*, 'words' as well as 'voices'; *mojadas*, 'wet'—*mojar* also being slang for 'drinking wine, wetting one's whistle'), this quatrain also provides the second hint, after *trampa* (3), of a recurrent concern in Quevedo's satirical writing: the poor quality of the wine on offer in taverns and the professional tricks of the innkeeping trade. Drinking in such hostelries was thus a form of the water torture commonly used in the

---

[6] Two of the most famous attacks on Galicia from the period come in Góngora's *letrilla* 'Oh, montañas de Galicia' (1609: G.203) and in the sonnet 'Pálido sol en cielo encapotado', often attributed to him (?1609: G.439).

interrogation of suspects (Eslava 1991: 175). Time and again, in both prose and verse, Quevedo attacks taverns where wine is watered down or in other ways adulterated to maximize profit. Another of his *romances*, probably written a year or two before ours, 'Parióme adrede mi madre', includes the quatrain (Q.696: 73–76) 'Agua me falta en el mar, | y la hallo en las tabernas: | que mis contentos y el vino | son aguados dondequiera', and a similar thought emerges in the much later *romance* 'Llorando está Manzanares' (Q.770: 9–12): 'Más agua trae en un jarro | cualquier cuartillo de vino | de la taberna, que lleva | con todo su argamandijo'.[7] The conviction that innkeepers were crooks was neither new nor a product of Quevedo's fertile imagination; a hundred years earlier the 1520 *Dança general de la Muerte* had Death dismiss the Innkeeper's plea of innocence with: 'Traidor, lisonjero, falso, mezquino | e robador de bienes agenos, | tú que tornaste del agua vino | hinchendo los cueros de vazíos llenos' (Infantes 1982: 195), and a contemporary of Quevedo paints a not dissimilar picture: 'El tabernero hurta de cien mil maneras, mezclando y confundiendo un vino con otro a más de la agua que le pone. Y quando su vino, de tan mezclado y bautizado, no tiene fuerça, cuelga dentro en el tonel un salchichote lleno de clavo, pimienta, gengibre y otras drogas, con que le haze parecer bueno' (García 1977: 145; see also Deleito 1942: 155).[8] There is a third sense for *mojada*, 'fight, scrap', and the implication would seem to be that, in an earlier, more boisterous phase of this bender, when the three *gallegos* were still capable of coherent participation, they—like Maroto whom we see by turns boastful, maudlin, and crapulous—have been arguing and shouting at or across each other (or, if you like, 'singing under wine/water torture').

[7] Quevedo harps on about the same issue in 'Yo, que nunca sé callar' (Q.651: 16–19), 'Desde esta Sierra Morena' (Q.711: 97–100), 'Hagamos cuenta con pago' (Q.753: 55–56) and an *entremés, La venta*, full of unflattering observations on the tavern trade (García Valdés 2005: 70; see below p. 142), while short measures and poor cellarage are his targets in 'Muchos dicen mal de mí' (Q.775: 35–38). His *Cosas más corrientes de Madrid, y que más se usan, por alfabeto* has an entry which reads 'vinos con aguas, como chamelotes' (Quevedo 1876–77: I.475). Identical concerns had surfaced in the *Sueño del juicio final*, a work circulating in manuscript as early as 1605 (Quevedo 1972: 83): 'En esto dieron con muchos taberneros en el puesto, y fueron acusados de que habían muerto mucha cantidad de sed a traición, vendiendo agua por vino... todos fueron despachados como siempre se esperaba.' The poet employs the verb *mojar* in connection with drinking in the sonnet 'De los misterios a los brindis llevas', on the writing on the wall at Belshazzar's feast after the king, as described in the Chapter V of the Book of Daniel, has drunk out of the golden vessels taken from the Temple by his father Nebuchadnezzar: 'después de haber, sacrílego, bebido | toda la edad a Baco en urna santa, | mojado el seso y húmedo el sentido' (Q.128: 9–11).

[8] Strenuous efforts were made by the Alcaldes de Casa y Corte to monitor the quality and check the provenance of wines sold in the city. In 1588, for example, it became illegal for an inn to have water anywhere on the premises. The huge influx of population in the early years of the seventeenth century and the need to import wine from an ever larger area made controls increasingly difficult to devise and enforce (Alvar 1989: 163–65; Ringrose 1983: 156–57); there is a small selection of seventeenth-century lyrics attesting to the futility of their efforts in Díaz (1992: 38–39).

The pun on *hierro*, 'iron, rust', and *yerro*, 'error, slip, sin' confirms the idea of slurred diction, as does the [rr] sound; it is a wordplay Quevedo employs elsewhere (e.g. Q.630, 'Este que, cecijunto y barbinegro': 21, 24; Q.735, 'Tres mulas de tres doctores': 22, 24; Q.759, 'Los médicos han de errar': 5–8, the last of these also fooling around with the mispronunciation of [rr] by foreigners). For an example of Góngora doing the same see above, p. 30. Meanwhile, the drinkers' lips are stained with the sediment (and much else) that comes from cheap red wine.

Yesca, defined by *Aut.* as tinder or kindling normally made of charred linen, dried fungus, or (most appropriately in this context) sponge, is also there described as a term used (compare English *tinder-box*) for anything 'que está sumamente seco, y por el consiguiente dispuesto a encenderse, o abrasarse', a further entry reading: 'en estilo familiar y festivo se dice privativamente de qualquier cosa, que excita la gana de beber, y con singularidad de beber vino' (see also Jauralde 1974: 77). A similar notion informs the early strophes of another Quevedo poem on drunks, the *baile* Q.873, in which the opening line has Bacchus's 'gentilhombres de boca' 'Echando chispas de vino'. Two of the drinkers, Pierres and Roque have names that mean, *inter alia*, 'stone, rock, flint' (*Pierres* was also a common name for a drunkard: Quevedo 1998b: 457n.). *Yesca* was used in street slang, *germanía*, to identify a likely candidate for a life-sentence in the galleys.

Gaznate, 'gizzard, craw', is a word normally reserved for animals and birds, often in contexts related to slaughter. Quevedo was given to caricature and fond of the cartoonist's standby of portraying men as animals (Smith 1991: 70); he not infrequently uses *gaznate* for the human gullet (as he does in his pen-portrait of Licenciado Cabra in the *Buscón* I.III: Quevedo 1990: 90), sometimes, as here, doing so in the context of wine drinking, as witness the sonnets 'Tudescos moscos de los sorbos finos' (Q.531: 9–11: 'liendres de la vendimia, yo os admito | en mi gaznate, pues tenéis por soga | al nieto de la vid, licor bendito'), and the first strophe of Q.581: 'Con la sombra del jarro y de las nueces, | la sed bien inclinada se alborota; | todo gaznate esté con mal de gota, | hasta dejar las cubas en las heces'). More significant, perhaps, is the entry in *Cov.* referring to the barking of dogs or croaking of birds (and hence to the fatal cawing of the Crow in the traditional tale): '*Gaznate*: la caña del cuello que está asida al pulmón, por la cual respiramos y echamos la voz; y la que se forma en él (como las sílabas, que empiezan en letras guturales) hace el sonido de *cah*, *gah*, *xah*, y por eso se dijo *gahnate*, y corruptamente *gaznate*. Del sonido desta pronunciación se dijo gañir el perro y graznar el ánsar, *interposita littera r*, y graznido ni más ni menos.'

Quevedo, when in this mode, seldom if ever resorts to tame repetitions of the same word; all is done with malice aforethought. One sense of *tener*, listed in *Aut.* and still in use today, is 'juzgar, reputar, y entender'. Lines 7–8 also read, then, as *tienen los gaznates secos por ser hechos de yesca*, 'they reckon their parched gullets are on fire (and so they carry on drinking)'. A similar sense of *tienen* may apply to 6.

> **Pierres, sentado en arpón,**
> **el vino estaba meciendo,**
> **que en un sudor remostado**
> 12 **se cierne por el cabello.**

Pierres, squatting cross-legged (?), was nursing his wine, which emerges as crusty sweat through his hair.

A recent edition of this poem observes of *sentado en arpón*: 'No vemos la imagen del todo nítida' (Quevedo 1998b: 457n.). An etching by the Flemish engraver Jan Saenredam after Hendrik Goltzius, touted by some (e.g. Harris 1982: 74) as a possible model for Velázquez's *Triunfo de Baco* and commonly known to the English-speaking public as *The worship of Bacchus,* depicts three drinkers imploring the wine god to relieve their pains and worries. The foremost of the three is shown squatting with his right leg tucked underneath him, his two legs forming a triangular shape one might describe as an *arpón*, 'harpoon, arrow, anchor'; Velázquez's Bacchus, more conventionally, sits atop a wine-cask with his legs crossed (Orso 1993: 1, 110). The phrase *en arpón* also appears, linked with *sentarse/sentado*, in the *entremés* entitled *La venta*: 'Sentáronse en arpón en un banquillo' (García Valdés 2005: 74; see above, p. 140); included in the 1635 *Segunda parte de las comedias de Tirso de Molina*, it is almost certainly by Quevedo. Towards the end of our poem (134), Pierres is described as having *mareta en el asiento,* which may make a reader suppose that the reference here to *arpón* is perhaps to a three-legged bar-stool, but *asiento* there probably means 'backside, seat', as it does in 'El alguacil endomoniado' (1606?: Quevedo 2003: I. 267).

A feature of verse in Quevedo's day is deliberate confusion between the subjects and objects of verbs. Here, Pierres may be *meciendo* his wine, mulling lovingly between his hands the *cuero* from which he is drinking, but the wine may also be warming/befuddling him ('menear una cosa, revolviéndola, como mecer las cubas; del verbo latino *misceo, es,* por mezclar', *Cov.*); when, later, he is shown swaying drunkenly from side to side (134), the rocking movement picks up on *meciendo* ('mecer o menear los [niños] de una parte a otra para adormirlos', *Cov., s.v. combleza*).

Quevedo now introduces an idea that will become a leitmotif of the poem: the various ways in which the cheap wine seeks to leave the bodies of the drinkers (see below, 25, 143–44). There may also be an allusion in 11–12 to the tradition that Bacchus garlands his champions, in this case not with the traditional crown of vine-leaves we see depicted by Velázquez and others, but with *un sudor remostado* reminiscent of the dandruff of another Quevedo drinking poem, 'Tudescos moscos de los sorbos finos' (Q.531), *mosto,* 'must', being grape juice added to wine before or during the fermentation period, and *sudor* regularly referring to the agonies associated with syphilis (see Q.694, 'Tomando estaba sudores'). Quevedo uses the same adjective to imply the slurred speech of drunkards, *la habla remostada*, in 'Sueño de la muerte' (1972: 235).

> **Hecho verga de ballesta,**
> **retortijado el pescuezo,**
> **Jaques, medio desmayado,**
> 16 **a vómito estaba puesto.**

Jacques, half fainting and with his neck twisted and strained into the shape of a cross-bow stock, was puking his guts up.

The delay of two lines before naming the person who (or whose *pescuezo*) is *hecho verga de ballesta* leaves the listener with a moment or two during which the most likely reading of 13 seems to involve *echo verga*, both 'I fuck' and 'I boast of my manhood', and *verga de ballesta*, 'prick like a crossbow stock'. *Jaque(s)/ Xaque(s)* was a term and nickname in *germanía* for 'pimp', and *medio desmayado* hints at *medio desmallado*, both 'semi-flaccid' and 'stabbed half to death'. Picking up on the notion that the drinkers are deformed by wine, a fancy introduced with *arpón* in 9, Jaques is now shown twisting his head to one side and straining. Thus Quevedo builds a multiple image of a person straining while vomiting or attempting to tauten the string of a crossbow by inching it up the stock, of the bow itself bending under tension, and of a semi-erect penis. Victims of the water torture (or *toca*), widely used in interrogation, strove in vain, firmly anchored as they were, to void the contents of a gut agonizingly distended with enforced liquid intake; they often passed out (*medio desmayado*) under such treatment. Near-asphyxiation also triggers other reflexes.

In common with *gaznate*, 'gizzard', in 8, and the coarse *verga*, 'prick', in 13, *pescuezo*, 'neck', is a word more commonly associated with animals than men, though all three crop up on occasion in gallows humour (e.g. Q.572: 'Pues que vuela la edad, ande la loza', 9–11), Quevedo being given, as we have seen, to making unflattering comparisons between men and beasts, as in his *romance* 'Yo, el único caballero' (Q.707) and his burlesque description of the sleeping Cid in the opening strophes of another *romance*, 'Medio día era por filo' (Q.764), both of which include a reference to a human *pescuezo*. He employs the same association of a *retortijón* with vomiting in another *romance*, 'Los médicos han de errar' (Q.759: 129–32).

> **Roque, los puños cerrados,**
> **más entero y más atento,**
> **suspirando saca el aire,**
> 20 **por no avinagrar el cuero.**

Meawhile Roque, his fists bunched tight, more alert and more together, is sighing/belching as a way of getting the air out of himself so as not to let the wine turn to vinegar.

Puños cerrados, '(with) bunched fists', picturing Roque's struggle to stay awake and not to vomit, may also refer to sleeves buttoned or tied at the cuff; hence, presumably, *más entero* 'more together', while *más atento* 'more awake', plays with *más a tento* 'more aware of (more preoccupied with) the wine', *tento/tinto* being, then as now, a common term for red wine (compare English *tent*, 'red wine from Spain'). As *cerrados* would have been pronounced by most as **serraðo**[h], we also have a neat sylleptic contraposition: *serrado(s) mas entero*, 'cut but intact'.

As has often been remarked, both Quevedo and Góngora were much given to visual conceits. The sense that visualization enhanced memory (Yates 1966) and the fashion in the early seventeenth century for visual description in poetry and for paintings that had to be read and decoded is reflected in the craze for emblem-books (see above p. 102) and succinctly summarized by the Madrid poet Gabriel Bocángel in a sonnet dedicated to the poet-painter Juan de Jáuregui, where he states that the latter's brush describes, while his pen paints: 'pues describe el pincel, pinta la pluma' (Bocángel 1985: 369, discussed in Schwartz 2002). Here, the notion of wine being transferred from leather wineskins to the walking wineskins that are the four drinkers, together with the ancillary fancy that Roque is belching deliberately to safeguard the wine in his belly, are suggested by the link *cuero*, 'hide, leather, wineskin', a word used of men and women in phrases such as *en cueros*, 'without a stitch of clothing' (compare Q.621, 'Oye la voz de un hombre que te canta', 18: 'que el vino y el amor andan en cueros'), and one of many words in *germanía* for 'a drunk' (Jauralde 1974: 76). Quevedo plays elsewhere with the image of man as wineskin: Q.594, 'Casóse la Linterna y el Tintero', in which (4) 'la boda fue entre carne y cuero', as the bride is a strumpet and the groom a sot (Arellano 1984: 486); Q.634, 'Este que veis hinchado como cuero', depicting an innkeeper; Q.773, 'Tardóse en parirme': 81–88, where the speaker contemplates the futility of amassing a fortune through abstinence only to have his son and heir fritter it away in the tavern ('que lo que yo anduve | ahorrando en cueros, | glotón y borracho, | él lo gaste en ellos'); and the *romance* 'Mirábanse de mal ojo' (Q.763: 361–68, where we again encounter Quevedo's obsession with adulteration): 'Andemos, como la borra, | en pelota, que es barato; | o repelemos la higuera, | que fue tienda del manzano; | o salgamos, como el vino | en cueros, ya que los charcos | no le consienten andar | *in puribus* en los jarros' (see also above p. 137). He will produce a memorable play on the phrase *quedar en cueros*, 'to be left stark naked', in *La hora de todos y la Fortuna con seso*, where a thief who has built himself an ostentatiously large house out of his ill-gotten gains, sees it disappear, stone by stone, on the Day of Judgement until 'el pícaro quedó desnudo de paredes y en cueros de edificio' (Quevedo 1987: 168, analysed by Pring-Mill 1968: 272–73).

Neither is the notion of releasing the air from one's gut to prevent the contents from turning to vinegar entirely new in Quevedo: he used it in the c.1603 lyric song 'Óyeme riguroso' (Q.622: 67–72): 'Con suspirar engañas | al amante que espera ser querido, | porque está persuadido | que, pues suspiras, penan tus entrañas, | siendo echar fuera el aire recogido, | porque no se avinagre lo bebido'. It is intriguing, however, to place alongside this strophe a short extract on the subject from the satirical pen of the poet and dramatist Juan de Zabaleta: 'Vinagre torcido llaman a un borracho, porque el vino que lleva en el estómago está hecho vinagre, y él lleva el cuerpo torcido, como le falta el gobierno de la razón' (Zabaleta 1983: 359, emphasis added). Quevedo will develop this notion of the behaviour of wine inside its new wineskins later in the poem, and a similar take on excess drinking is to be found in his mock-heroic poem on 'Orlando el Enamorado', 'Canto los disparates, las locuras' (Q.875: I. 361–68): 'Ferraguto, agarrando de una cuba | que tiene una vendimia en la barriga, | mirando a Galalón hecho una uva, | le hizo un brindis, dándole una higa: | "No tengas miedo —dijo— que se suba | a cabeza tan falsa y enemiga | el vino; que sin duda estará quedo, | por no mezclarse allá con tanto enredo".'

> **Maroto, buen español,**
> **hecho faja el ferreruelo,**
> **vueltos lágrimas los brindis**
> 24 **y bebido el ojo izquierdo,**

Maroto, a good Spaniard, has twisted his cape into a kerchief, all the toasts he has drunk having ended in tears, and his left eye now watering.

After the three *gabachos*, we now turn to the *gallego*. *Maroto*, although found as a surname and toponym in Mallorca and elsewhere (Nieto 2002), is not a Christian name, even in Galicia; hence the heavy irony of *buen español*. In one version of this poem (Biblioteca Nacional de España, MS 3985) his name is given as Marloto; just a hint, then, of *malroto*, 'decrepit'. A *ferreruelo*, or *herreruelo*, is a short cape, without hood or collar (illustration in Castillo Solórzano 1985: 91), the archaic initial <f-> presumably being preferred because of the resulting alliteration with *faja*, rather than as some kind of linguistic archaism (there is little such archaism in this poem, even in 35–48 which conjure up the world of medieval heroic literature—but see 'De un molimiento de güesos', above, pp. 83 and 88). At least two of the senses of *faja* listed in *Cov.* may apply here: 'los antiguos usaban, en lugar de calzas, unas fajas que se rodeaban a las piernas, desde el tobillo hasta la rodilla…; hoy día usan dellas algunos labradores, gente del campo y pastores, y algunos pobres; a veces las han menester traer también los ricos, disimuladas debajo de las medias de seda, por la poca firmeza de las piernas', and (*s.v. faisa*) 'este nombre se extiende a sinificar la guarnición de tiras que se echan en las ropas, y ciertos levantales de las labradoras con que algunas veces se cubren y usan dellos como mantellinas, y otras traen sobre las sayas'. Both meanings, then, suggest that the *faja* is an indicator of poverty.

Lines 23–24 return to the notions of watered wine, with the pun on three meanings of *bebido*, 'watery, drunk, lazy (of an eye)', a reference to another of the ways (*lágrimas*) by which the wine emerges from its new, human wineskin, and the perennial, short-lived regrets of a drinker on the verge of crapulousness.

> **con palabras rocïadas**
> **y con el tono algo crespo,**
> **después que toda la calle**
> 28   **sahumó con un regüeldo,**
>
> **dijo, mirando a los tres**
> **con vinoso sentimiento:**
> **'¿En qué ha de parar el mundo?**
> 32   **¿Qué fin tendrán estos tiempos?**

After perfuming the length of the street with a belch and turning to the other three with that sentimental look in his eye that is born of wine, he lets fly somewhat querulously in dew-spattered words: 'What is the world coming to? Where will it all end?'

The wine-water mix comes out also as spittle (*palabras rocïadas*) the minute Maroto opens his mouth to start ranting; Elizabethan English had a delightful term for this, *Bacchus' dew* (compare the 'habladores que llaman del río o del rocío' in 'Sueño de la muerte': Quevedo 1972: 193). *Crespo*, normally implying 'wavy', is now partnered with spittle rather than ocean waves; often used to describe a person's hair, 'curly, wavy', it can also be employed to denote a style or tone of voice either pompous or 'irritado, alterado y enemistado' (*Aut.*); compare Quevedo's pun on this last meaning together with that of 'wavy' in his well-known love sonnet (Q.449), which begins with the lines 'En crespa tempestad del oro undoso, | nada golfos de luz ardiente y pura | mi corazón'. It may be that Quevedo is here using *crespo* in the sense of Latin *crispus*, 'querulous, quavering', and that he recalled Juvenal's pen-portrait of another case of self-indulgence: that of a wife wallowing in the sweetness of her musical instruments: 'crispo numerantur pectine chordae' (VI. 382; Juvenal 2004: 270–71). Cervantes (1986: I.203; 2005: 71) also enjoyed playing ironically with the associations of *sahumar* ('dar humo a alguna cosa para purificarla, o para que huela', *Aut.*; 'Volver una cosa a su dueño sahumada, es volverla más bien tratada que él la dio', *Cov.*), though here it is presumably the wine in Maroto's sails that provides the bouquet (compare Quevedo 1972: 117). *Regüeldo*, 'belch', was also a slang term for 'boast'.

The 100-line rant that now follows includes many of the concerns that dominate Quevedo's satirical verse.

> **Lo que hoy es ración de un paje**
> **de un capitán era sueldo**

cuando eran los hombres más
36   y habían menester menos.

What they pay a pageboy these days was an army captain's wage in the
days when men were men and could manage on a shoestring.

The first of these is inflation. 'Most contemporary poets, playwrights, and
men of letters lived precariously on the borderline between survival and
starvation'.[9] As someone who depended on fixed rents from his estates at La
Torre de Juan Abad, in La Mancha (and even those were notoriously difficult to collect), Quevedo found the spiralling cost of living in the capital a
constant source of concern, especially after the cut in the interest payable on
juros (or bonds) and the State bankruptcy of January 1627. He ascribed it to
a number of factors, among them the demands of women, the rapacious
nature of social climbers, the surge in the minting of *moneda de vellón*
(copper coinage not worth its face value: 'money that lies', then, 'worthless
money'; see the sonnet 'Mal oficio es mentir, pero abrigado', Q.579), and,
as did many at the time, the greed of merchants supplying the Court.[10] His
letrilla 'Madre, yo al oro me humillo' (Q.660), of which versions exist from
before 1603 right through to the late 1630s, is just the best known of many
to disparage the role of money and lampoon the lure of wealth. The same
attitude surfaces in his prose writings. In 'Sueño de la muerte' (1622),
money emerges as the arch-enemy of the Christian: '—¿Quién es —dije
yo— aquel que está allí apartado haciéndose pedazos con estos tres, con
tantas caras y figuras? Ese es —dijo la Muerte— el Dinero, que tiene puesto
pleito a los tres enemigos del alma [i.e. the world, the flesh, and the Devil],
diciendo que quiere ahorrar de émulos, y que a donde él está no son menester, porque él solo es todos los tres enemigos', while *La cuna y la sepultura*
(1634) portrays money as the major impediment to anyone seeking to perfect his or her soul: '¿qué otra cosa es esso que desigual carga al que aun
desnudo camina cargado de sí proprio?' (Quevedo 1972: 19; 1969b: 42; see
Alarcos 1942: 10–11).

Eran los hombres más reads as both 'when there were more (real) men'
and 'when men were (more like real) men'. There is a lengthy and erudite
commentary on the uses of *ración*, 'parte que se da a cada uno de los
criados por cada día' (*Cov.*), in Crosby's commentary on 'Sueño del Infierno'

---

[9] Elliott (1986: 175; on inflation see 267–70, 298–99); also Jauralde (1988a: 504,
512, 524) and Quevedo (1998a: 80, 91–92).
[10] As early as May 1621, the Junta de Reformación was advising the king to encourage
nobles living in Madrid to return to their estates, not only to staunch the demographic
haemorrhage from countryside to capital but also because 'el estado y grandeza de la
Corte' obliged them to spend 'más de lo que sus rentas sufren, con que muchos an
descompuesto sus estados, y puéstolos en el empeño que los vemos'. The supposed
inflationary effects of 'la mala calidad de la moneda de vellón' were highlighted in a
letter of August 1627, this time from the Junta de Diputación General (González
Palencia 1932: 77–87, 536–39, docs XV and LXXXVI).

(Quevedo 1993: II. 1177). *Menos*, 'less', is also a *germanía* word for 'page-boy, servant'.

> **Cuatro mil maravedís**
> **que le dan a un escudero**
> **era dádiva de un rey**
> 40   **para rico casamiento.**
>
> **Apreciábase el ajuar**
> **que a Jimena Gómez dieron**
> **en menos que agora cuesta**
> 44   **remendar unos greguescos.**

These days a servant gets four thousand maravedís; that used to be a princely dowry for a society wedding. The trousseau they gave Jimena Gómez when she married cost what you have to pay these days to get a pair of breeches mended.

The reference here to the *maravedí*, a money of account equivalent to one thirty-fourth of a silver *real*, as well as the archaic references to a *dádiva de un rey* prepare the listener for the cod-medieval content of 41–42, with their allusion to the marriage of one 'Jimena Gómez', and for the consequent bathos of 43–44. These references reflect unfavourably on contemporary currency. Dádiva is used ironically elsewhere by Quevedo (2003: ii. 643: 'Miren qué gentil dádiva'; Q.682, 1–2: 'Anilla, dame atención, | que es dádiva que no empobra'; and Q.704 'Quitándose está Medoro', 25–28: 'A una mujer que se espanta | de ver una lagartija, | una dádiva de muerto | es una cosa muy linda'). The exact social status of an early seventeenth-century *escudero* is unclear, but, as a group, they were popularly supposed to be given to excessive wine drinking (as were *gallegos*: Quevedo 2003: I. 301, II. 657). The fact that the Cid, Ruy (Rodrigo) Díaz de Vivar, the conqueror of Valencia (d. 1099), also the subject of a mocking allusion in Q.853, 'Allá va en letra Lampuga', puts in an appearance in 45, leads the listener to conclude that the marriage invoked here is that of the hero of the epic *Poema de mio Cid* and Jimena Gómez, whom, with the encouragement of King Alfonso VI, he wed in 1074 or 1075 (this strophe is not present in any of the variant versions of the poem listed in Blecua). There is a traditional *romance* on the figure of Jimena Gómez, probably originating in an unknown version of *Las mocedades de Rodrigo* (Díaz Roig 1985: 136–37).

It may be that the use of the form *agora* is well suited to a context in which the Cid and his wife appear, but it is commonly preferred by Quevedo to *ahora* (as it is in 62, 109, and 115), even in works where no attempt is apparently afoot to conjure up some kind of archaic diction; here it probably functions, like *agüelos* (118), as an indication of the unrefined nature of the speaker. *Greguescos*, a word of which Quevedo was fond, possibly because of its sound (especially when he can add further [g] sounds, as here with *Gómez*), are 'leggings'; illustrations are provided of both these and *calzas enteras atacadas* (see 59, below) in a recent edition of *Don Quijote* (Cervantes 2005: II. 1002, 1005, 1007).

The reference to patching and mending (*remendar*) is a harbinger both of the literary world of ungenteel poverty that will emerge with the late introduction of drinkers' masters as *hidalgos hambrientos* (126) and hints slyly of the practice of repairing maidenheads (see pp. 166 and 207, below, and above, p. 127).

> Andaba entonces el Cid
> más galán que Gerineldos,
> con botarga colorada
> 48   en figura de pimiento:

In those days the Cid was able to go about better dressed than Gerineldos, in red breeches the same shape as a pepper.

Gerineldo(s), the protagonist of a traditional *romance* (Díaz Roig 1985: 257, adulterated through contact with another, known variously as *La Condesita* or *La boda estorbada*: Menéndez Pidal 1920), is a young pageboy (*paje, menos*, 33, 36) who enjoys the favours of a princess, only to be discovered asleep in her bed by her father. The direct reference here, though, is not to that ballad but to another from the *Cancionero de 1600* relating the marriage of the Cid and Doña Jimena ('A Jimena y a Rodrigo'), which has the lines: 'Más galán que Gerineldos | bajó el Cid famoso al patio' (Menéndez Pidal 1963: 127). *Andar galán* is a phrase used in *germanía* to describe the gait of those affected by syphilis; there may be an undercurrent of references of this kind in the poem (see the notes on *sudor*, 11, and *hocicos*, 135) and one should not forget that several slang terms for venereal disease derive from the lexicon of torture and punishment (Arellano 1997).

The quatrain we have here is quoted in *Aut.* as an illustration of the first of the five meanings there listed for *botarga*: 'Una parte del trage que se trahía antiguamente, que cubría el muslo y la pierna, y era ancha. Pudo decirse quasi Bota larga, por ser toda de una pieza, que empezaba en la cintura, y llegaba hasta el tobillo.' However, it is clear, from the outlandish colour of the costume and the references back to *greguescos* and to the shape of a pepper, that another, more absurd sense is in play. The *botarga* was part of the wardrobe of the player of minor dramatic entertainments, such as *mojigangas* and *entremeses* (for these see Rodríguez & Tordera 1983: 35–68), the name probably deriving from a Pantaleone costume worn in Spain by Estefanel(l)o Bot(t)arga, a one-time partner of Ganassa who seems to have had his own *commedia dell'arte* company of Spanish actors in the 1580s (from this comes the modern meaning of *botarga*, '(red) clown costume'). Lope de Vega appeared dressed in a Botarga costume at the 1599 Valencia celebrations to mark the wedding of Philip III (Shergold 1967:

187–88, 244–45), and, in one of his *entremeses*, Quevedo dresses the male lead in one.[11]

> **y hoy, si alguno ha de vestirse,**
> **le desnudan dos primero:**
> **el mercader de quien compra**
> 52   **y el sastre que ha de coserlo.**

But when you have to buy clothes these days they have the shirt off your back twice over, once when you buy the material and then again when you pay the tailor.

The second of Quevedo's satirical targets, linked here (as elsewhere) with the first and with a general sense that the world is out of kilter, or *al revés*, 'upside-down' (see Q.642, 'Sin ser juez de la pelota': 30; Q.668, 'Que no tenga por molesto': 24; and above p. 128), now takes centre stage. Many writers in the early years of the seventeenth century comment adversely on the craze for swiftly changing trends in male attire (Jauralde 1998b: 65). Here, the insistence on parading in the latest fashion, seen in turn as responsible for undermining the masculinity of courtiers, leaving them uncertain of their proper roles as husbands and lovers, and bankrupting them in the process, is one such symptom of a world out of sync. *Sastre* and *mercader* were both slang terms for 'thief', and *coser* for 'fighting', the implication being, thanks to the ambivalence of *–lo* ('it'?, 'him'?) that the two will struggle with each other over who gets the lion's share of the money they have fleeced from the client, *–lo* referring both to the cloth purchased from the *mercader* that has to be 'sewn, worked into garments' and to the client who is to be 'stitched up' by his tailor. *Coserlo* also has the vulgar sense of 'fuck him (it?) up' (Delicado 1994: 97, 227n.). The conceit that the tailor, together with the perfidious and grasping cloth merchant ('los siempre condenados mercaderes', line 52 of '¿Por qué mi musa descompuesta y bronca', Q.639), will have the shirt off your back is a traditional one, and the *sastre* prominent among the blackguards paraded, to Quevedo's evident glee, in 'Sueño del Juicio Final' where 'una legión de demonios con azotes, palos y otros instrumentos… traían a la audiencia una

---

[11] García Valdés 2005: 123. For references to *botargas*, see: the costume changes in 'Dígote pretendiente y cortesano' (Q.564; Arellano 1984: 445–46); the burlesque description of Alexander the Great's visit to the philosopher Diogenes 'En el retrete del mosto' (Q.745: 105–06: 'El vestido era un enjerto | de cachondas y botargas'); a further *romance* where, as here, he is lamenting the passing of past glories, 'Lindo gusto tiene el Tiempo' (Q.757: 121–24: 'Las galas de los antiguos | ha convertido en botargas, | y las marimantas viejas | las ha introducido en galas'); and the pre-1621 *romance* 'Don Repollo y doña Berza', where, among a guest-list of fruit and vegetables, we find 'el señor don Pimiento, | vestidito de botarga' (Q.683: 85–89). *Pimiento* adds a further touch of ridicule (compare *no valer un pimiento*, 'to be worthless'). On outlandish theatrical costumes, see Calderón (1982: 44–45).

muchedumbre de taberneros, sastres, libreros y zapateros' (1993: II. 1160–62, 1425–26).[12] Some of the same cast are mocked mercilessly in Q.677, 'Contando estaba las cañas': 29–32 and Q.849, 'Ya está guardado en la trena': 17–20 (*sastres*), and Q.750, 'Debe de haber ocho días': 197–200 (*sastre* and *zapatero*).

> Ya no gastan los vestidos
> las personas con traerlos :
> que el inventor de otro traje
> 56   hace lo flamante viejo.

Clothes no longer wear out because you wear them; the arrival of a new fashion means that the old one is passé.

Traerlos involves a pun following *gastan*: between 'wearing clothes' and 'wearing them out'. The presence of a simple game around *inventor de traje*, 'fashion designer', *otro traje*, 'another style of clothing, a fresh set of clothes', and the phrase *de otro traje*, 'of another stamp, in another way', does not prevent Quevedo from essaying further word games. As was the case with 45–48 above, *Aut.* cites 55–56 by way of illustration of the second of the three definitions it gives for *inventor*, thus picking up on Quevedo's twin accusation that old goods are being sold as new and that men feel pressured into acquiring the latest fashion and ditching clothing that is still serviceable: 'Se llama también el que introduce de nuevo algún uso, costumbre o moda en qualquier materia'. The word, however, also carries within it the twin notions of *venta*, 'sale', and—especially appropriate in the case of fashionably slashed designs (see 61)—of 'vents to allow air/wind', to penetrate the cloth.

Aut. also cites the whole strophe as an example of the use of *flamante* (normally *resplandeciente*, 'colourful') to denote 'lo que está nuevo, que no se ha ajado ni deslucido' (a meaning of the word Quevedo also employs in the opening strophe of *romance* Q.721: 'Ansí a solas industriaba, | como un Tácito Cornelio, | a un maridillo flamante | un maridísimo viejo').

> Sin duda inventó las calzas
> algún diablo del infierno,
> pues un cristiano atacado
> 60   ya no queda de provecho.

Some devil in Hell must have designed the leggings [they sell these days], because there isn't a single normal man left wearing anything half-way decent.

---

[12] The idea that *sastres* were untrustworthy and mendacious can be found in, among others: the 1520 *La dança de la Muerte*, lines 793–800 (Infantes 1982: 193) ; Part II of the *Segunda parte del Lazarillo* (Luna 1988: 299); and *El licenciado Vidriera* (Cervantes 1986: II. 65).

Atacado, 'buttoned, tied' (of leggings, normally to the jerkin), was also a
term for the victim of a hired murderer or hit-man (hence *ya no queda*).
Quevedo frequently refers deprecatingly to the affectation of the day for
attaching leggings to the upper garment with multiple ties (2003: I. 298; see
above p. 149); the failure to do so, however, would leave a gaping hole (the
pun with *inventor* is repeated here with *inventó*, 'designed/ made holes in').
There may also be here an allusion to the sense of *calzarse a alguno* (used
elsewhere by Quevedo; see Crosby 2005: 106) as 'to stitch someone up',
defined in *Aut.* as 'levantarse con la voluntad de alguno enteramente y
conseguir alguna cosa que se deseaba'.

He now, via the more common meanings of *atacar*, 'to attack' (and, in
germanía, 'to stab to death'), introduces the lexicon of warfare, and proceeds
to sprinkle the following strophes with words and phrases associated with
those activities, alluding in passing to the lost world of the *romances viejos*,
and openly introducing the topos of *el mundo al revés*. Yet, as before with
the language of criminality, he employs these terms not with their common,
military meanings but in other senses: *cristiano* (59) 'a normal man, a decent
man', *de provecho* (60) 'at an advantage, in a state of grace', *cuchillada*
(61) 'a fashionable slit or slash in costume', *caballero* (62) 'gentleman,
courtier', *pendencia* (63) 'bagginess, sagginess' (and perhaps something
more, see comments on the following strophe), *paz* (64) 'peace of mind',
and, a little further on, *soldados* (67), *acero* (70), *armas* (71), *petos* (72),
barbacana (77) and *castillos* (78).

Quevedo elsewhere uses the phrase *de provecho* in the sense of 'useful,
ideally suited to a purpose', as in the poem we saw earlier depicting an
innkeeper: 'y no le fue el dinero de provecho' (Q.634: 22) and also in a
burlesque *romance* 'Ya que descansan las uñas' (Q.780: 147–48) where
provecho is paired with its opposite, *daño*: 'eres daño provechoso, | eres
dañoso provecho'. Here it is possibly an allusion to an Old Christian
(compare *cristiano provecto* in *La culta latiniparla*: Quevedo 2003: I. 115),
reminding us of the proverb *Honra y provecho no caben en un saco*. The
last line thus offers: *cristiano ya no, que da de provecho*, 'now longer an
honourable man, since, with his leggings sagging down, he offers himself
for free'.

> **¡Qué es ver tantas cuchilladas**
> **agora en un caballero;**
> **tanta pendencia en las calzas,**
> 64 **y tanta paz en el dueño!**

*What you see these days are 'gentlemen' blithely going about with slits in
their clothing unconcerned that their leggings sag down round their ankles.*

For several years before the early spring of 1623 when Olivares drew up the
Capítulos de reformación para el gobierno del reino, or Articles of Refor-

mation, the Madrid authorities had been exercised by fashions in dress that they saw as excessive and excessively expensive. They did so in terms which closely reflect the stance taken by Quevedo's *buen español* in this poem. In the seventh of the *Discursos* in his *Restauración política de España* (1619), entitled *Censura de las causas a que se carga el daño general de España*, the *arbitrista* and Toledo biblical scholar Sancho de Moncada informed Philip III that his courtiers were spending more on clothes than they could possibly afford: 'Gran lástima es de ver que hay pocos que no tengan todas sus haciendas encima de sí en un vestido' (1974: 195), and the Junta de Reformación, writing to the new king in June 1621, issued its own warning on the subject, suggesting that its effects were of concern on a number of counts: 'La reformación y moderación en los trajes y vestidos es muy neçessaria en estos Reynos, por hauer llegado lo que a esto toca a tan grande exçeso que haze mucho daño en ellos, assí en los gastos como en criarse los hombres en demasiado regalo, y por esto ser menos útiles en la guerra que lo que esta nación Hespañola solía ser, y las mugeres, tan costosas e intolerables en sus galas, exçediendo tanto a lo que el estado de cada una pide y puede, y hazen vivir a sus maridos con neçesidad y aun a muchos a no se atrever a casarse' (González Palencia 1932: 97–98, doc. XIX). Prominent among the measures eventually taken were new sumptuary laws, which came into immediate effect and were designed to prune these excesses. In his 'No he de callar, por más que con el dedo' (Q.146), addressed to Olivares himself, Quevedo celebrated this austerity drive and, in a sonnet probably written soon after the publication of the Articles, he hailed the proscription of outer garments deliberately slashed to display rich undergarments of another colour and/or material: 'No quieres ver en calzas de españoles | cuchilladas, por verlas con la sola' (Q.607, 'Rey que desencarcelas los gaznates': 12–13, 'la sola' here presumably referring to a single *cuchillada*, i.e. a sword-stroke, thus linking fashion, as in the following few strophes of the poem we are examining here, with effeminacy and the loss of proper soldierly virtue; see above, p. 117, also Arellano 1984: 504). The new norms may have been effective in the short term—and what is arguably Velázquez's first portrait of Philip IV, executed in August 1623, shows the king wearing what Quevedo called a *golilla perdurable* (1998a: 116), or simple collar, and not the elaborate starched ruff previously in vogue—but they do not seem to have exercised a lasting influence on Court behaviour, possibly because austerity was gleefully abandoned for the surprise visit in March 1623 of the wife-prospecting future King Charles I of England, then Prince of Wales.[13].

In Quevedo's works, *caballeros* are often anything but (e.g. 2003: I. 239, 362, 450), and the 'gentleman' in 62 compares unfavourably with the *caba-*

---

[13] See Elliott 1986 : 146–47, 173. For an example of the starched ruff, see El Greco's *Retrato de un caballero desconocido* (1603–07), in the Museo del Prado.

lleros, or knights of old, whose military prowess and sense of honour would have ensured that no such *cuchilladas* were seen on them, but only their *cuchilladas*, 'sword-cuts', on their enemies. The display of *cuchilladas* is also associated by Quevedo, as is the phrase *cabos de cuchillo*, with the status of 'being a public cuckold' (see the speech of Diego Moreno, *prototipo de cornudos*, at the close of 'Sueño de la muerte': 1993: II. 1523–24).

Pendencia, 'quarrel, scuffle, brawl' (and it is in this sense that Quevedo employs it in Q.641, 'Que pretenda dos años ser cornudo': 219), is also a slang term for 'pimp' (*Aut.*). Here it is also used to mean 'sagging': an indication that the fashion for not tying one's leggings securely to an upper garment led to the former's slipping down and becoming crumpled. But this is not the only example in which, given the increasingly sexual tone of what follows, a salacious further meaning may be involved: compare Q.763, 'Mirábanse de mal ojo': 247: 'rica pendencia de muslos' and the note in Alzieu *et al.* (1975: 113) on 12–24 of 'Dale si le das | mozuela de Carasa' (described by Asenjo as an 'obscena canción populachera y tabernaria': 1890: 211): 'Otra mozuela de buen rejo | mostrado me ha su pende | con qu'ella pendaba'.[14]

> **Todo se ha trocado ya;**
> **todo al revés está vuelto;**
> **las mujeres son soldados,**
> 68   **y los hombres son doncellos.**

Everything has changed; the world has gone mad; women are on the warpath and men have become pansies.

We have been building towards the third Quevedo literary obsession for some lines now. One of the lengthiest studies in English of Quevedo concludes that 'if there were any term that could encompass the entire tenor of his satirical and burlesque works... it would be *el mundo al revés*' (Iffland 1978–82: I.69), and Quevedo himself was to make hay with the idea in the mid-1630s in *La hora de todos y la Fortuna con seso*.[15] He was not alone in voicing such sentiments. The medieval topos of the world 'upside-down' enjoyed a revival at the turn of the seventeenth century (Curtius 1953: 94–98; Maravall 1986: 152ff.; Grant 1973); one has only to recall the famous *letrilla* of a few years earlier, sometimes attributed to Góngora, satirizing the live-now-pay-later culture of the Spanish capital: 'Todo el mundo está

---

[14] The sexual innuendo to much of Maroto's rant recalls Julián de San Valero's description of the Court of Philip IV as a place which 'sólo con Sodoma podría compararse' (Deleito 2005: 9).

[15] Among epigraphs chosen for a modern edition of the *Sueños* (Quevedo 1993: I. vii) are the four snippets : 'Al revés lo haces...', 'Todo lo entendéis al revés...', 'Todo lo hacen al revés...', and 'Al fin, es gente hecha al revés...'. The only essay known to me that involves detailed analysis of at least part of our poem (Vaíllo 1982) takes as its subject *el mundo al revés*.

trocado, | sólo reina el recibir, | ya nos venden el vivir, | y vivimos de prestado' (Góngora 1980: 277, no. CI). There is the odd ballad in the *Romancero general* that portrays a world whose values have been turned upside-down (e.g. 'Cantemos, señora Musa', González Palencia 1947: I. 226). Quevedo here is more specific, with his suggestion that a supposed recent breakdown of traditional gender roles has empowered women to run circles round men and left men themselves bewildered and sexually ambivalent—a commonplace in the *entremeses* of the period (Asensio 1965), as illustrated by the extraordinary career of 'Juan Rana', the stage name of the gay actor Cosme Pérez, whose notorious offstage behaviour only served to fuel his rise to stardom (Thompson 2006). *Trocado*, 'changed (in particular of dress)', is a slang term for 'puked (up)'; *revés* a sword-thurst from left to right and the wound resulting from it (and Quevedo puns with this and its mirror-image, the *tajo*, in 'Parióme adrede mi madre', Q.696: 36; below, p. 191); and both are also technical expressions from the world of card games, as is *soldados* (Chamorro 2005).[16]

Soldados, 'soldered together', also contrasts playfully with *cuchilladas* and *pendencia* (compare the Prologue to *Sueños y discursos*: 'más desgarrado y rompido que soldado', Quevedo 1972: 69). *Doncello*, calqued upon *doncella,* 'maiden', may be a neologism of Quevedo's own coinage. Most speakers in early seventeenth-century Madrid would have pronounced this as **doŋş'eλo/δoŋş'eλo**, as would all the Andalusians who had flocked to the capital, making this a further allusion to pimping and male complaisance: *don Sello*, 'Sir I Consent' and/or 'Sir Mum's the Word' (*Aut: sellar*: 'obligar a alguno con beneficios, para que de agradecido le siga siempre en lo que se le ofrezca, como si le hiciera su esclavo'; *sellar los labios*: 'callar, enmudecer, o suspender sus palabras'). This is not the only outing Quevedo gives his *don Sello*: the sonnet 'Cornudo eres, Fulano, hasta los codos' (Q.590), has tercets which read 'Taba es tu hacienda; pan y carne sacas | del hueso que te sirve de cabello; | marido en nombre, y en acción difunto, | mas con palma o cabestra de las vacas: | que al otro mundo te hacen ir doncello | los que no dejan tu mujer un punto' (*marido* implying 'sexually active', as it did in the 'Sueño de la muerte' of 1622: '¿Pensáis que todos los casados son maridos? Pues mentís, que hay muchos casados solteros y muchos solteros maridos. Y hay hombre que se casa para morir doncel y doncella que se casa para morir virgen de su marido', Quevedo 1972: 219), while, in an *entremés*, *El Marión*, he has Don Costanzo refer to a friend who allows himself to be seduced by 'una mujer en pretendelle loca' as a *doncello* (Quevedo 1961: II. 555).

---

[16] 'Reversal' also figured among the *hampa*, or underbelly of society, which practised a 'dog-Latin' or backward slang, not unlike that once current among street traders in London (e.g. *dlo woc*, 'old cow'). The precise word formation varied: as witness, for example, *greno* for *negro*, itself slang for 'skilled' (see above p. 122, and compare English *wicked*, 'good').

Los mozos traen cadenitas;
las niñas toman acero:
que de las antiguas armas
72   **sólo conservan los petos.**

Young lads sport little chains while women have taken up arms; all that's left
of the arms of yesteryear are the breastplates.

This strophe, right at the heart of our ballad, is the most densely packed of
all. The immediate link between *mozos*, 'hooks', and *cadenitas*, 'chains', is
obvious enough: both belong to the lexicon of entrapment. Chains were worn
by women as a display of wealth and status, as Quevedo himself recognizes
when he gets the lady in one of his *letrillas* to respond to a *galán*'s offer of
undying love with 'Dinero fuera mejor' and 'Mejor será una cadena'.[17] Men
also wore them on formal occasions, often as a outward sign of the esteem
in which they were held by their lords and masters, as witness many a
painting of the period.[18] But those are *cadenas*, 'gold, wealth, status', not
cadenitas, 'bling'. Despite the Articles of 1623, it was fashionable for the
dandies and male prostitutes of Madrid to affect bracelets and necklaces
(and the diminutive here continues the undertone of sexual ambivalence, as
does the notion that they no longer seek to *dar el acero*, 'fuck', even though
women still *toman el acero*). Yet *caden(it)as* has more than one meaning,
and men are everywhere in chains principally because they are henpecked.
They have failed to behave like real men and to profess arms (have *armas*,
'erections'), substituting sumptuary *cuchilladas* for real ones, military and
sexual, and, abandoning their proper calling as *soldados* and husbands, have
allowed their womenfolk—or *niñas*, 'young girls, harlots', at least—to
behave 'unnaturally', wearing the trousers and taking up the sword for
themselves.[19] The 1610s and early 1620s had seen a number of *arbitristas*,
or political theorists, making similar assertions of widespread effeminacy
and its consequences.[20] Yet a further sense of *cadenita*, in a poem that plays
with hair and hairlessness (*cabello*, 4, 94; *lampiños*, 75; *barba/barbero*, 73,
76, 77), is the fashionable lovelock, popular with European youth but a
target of moralists across Europe, that had originated at the French Court in
the mid-1620s, where it was known (after Honoré d'Albert, seigneur de
Cadenet) as a *cadenette* (Schama 1999: 8–9).

---

[17] 'Si queréis alma, Leonor' (Q.664: 20, 22); also 'Helas, helas por do vienen'
(Q.866: 133–38): 'La universal es el dar; | cuarto círculo, cadena; | atajo, todo dinero; |
rodea, toda promesa. | *Cuchilladas no son buenas;* | *puntas, sí, de las joyeras'*.
[18] See, for example, Pantoja de la Cruz's portrait (1600–10) of the Duke of Lerma,
reprod. in Brown (1998: 85), and Velázquez's of Olivares (1624) in Carr *et al.* (2006: 165).
[19] *Arma*, 'erection', features in several pieces in *Cancionero de burlas* (Jauralde 1974).
[20] For example, Sancho de Moncada, *Restauración política de España* (1619),
Cristóbal Suárez de Figueroa, *Varias noticias importantes de la humana condición*
(1621), and Pellicer de Tovar, *Avisos* (1639–44). For an analysis of further critiques of
the state of Spanish society before the 1620s see Truman (1999).

Yet male-female role reversal and the odd, barbed sexual allusion are not the only wordgames in play with *las niñas toman acero* (70). Time and again, Quevedo complains in his satirical writings of the rapaciousness of women and the crippling cost of liaisons.[21] *Acero* also reads as *a cero*, suggesting that women take, but give nothing in return for the outlay they demand of their *galanes*. The second double-entendre, found also in both the *estribillo* of Q.655, 'La morena que yo adoro', which runs 'en verano toma el acero | y en todos tiempos el oro', and in 'A la Corte vas, Perico' (Q.726: 57–58: 'Toman acero en verano, | que ningún metal desprecian'; see above p. 125), depends on yet another meaning of *acero* frequently returned to by Quevedo, and used by Lope de Vega in the title of his play *El acero de Madrid*, probably written 1607–09.[22] The ladies of Madrid went to great lengths to acquire and sustain a fashionable pallor. This they did, in the first instance, by avoiding exposure to the elements, especially in summer, but for those of a naturally dark complexion this alone did not always produce the desired effect. One popular way to ensure a fashionable pastiness was to add clay to the diet as an oppilant, a proceeding referred to by contemporaries as *comer búcaros* or *comer barro* (as witness the anonymous *canción* 'Niña del color quebrado, | o tienes amores o comes barro',[23] and Quevedo's own *madrigal* 'Tú sola, Cloris mía', Q.624). The chlorosis or iron-deficiency that resulted from this practice, and to which younger women were apparently particularly prone,[24] was then treated with a regime of long walks (allegedly adopted by some as a smokescreen for clandestine meetings with a *galán*) and with an iron-based specific known as *agua acerada*, or *acero*, the process alluded to here in 70 and also in *letrillas* by both Quevedo (Q.649, 'Pues amarga la verdad': 27–28: '¿Quién gasta su opilación | con oro y no con acero?') and (with a further pun involving the phrase *dar el/su acero*) Góngora: 'Opilóse vuestra hermana | y diola el doctor su acero' (G.122, *'Allá darás, rayo'*; Góngora 1980: 89, xv : 35–36). A further supposed property of *agua acerada* was to trigger amenorrhoea, thus (or so it was believed) acting as a

[21] Good examples are the two *romances* 'A la Corte vas, Perico' (Q.726, see pp. 115–33, above), and '¿Quién me compra, caballeros?' (Q.754). Quevedo often adds sexual innuendo to his complaints: e.g. 'Si el tiempo que contigo gasté lloro' (Q.626: 17–18, 23–24): 'Pues ¿qué ley manda, niña, o qué alcalde | que valgas tú dinero, y yo de balde?', '¡Cómo saben, mis ojos, que te olvidas | pues me diste en la bolsa las heridas!' (*bolsa* meaning both 'purse' and 'scrotum', and *ojo* both 'eye' and 'anus' as well as 'vagina') and 89–92, below.

[22] 'Quevedo was as wont to return repeatedly to particular phrases or comparisons as he was to favorite targets . . . and themes' (Iffland 1978–82: I.109).

[23] This poem, which first appears in the 1589 *Flor de varios romances nuevos y canciones* (Huesca: Juan Pérez de Valdivielso), fol. 50, is reproduced entire as part of a lengthy discussion of clay-induced iron-deficiency and its treatment in Stefano Arata's edition of Lope's *comedia* (Vega 2000: 30–35). A complexion *de color quebrado*, 'yellow', was widely supposed to be an indication that a person had fallen prey to love.

[24] Though, if Quevedo is to be believed, not only younger women: 'El otro día llevé yo una de setenta años que comía barro y hacía ejercicio para remediar las opilaciones' ('El alguacil endemoniado', in Quevedo 1972: 101).

contraceptive by suppressing menstruation (several literary references to this are listed in Plata Parga 1997: 182–86).

Quevedo had a fine personal collection of arms, much of it inherited from his father. Such collections were becoming increasingly rare. The disappearance of these *antiguas armas* (see Crosby 2005: 285–86, 312) only served as a further reminder of the decay of the supposed old order. The final word of 72, *petos*, a reference both to the breastplate traditionally worn as part of a suit of armour (compare the burlesque on the will of Don Quijote, Q.733: 69, analysed in Chapter 5) and, by extension, any costume covering the upper part of the body (see Q.749, 'Cansado estoy de la Corte': 67), is presumably an indication that the *cadenitas* to which Quevedo refers were worn round the neck. Poems of this period are often constructed around pairs of contrasting words: *mozos/niñas, hombres/mujeres*, and so on. The presence of *antiguas* alongside *niñas* provides a hint that the former, too, may be read as a noun, while *acero/a cero* is not the only instance in this poem of punning with word division. Thus: *los petos de las antiguas se van, sólo con ser armas*, reads: 'as for the old women, the moment there's an erection in the offing, off comes their kit'. *Petos* also hints at the farts (*pedos*) that were a side-effect of regular doses of *agua acerada*.[25] As late as the 1650s, another satirical chronicler of Madrid life was to complain, via an almost identical pun to the one we have here, of the regularity with which fashionistas of the day were given to breaking wind (Zabaleta 1983: 117).

> **De arrepentidos de barba**
> **hay infinitos conventos,**
> **donde se vuelven lampiños**
> 76   **por gracia de los barberos.**

There are any number of monasteries full of men who have turned their back on manhood and who are there shaved and cosseted thanks to the ministrations of barbers.

In medieval Spain, as in many civilizations both ancient and modern, beards had especial significance as markers of rank, status, and much else besides (Menéndez Pidal 1954–56: II.494–99). The cluster of associations between beards and honour persisted in Spain into the seventeenth century and beyond, and it emerges here in what was for the day a common accusation against barbers, whose profession involved shaving and removing beards (compare English 'fleece', 'trimmer'). The link is suggestively made in the *Guía y avisos de forasteros que vienen a la Corte* (1620), purportedly written by a Madrid resident styling himself Antonio Liñán y Verdugo: 'cierto barbero que tenía una mujer moza y hermosa, porque acudiesen muchos a quitarse la barba a su casa, tenía puesta la mujercilla sentada a una ventana

---

[25] See Quevedo 1998: 459, for a suggestion that *petos* may also be an allusion, via Latin *peto*, 'I beg', to begging women, *pidonas*, of the kind we meet in lines 87–89, below.

baja' (Liñán y Verdugo 1980: 69). Allusions to the supposed sexual prowess of *barberos*, often expressed through the verb *sangrar*, 'to let blood' (a mainstream occupation of a barber-surgeon) but also 'to furnish an orgasm', are legion in the poetry of the time, as witness the comments of Alzieu *et al.* on the *seguidilla* 'Madre el barberillo, que entra en mi casa | es verdad que me pica, más él se sangra', the dialogue of the two *comadres*, 'la de Tortuera' and 'la de Garrido': 'Pues llamemos al barbero |... | que nos haga una sangría; | Darémonos un buen día'; and a *zarabanda* 'Madre que me muero, | llamadme al barbero' (1975: 100, 170–72, 264; poems 63: 1–2 etc.; 92: 8, 13–14; 133: 5). *Barberos* are also 'cutpurses', whose ministrations clean out many a *convento* client, *convento* also being a slang term for 'brothel' (in Salas Barbadillo, *La ingeniosa Elena* of 1614, for example: Salas 1983: 110, 160; see also Molina 1998: 133 and Rioyo 2003: 48–51). Quevedo makes his *Buscón*, Pablos, the son of a *tundidor de mejillas y sastre de barbas* and on several occasions puts *barberos* in the firing line, alongside tailors and cobblers (for example, in *Historia y vida del Gran Tacaño*: Quevedo 1699: 344).

The subtext of alleged male heterosexual inadequacy, hinted at earlier in the contrast between *paz* and *pendencia* and the references to *doncellos* and *cadenitas*, is now brought further into the open. One of the reforms proposed by Olivares at the second Junta de Reformación in October 1622 (the Junta Grande) was the closure of the city's bordellos. It is a nice irony that his King continued meanwhile to cut a swathe through the ladies of Court and capital and that several of his cast-offs ended their days in *conventos* of a more conventional stamp (Rioyo 2003: 141). The women rounded up off the streets after this decree was enacted were shipped off to houses of reform, or *conventos de arrepentidas*; *Cov.* refers to these (*s.v. arrepentida*): 'de arrepentidas ay monesterios de gran religión y penitencia en España y en toda la christiandad' (see also Quevedo 1998a: 117). The regime established in such *conventos*, or *galeras* as they became known, was designed to terrify inmates into conformity: torture and deprivation were routine, as perhaps we might conclude from the title alone that Magdalena de San Gerónimo, who at the end of the previous century had run one such *convento* in Valladolid (known officially as the Casa Pía de Arrepentidas de Santa María Magdalena) and was later to help shape a similar establishment in Madrid, gave to a pamphlet setting out her thinking on the reform of fallen women: *Razón y forma de la galera y casa real que el Rey, Nuestro Señor, manda hacer en estos reinos para castigo de las mujeres vagantes, y ladronas, alcahuetas, hechiceras, y otras semejantes* (1608). One of her house rules was that inmates should have their heads shaven on arrival: 'En entrando cualquiera mujer en esta galera ha de estar despojada de todas sus galas y vestidos, y luego la raparán el cabello a navaja como hazen a los forzados en las galeras'. *Conventos de arrepentidos*, 'houses of penitents', is, then, a sly allusion to these prisons-cum-*conventos*-cum-*galeras*: a male, *al revés* version of communities of reformed *mujeres perdidas*, with *arrepentidos de barba*, 'forsaking maleness and/or male (i.e. heterosexual) behaviour', *lampiños,* 'shaven', like those entering service in a real *galera* (compare 'Juan Redondo, está en gurapas, | lampiño por sus pecados', Q.867: 1–2), and yet, presumably, still sexually active.[26]

Lampiños ('aplicándose al hombre que no tiene pelos en la barba, estando de edad de que le nazcan', *Aut.*), is a term Quevedo uses elsewhere both of effeminate men and of clothes that have become threadbare (Quevedo 1699: 384; 1972: 204). The context in which the word appears in *El Buscón* is certainly one in which homosexuality is in play: '—¡Algún puto, cornudo, bujarrón y judío —dijo en altas voces— ordenó tal cosa! Y si supiera quién era, yo le hiciera una sátira con tales coplas, que le pesara a él y a todos cuantos las vieran de verlas. Miren qué bien le estaría a un hombre lampiño como yo la ermita; o a un hombre vinajeroso y sacristando ser mozo de mulas. ¡Ea, señor, que son grandes pesadumbres esas!' (Quevedo 1990: 150). It may also be significant that the word appears in the company of *barba cana* (see 77, below) in the sonnet '¿Tú, dios, tirano y ciego Amor?' (Q.327: 6). In addition to this, those entering a religious order other than the Franciscans would be shaven, or at least tonsured, as a visible sign of their changed way of life (hence *conventos de arrepentidos*) and a frequent complaint among *arbitristas* in the 1620s is what many saw as an excessive growth in the ecclesiastical estate (*infinitos conventos*), especially in Madrid, producing, or so they alleged, demographic imbalance, depleting the size of the potential labour force, and sapping the vitality of the nation (Rawlings 2006).

Hair loss was also the most visible effect of the standard mercuric treatment for syphilis—one of the great scourges of the day in the New Babylon that was Madrid, as Magdalena de San Gerónimo herself recognized (Dopico Black 2001: 83; Michael 2000: 117)—and hospices such as that in Madrid's Antón Martín were, presumably, full of patients who had good cause to regret their sexual past.

Pendencia en las calzas and *petos* serve as reminders of the sexual and scatological obsessions of 'the powerful persona which seems to emerge from many of the poems' (Terry 1993: 153). Quevedo more than once likens pubic hair to a *barba (de letrado o médico)*, most notably in *Gracias y desgracias del ojo del culo, dirigidas a Doña Juana Mucha, Montón de Carne, mujer gorda por arrobas* (1628?) but also in the sonnet 'Un tenedor con medias y zapatos' (Q.597), analysed by both Iffland *(*1978–82: I.78–84) and Arellano (1984: 489–91).

Never one to turn down an opportunity to dip into a specialized lexicon for the challenges it might afford, Quevedo now follows up the term *arrepen-*

---

[26] Text in Barbeito (1991: 78); See also Dopico Black (2001: 82) and Morel d'Arleux (1994: 117–18). Carrasco (1994a: 108) lists a number of terms for a male prostitute, among them *sin pelo, muy afeitado, afeitadito, sin barbas, sin vello,* and *muy pulido.*

tidos, commonly encountered in religious contexts, with two more words from that same semantic area: *conventos* and *gracia*. Each, in the manner we have now come to expect, is imbued here with a non-religious primary sense: *arrepentidos* 'rejecting', 'regretting', and *conventos* picking up on the implications of *inventor/inventó* (55, 57) and on *petos* from the last line of the previous stanza (and perhaps having an ironical sense, such as 'cabal, conventicle'?), while *gracia* here means, with heavy irony, 'through the good offices of'. We shall hear an echo of this religious vocabulary later, in 121–24.

> **No hay barba cana ninguna,**
> **porque aun los castillos pienso**
> **que han teñido ya las suyas,**
> 80 **a persuasión de los viejos.**

There isn't a greybeard left, and I'm told that even the chaste lads have dyed theirs at the insistence of the old men.

Quevedo persists with the military lexicon (*barbacana*, 'barbican', and *castillos*, 'castles'), though, as before, the words are shorn of their primary sense. The first is presented as two words on the written page ('greybeard'); it also had the meaning, in *germanía*, of 'thieves' den' (Chamorro 2002: *s.v. vara*). The second is an ironic diminutive of *casto*, 'chaste', though, as elsewhere in the poetry of the period, it carries with it a subtext of impotence and sexual deviancy. *Cov.* makes the same link between barbican and greybeard in his entry for *barbacana*: 'La muralla baxa, cerca del foso, que está delante del muro. *Latine antemurale pomerium*; dicho assí, porque defiende y adorna la fortaleza en lo exterior, como ya dentro de los palacios los hombres ancianos autorizan y defienden la honra y honestidad dellos.'

We may think the practice of tinting hair to avoid the appearance of age a modern development, yet it was common in Quevedo's day, and he not infrequently mentions it (Q.557, Q.632, Q.651, etc.). But *teñir* carries also the sense of 'soil, bespatter', found in contexts involving *tinte*, 'ink, dye, semen', and *tintero*, 'inkwell, vagina' (e.g. Alzieu *et al.* 87: 23; Quevedo 1993: II. 1335–36), and it would here seem to explain the choice made by men driven to such practices by the behaviour of the harpies depicted in the stanzas that follow. There is also presumably a further suggestion here of (grey) pubic hair, dyed at the behest and for the pleasure of ageing male clients.

> **Pues, ¿quién sufrirá el lenguaje,**
> **la soberbia y los enredos**
> **de una mujer pretendida,**
> 84 **de éstas que se dan a peso?**
>
> **Han hecho mercadería**
> **sus favores y sus cuerpos,**
> **introduciendo por ley**
> 88 **que reciban y que demos.**

Since who could abide the hauteur and tricks of ambitious women prepared to sell themselves to the highest bidder, or the language they use? They've turned their favours and their bodies into commodities, decreeing it a gold standard that they receive and we give.

Mercadería, 'merchandise', was also, in popular parlance, 'swag, stolen or fake goods', and both it and *pretendida*, with its connotations of falsity, pretension, and ambition, provide a link back to the obsession we noted earlier with the commercial nature of relationships between women and the men they ensnare. Quevedo once described *pretensiones* as the bane of social existence: 'de las dos plagas de la vida (que son pleitos y pretensiones), es la mejor y más honrada el pleito' (letter of 1627: Sliwa 2005: 397). *Una mujer pretendida*, 'a sought after woman', also conjures up an image of male crossdressing to accompany *conventos... de arrepentidos*; compare the laconic entry 'Putas, *ambigui generis*' in Quevedo's *Cosas más corrientes de Madrid, y que más se usan, por alfabeto* (1876–77: I.475). *Enredos*, 'falsedad y engaño artificioso, mentira' (*Aut.*), repeated in 108—a term often associated with womanly wiles—is used elsewhere by Quevedo to denote fake goods, as for example in 'Sueño de la muerte': 'Echad los ojos por esos mercaderes, si no es que estén ya allá, pues roban ojos. Mirad esos joyeros, que a persuasión de la locura, venden enredos resplandecientes y embustes de colores, donde se anegan los dotes de los recién casados' (1972: 218–19).[27]

Notice is thus given that we are about to be treated once again to a stream of words connected with a single semantic field: not this time arrests or interrogation, religion or sex or soldiering, but trade: *enredos* (82), *(dar a) peso* (84), *mercadería* (85), *favores* (86), *cuerpos* (86), *ley* (87), *reciban* (88), *demos* (88), *pagar (al momento)* (90), *interesable* (92), *cueste* (93).

The implications of *se dan a peso* are not only that women sell themselves (by weight), but also that they do so to the highest bidder, as though at a market-stall or an auction, a sense of *peso* being 'street-market' ('el puesto u sitio público donde se venden por mayor varias especies comestibles, especialmente de despensa', *Aut.*) and *darse a* one way of saying 'being into, becoming obsessed by' as well as 'trading (themselves) for'. *Peso* also has the sense hinted at by *Cov.*: 'hombre de peso, hombre grave'. Women, then, sell themselves to 'the highest roller'. *Peso* also implies 'burden, sadness', one result of this alleged trade, as well as 'coin, money'. Possibly the most direct account in Quevedo's poetry of a woman *dándose a peso* comes in an exchange between a Galán and a Dama: 'GALÁN: Como un oro, no hay dudar, | eres, niña, y yo te adoro. | DAMA: *Niño, pues soy como un oro | con premio me has de trocar.* | GALÁN: De oro tus cabellos son, | rica ocupación del viento. | DAMA: Pues a sesenta por ciento | daré cada repelón' (Q.663:

---

[27] See 'Fue más larga que paga de tramposo' (Q.521: 10), and 'Ya que a las cristianas nuevas' (Q.708: 33–36). Also 'Sueño de la muerte', where gatherings of females spawn 'calamidades y plagas, los enredos y embustes, marañas y parlerías' (1972: 225).

1–8). But it is a complaint to which he returns time and again (e.g. Q.713, 'Una picaza de estrado': 23–24), the choice of *ley* here not only emphasizing the demands upon the male purse that are an invariable feature of relationships and focusing on the commerce involved in sexual transactions, but also acting as an ironic commentary on the question of fidelity, two of the meanings of *ley* recorded by *Cov.* being 'fidelidad, como el criado que tiene ley con su amo' and '*ser de ley una mercaduría*: estar conforme a las leyes y aranzeles'.

Favor (compare English *favour*, 'token of affection' as well as 'sexual reward') was not only slang for 'brothel-keeper, Madame' but also a term in wide use in commerce, as was *cuerpo(s)*, 'substance, quantity (in a contract)'. Line 88, which recalls Q.626: 17–18, commented on above (p. 157), contains a pun (compare *acero/a cero* in 70 and *barbacana/barba cana* in 77) between *que demos* 'that we (men) have to give' and *quedemos* 'we have to stand there (when they leave [with our cash])'.

> ¡Que si pecamos los dos,
> yo he de pagar al momento,
> y que sólo para mí
> 92 sea interesable el infierno!
>
> ¿Que a la mujer no le cueste
> el condenarse un cabello,
> y que por llevarme el diablo,
> 96 me lleve lo que no tengo?

If both man and woman sin, why should I have to pay upfront when the only interest I'll get on my money is a place in Hell? How can it be right that it doesn't cost the woman a single hair from her head to secure condemnation, while in order to get the Devil to carry me off, she takes everything I possess, and then some.

Salacious innuendo rolls on. The pun on *infierno*, 'Hell, cunt, pox', is one found in the sonnet 'A la orilla del agua', sometimes attributed without foundation to Quevedo: 'A la orilla del agua estando un día | ajena de cuidado, una hermosa | de mirarse su infierno deseosa, | por verse sola allí sin compañía, | la saya alzó que ver se lo empedía' (Alzieu *et al.* 1975: 48–49; compare Q.593, 'Cuernos hay para todos, sor Corbera': 11), while the phrase *no le cueste... un cabello* (compare modern Spanish *pelo*, 'hair, small or insignificant amount') not only echoes the string of words we have recently encountered to do with hair (*barba, barberos, lampiños*) and, by extension, prosperity (*gente de pelo* are those with 'conveniencas, dinero o hacienda', *Aut.*), but also alludes to a woman's infinitely renewable claims to maidenhood, *Aut.* defining the phrase *moza en cabello* as a synonym of *doncella o virgen*. Both this and references to venereal disease are commonplace in Quevedo.

Line 95 provides a good example of the poet's ability to create multiple meanings by playing with syntax. If *diablo* is the agent of *llevar*, then the speaker is either talking of his own eternal punishment for sin or admitting that he was led by the tail (or both); if *diablo* is the object of *llevar* and *mujer* its subject, the implication is that the speaker has contracted the pox (*infierno*) from a sexual encounter (which, perversely, has not cost his accomplice a single hair) and has paid for his pleasure by losing (use of) his *diablo*, 'penis' (though he still hopes to recover it one day: *demonio*, 99).

> **¡Vive Dios, que no es razón,**
> **y que es muy ruinmente hecho,**
> **y se lo diré al demonio,**
> 100   **si me topa o si le encuentro!**
>
> **Si yo reinara ocho días,**
> **pusiera en todo remedio,**
> **y anduvieran tras nosotros**
> 104   **y nos dijeran requiebros.**

My God, it's not! It's so unfair that, if I run into the Devil in the street, I'll bloody well tell him so! If I ruled the world for just a week, I'd sort it all out. Women would have to come looking for us and they'd be the ones who'd have to make the running and whisper honeyed words.

To put the world back on an even kilter, then, women must be made once again subservient to men, *anduvieran tras nosotros* suggesting that they would have come running after men and at the same time alluding to the common courtesy of allowing women to walk ahead and also, by implication, permitting them by default to run the show.

Line 101 represents the high point of this long rant, the idea of 'If I ruled the world', with its echo of the first line of the ballad, being one found in many a literary description of drunkards laying down the law as well as in the traditional addresses of the (often equally inebriated) Carnival King. The word *reinar*, 'to reign (over)', meanwhile, triggers another of Quevedo's semantically linked wordstreams, this time one based on the lexicon of army, governance, and administration: *remedio*, 'reform' (102), *gobernán-dose* (106) 'ruling the roost', *sostitutos* (107) 'stand-ins', *alcaides* (107) 'military governors, gaolers', *comisiones* (108, 114) 'orders, delegated duties', *lugarteniente* (111) 'lieutenant'. It is because we have been alerted by *reinar* that we pick up, behind the then common meaning of *remedio*, 'remedy, solution', the sense that the word has, in *germanía*, of 'attorney, prosecutor' (*Aut.*). *Requiebros* are the honeyed words which, as Diego de Saavedra Fajardo explains, are central to courtship and to love poetry: 'la que mantiene vivos los afectos amorosos, cebando con tiernos encareci-mientos y blandos requiebros las llamas proprias y ajenas' (Saavedra 1967: 81; compare above, p. 38).

Yo conocí los maridos
gobernándose ellos mesmos,
sin sostitutos ni alcaides,
108 sin comisiones ni enredos;

y agora los más maridos
(nadie bastará a entenderlos)
tienen por lugarteniente
112 la mitad de todo el pueblo.

No se les daba de antes
por comisiones un cuerno,
y agora por comisiones
116 se les dan más de quinientos.

Solían usarse doncellas:
cuéntanlo ansí mis agüelos;
debiéronse de gastar,
120 por ser muy pocas, muy presto.

I remember the old days when a husband was master in his own house, with no third parties or officials to run his life, and no contracts or scandals. Nowadays, most husbands (why, I'll never understand) have half the town standing in for them. In the old days, they didn't give a damn for commissions while today they stump up for five hundred and more of their wife's lovers. There used to be such a thing as a virgin, or so my grandparents say. They must have all been used up very quickly, because there were so few of them.

Alcaide, 'governor of a castle', had the sense in underworld slang of 'boss of a bordello', a sort of male counterpart to 'Madame', most brothels having a male overseer (often styled *padre*), who was licensed to run them; echoes, then, of those *conventos de arrepentidos*. *Lugarteniente*, 'lieutenant', is a military rank, but the play here is with its etymological meaning of 'one who stands in for another'. As noted earlier, Quevedo does not use the same word three times in eight lines unless he wishes to do something with it: *comisiones,* 'commissions, authorities to act', means also 'instructions/orders to be obeyed' (see also Quevedo 2003, I. 247), and, when it is repeated for a second time, can also be read as *co-misiones*, 'joint enterprises, company orders', with more than 500 men under orders to perform the conjugal duties of a complaisant husband.

Cuckoldry is frequently alluded to by Quevedo through *cuerno* (most notably in Q.601, 'Cuando tu madre te parió cornudo', and Q.615, 'A las bodas que hicieron Diego y Juana', both of which run the gamut of multiple meanings for the word and its derivatives: horn, hunting horn, drinking horn, inkwell, horn urinal, crescent moon, etc.); *poner/dar un cuerno*, 'to cuckold someone', is here linked with *dar un cuerno*, 'give a damn'. *Gastar* has the meaning of 'spend' and *gastarse* 'to use up, to wear out'.

The last of these four stanzas, 'Solían usarse doncellas', reminiscent of Juvenal (*Satires*, VI. 38–59), is quoted by Deleito (2005: 30), who lists several other early seventeenth-century Spanish texts expressing identical sentiments, among them this from Act I of a *comedia de tramoya* attributed to Tirso de Molina, *En Madrid y en una casa* (before 1635): 'Iba a decir que me tiran | más las señoras doncellas; | pero están fuera del mundo, | y no hay quien hallarlas pueda'. San Valero chronicles the emergence in the early years of the reign of Philip IV of what he sees as a new phenomenon: mothers who sought or obtained notarial 'certification' of their daughter's virginity, often in the process having recourse to professional assistance from *remendadoras de doncellajes desgarros* (Deleito 2005: 9), and Quevedo alludes to the practice in his *Tasa de las hermanitas del pecar*: 'Las doncellas valen tanto como costaron los juramentos para parecerlo; y si fueran de las finas aprobadas por el contraste de virgos, valen lo que costare el descubrir y hallar una de las tales doncellas' (1961: I. 94). The impact of using *usarse* instead of, say, *haber* ('además de la passiva del verbo usar, vale estar una cosa en estilo, u práctica', *Aut.*) and then twinning it with *doncellas* derives not only from the internal contradiction (once *usada* no longer *doncella*) and the sense of *usar*, 'to wear, to wear out', but also from the reader/listener's familiarity with the term *puta usada* that we find in *La Lozana andaluza* and elsewhere (Delicado 1994: 269).

> **Bien hayan los ermitaños**
> **que viven por esos cerros,**
> **que si son buenos, se salvan,**
> 124 **y si no, los queman presto;**

Blessed be the hermits who live in the wilds around here, for they are saved if they are good, and if not they are burned pretty quickly.

On the face of it, this is possibly the most puzzling quatrain of all. Up to now, Maroto's rant may have been rambling, shifting drunkenly from one grouse to the next, but there has always been a measure of continuity, if only at the lexical level. Line 121 would seem to mark a lunge in a different direction, and it is initially difficult to see what a reference to local hermits might be doing here, save as a distant echo of *conventos* in 74. The poem is set in a tavern, possibly in Madrid but certainly on a street (27). As Don Quijote advises Sancho Panza, it is no longer the case that all hermits live in deserts, where 'se vestían de hojas de palma y comían raíces de la tierra' (Cervantes 2005: I. 907), but we do still associate a hermitage with a relatively isolated, solitary location, often rural, as suggested here by *cerros,* 'slopes, hills'.

Part of the solution to the first piece of the problem posed by this quatrain lies, I suspect, in the phrase *por esos cerros*, defined by *Aut.* as 'phrase metaphórica, que explica ir alguna persona descaminada, no tener orden ni razón en lo que dice o hace', and in a reading of *ermitaños* as both 'thieves' and 'tavern-dwellers', the latter calqued upon the common *germanía* sense of *ermita* as 'tavern' (Deleito 2005: 123; *Aut.* cites as an example the description of Carriazo from the opening of Cervantes's *La ilustre fregona*: 'Visitaba pocas veces las ermitas de Baco': Cervantes 1986: II. 44).[28] In play also is a link between hermits and homosexuality that one finds elsewhere in the poet's work, a good example being '¿Ermitaño tú? El mulato' (Q.636). Quevedo's admiration for those who forsook the world in favour of the religious life only serves to make more bitter his use of the word *ermitaños* here. Thus, this verse becomes the final *brindis* of a mammoth drinking session: 'Here's to all drinkers' or 'Here's to a life like this'. Maroto's long complaint, ever shambolic, is now itself *andando por los cerros.*

Lines 123–24 are opaque, however, and the problem, once again, is one of syntax. *Ermitaños* also has the sense of 'prisoners', which would give a fairly simple surface meaning to *si son buenos se salvan | y si no, los queman presto.* But what is the subject of *si son buenos?*: *ermitaños,* or *cerros?* If the latter, there is presumably a suggestion here of the practice of burning stubble or scrub prior to ploughing. Similarly, what is the meaning of *se salvan?* Is it eschatological, 'they will be saved', and paired with *queman,* 'they (the *ermitaños*) burn (in Hell)', or does it mean 'they will escape' rather than 'be burned' (the usual sentence for those found guilty of sodomy: Rioyo 2003: 74–76) or 'be infected by the pox' (compare *infierno,* 92)? And if they do escape will it be because they are good or because they are good devotees of the pothouse?—the corollary being that, if they are not, they will be found guilty and will burn (presumably of thirst; compare *yesca* (7) and *gaznates secos* (8), above). *Salvarse* may even be a further example of cardsharpers' jargon (*Aut.:* 'retener el naipe el fullero'). And, once again, what is the subject of *se salvan?* Finally (and the answer(s) will depend on how one parses the previous line), which of the two candidates is the subject of *queman* and to which does the object, *los,* refer? Are we to understand that, if they get off scot-free (from prison) and leave (the tavern), the *ermitaños* will find that their *cerros,* 'bodies, flanks', *los queman,* 'will burn', or that they, the *ermitaños,* will 'burn up' the neighbourhood (with *los* in apposition to *esos cerros*)?

Whatever the answers to these questions, the suggested reading of this strophe as a toast provides a solution to what otherwise would seem to be a second, abrupt shift: that from *se queman presto* to Maroto's addressing his fellow drinkers (*y no vosotros*), rather than the world at large:

y no vosotros, lacayos
de tres hidalgos hambrientos,

---

[28] Jokes based on the idea that inns have their faithful adherents, with services offering solace and shriving the devout of their cares, are legion in the verse of Quevedo's day. An example is the *letrilla* 'Algunos hombres de bien', often attributed to Góngora (1980: 95).

                    alguaciles de unas ancas
        128   con la vara y el cabestro.

                    Y yo, que en diez y seis años
                    que tengo de despensero,
                    aun no he podido ser Judas,
        132   y vender a mi maestro.'

Not like you three, servants to three penniless hidalgos, put in charge of a set
of backsides, complete with staff of office and head of horns. In all the sixteen
years I've been in charge of provisions, I've never had a chance to play Judas
and cheat my master.

The eleventh-hour introduction of (penniless?) *hidalgo* masters takes us back,
of course, to where we came in with Maroto's whine about the spiralling cost
of living. But it is also a nod, readily appreciated, in the direction of the taste
for the picaresque: stories told in the first person by narrators recounting a
version of their past. The fashion for tales of this kind began in the middle
of the sixteenth century with the anonymous *Lazarillo de Tormes* and took
off at the close of the century with the publication of the two Parts of Mateo
Alemán's European best-seller *Guzmán de Alfarache* (1599/1604). Quevedo
himself was to flirt with aspects of the genre in *El Buscón*, published in
1626 but drafted only a few years after the publication of Part II of *Guzmán*.
A feature of such tales is the way in which narrators represent hunger as the
motor driving their actions when young. In 126, it is unclear whether *ham-*
brientos qualifies *hidalgos, lacayos*, or both, punctuation in poems from this
period being a choice made by the printer or editor; certainly there are picaresque tales that depict starving *hidalgo*s as well as starving servants.

    As with *gaznates* (8), *verga* (13), *pescuezo* (14), and *hocicos* (below, 135),
ancas, 'haunches, hind quarters', is a word normally associated with animals,
often in contexts where someone is riding pillion. *Alguaciles de unas ancas*
may suggest that the *lacayos* are 'in charge of' (live off? organize? enjoy?)
the *ancas* of their master's wife (or their master?), thus ensuring the three of
them *se salvan* financially; *alguaciles* also has the sense, as often in Quevedo,
of 'drunks'.

    The *vara* (slang also for 'prick') was the ubiquitous staff of office of
those in authority, military and civil ('*alguacil*: ministro de justicia, con
facultad de prender y traher vara alta de justicia', *Aut*.), as witness countless
portraits of the period (Brown 1998: nos 156, 159, 161, 162, etc.), and also,
by extension, the *ministro de justicia* himself (Chamorro 2002), while *algua-*
ciles was common slang for 'thieves', as both 'Coloquio de los perros' and
'Rinconete y Cortadillo' bear witness (Cervantes 1986: II. 324, I. 217).

    Cabestro, 'leading-rein', a term widely used to denote a complaisant
cuckold, and more specifically one who pimped for his wife, was used in
that sense by Quevedo's in a *letrilla*, 'Prenderánte, si te tapas' (Q.650: 20–

23): 'Tendrá la del maridillo | si en disimular es diestro, | al marido por cabestro | y al galán por cabestrillo'.[29]

The *despensero*, defined by *Cov.* (*s.v. despender*) as: 'el que tiene a su cuenta la despensa y el gasto de lo que se compra en las casas de los señores', was another of the writer's pet targets: an entry in *Cosas más corrientes de Madrid, y que más se usan, por alfabeto* reads 'Ladrones de privilegio, como son las despensas' (1876–77: I. 475). Judas Iscariot, the disciple who betrayed Christ, is described in St John's Gospel (12: 6) as the keeper of the *loculus*, 'coffer, purse' (from which he steals 'for he was a thief'), and Pablos, in Quevedo's *Buscón*, once promoted to steward, likens himself to 'el despensero Judas' (Quevedo 1990: 122; see Vilar 1978: 108–09). *Vender a mi maestro* can be read as both 'sell my master' and 'sell to my master'. *Diez y seis años* (129) may or may not be a bitter-sweet allusion to the poet's lengthy and troubled acquisition and tenure of the *señorío* of La Torre de Juan Abad, but that must remain a matter for conjecture.

> **En esto Pierres, que estaba**
> **con mareta en el asiento,**
> **dormido cayó de hocicos,**
> 136 **y devoto besó el suelo.**
>
> **Jaques, desembarazado**
> **el estómago y el lecho,**
> **daba mil tiernos abrazos**
> 140 **a un banco y a un paramento.**

At this point, Pierres, who had passed out and was swaying on his stool, fell flat on his face, kissing the floor like a penitent. Jaques, who had unburdened his stomach and the litter he was lying on, was busy fondly embracing a bench and a wall hanging.

Maroto falls silent, having having given vent at length to his (and Quevedo's) obsessions. We have had the boastful drunk and the drunk maudlin. Now it is the turn of the drunk paralytic, the dead drunk. Having passed out some time back from his ordeal by wine, Pierres is swaying on his *asiento* (see note on 9, above) in the manner of a sailor aboard ship in a swell (*mareta*, 'motion of the waves, sea-sickness'); the notion that, when he falls flat on his face, he kisses the ground recalls the age-old seafarer custom of doing just that when making landfall at the end of a voyage, as well as conjuring up images of religious contexts (*devoto*) in which penitents do the same. Pierres is a regular in the temples to Bacchus. *Mareta*, also slang for the swinging motion of a hanged man on the gallows (see Q.541, 'Esta redoma,

---

[29] 'Antiguamente sacavan en París al cornudo por las calles públicas de la ciudad, *cavallero* sobre una burra, *sentado al revés* y llevando en la mano por *cabestro* la cola de la jumenta, y *su muger delante llevándola* de diestro' (*Cov.*, *s.v. cornudo*, emphasis added).

rebosando babas': 7), recalls a cluster of slang terms for 'thief' (*mareador* and *marear* amongst them, but also *devoto*: Deleito 2005: 135).

Hocicos, 'snout' (see the comment on *ancas* in 127, above) gives us our final glimpse of this particular toper with his facial muscles relaxed by drink and his mouth agape ('Ambos labios, cuando son preeminentes, los llamamos hocicos', *Cov. s.v. labio*; 'y por semejanza se llama assí la boca del hombre, quando tiene los labios mui salidos afuera, formando con ellos como punta', *Aut.*); it may also be that, given the known effect, alluded to several times by Quevedo, of syphilis on nasal tissue, he is here revisiting earlier sexual resonances.

Quevedo was fond of the rhetorical device known as syllepsis or zeugma (see the examples cited above, pp. 49–50, 86, 118); here Jaques's stomach is *desembarazado*, 'unburdened', because he voided its contents in 15–16, while his *lecho*, 'bed, seat, rack' is *desembarazado* because he has rolled off it and is now hugging a *banco*, 'bench', and clinging to a *paramento*, 'wall hanging'. But, even now, we are not done with puns and double-entendre. Firstly, the leitmotif of men transformed into beasts by drink is kept afloat by another meaning for *paramento*, 'animal blanket' (and it appears in that sense in *Don Quijote* II. 34: Cervantes 2005: I. 1004). And, secondly, where the description of Jaques's vomiting near the start of the poem was bedecked with words taken from the world of crime and punishment and spiced with underworld sexual slang, that continues to be the case: *banco* also had the senses of 'prison', 'removable support used in torture', 'rack (for torture)', and 'seat in a galley' (compare *yesca*, 8), while a *paramento* was a whore, usually one operating in a tavern (hence the play with *mil tiernos abrazos*).

> **Sirviéronle de orinales**
> **al buen Roque sus greguescos:**
> **que no se halló bien el vino,**
> 144   **y ansí se salió tan presto.**
>
> **Maroto, que vio el estrago**
> **y el auditorio de cestos,**
> **bostezando con temblores,**
> 148   **dio con su vino en el suelo.**

Roque's breeches were serving him as a pisspot, since the wine in his body felt unwell and so shot straight out again. Maroto, surveying the damage and his audience of empty wine baskets, began to shudder and yawn and then dropped his wine [threw up] on the floor.

We commented earlier about the (watered) wine seeking ways to leave its new *cueros*, first as a *sudor remostado* (11) and then as *vómito* (16), *palabras rocïadas* (25), and the *lágrimas* in Maroto's *ojo bebido* (23–24). The motif has been kept alive in the mind's eye of the reader/listener with *trocado* (65) and it recurs in *desembarazado el estómago* (137–38) and, now, *orinales* (141), before finally emerging *en clair* in 143–44, where we are made to revise our (correct) assumption that Roque *no se halló bien* by the merry addition of a new subject for the verb, *el vino*. In addition to the meaning of 'pisspots, urinals', *orinales* had the sense of 'specimen jars/ dishes', of the kind routinely used by medics of Quevedo's day in diagnoses based on the colour and consistency of a patient's urine. Feeling unwell, then, the wine is offering itself up as a specimen for analysis.

The poem opened with four drinkers *cogidos* (2), and *cogidos* they still are: both taken in wine and imprisoned or tricked by it, *cesto* being yet another slang term for 'gaol', and *bostezando*, 'yawning', one of many terms in *germanía*, based on *bostezo* ('hierro llamado bostezo, que es como tenaza de forja', Duque de Estrada 1982: 127), for 'turning informant under torture'. Just before collapsing, wine and all, Maroto surveys the wreckage (*estrago*) of an *auditorio*, 'group of legal or administrative officials gathered to judge a case' ('*Auditor*: el tal juez que oye causas, dicho en castellano oydor de chancillería o Consejo. El nombre auditor es usado en Roma: auditor de rota y auditor de la cámara', *Cov.*), though those hearing (and not hearing) his case are *cestos,* 'empty vessels', the wineskins now voided and the human *cueros* having respectively sweated, puked, and pissed their way to oblivion. *Aut.* explains that *estar hecho un cesto* is a 'phrase familiar con que se explica estar alguna persona embriagada, o durmiéndose', while *Cov. (s.v. cesta),* after stating that 'es un vaso de mimbres tejidas unas con otras, y cuando es grande y hondo le llamamos cesto', goes on to explain that 'en estos se trae la fruta y en los que llaman de vendimiar las uvas, son grandes' and that 'por afrenta se dice a uno que es un cesto, por cuanto está vacío del licor de sabiduría y discreción, como hombre incapaz... como acontecería si uno quisiese echar agua en cesto, que se toma por cosa perdida y sin provecho'.

Our ballad began with a phrase involving *con* that could be read in more than one way (2). It closes with another. *Dio con su vino en el suelo* reads as 'dashed his wine to the floor' and, appropriately for a drinker with bloated gut, as 'slumped to the floor along with his wine'. Both readings would leave Moroto, *el buen español*, as the only one of the four *cueros* still carrying his drink. A more likely sense of 148, however, and one that would take us back to the traditional tale of the Fox and the Crow, is that, just as the crow opens his beak to sing and drops his prized cheese, Maroto now opens his and—the final trick of the wine that has flattered only to deceive— throws up.

*   *   *   *   *

It is tempting to speculate whether Quevedo, resident in Madrid and a regular at Court, may have had contact during the winter of 1627–28 with another Olivares protégé engaged on a composition featuring drunks.

It is not known when Diego Rodrigo de Silva Velázquez, one of the many Sevillans to converge on Madrid after Olivares's role in the new regime became clear, began work on 'a striking departure from the path his career had thus far taken': his first large-scale mythological painting, *Triunfo de Baco* (more famous today as *Los borrachos*).[30] The sole authority for the notion that the subject was suggested by the envoy despatched to Madrid in 1628 by the English to help negotiate a alliance by marriage between that nation and Spain, is a not disinterested source, but rather the painter's father-in-law and erstwhile apprentice-master Francisco Pacheco. The envoy himself, Sir Peter Paul Rubens, was some seven months at the Spanish Court, from September until the April of the following year, spending much of his time painting and making copies of the royal collection of Titians.[31] Three months after his departure, Philip IV ordered his *tesorero general* to pay Velázquez four hundred ducats, one hundred of them 'por la [cuenta] de una pintura de Baco que hizo para servicio de Su Mgd' (Gallego y Burín 1960: II.231, doc. 42). The finished painting would hang in the King's apartments for the rest of his life (Orso 1993: 6, 118–20).

Whatever the truth of Velázquez's relationship with Rubens and of the latter's possible role in the gestation of *Triunfo de Baco,* Velázquez and Quevedo were known to each other (Schwartz 2002: 131). The former was no stranger to the world of letters, having spent six years from the autumn of 1611 as apprentice to Pacheco, a cultivated man whose house and studio were the hub of much of the literary and artistic life of Seville (Pacheco 1990: 21, 32; Cherry 1996: 67; Lleó Cañal 1996; Elliott 2006: 14) and the author of an erudite set of pen-portraits (Cacho 2007a). Pacheco and Quevedo were both prominent, albeit on different sides, in the controversy over the possible elevation of St Teresa of Avila to the co-patronage of Spain; they corresponded on this and other issues (Pacheco 1990: 15, 26; Jauralde 1998a: 157, 541–42; Nalle 2002: 116–17). Quevedo paid his own tribute to Velázquez around this same time (1629?) in his 'Tú, si en cuerpo pequeño', normally known as 'El pincel' (Q.205: 85–90, version *C*; López Grigera 1975: 233–34). Yet we have no proof of any close association between them.

Quevedo's rival, Luis de Góngora y Argote, at Court for nearly ten years before returning to his native Córdoba in 1626, did sit for Velázquez in 1622, the result being the luminous portrait of the 61-year-old poet in the

---

[30] 'With the capture of power by Olivares and his relatives and dependants, Seville itself may be said to have come to Madrid' (Elliott 2006: 16). On *Triunfo de Baco* see Orso, who speculates that the daily *ración* paid to Velázquez from the royal household from 18 September 1628 may provide a *terminus post quem* for his beginning the work. The nickname *Los borrachos* attached quite late to the painting, certainly after its entry into the Prado collections in 1819 (Orso 1993: 4–8).

[31] Pacheco claimed that Velázquez was the only artist with whom Rubens had any real contact during his time at the Spanish Court. Borelius, for one, sees the painting as evincing a 'contradictorio dualismo de lo español y lo flamenco' (1960: 248).

Museum of Fine Arts in Boston.[32] It used to be believed (and until recently was still often said, e.g. Jauralde 1998a: 466, 892–94; 1998b: 66) that the well-known image of our poet, wearing the distinctive spectacles that came to be known as *quevedos*, was also painted by Velázquez in the 1620s (the original of the portrait has been lost but several contemporary copies still survive: López-Rey 1963: nos 530–33). Doubts have now been raised over that attribution (Schwartz 2002: 132–33).

Yet drunkenness was hardly an esoteric subject for either painter or poet. As the price of wheat in the capital shot up in the wake of failed harvests, wine proved a popular substitute. Consumption soared, the inn-trade enjoyed a boom with some 500 taverns in the early 1620s compared with 391 in 1600 (this for an lay population of some 125,000, women and children included: one tavern for every hundred men of drinking age) and the drunkard held sway.[33]

The two compositions, nicknames apart, could not be more different in mood and tone. There is a case for seeing the painting as a burlesque of Classical mythology of the kind discussed in Chapters 2 and 9, but Quevedo's poem is hardly mythological. Velázquez's composition includes nine life-size figures in an open-air scene on a sunny day; Quevedo's has just the four, and they are stuck in a tavern. Velázquez's drinkers, or those that we can see clearly (the picture was damaged in the fire that gutted the Royal Palace in 1734 and subsequently cropped) are at the stage where 'a silly grin of intoxication spreads across the faces of the two drinkers in the centre of the composition' (Brown & Garrido 1998: 34); Quevedo's are fast approaching collapse. Velázquez's figures, possibly drawn from life, are framed by Bacchus and his cupbearers; if Quevedo's topers have any company at all that has not retreated in the face of Maroto's liquored rant and the boorish incontinence of his three fellow-revellers, it consists of a cozening inn-keeper and his pothouse drabs. And, most importantly of all, there is an astonishing, radiant humanity in the unfocused gaze of the central drinkers in the Velázquez canvas which finds no echo in our poem. Even the *buen español* here is just the pub bore heading for a fall.

* * * * *

Jorge Luis Borges suggested in *Otras inquisiciones* that much of Quevedo's output as a writer of both prose and verse was admirable not so much for its content as for its polished craftsmanship:

[32] Carr *et al.* (2006: 144–45). Pacheco claimed the idea for the portrait was his (1990: 203).

[33] For a best estimate of the population during the period of expansion that followed the return from Valladolid see Carbajo (1987: 41, 51, 134, 144, 149–50). On wine consumption in the capital see Ringrose (1983: 112–14, 120, Fig. 6.2).

> La grandeza de Quevedo es verbal. Juzgarlo un filósofo o... un hombre
> de estado, es un error que pueden consentir los títulos de sus obras, no el
> contenido... Las mejores piezas de Quevedo... son (para de alguna
> manera decirlo) objetos verbales, puros e independientes como una
> espada o como un anillo.   (Borges 1974: 661, 666)

As we have seen elsewhere in this volume, Quevedo wrote serious verse addressing directly the essential human agonies. Here, too, beneath the rumbustuous humour, lies criticism both trenchant and damning. It is a case, if ever there was one, of *in vino veritas*. But this poem is also an end in itself: forged and wrought, twisted and tortured, like his drinkers, to provide the reader with entertainment and no small measure of intellectual satisfaction.

SALVADOR JACINTO POLO DE MEDINA

'A VULCANO, VENUS Y MARTE' (c.1630)

El jaque de las deidades,
todo bravatas y rumbo,
que vive pared en medio
del planeta boquirrubio;

5   el de los ojos al sesgo,
caribajo y cejijunto,
de la frente encapotada
y mostachos a lo ruso;

de Venus se enamoró,
10   que en la orilla del Danubio
muy arremangada estaba
enjabonando un menudo,

para que comiese Adonis,
que estaba de ciertos pujos
15   desmayado; que el mozuelo
come poco y anda mucho.

Era, pues, madama Venus
moza redomada al uso,
con más panza que un prior,
20   más enaguas que un diluvio;

pelinegra y ojos grandes,
más claros que dos carbunclos,
si es que puede ser verdad
lo que de ellos dice el vulgo.

25   No hay más asentada cosa
que su cara en todo el mundo,
y se levanta a mayores
sólo la nariz por puntos.

Es mujer de pelo en pecho,
30   muy varonil y forzudo,
aunque pasa por lunar
en el concepto de muchos.

Es más ancha su cintura
que el trato, la vida y uso
35   de hombre que se va al infierno,
mercader, que todo es uno.

A lo jinete, estevadas
son sus piernas y sus muslos,
frisadas de vello, y gordas
40   como las letras de algunos.

Muy avarienta de pie,
de quien eran dos sepulcros,
con listones noguerados,
zapatillas de a diez puntos.

45   Esta es la estampa y bosquejo
de la diosa de los gustos:
adivine el estrellero,
zahorí de los influjos.

Por mirarla más de cerca,
50   sobre las guijas se puso,
haciendo antojo del agua,
Marte, transformado en pulpo;

echando dos mil conceptos
a los hermosos tarugos
55   con que fregaba el mondongo,
sin hacer asco del zumo.

Hizo Venus dos melindres,
que el monstruo la dio gran susto;
y el cuajar que enjabonaba
60   soltó al agua, abriendo el puño.

Bien quisiera el dios amante,
más blando y menos sañudo,
dejar de pulpo la forma
por transformarse en besugo.

65 El niño desabrigado,
    por vengarla de este insulto,
    veloz se llegó encubierto
    por un florido arcabuco,

    y apuntando al corazón,
70 le arrojó con fuerte impulso,
    con el arco cornicabra,
    un virote zapatudo.

    Dejóle escrito en el alma,
    por más discretos y agudos,
75 con caracteres vascuences
    de la diosa el nombre augusto.

    No pudiendo por los ojos
    su divino bello bulto
    trasladar a sus entrañas,
80 bebió en el agua el trasunto.

    Para decirla sus ansias
    en dulces conceptos cultos
    dejó el disfraz de cuaresma
    y el carnal tomó del suyo.

85 Miróla Marte amoroso,
    y ella con desdén y zuño;
    que es la moza por extremo
    socarrona, si él astuto.

    Diferentes se contemplan,
90 si unánimes en lo culto;
    él tierno a lo portugués,
    ella arrogante a lo turco.

    Después de haberse ostentado
    ella grave y él confuso,
95 la dijo en razones verdes
    estos requiebros maduros:

    'Diosa nacida entre conchas,
    de cuyo principio arguyo
    que las tienes en el trato,
100 si las niega el disimulo;

    alhóndiga de belleza,
    hija del capón Saturno,
    de cuya capona tacha
    no heredaste ni un minuto;

105 yo soy el dios revoltoso,
    el que alcanzó sin segundo,
    con las fuerzas de mis armas,
    muchas victorias y triunfos.

    Yo inventé la caja y trompa,
110 instrumentos tremebundos,
    que el uno anima a los hombres,
    y el otro alienta a los brutos.

    Mas tanto poder, ¿qué importa,
    si con sólo un estornudo
115 de tus basiliscos ojos
    me tiene tu amor sin pulsos?

    Cordero a tus pies me postro
    si bien de tu humor presumo
    que para ciencia tan mansa
120 es sutil ingenio el tuyo.

    Permite que mis deseos
    den fondo en tu mar profundo,
    si acaso de él no heredaste
    sus borrascas y reflujos.

125 Consiente, pues, diosa bella,
    que sea de sus ondas buzo,
    si no quieres verme en ellas
    infelice Palinuro.

    Serás, oh Venus, mi manfla,
130 yo seré, Venus, tu cuyo;
    serás de este Marte marta,
    que lo abrigues aun por julio;

    que si vengo a verme cuervo
    de esas bellas carnes, juro
135 de darte seis tabaqueras
    para tabaco con humo.'

    Respondióle la taimada:
    'Marte, ofendida te escucho
    de que pienses conquistarme
140 con bombardas y con chuzos.

    Las tusonas de mi porte
    no temen fuerzas ni orgullos;
    que en su golfo y mar sin norte
    no se camina por rumbos.

145 Todas son Troyas de bronce,
    y sólo rompen su muro
    un doblón con "Vida mía,
    tómalo, que todo es tuyo".'

    Marte le replica, y Venus
150 siempre en sus trece se estuvo;
    al fin venció sus desdenes
    con las armas de un escudo.

Concertáronse en secreto
de ser los dos para en uno,
155 antes que la Aurora calva
despertase el dios greñudo;

que era el tiempo en que a Vulcano
deleitaban importunos
del yunque las consonancias,
160 del fuelle los contrapuntos.

Despidiéronse abrazando
Venus al amante adusto,
volviéndola dulces paces
el dios que nunca las tuvo.

165 Vulcano, que ya por cierto
tiene del ave el abuso
que cantando hados presentes,
predice agravios futuros,

y que se sueña animal
170 jarameño y corajudo,
convertido en puerco espín
a garrochas y repullos,

y en un sueño vio dos cañas
que tenían sus cañutos,
175 en su mujer las raíces,
y en su cabeza los ñudos,

para vengarse, prendiendo
al autor de sus disgustos,
viéndose en su oficio y arte,
180 con ingenio peliagudo,

labró de templado acero
una red sutil, que dudo
pudiera verla un vecino
ni el pastor frisón de Juno.

185 En el lecho conyugal
de manera la dispuso,
que no pudiera escaparse
el cobarde más astuto.

Cuando la tierra enlosaba
190 de la noche el manto oscuro,
dejó las fraguas Vulcano,
y a su alcoba se retrujo,

a lo que a dormir llamamos
los que somos algo rudos,
195 de la vida intermisión,
del dios Morfeo tributo.

Ya que la noche enfaldaba
la cola al monjil de luto,
huyendo del dios cochero,
200 de sus tinieblas verdugo,

Bronte y sus dos compañeros,
tres oficiales machuchos,
ayudantes de Vulcano
ojinones y membrudos,

205 dieron voces al maestro,
que lo dispertó el retumbo
de las fugas que formaban
los martillos campanudos.

Salió del lecho y vistióse
210 micer Cornelio Castrucho,
cuyos pies de copla estaban
de sílabas diminutos.

En un tronco de alcornoque
tropezó, terrible augurio,
215 y mirando la escalera,
llegó al suelo en cuatro tumbos.

Marte, que acechando estaba,
puesto en vela como grullo,
oyó un suspiro, que Venus
220 le despachaba por nuncio.

Bajó por la chimenea,
transformado en avechucho
y el lado ocupó de Venus,
de marido sustituto.

225 Ya cuando Marte empezaba
las jerigonzas del gusto,
sin encanto de hechiceros
se vio ligado y compulso.

Venus dice: '¡Que me aprietan!'
230 y él dice: 'Yo me escabullo.'
Prueban a desenredarse,
mas ninguno de ellos supo.

En su magna conjunción,
de su mismo ardor combustos,
235 en orbes de red quedaron
los dos planetas conjuntos.

Salió el sol con luz escoba,
barriendo sombras y nublos,
según versistas lo mienten
240 en sus cantos o rebuznos;

y enhilando un sutil rayo
por el ojo de un rasguño
que él hizo en una ventana
con las uñas de sus cursos,

245 entró, y vio los dos amantes
hechos al vivo un dibujo
de aquel signo que a sus potros
sirve de establo por junio.

Dio al punto a Vulcano el soplo,
250 que estaba en lugar de puño
echando cachas de cuerno
al puñal de un hombre zurdo.

Tomó el martillo, furioso,
y aunque zompo y barrigudo
255 embistió con la escalera,
sin ser capa, echando bufos.

Subió el primer escalón,
mas no pasó del segundo;
que como cojo y pesado
260 de cabeza, se detuvo.

En culta voz de becerro,
porque en la humana no pudo,
llamó a los dioses que bajen
a vengar su agravio injusto.

265 Luego que la oreja el bramo
oyó de los dioses sumos,
rompiendo golfos de estrellas,
descendieron a pie enjuto.

Halláronlos jadeando,
270 por salir de aquel tabuco,
y aunque de sudor aguados,
estaban en cueros puros:

Venus, desgreñado el moño,
desrizado su apatusco,
275 y medrosa de otra espina,
dos argentados pantuflos;

Marte, con un tocador
y escarpines que se puso,
teniendo un francés catarro
280 con dolores de Acapulco.

Y porque el rumor no fuese
despertador de tumultos,
unos renuncian zapatos
y otros repudian coturnos.

285 Sonó al punto, en risa envuelto,
entre los sacros alumnos,
como en corro de poetas,
un murmurador susurro.

Juno, que del matrimonio
290 ostenta celosa el yugo,
mal contenta lo miraba,
haciendo varios discursos.

Palas, cuya flor estaba
recogida en su capullo,
295 los mira, haciendo en sus ojos
mil melindrosos repulgos.

Dïana, que estaba hecha
a pisar bosques incultos,
donde de virgen silvestre
300 guardaba los estatutos,

viéndolos tan descompuestos,
a su memoria redujo
de Acteón la vista osada,
de Susana el rigor justo,

305 cuando desnuda en la fuente,
vio por cuartos y por puntos
de su claustro virginal
los lunares más reclusos.

'¡Miren, y qué desvergüenza!',
310 dijo con un rostro turbio,
y en él la mano miraba
por los dedos al descuido.

Momo, el fisgón de los dioses,
haciendo un gesto a Vertumno,
315 por festejar maldiciente
tan soberano concurso,

dio tres silbos a Vulcano
que estaba como un lechuzo,
contemplando en un rincón
320 sus presentes infortunios.

Ignorando el nombre propio,
llamaba al bicorne búho,
como a animal de carreta,
ya Naranjo, ya Aceituno.

325 Él, corriendo como un toro,
quisiera ser de un saúco,
si no pendiente espantajo,
cabrahígo de su fruto.

Sueltos de la red los presos,
330 cubrieron sus miembros rucios,
Venus con baquero verde,
Marte con ropón lobuno.

Condénanle por sentencia,
con un falso y un pronuncio,
335 a que sirva de atambor
en las islas del Maluco.

Y a Venus a que se vaya
sin coche y sin moño a Burgos,
donde, sin gustar la carne,
340 tenga tres meses de ayuno.

Y a Vulcano, por paciente,
le dejaron por indulto

que de maridos de cachas
fuese abogado absoluto.

345 Con esto, dioses y diosas
al cielo hicieron recurso,
ellas en forma de urracas,
y ellos como abejorrucos.

Vulcano, que iba esparciendo
350 olor de secretos flujos,
no quiso salir de casa
sin guantes de calambuco;

y por cubrir de sus sienes
ciertos renuevos talludos
355 dicen que fue el inventor
de las guedejas y tufos.

*   *   *   *   *

Little is known about the life of Salvador Jacinto Polo de Medina. Born in Murcia in 1603, he benefited from both a religious education and the tutelage of Francisco Cascales, an outspoken detractor of *culto* forms of discourse. In 1630, he undertook his first trip to Madrid where he became associated with the circle of Lope de Vega and Pérez de Montalbán. Late that same year, under Lope's supervision, he published his earliest known works, the *Academias del jardín* and *El buen humor de las musas*, the volume of poetry in which 'A Vulcano, Venus y Marte' first appears. Published for a second time in 1637, *El buen humor* includes eighty-two poems, of which thirty-one are *romances*. In 1645, after fifteen years of moving between Madrid and Murcia, Polo returned home for good where he took up religious office. Almost nothing is known about the last thirty years of his life leading up to his death in 1676. He is now best known as an academy poet and writer of burlesque poetry.

In the late sixteenth and early seventeenth centuries a vogue for mythological burlesque developed (see above, pp.27, 44). Góngora's ballads on Hero and Leander (1589 and 1610, GR.28 and GR.63) and on Pyramus and Thisbe (1604 and 1618, GR.55 and GR.74) mark important stages in its birth and evolution. Polo's two most famous exercises in the genre of mythological burlesque are his poems dedicated to the myths of Apollo and Daphne (*Fábula de Apolo y Dafne*, 1634) and Pan and Syrinx (*Fábula de Pan y Siringa*, 1636), the former written in *silvas*, the latter in *romance* form. 'A Vulcano, Venus y Marte' represents, I suggest, a more challenging and entertaining text than either of its more illustrious companions.

The myth of Mars, Venus, and Vulcan is first recounted in *Odyssey*, VIII. 266–369. In order to dispel the tension between the wanderer Odysseus and the Phaeacian Euryalus, the Homeric bard, Demodocus, introduces the story of the love of Ares (Mars) and Aphrodite (Venus). Unbeknown to her husband Hephaestus (Vulcan), Aphrodite is engaged in an affair with the god of war. One day, the sun-god Apollo catches Aphrodite and Ares making love. As we see him do in Velázquez's 1630 *La Fragua de Vulcano* (Carr *et al.* 2006: 154–57; also below pp. 209, 219), he informs Hephaestus, who, on hearing of his wife's infidelity, forges an invisible and unbreakable network of chains. The smith-god then erects the chains around his marriage bed and feigns departure for Lemnos. Ares and Aphrodite seize the opportunity to renew their affair, but when they climb into bed they are immediately ensnared in Hephaestus's cunning trap. Hephaestus returns home and calls out to Zeus and the gods of Olympus, entreating them to bear witness to the spectacle. The male gods descend whilst the female deities stay at home out of modesty. In response to the lovers' entrapment, the gods are seized by a fit of uncontrollable laughter, a classic example of Homeric *Schadenfreude*. The gods pass comment upon the spectacle before Apollo and Hermes share a joke about what they would give to be in Ares's position. When Poseidon intervenes and negotiates the freedom of the lovers, Hephaestus eventually agrees to set them free. Whilst Ares heads for Thrace, Aphrodite flees to Paphos where she is bathed, anointed, and clothed by her attendants, the Three Graces.

Like most Homeric embedded narratives, the song of Demodocus ends without fanfare, with a passing aside on the delight shown by Odysseus and the Phaeacians. It is important to note that the primary objective of Demodocus's narrative is to please and to entertain. The laughter of the gods, mirrored by the response of the bard's audience, is liberating, dissolving the tension of an otherwise serious matter. The visual comedy of the lovers struggling to free themselves whilst attempting to maintain some sense of personal dignity is complemented by the verbal comedy of the exchange between Apollo and Hermes, to which Lucian's *Dialogues* introduce additions (*Dialogi Deorum*, XVII, XXI).

The episode is reworked by a young Ovid, in *Ars Amatoria*, II. 561–92, to lend weight to the argument that a lover gains nothing by establishing the infidelity of his love, since she simply becomes more openly instead of stealthily unfaithful. Ovid develops the comic potential inherent in the myth when he recounts how Venus would laugh at her crippled husband's legs and imitate his limp when left alone with Mars (567–70). An element of more salacious humour is introduced when the sun-god is reproached for having informed Vulcan of his wife's affair. Had he kept quiet, we are told, he too would have been granted his privilege by Venus (575–76). In the *Metamorphoses*, IV. 169–89, the story is retold in just twenty-one lines, as an introduction to a much longer section on the amorous trials and tribulations of Apollo: 'Solis referemus amores' (IV. 170), 'the Sun's love we will relate' (Ovid 1984: I. 191). Whilst he is faithful to the Homeric account, Ovid refuses to restore the compensatory aspect of the lovers' majestic or ideal roles: there is no mention of the lovers' release and no restoration of their dignity and divine authority. Whereas the most famous and frivolous of the Homeric love stories includes the more solemn note of Poseidon's guarantee for the redress demanded by Hephaestus, Ovid's cursory ending to the telling in the *Metamorphoses* offers an oblique reference to an exchange between Apollo and Hermes before focusing entirely on the laughter and notoriety associated with the spectacle: 'illi iacuere ligati | turpiter, atque aliquis de dis non tristibus optat | sic fieri turpis; superi risere, diuque | haec fuit in toto notissima fabula caelo' (IV.186–89), 'There lay the two in chains, disgracefully, and some one of the merry gods prayed that he might be so disgraced. The gods laughed, and for a long time this story was the talk of heaven' (Ovid 1984: I. 191).

Polo's poem is typical of the genre established by Góngora in that it takes a specific Classical story and debases it by ridiculing figures from the world of Classical mythology, by trivializing the affairs of the gods, and by mixing high and low styles. Throughout his 356–line romp, Polo employs the *ú–o* assonance associated with comedy (see above, p. 45) and used, for example, by Góngora in his 1618 *romance* on Pyramus and Thisbe, 'La ciudad de Babilonia' (GR.74). Like many of Góngora's burlesques, Polo's poem also stands in counterpoint to an earlier Spanish version of the myth. Just as Góngora's ballads on Hero and Leander are, in some measure, burlesque commentaries on Boscán's lengthy and serious reading of Musaeus (see above, pp. 43–44), Polo's poem is, in part, a form of response to Juan de la Cueva's 'Los amores de Marte y Venus' (1604), a pseudo-epic in 137 *octavas* offering a predominantly serious treatment of Homer's humorous embedded narrative. However, Polo's poem differs in one regard from the standard model for the mythological burlesque: as we have seen, the myth of Mars, Venus, and Vulcan, unlike the tragic tales of Hero and Leander and Pyramus and Thisbe, is generally treated lightly. In Homer and Ovid, the tale is something of a joke: it provokes hysterical laughter and malicious gossip and is associated with the art of storytelling and the need to entertain an audience. The divine cast are thoroughly humanized; their role as gods is at best implied or at least suspended until after the denouement of the tale. Thus, Polo subverts a myth that is already in some sense a parody of the actions of the gods of Olympus. By electing to gloss a myth that is associated with the response of laughter, Polo prepares his audience for a subject replete with comic potential.

*   *   *   *   *

> El jaque de las deidades,
> todo bravatas y rumbo,
> que vive pared en medio
> 4   del planeta boquirrubio;

>   el de los ojos al sesgo,
>   caribajo y cejijunto,
>   de la frente encapotada
> 8   y mostachos a lo ruso;
>
>   de Venus se enamoró,
>   que en la orilla del Danubio
>   muy arremangada estaba
> 12   enjabonando un menudo,
>
>   para que comiese Adonis,
>   que estaba de ciertos pujos
>   desmayado; que el mozuelo
> 16   come poco y anda mucho.

The pimp of the gods (Mars), who lives in the house next door to the pretty-boy planet (Apollo), is all bravado and show, with shifty eyes, head down and monobrow, lowering forehead, and Russian-style moustachios. He fell in love with Venus, who was on the banks of the Danube, with her sleeves all rolled up, dressing some giblets, so that Adonis, who had fainted from some serious stresses and strains, could have something to eat, for the young lad eats little and gets about a lot.

The poem opens with an eight-line description of Mars, the Roman god of war. In the lyric poetry of the sixteenth century, Mars's appearance is rarely described. More often than not, a solitary epithet, such as *airado, fiero,* or *belicoso,* is sufficient to evoke a picture of the warrior-god in all his military splendour. In contrast, Polo foregrounds the description of Mars and plays it off against the reader's knowledge of Classical authority and Renaissance shorthand. The traditional picture of Mars as a young, powerfully muscular, and awe-inspiring embodiment of war is undermined. Mars does not strike fear into the heart of the reader. Instead, his facial appearance invites a snigger; with his shifty eyes, lowering monobrow, and Russian-style moustachios, he is a deceitful and fearsomely ugly representative of the Olympian criminal underworld, a fitting companion for Cervantes's Monipodio, 'el más rústico y disforme bárbaro del mundo' (1986: I.211). The opening noun, *jaque,* 'rufián a cuyo cargo está una prostituta' (Alonso 1976: 453), sets the tone for the rest of the poem, introducing not the elevated and noble world of Classical mythology but an underworld associated with *germanía,* prostitution, and the picaresque. Mars is a common pimp who would not be out of place in the sphere of the *Celestina* and its imitations, Quevedo's *jácaras,* or *El Buscón.* Following in the footsteps of the Latin playwright Plautus's *Miles Gloriosus,* he is a pompous, posturing, and boastful soldier/pander. The opening lines remind us of Quevedo's representation of Mars as the Don Quixote of the gods of Olympus in *La hora de todos y la Fortuna con seso*: 'Marte, don Quijote de las deidades, entró con sus armas y capacete, y la insignia de viñadero enristrada, echando chuzos' (Quevedo 1987: 149–50). Whereas Quevedo's Mars is accompanied by Bacchus, the divine alcoholic, here Mars has Apollo for his planetary neighbour. The absurd periphrasis of 4 exposes Apollo as a naive youngster who is unable to keep his mouth shut, the sense of *boquirrubio* being 'jovenzuelo fatuo, ingenuo, fácil de engañar, no malicioso. Lo contrario de rufián y valiente' (Alonso 1976: 122). According to Homeric tradition, it is the sun-god who will inform Vulcan of Venus's infidelity. Polo's portrayal of Mars is so unflattering that it has given rise to the suggestion that 1–8 provide the literary source for Velázquez's equally unexpected and profoundly unsettling representation of the god of war, *Marte* (c.1640), which hangs in the Museo del Prado in Madrid (Noble Wood 2007: 143–44).

In 9, the main verb of the opening sentence introduces the narrative content of the Homeric and Ovidian myth: Mars has fallen in love with Venus. Like Lope's Juana in the *Rimas humanas y divinas del Licenciado Tomé de Burguillos* (1634), the Classical goddess of love and beauty is portrayed as a common washerwoman. Whereas Lope's Juana carries out menial tasks on the banks of the Manzanares, Polo's Venus is on the banks of the Danube preparing some tripe, the *menudo* of 12 (also the *mondongo* of 55 and the *cuajar* of 59), for Adonis, another of her lovers according to Classical tradition. The Golden-Age divinities, it seems, are content to gorge themselves on base comestibles rather than on the ambrosia associated with the gods of Classical Antiquity. In Góngora's 'Arrojóse el mancebito', Venus is unable to come to Leander's rescue as the foolish *mancebito* struggles to cross the Hellespont, for she is otherwise engaged: 'Pero Amor, como llovía | y estaba en cueros, no acude, | ni Venus, porque con Marte | está cenando unas ubres' (45–48; see above p. 50). As a noun, *menudo* denotes 'el vientre, manos y cabeza de carnero' (Alonso 1976: 526); the plural, *menudos*, refers to 'las monedas de cobre, a diferencia de las de plata y oro' (*Cov.*), 'small change', or *moneda de vellón*. Thus, Venus is not only preparing some tripe but also washing a coin of insignificant real monetary value, a suggestion that fits in with the image of Venus as a tightfisted, penny-pinching prostitute developed in the rest of the poem.

The Danube is a river that contemporary readers would have associated with the poetry of the first generation of Spanish Petrarchist poets. In poems by writers such as Garcilaso and Diego Hurtado de Mendoza, it is the setting for serious lyric or epic poetry, as in Garcilaso's Canción III and Égloga II. Elsewhere, the Danube is occasionally associated with greed. In the pseudo-Ovidian *Consolatio ad Liviam*, for example, the river is referred to as 'Danuviusque rapax' (387), a fast-flowing body of water that consumes and carries away anything that is within its grasp. While, as a noun, *menudo(s)* denotes 'tripe' or 'small change', as an adjective, *menudo* may have the sense of 'pobre, bajo, desvalido' or 'avaro' (Alonso 1976: 526).

Thus, the juxtaposition of *un menudo* and *el Danubio* via the *ú–o* assonantal rhyme reinforces the link between the Danube and the deadly sin of Greed. Through his choice of the Danube, Polo not only parodies some serious strains of sixteenth-century poetry but also hints at the link between Venus, the archetypal woman, and Greed, a link that is reinforced later on when Venus is said to be *muy avarienta de pie* (41). The scene set by Polo also reflects the fact that 'the area designated for *mancebías* was usually outside the city walls, far away from the heart of the city, from churches and streets, and often close to the river' (Hsu 2002: 63–64).

Adonis is not the strikingly handsome young hunter of Classical mythology, whose death, which according to some traditions was orchestrated by Mars, provoked such an emotive response from Venus, but a picaresque layabout accustomed to extensive wanderings on an empty stomach punctuated by spurts of vigorous activity (presumably sexual): *que el mozuelo | come poco y anda mucho* (15–16). Given the link established later between eating (meat) and having sex, and the obscene implications of *fregaba el mondongo | sin hacer asco del zumo* (55–56), Venus's comical culinary preparations may suggest that she is, in fact, either recharging Adonis's batteries for another bout of lovemaking or already engaged in some sort of sexual practice with her young lover. Like many a picaresque figure, Adonis is subjected to the ravages of scatological humour. In 14–15, we find him having fainted from the stresses and strains of *ciertos pujos*, *pujo* being defined by *Aut.* as an 'enfermedad muy penosa, que consiste en la gana continua de hacer cámara, con gran dificultad de lograrlo, lo cual causa graves dolores en el seso'. Metaphorically, Adonis is worn out, having made a concerted effort to achieve a desired goal, presumably that of satisfying his own sexual desires or those of Venus. Literally, however, the young hunter has passed out, having undoubtedly gone bright red, due to the trials and tribulations associated with forcing something out of a bodily orifice: poor old Adonis has experienced the pain associated with either childbirth or tenesmus, the excruciatingly painful inability to defecate.

> **Era, pues, madama Venus**
> **moza redomada al uso,**
> **con más panza que un prior,**
> 20 **más enaguas que un diluvio;**
>
> **pelinegra y ojos grandes,**
> **más claros que dos carbunclos,**
> **si es que puede ser verdad**
> 24 **lo que de ellos dice el vulgo.**
>
> **No hay más asentada cosa**
> **que su cara en todo el mundo,**
> **y se levanta a mayores**
> 28 **sólo la nariz por puntos.**

Es mujer de pelo en pecho,
muy varonil y forzudo,
aunque pasa por lunar
32   en el concepto de muchos.

Es más ancha su cintura
que el trato, la vida y uso
de hombre que se va al infierno,
36   mercader, que todo es uno.

A lo jinete, estevadas
son sus piernas y sus muslos,
frisadas de vello, y gordas
40   como las letras de algunos.

Muy avarienta de pie,
de quien eran dos sepulcros,
con listones noguerados,
44   zapatillas de a diez puntos.

Esta es la estampa y bosquejo
de la diosa de los gustos:
adivine el estrellero,
48   zahorí de los influjos.

Madame Venus, who was a crafty little whore with bags of experience, had a belly bigger than that of a prior and more petticoats than a chorus line [literally, 'more petticoats than a deluge']. She had black hair and big eyes, brighter than two carbuncles, at least if what's said about them in the brothel's true. In the whole wide world there's nothing more set in stone than her face—only her massive nose is out of proportion with the rest of it. Very manly and strong, she's one of those women with a hairy chest, though it passes for a birthmark in the minds of many. Her waist's wider than the dealings, way of life, and practices of a man who goes to hell, or a merchant—they're one and the same. When she's riding, her legs and thighs are bandy, covered in down, and ungainly like some people's aimless ramblings. She's very greedy when she's on her feet, which are entombed in two size-10 shoes with thick walnut-coloured laces. This is the brief sketch or illustration of the goddess of desire: may the astrologer, diviner of celestial influences, try to predict what the future holds in store.

The description of Venus's physical appearance in 17–48 makes a mockery of the pictorial tradition of the Toilet of Venus and subverts the traditional function of Venus as a metonym for beauty and virtuous love. That Venus belongs to the world of the picaresque is confirmed when she is given the epithet *madama* (17), which carries the connotations of a married woman, a prostitute or brothel madame, or a midwife (Alonso 1976: 496), the last of these tying in with the suggestion that Adonis might be going through labour; Quevedo also plays with the absurd notion of male pregnancy in his *romance* 'Parióme adrede mi madre' (Q.696: 129–32). The connection between Venus and prostitution derives from the Classical distinction between the celestial Venus and the terrestrial Venus, as seen in the writings of Plato, Cicero, Boccaccio, Ficino, and Pérez de Moya, to list but a few. Throughout the poem, Polo's Venus is repeatedly shown to be the terrestrial, libidinal figure responsible for establishing the art of prostitution in Cyprus. In 18, we learn that she is a *moza redomada al uso*; as *Cov.* notes (*s.v. redomar*), 'llamamos redomado al hombre cauteloso y astuto, porque está recozido en malicia'. She has become a skilled tradeswoman after years of practice as a 'mujer astuta buscona' (Alonso 1976: 663). In 20, Venus's association with *enaguas* strengthens the image of her as a prostitute. In Polo's *Fábula de Apolo y Dafne*, the sun-god tries to seduce the fleeing nymph with a present of *enaguas*, 'petticoats', a symbol of extravagant *coquetería*. Here, Venus not only wears them but has *más enaguas que un diluvio* (20), a hyperbolic conceit based upon the play between *enaguas* and *en aguas* (compare the similar games with word division described above, pp. 157–58, 163).

Though the description of Venus follows the traditional Petrarchan order, the classical depiction of Venus as the paragon of female beauty is subverted as we are shown a muscular and manly woman with a potbelly, hairy chest, and massive nose (the last of these features drawing our attention to Venus's possible lack of *limpieza de sangre*; compare Quevedo's sonnet 'Érase un hombre a una nariz pegado', Q.513). She has black hair, a large waist, and gigantic feet. Her legs are fat, bandy, and hairy: '*gordas | como las letras de algunos*'. While *letras* could be 'palabrería o jerigonza de mendigos; el hecho de recitar las oraciones o lamentos en voz alta a fin de mover a compasión' (Alonso 1976: 479), *letras gordas* are 'las maçorrales y de hombres de poco ingenio' (*Cov.*). Thus, Polo refers in passing to the ramblings of both blabbering beggars and, as will become apparent, *culto* poets, 'hombres de poco ingenio'. Details of the physical appearance of Venus have been passed down through *el vulgo*, 'la gente ordinaria del pueblo' (*Cov.*) and the community of the *mancebía*, 'brothel' (Alonso 1976: 787). Polo acknowledges the disparity between this image of Venus and that to which his audience would have been more accustomed through an ironic aside to the fact that Venus's face is the most firmly established image in the poetic world (25–26). The description of Venus recalls Sancho Panza's decidedly unflattering portrayal of Aldonza Lorenzo in *Don Quijote*, I. XXV. When Don Quixote finally reveals to his squire the identity of his lady, Dulcinea, Sancho is amused to find that he knows his master's 'princess' only too well. He delights in telling Don Quixote, who has just declared his muse to be 'la que merece ser señora de todo el universo', that she is in fact none other than Aldonza, a humble peasant girl 'de pelo en pecho' and with a booming voice to boot (2005: I. 309–10). That description may, in turn, owe something to the *serranas* discussed in Chapter 1, above (18–20; see also Redondo 1983).

In 33–36, Polo combines a topical attack on merchants, whose greed and cheating secure their ticket to hell (see above, p. 150), with an allusion to the more lurid side of Venus's profession: *Es más ancha su cintura | que el trato, la vida y uso | de hombre que se va al infierno, | mercader, que todo es uno.* *Cov.* explains that *ancha* may be an allusion to 'vida ancha y conciencia ancha, libre y desalmada', while Alonso (1976: 41) explains that, in the phrase *venir algo muy ancho a uno,* '*ancho* alude también al coño, sobre todo el de las prostitutas o de las no doncellas, en el sentido de que, por carecer de virgo, es más ancho o abierto de lo que fuera menester en la idea de alguien que pretende mantener relaciones sexuales con vírgenes y, en consecuencia, esperaba encontrarlo estrecho'. While Polo alludes to the immoral behaviour of the *mercader*, 'ladrón que anda siempre donde hay trato' (Alonso 1976: 526), he also leads us to the obscene thought that Venus might literally be getting *más ancha* with every day that she plies her trade. As we shall see, the base sexual humour of Polo's meditation on the word *ancha* is developed in 229, when he plays with slang connotations of the verb *apretar*.

Lines 45–48 bring the portrait of Venus to a close. She is described as the *diosa de los gustos*: *gustos* being, in one sense, 'el trato ilícito o la relación de la prostituta con su cliente', and *una mujer del gusto* a prostitute (Alonso 1976: 425–26). The final two lines (47–48) call on the *estrellero* (47), 'astrologer' (or 'stargazer'), to try to predict what the future holds in store for Venus, both the goddess and the planet; the sense of the verb *adivinar* (47) being 'dezir lo que está por venir sin certidumbre ni fundamento, con temeridad y gran cargo de conciencia' (*Cov.*). The suggestion that 'astrology' is held in low esteem is then confirmed by the epithet *zahorí de los influjos* (48); *Cov.* has a rather negative view of the *çahorí*: 'El que dize ver lo que está debaxo de la tierra o detrás de una pared o encerrado en un arca, o lo que otro trae en el pecho, como no tenga algún aforro de grana. Ésta es una muy gran burlería y manifiesto error; pues naturalmente no puede ser... Digo, pues, que los *çahoríes*, sin intervención de pacto con el demonio, no pueden ver lo que está escondido debaxo de tierra, o de otra parte.' In Lope de Vega's c.1612–14 play *Fuente Ovejuna*, Laurencia's father Esteban offers a damning assessment of astrologers and their practice. In three octaves at the start of Act II (868–91), he attacks them for claiming to know things known only to God, for seeing themselves as theologians (yet knowing nothing about the present), for telling others what crops to sow (while they themselves are *calabazas*, 'pumpkin heads' or 'idiots'), and for making absurd predictions relating to far-off regions, such as Transylvania, Germany, and Gascony (Vega 1984: 123–24). While Polo appears to reflect this derogatory attitude towards astrologers, the suggestion that such figures could cast a horoscope for the goddess of love is ironic, for she would not normally be subject to their wild conjectures. At the same time, 47–48 suggest that one does not even have to be an 'astrologer' to read this woman's character or future, for the description of her external appearance in 17–44 makes it only too clear what is expected of her.

> **Por mirarla más de cerca,**
> **sobre las guijas se puso,**
> **haciendo antojo del agua,**
> 52 **Marte, transformado en pulpo;**
>
> **echando dos mil conceptos**
> **a los hermosos tarugos**
> **con que fregaba el mondongo,**
> 56 **sin hacer asco del zumo.**
>
> **Hizo Venus dos melindres,**
> **que el monstruo la dio gran susto;**
> **y el cuajar que enjabonaba**
> 60 **soltó al agua, abriendo el puño.**
>
> **Bien quisiera el dios amante,**
> **más blando y menos sañudo,**
> **dejar de pulpo la forma**
> 64 **por transformarse en besugo.**
>
> **El niño desabrigado,**
> **por vengarla de este insulto,**
> **veloz se llegó encubierto**
> 68 **por un florido arcabuco,**
>
> **y apuntando al corazón,**
> **le arrojó con fuerte impulso,**
> **con el arco cornicabra,**
> 72 **un virote zapatudo.**
>
> **Dejóle escrito en el alma,**
> **por más discretos y agudos,**
> **con caracteres vascuences**
> 76 **de la diosa el nombre augusto.**

In order to get a better view of her, Mars went out onto the shingle, disguised as an octopus, turning the water into a pair of spectacles (i.e. he contemplates Venus's reflection on the surface of the water). He launched two thousand conceits at the beautiful wooden pegs with which she was scrubbing the tripe without turning her nose up at the juices. Venus made a couple of gestures of affected daintiness, for the monster gave her a great fright and the fourth stomach, which she was dressing, leapt into the water as she opened her fist. The amorous god, more docile and less aggressive

*than before, really wanted to give up the form of an octopus to transform
himself into a red bream (to kiss Venus). In order to avenge this insult
against his mother, the naked child (Cupid) quickly arrived on the scene
hidden behind an elaborate harquebus. Aiming the cuckolding bow at
Mars's heart, Cupid instinctively fired off a dart that always hits its mark. It
left the venerable name of the goddess written on his soul in Basque letters,
for they are more clear and distinct.*

In the world of Classical mythology, Mars is one of the traditional lovers of
Venus. However, in the Classical sources of the myth it is not clear how he
came to find himself in such an enviable position. The first 160 lines of 'A
Vulcano, Venus y Marte', well over a third of Polo's poem, satisfy our desire
to know how Mars came to conquer the goddess of love and beauty. Like
Cueva, in his poem 'Los amores de Marte y Venus' (see above, p. 181),
Polo recounts the process of Mars's courtship of Venus, from his initial
declaration of love, to Venus's response, and the subsequent consummation
of their passion. By expanding the myth to include a series of events that
take place before the start of the traditional narrative, Polo establishes a
creative dialectic between invention and imitation, whilst giving free rein to
his own imagination and wit.

In the above lines we see the start of Mars's absurd courtship of Venus.
In 49–52, he settles on the banks of the Danube metaphorically transformed
into an octopus, a creature at home in the element of water. Mars's association with an octopus is absurd: he is exposed as a twit who is all arms in
his attempts to get closer to Venus. In order to eye her up, he turns the water
into an *antojo*, *antojos* being both 'caprichos' and 'los espejuelos que se
ponen delante de la vista para alargarla a los que la tienen corta' (*Cov.*). In
other words, he contemplates the reflection of Venus on the surface of the
water. He launches *dos mil conceptos* (53) in the direction of *los hermosos
tarugos | con que fregaba el mondongo | sin hacer asco del zumo* (54–56).
Tarugo is given by *Cov.* as 'un clavo de madera con que se aprietan las
junturas y ensambladuras de dos maderos'. Venus's fingers, which one might
otherwise expect to be feminine and dainty, are described as 'wooden pegs'.
We return to the image of the common washerwoman engaged in a menial
task. However, *mondongo*, 'tripe', can also, in *germanía*, denote both 'la
barriga de una persona' (Alonso 1976: 537) and the male sexual organ
(Chamorro 2002: 591). Accordingly it comes as no surprise to learn that
zumo was slang for 'semen' (*ibid.*: 827). While Venus is still preparing the
menudo of 12, she is also both scrubbing her belly and pleasuring Adonis.

Mars's movements do not have the desired effect upon his target. *Cov.*
defines *melindre* (57) as 'un género de frutilla de sartén hecha con miel;
comida delicada y tenida por golosina. De allí vino a sinificar este nombre
el regalo con que suelen hablar algunas damas, a las quales por esta razón
llaman melidrosas'. Venus is the sort of lady who affects airs and graces;
she pretends to be prim and proper (*parecer*) but is, as we shall see, any-

thing and everything but (*ser*). In this regard (and many others), Polo's Venus is a decidedly more unsavoury figure than Aldonza Lorenzo, of whom Sancho says, in I. XXV: 'lo mejor que tiene es que no es nada melindrosa, porque tiene mucho de cortesana: con todos se burla y de todo hace mueca y donaire' (2005 : I. 310). The monstrous apparition scares Venus into dropping the absurdly specific *cuajar* (59), 'fourth stomach', into the river. In 61–63, Mars subsequently wishes to transform himself into another creature of the water, a red bream. Such a metamorphosis would allow him to kiss Venus, for the expression *jugar de besugo* means 'besar mucho' (Alonso 1976: 110). Mars's natural instincts are tempered by his amorous desires. The suggestion that he is now *más blando y menos sañudo* (62) is a subtle allusion to the Neoplatonic doctrines of Ficino and Hebreo, according to which Venus alone can pacify Mars. As we shall see, Polo implicitly parodies the concept of *discordia concors* and the Neoplatonic belief that the negative qualities associated with the god of war may be held in equilibrium with the positive virtues of Venus. Though *blando* denotes someone who will comply with the wishes of others, as *Cov.* explains, *blandura* is often feigned: 'Lo que es blando déxase tratar, y hazemos dello lo que queremos, obedeciendo a nuestra voluntad, y esso mesmo haze el hombre apazible de condición y fácil, que se acomoda a la voluntad de qualquiera, aunque muchas vezes es fingida esta blandura, para asegurarnos y engañarnos a la fin.'

Cupid, *el niño desabrigado* (65), comes to his mother's rescue armed with a *florido arcabuco* (68), which is then described as an *arco cornicabra* (71). Cupid's harquebus is made out of the wood of the *terebinto* or turpentine tree. The *cornicabra* is chosen for its association with both horns (*corn-*) and an animal that has horns (*cabra*). Cupid's bow will make Vulcan a cuckold, but, in time, Mars will also become a cuckold, for Venus will forget about the warrior-god and turn her attentions elsewhere. By shooting Mars with the phallic *virote zapatudo* (72), Cupid ensures that Mars will fall for Venus. As *Cov.* explains, *virote* 'se dixo de vira. Éstos sirven tan solamente para matar conejos, liebres o algunas aves, como la perdiz', while *zapatudo*, according to *Aut.,* 'vale también lo que está asegurado, o tiene puesta alguna zapata'. Drawing on the tradition of Petrarchan lyric, Venus's name is inscribed on Mars's soul by Cupid's arrow, or pen. However, the topos of the engraving of the beloved's name on the lover's soul is parodied as Venus's name is inscribed *con caracteres vascuences* (75), *vascuence* denoting 'lo que está tan confuso, y obscuro, que no se puede entender' (*Aut.*). The suggestion that Cupid's *caracteres vascuences* are *discretos y agudos* (74), and thus easy to read, is ironic, for Venus's name is written in a script that is almost impossible to understand.

> **No pudiendo por los ojos**
> **su divino bello bulto**
> **trasladar a sus entrañas,**
> 80   **bebió en el agua el trasunto.**

Para decirla sus ansias
en dulces conceptos cultos
dejó el disfraz de cuaresma
84   y el carnal tomó del suyo.

Miróla Marte amoroso,
y ella con desdén y zuño;
que es la moza por extremo
88   socarrona, si él astuto.

Diferentes se contemplan,
si unánimes en lo culto;
él tierno a lo portugués,
92   ella arrogante a lo turco.

Because he couldn't transfer her divine and beautiful bulk to his insides through his eyes he drank up her refection in the water. In order to convey his amorous desires to her in sweet culto conceits, he abandoned the disguise associated with Lent and took on his customary carnal appearance. Mars looked longingly at Venus and she responded with a look of disdain and irritation—for if he is cunning she is extremely sly. Though their attitudes to one another differ, they are united in their use of culto language: he as affectionate as a Portuguese lover, she as boastful as a Turk.

Unable to satiate his desires by merely admiring Venus from afar, Mars changes his appearance once again in 77–84. The first quatrain develops the parody of the topos of the lover gazing at the beloved's imagined reflection in a stream, a parody that is reinforced by the alliteration of the absurd description of Venus as *su divino bello bulto* (78). *Cov.* (*s.v. bulto*) notes that 'Los cortos de vista dizen ver de las cosas el bulto, que es la corpulencia', further confirmation that Mars is shortsighted (a stigma both physical and moral). The *entrañas* of 79 stand in opposition to the *alma* of 73. In Góngora's *romance* 'Ensíllenme el asno rucio' of 1585 (GR.18), a burlesque reworking of Lope's serious *romance morisco* 'Ensíllenme el potro rucio' (1583; Vega 1982: 70–73), the Cordoban poet replaces Lope's valiant and aristocratic Moor with the simple peasant Galayo. Whereas Lope's Azarque, who is preparing to leave for battle, opens his appeal to the beloved with the hyperbolic 'Adalifa de mi alma', Góngora's rustic anti-hero appeals to 'Teresa de mis entrañas' before heading off for the riverside brothel: 'A dar, pues, se parte el bobo | estocadas y reveses, | y tajos, orilla el Tajo, | en mil hermosos broqueles' (81–84). As in Góngora's parody of Lope, here it becomes apparent that the male protagonist is more interested in the physical pleasures associated with sex than anything approaching the more sophisticated forms of Platonic love.

In the next quatrain (81–84) religious and sexual frames of reference are combined to suggest that after a period of abstinence from eating meat Mars is ready to resume normal service: he abandons his disguise associated with Lent and takes up *el carnal... del suyo* (84). *Cov.* (*s.v. disfraz*) notes that 'Particularmente se usan estos disfraces en los días de carnestolendas'. He also explains (*s.v. carnal*) that 'al hombre que es muy dado a la sensualidad y vicio de la carne, le llamamos carnal. También llamamos carnal el tiempo del año que se come carne, en respeto de la quaresma, y los días cercanos a ella llamamos carnaval, porque nos despedimos della, como si le dixésse-mos; *carne vale*'. Thus, the word *carnal* refers not only to Mars's sexual proclivities but also to a specific period outside Lent. Throughout the poem references to eating and, in particular, to meat are surcharged with sexual connotations; *carne* refers to 'la de la prostituta y a la prostituta misma o a sus actividades' (Alonso 1976: 183). After a period without the pleasure of sexual intercourse, Mars intends to have his wicked way with Venus. Polo's description of the start of Mars's courtship of Venus informs the reader of exactly how the god of war intends to continue, from voyeurism (*pulpo*), through the foreplay of petting and kissing (*besugo*), to the desired goal of full sexual intercourse (*carnal*). The whole sequence is reminiscent of the battle between Don Carnal and Doña Quaresma in stanzas 1067–1209 of the fourteenth-century *Libro de buen amor*.

The final two quatrains of this section present a series of oppositions between Mars and Venus. Whilst they are alike in their usage of *culto* forms of discourse, in all other respects we see a reversal of the roles ascribed to them by Classical tradition. In 85–86, it is Mars who is presented as the tender lover and Venus who is characterized by *desdén y zuño*. Being *portugués* (91) is synonymous with being in love, as 'el portugués aparece frecuentemente en la literatura de la época como el prototipo del enamo-rado' (Alonso 1976: 630), while to call someone *turco* (92) is to insult them: 'esta nación es más conocida de lo que avíamos menester, por aver venido a señorear tan gran parte del orbe; gente baxa y de malas costumbres, que vivían de robar y maltratar a los demás' (*Cov.*). Venus is described as *socarrona* (88), a word relating to the craftiness of a 'mujer desvergonzada' and one frequently used to describe swindlers (Chamorro 2002: 740–41). As we can see already, Polo exploits the slang connotations of many words in order to underline the negative characteristics of both Mars and Venus.

> **Después de haberse ostentado**
> **ella grave y él confuso,**
> **la dijo en razones verdes**
> 96 **estos requiebros maduros:**
>
> **'Diosa nacida entre conchas,**
> **de cuyo principio arguyo**
> **que las tienes en el trato,**
> 100 **si las niega el disimulo;**

> alhóndiga de belleza,
> hija del capón Saturno,
> de cuya capona tacha
> 104 no heredaste ni un minuto;

Having paraded themselves in front of one another, she serious and he disconcerted, Mars conveyed to her in dirty words the following tried and tested sweet nothings: 'Goddess born amongst shells, from whose origin I infer that you employ them in your dealings even if you mask them through deceit (i.e. that it is clear that she is a prostitute despite her attempts to conceal her trade). Oh, corn-exchange of beauty, daughter of the emasculated Saturn, of whose castrated mark you didn't inherit even the smallest part.'

The Classical authority of Mars is further undermined through the presentation of his verbal exchanges with Venus: first, we are told that he addresses her with *dos mil conceptos* (54); next, in order to express his *ansias*, a word that relates specifically to the relationship between a pimp and his prostitute (Chamorro 2002: 94), Mars employs *dulces conceptos cultos* (82), *razones verdes* (95) and *requiebros maduros* (96), only for Venus to dismiss them as *bombardas y chuzos* (140); and when Mars, metaphorically transformed into an *avechucho* (222), drops in to see Venus on the occasion of their capture, he conducts himself in accordance with *las jerigonzas del gusto* (226). As we shall see, by associating *culto* forms of expression with a mythological god who is exposed as a member of the underworld of pimps and prostitutes, Polo ridicules one of the predominant contemporary modes of poetic discourse. The full extent of the disparity between how the words of Mars are described and what he actually says is confirmed in his mock serenade to Venus.

The opening of Mars's address to Venus is absurd. The warrior-god begins with a comical eulogy of the birth of Venus, based on Hesiod's account of the conjunction of Saturn's castrated member and the waters of the ocean (97–100). Saturn is remembered not for ruling over the Classical Golden Age but for being emasculated by his son. The shell on which Venus traditionally arrives on the shore of Cyprus allows the poet to associate her with the vice of prostitution through the double meaning of the word *concha*, both a shell and a symbol of the female genitalia. Mars comments that Venus's line of work involves *conchas* yet notes her attempts to disguise her trade through *el disimulo* (99–100). While, in *germanía*, *trato* (34 and 99), 'dealings', also means 'sexual relations', a *mujer del trato* is a prostitute and *los del trato* are those involved in *la vida rufianesca* (Alonso 1976: 751). Thus, *el trato* makes the art that she practises abundantly clear. By describing Venus as an *alhóndiga de belleza* (101), a place where beauty or sex, like corn, is bought and sold, Mars introduces us to the commercial side of Venus's trade, in a way reminiscent of Quevedo's account of the relations between men and women (see above, p. 162). Questions of setting prices and of buying and selling return when Mars and Venus haggle over the price of their transaction. The last three lines turn to questions of lineage and astrology. Polo returns to the sphere of the *estrellero* (48) who divides 'círculos esferales y el zodíaco en grados y minutos' (*Cov.*). According to Mars, Venus has inherited none of the scars associated with Saturn's emasculation. However, the description of Venus in 17–44 allows us to see through the thin veneer provided by Mars's flattery and self-deception.

> yo soy el dios revoltoso,
> el que alcanzó sin segundo,
> con las fuerzas de mis armas,
> 108   muchas victorias y triunfos.
>
> Yo inventé la caja y trompa,
> instrumentos tremebundos,
> que el uno anima a los hombres,
> 112   y el otro alienta a los brutos.
>
> Mas tanto poder, ¿qué importa,
> si con sólo un estornudo
> de tus basiliscos ojos
> 116   me tiene tu amor sin pulsos?
>
> Cordero a tus pies me postro
> si bien de tu humor presumo
> que para ciencia tan mansa
> 120   es sutil ingenio el tuyo.
>
> Permite que mis deseos
> den fondo en tu mar profundo,
> si acaso de él no heredaste
> 124   sus borrascas y reflujos.
>
> Consiente, pues, diosa bella,
> que sea de sus ondas buzo,
> si no quieres verme en ellas
> 128   infelice Palinuro.
>
> Serás, oh Venus, mi manfla,
> yo seré, Venus, tu cuyo;
> serás de este Marte marta,
> 132   que lo abrigues aun por julio;
>
> que si vengo a verme cuervo
> de esas bellas carnes, juro
> de darte seis tabaqueras
> 136   para tabaco con humo.'

I am the rebellious god, the one who through the force of my arms achieved an unparalleled number of victories and triumphs. I invented the drum and the

*horn, fearsome instruments, for one arouses men while the other stirs up beasts.
But what use is all this power, if your love knocks me out with a simple blink
from your basilisk-like eyes? I prostrate myself like a lamb at your feet even
though judging by your mood I reckon your skill is subtle when it comes to
this gentle science. Allow my desires to drop anchor in your deep sea, if that is
you haven't inherited its ebbs and squalls. Beautiful goddess, let me dive into
your waves, if you don't want to see me as an unfortunate Palinurus in them.
Oh Venus, you'll be my courtesan and I'll be your lover. You'll be this Mars's
prostitute—may you keep him warm even in July, because if I get to pick at that
lovely flesh like a crow, I swear I'll give you six pouches for smoking tobacco.*

In 105–12, Mars proceeds with a boastful description of his own military, and
by extension also sexual, achievements, thus confirming the identification of
him as a Plautan *Miles Gloriosus*. The warrior-god claims that his skill on
the battlefield is unparalleled and that he invented *la caja y trompa* (109),
two *instrumentos tremebundos* (110) associated with war. However, whilst
la caja inspires men in battle, as slang for 'brothel' (Alonso 1976: 153) it also
leads men astray. Mars presents himself as a sacrificial *cordero*, or cuckold
(*ibid.*: 226), at the goddess's feet. The context of this commonplace form of
prostration or submission, depicted in works such as Francesco del Cossa's
Aprile (1469–70), renders it absurd. One of the most arresting descriptions
of Venus is given in 113–16 when Mars complains that all his power is use-
less in the face of *un estornudo | de [sus] basiliscos ojos*, a burlesque re-
minder of Venus's unique ability to subdue and tame the god of war. As *Cov.*
explains, the *basilisco* is 'Una especie de serpiente, de la qual haze mención
Plinio, lib. 8, cap. 21. Críase en los desiertos de África, tiene en la cabeça
cierta crestilla con tres puntas en forma de diadema y algunas manchas blancas sembradas por el cuerpo; no es mayor que un palmo, con su silvo ahuyen-
ta las demás serpientes y con su vista y resuello mata'. The identification of
Venus with the basilisk, whose evil eye was a symbol of destructive power
and moral degeneration, allows for an economical reference to the Petrarchan commonplace that the look of a woman had the power to kill a man, as
reworked in the opening to Quevedo's ballad 'Los médicos con que miras, |
los dos ojos con que matas' (Q.706). The basilisk, which is an integral
component of many descriptions of unspeakable monsters in Gracián's *El
criticón*, is also the subject of Quevedo's poem 'Al basilisco': 'si está vivo
quien te vio, | toda tu historia es mentira, | pues si no murió, te ignora | y si
murió, no lo afirma' (Q.700(3): 53–56; see Arellano 2002). Significantly,
the basilisk could not stand its own appearance. It is ironic that a narcissistic
Venus, so often seen in Renaissance and Baroque painting contemplating
her reflection in a mirror (e.g. Velázquez's *Rokeby Venus*, which hangs in
the National Gallery in London), should be compared to an animal that has a
fabled aversion to reflective surfaces.

The fact that Mars is confronted by an *estornudo* is more problematic.
Common sense dictates that, here, *estornudo*, 'sneeze', has the meaning of

'blink', in that most people involuntarily close their eyes upon sneezing. We are thus presented with an asburd description of what Mars presumably takes to be flirtatious behaviour from Venus: when she sneezes, she cannot prevent herself from blinking, or batting her eyes at him. However, Polo is also drawing on the link between sneezing and death, as given by *Cov.* (*s.v. estornudar*): 'En un tiempo huvo en Roma un género de peste tan subitánea que, estornudando, los hombres se quedavan muertos.' This link between death and sneezing, one of the main symptoms of the plague, suggests that Polo's Venus may be a victim of one of the many epidemics that swept through Europe periodically after the fourteenth-century Black Death. However, whilst plague victims were themselves thought to be close to death when they sneezed, here the suggestion is that Mars will contract the plague and die as a result of Venus's violent exhalation. While idealized Petrarchan women metaphorically had the ability to render a man lifeless, and could thus be compared to basilisks, Polo's ugly brothel madame literally has the ability to kill Mars. Yet another nail is driven into the coffin of serious adherence to both Petrarchan metaphor and the authority of the pagan gods.

This mock eulogy soon gives way to the expression of Mars's true desires in 121–28. Here, periphrasis and erudite Classical allusion are employed for the purpose of parodying *culto* forms of discourse in which such devices had become the normal mode of expression. Mars thinly veils his intentions through a range of associated euphemisms based on references to navigation and diving: he wants to drop his phallic anchor in Venus's deep sea and dive into the waves of her genitalia. While Polo draws a parallel between the movements of the anchor or diver, as each penetrates the surface of the water, and the motions of the male member in sexual intercourse, he also develops both base and erudite wordplay to suggest that the waters of the ocean are not without their own dangers. Mars wants to have sex with Venus but recognizes that this might be made problematic by the presence of *borrascas y reflujos* (124). On the one hand, the *borrascas y reflujos* are the 'ebbs and squalls' that pose a danger to those navigating the waters of the oceans; on the other, they represent forms of Venus's menstrual flow, *fluxo* denoting 'Fluxo de sangre, enfermedad enfadosa y peligrosa, por otro nombre sangre lluvia' (*Cov.*). The erudite reference to *infelice Palinuro* (128) is to Aeneas's helmsman, Palinurus, who in Virgil's *Aeneid*, V.779–871, fell asleep on deck and was cast into the water. He swam for four days and reached the Italian coastline, only to be killed by the Lucanians on his arrival. The allusion to the death of Palinurus represents another aspect of Polo's reworking of the Petrarchan commonplace introduced in the description of the effects of Venus's *ojos basiliscos*.

In 129–32, Mars offers to be Venus's *cuyo*, 'marido, o amante, en el caso de los rufianes y de las prostitutas que los mantienen', if she agrees to be his *manfla*, a 'mujer con la que se tiene trato ilícito' (Alonso 1976: 253, 506). In an absurd play on his own name, *Marte/marta* (131), Mars then invites Venus to be his pine marten (whose Latin name is *Martes martes*), an animal that is active predominantly at night and thus an appropriate slang term for a 'prostitute'. *Marta* also refers to the proverbial character who is 'a hypocritical woman who puts on the front of piety for show' (Hayes 1939: 316), as in Tirso de Molina's 1615 play *Marta la piadosa*. The figure of Marta is the subject of many contemporary *refranes*, such as 'Kókale, Marta' and 'Habla Marta, rresponde Xusta; una puta a otra buska' (Correas 1967: 176, 585), the second of these revealing a clear link between the figure of Marta and prostitution (one also drawn on in Quevedo's sonnet 'A quien hace el Amor tantas mercedes', Q.616: 11). In a second play on Mars's name, this time based on the months of the Gregorian calendar, Mars asks Venus to keep him warm even in July, one of the hottest months of the year (the marten was also noted for its warm fur). The implication is that Mars wants to have sex with her all year round. Ironically, in the language of *germanía*, *abrigo* signifies the 'protección que el rufián dispensa a la prostituta a la vez que la ejercita en las mañas del oficio' (Alonso 1976: 4). We are brought back to the relationship between the *cuyo/jaque* and the *manfla/madama*, yet here, in an inversion of the standard relationship between pimp and prostitute, it is Venus who will provide protection, or *abrigo*, for Mars. This complements the role reversal suggested above (91–92).

Mars promises to give Venus *seis tabaqueras | para tabaco con humo* (133–34) if he gets to pick at her flesh like a crow. The *cuervo* (133), perhaps best rendered here as 'raven', is not only an 'ave conocida, y entre todas las más negra' and thus a 'símbolo de la noche', but also a bird associated with flattery: 'Compararon los egypcios, en sus hieroglíficos, los aduladores a los cuervos, y dixeron ser más perjudiciales aun que ellos; porque el cuervo saca los ojos corporales al hombre muerto que halla en la horca, y el lisongero adulador saca los ojos del alma y del entendimiento al hombre vivo' (*Cov.*). One is reminded once more of the tale of the Fox and the Crow (see above, pp. 136, 171). On the one hand, the image of the flatterer Mars picking at Venus's flesh like a raven functions as another grotesque metaphor for sexual intercourse. On the other, since scavengers usually pick at dead flesh or carrion, the same image shows Mars feeding on the necrotic tissue of a woman riddled with disease. The offer of six tobacco pouches might seem to represent an exotic present connected with the New World, but tobacco was also taken as a restorative cure for syphilis and gonorrhoea and as a means of purging the brain; as *Cov.* suggests, tobacco snuff was used to 'expeler las humedades del cerebro' (compare Quevedo's sonnet 'Al tabaco en polvo, doctor a pie', Q.524).

> **Respondióle la taimada:**
> **'Marte, ofendida te escucho**
> **de que pienses conquistarme**
> 140 **con bombardas y con chuzos.**

Las tusonas de mi porte
no temen fuerzas ni orgullos;
que en su golfo y mar sin norte
144 no se camina por rumbos.

Todas son Troyas de bronce,
y sólo rompen su muro
un doblón con "Vida mía,
148 tómalo, que todo es tuyo".'

Marte le replica, y Venus
siempre en sus trece se estuvo;
al fin venció sus desdenes
152 con las armas de un escudo.

The crafty woman replied: 'Mars, I'm offended to hear that you think you can conquer me with bombards and pikes. Prostitutes of my standing are not afraid of force or boasting, for one does not get by with lavish show in such gulfs and seas without setting a course. They (i.e. high-class prostitutes) are all bronze Troys, and their walls can be breached only with a doubloon accompanied by the words "Love of my life, take it, for everything is yours".' Mars responds, but Venus continued to stand her ground. In the end he conquered her disdainful indifference by arming himself with a shield/employing a gold coin as a weapon.

Venus's identification with the oldest trade in the world is confirmed when Mars has to pay her for sex. In 137–52, Venus responds to Mars's verbal advances, undermining his mock serenade with her insistence on the language of commercial exchange. Mars's *bombardas*, 'bombards', and *chuzos*, 'pikes', are both military weapons associated with his profession as a soldier and forms of flattery and boasting, though *chuzo* is also slang for 'prick' (Chamorro 2002: 161, 314). Venus will not succumb to his verbal advances, nor will she be deceived by his tricks or tempted by his bribes. She is adamant that her defences, likened to the walls of Troy, *bronze* (145) marking something that is 'de gran fortaleza' (*Cov.*), can be breached only through the vehicle of money, Mars's equivalent of Odysseus's Trojan Horse.

Venus is a prostitute but she is no mere *buscona de Chipre* (see Quevedo's 'Anilla, dame atención', Q.682: 287), for she is from the very highest order of contemporary courtesans. Her status is confirmed when she speaks of *las tusonas de [su] porte* (141). The general Golden-Age concern for hierarchy and rank extends even to the sphere of prostitution, as Tristán explains to the young Don García in the 1634 play *La verdad sospechosa*: 'Hay una gran multitud | de señoras del Tusón, | que entre cortesanas son | de la mayor magnitud' (Ruiz de Alarcón 1999: 71–74). A *tusona*, the female equivalent of a member of the Order of the Golden Fleece, was a high-class escort, the cause of many a man's ruin: 'Las *tusonas*, o *damas del tusón*, constituían la aristocracia del oficio, como si dijéramos las modernas *cocottes* de alto copete; y se las denominaba de tal modo para determinar su preeminencia, así como entre las Órdenes militares ocupaban el primer puesto los *caballeros del tusón* o *del toisón'* (Deleito 1948: 37). Like Elicia and Areúsa in the *Celestina*, Venus is not attached to a public brothel, nor does she solicit in the streets or in public squares like mere *cantoneras*. Unlike Elicia and Areúsa, however, she is neither beautiful nor well dressed. Whilst the reference to *tusonas* points to the highest rank of prostitutes, it also suggests that Venus may have lost her hair on numerous occasions as a result of punishments meted out, or diseases encountered, during the course of her day-to-day business; *Aut.* defines *tusona* as 'Ramera, o dama cortesana. Pudo decirse así, porque les cortan el pelo por castigo, o ellas le pierden por el vicio deshonesto' (compare pp. 159–60, above). Picking up on Mars's seafaring metaphor, Venus claims that Mars is ill equipped to venture out on the waters associated with high-class prostitutes: *que en su golfo y mar sin norte | no se camina por rumbos* (143–44), *norte* here being a 'guiding star'. While *rumbo* denotes 'una figura de cosmógraphos en forma de estrella, en la qual forman los vientos y sirve a los marineros con la carta y aguja de marear' (*Cov.*), it is also, as in 2, 'distinción, elegancia, pompa' (Alonso 1996: 686–87). Just as the Greeks could gain access to Troy after almost a decade of besieging the city only through the medium of the Trojan Horse, so Mars can hope to enter the city of Venus only through payment. Venus demands a *doblón* (147), an 'escudo de a dos' (*Cov.*), but also, given the context of the poem, another form of tripe, for *doblón de vaca* is 'la tripa doblada que haze callo... y para la gente grosera es un goloso bocado si después de bien cozido lo asan y lo untan con azeyte y ajo, o lo comen con su ajo nuez' (*Cov.*).

Lines 149–52 suggest that the gods reach an impasse, before an extensive period of bartering leads to a financial transaction. It is noteworthy that Mars should end up paying one *escudo* when the original asking price was a *doblón*, worth exactly twice as much. Either Mars is proficient in the art of haggling or business is slow for Venus. Whilst the agreement reached by Mars and Venus is made on the conventional battlefield of love, the trappings of Mars's past military splendour are transformed through simple punning into cash for sexual favours. Their exchange is based not on friendship, honour, and love but on the buying and selling of brothel language. The *doblón/escudo* wordplay also draws on the fact that in medieval iconography soldiers armed with a shield or mirror were often shown fighting the basilisk. Perhaps it is in this light that we should view Mars when he breaks down Venus's defences *con las armas de un escudo* (152), both a gold coin and an impressive military shield.

> Concertáronse en secreto
> de ser los dos para en uno,
> antes que la Aurora calva
> 156 despertase el dios greñudo;

que era el tiempo en que a Vulcano
deleitaban importunos
del yunque las consonancias,
160 del fuelle los contrapuntos.

Despidiéronse abrazando
Venus al amante adusto,
volviéndola dulces paces
164 el dios que nunca las tuvo.

Vulcano, que ya por cierto
tiene del ave el abuso
que cantando hados presentes,
168 predice agravios futuros,

y que se sueña animal
jarameño y corajudo,
convertido en puerco espín
172 a garrochas y repullos,

y en un sueño vio dos cañas
que tenían sus cañutos,
en su mujer las raíces,
176 y en su cabeza los ñudos,

para vengarse, prendiendo
al autor de sus disgustos,
viéndose en su oficio y arte,
180 con ingenio peliagudo,

labró de templado acero
una red sutil, que dudo
pudiera verla un vecino
184 ni el pastor frisón de Juno.

En el lecho conyugal
de manera la dispuso,
que no pudiera escaparse
188 el cobarde más astuto.

They agreed in secret that the two of them would become one, before bald Dawn woke up the dishevelled god (Apollo); for it was the time when Vulcan took pleasure in the inopportune consonances of the anvil and the counterpoints of the bellows. When they said goodbye to one another, Venus embraced the severe lover, and Mars, the god who had experienced nothing but war, returned her to the world of sweet peace. Vulcan has already got wind of the outrage from the bird that singing about present fates predicts future problems. He dreams of himself as a brave animal from Jarama,

*turned into a porcupine with spikes and little arrows. In a dream he saw two
canes with their shoots, the roots of which were in his wife, and the knots of
which were in his head (i.e. another man sleeps with Venus and horns begin
to sprout from Vulcan's temples). In order to get revenge by catching the
author of his misfortune, and since he was in his forge surrounded by his
tools, with cunning skill, he forged a subtle net out of tough metal, which I
doubt even a neighbour or Juno's Friesian shepherd (Argos) could see. He
erected it round the marriage bed in such a way that not even the most astute
coward could escape.*

Mars and Venus spend the night together before the arrival of Dawn heralds
the appearance of Apollo. Before they part company, they agree to be *los
dos para en uno* (154), 'two as one'. The irony here is that the phrase *ser los
dos para en uno* usually relates to the marriage or indissoluble union of one
man and one woman. The phrase is used, for example, in *Fuente Ovejuna* to
describe the exemplary couples in both the main plot (Laurencia and Fron-
doso, lines 738, 1298, 1545) and the subplot (the Reyes Católicos, Ferdinand
and Isabella, line 2037; Vega 1984: 117, 141, 149, 171). Here, of course,
Mars and Venus are committing not to marriage but to a clandestine extra-
marital affair. Polo plays with the Classical tradition of lending epithets to
Dawn; here she is not 'rosy-fingered' but *calva* (155), pointing once more
in the direction of the bald syphilitic (see above, p. 199). In contrast, Apollo
is described as *el dios greñudo, greñas* denoting 'la cabellera rebuelta y mal
compuesta, quales suelen traerlas los pastores y los desaliñados, que nunca
se la peinan' (*Cov.*). This very brief reference to Apollo's dishevelled state
stands in contrast to Don Quixote's comically elevated description (I. II) of
how he imagines his first sally will be recorded: 'Apenas hubo el rubicundo
Apolo tendido por la faz de la ancha y espaciosa tierra las doradas hebras de
sus hermosos cabellos, y apenas los pequeños y pintados pajarillos con sus
harpadas lenguas habían saludado con dulce y meliflua armonía la venida de
la rosada aurora, que, dejando la blanda cama del celoso marido, por las
puertas y balcones del manchego horizonte...' (2005: I. 50). When, in
Polo's *romance,* the new day is ushered in by the now less than impressive
Aurora and Apollo, the lovers part company and the scene switches to
Vulcan's forge. The reader is invited to picture the smith-god hard at work
surrounded by his anvil, bellows, and other tools (compare the description
of Vulcan's forge in Virgil's *Aeneid*, VIII. 407–53).

Many seventeenth-century prostitutes pretended to be married in order to
evade prosecution. In this case, however, Venus is actually married. The
arrival of Venus's husband is deliberately held back until 165; Vulcan
becomes the principal protagonist of the second half of the poem. The
majority of seventeenth-century poets regard Vulcan as a figure of fun. In
Quevedo's satirical poems, Vulcan is introduced as the archetypal cuckold.
In a ballad written against the power of Cupid, Venus is seen as a prostitute
who allows her husband to rest while she evaluates Mars's erotic attributes

(Q.709: 17–28). In another, the poetic voice claims that Venus made him Vulcan and that Mars made him a cuckold: 'Menguó mi luna en mi esfera | y mi sol vino a eclipsarse, | Venus me dejó Vulcano | cornudo me dejó Marte' (Q.680: 101–04).

In a modification of the Homeric original, Vulcan is already aware of his wife's infidelity: *Vulcano, que ya por cierto | tiene del ave el abuso, | que cantando hados presentes, | predice agravios futuros* (165–68). While the *ave* in question could be the *búho*, 'Ave noturna, infeliz y de mal agüero' (*Cov.*), it seems more likely that it is, in fact, the *cuclillo*, 'ave conocida y de mal agüero para los casados celosos'. As *Cov.* goes on to explain, there is a strong link between the cuckoo and the cuckold: 'siendo esta avecica, dicha corruca, tan simple que saca los huevos de qualquier otra, poniéndoselos en su nido, el cuclillo de pereza, por no criar los suyos, derrueca en el suelo del nido abaxo los huevos de la corruca, o se los come, y déxale allí los suyos para que se los saque y críe. Esto mesmo haze el adúltero, quando la adúltera ha concebido dél, y el marido cría y alimenta el hijo que pare, creyendo ser suyo.' The *cuclillo* is also associated with the verb *cantar*, as in the phrase 'Por vos cantó el cuclillo' (*Cov., s.v. cantar*). Vulcan has heard the song of the cuckoo and has thus been informed of his wife's infidelity; aware of the *hados presentes* (167), the situation that he is now in, he is also conscious of the *agravios futuros* (168) associated with the end of the narrative.

In 169–72, Vulcan dreams of revenge. However, what he aspires to be, namely an agile and brave fighting bull, is the antithesis of what he actually is. The parallel between Vulcan and the finest fighting bulls in Spain, those from the region bordering the river Jarama, is patently absurd, for he is lame and clumsy. The only point of comparison between Vulcan and a bull is that both possess horns: 'cual suele arremeter a jarameño, | toro feroz, de media luna armado' (Lope de Vega, *La Gatomaquia*, III. 240–41; Vega 1983: 136). Vulcan imagines himself as an *animal | jarameño y corajudo | convertido en puerco espín* (169–71). *Cov.* says of the *puerco espín*: 'Está todo lleno de unas púas muy fuertes y agudas, las quales arroja a los perros, quando se ve fatigado dellos y se las enclava como si fuessen saetas.' For Louis XII, King of France from 1498 to 1515, the porcupine had been a symbol of invincibility. The French king's motto *Cominus et eminus* alludes to both the animal's inbuilt defence mechanism, based on *garrochas* ('la vara que se tira al toro para embravecerle con un hierro de lengüeta, que es como gorra', *Cov.*) and *repullos* ('se llama asimismo una saetilla, vestida por la parte superior de plumas o papel, para arrojarla derecha, y clavarla en alguna cosa', *Aut.*), and its mythical ability to throw such spines at any attackers. As we shall see, the full comic potential of these animal comparisons is explored in the poem's denouement.

Vulcan forges his net in response to a dream in which he sees other men enjoying the benefits of his wife's company (173–84). *Cov.* defines *cañuto* (174) as 'qualquiera caña o palo horadado y hueco', but it is also, by extension, 'prick' (Chamorro 2002: 218). On the one hand, the *cañutos* are the penises of Venus's lovers, or clients; on the other, they are the horns of Vulcan's cuckoldry. Thus, it is entirely appropriate that their *raíces* (175), 'los orígines y principios dellos' (*Cov.*), should be found in Vulcan's wife, Venus, while their *ñudos* (176)—'por metáfora... en los árboles, el nacimiento de los ramos' (*Cov.*)—appear as shoots from Vulcan's temples. As Venus beds more and more men, the horns of her husband's cuckoldry continue to grow.

For Homer and Ovid, the forging of the net represents a set piece in which the quality and ingenuity of Vulcan's craftsmanship are eulogized. Here, however, Vulcan's net is forged with *ingenio peliagudo* (180), *peliagudo* referring to 'el cabrito, ternero, conejo y otros animales semejantes' (*Cov.*). Whereas Homer suggests that the net is invisible even to the gods, and Ovid suggests that it surpasses the finest products of Nature, a thread of silk or a spider's web, Polo combines contemporary social satire and erudite Classical allusion by stating that it is made invisible even to neighbours and to Argos, the hundred-eyed shepherd left by Juno to guard the heifer Io. While Homer stresses the fact that the net is unbreakable, Polo suggests that it would be impossible for even the most cunning coward (another popular figure of contemporary satire) to escape from the trap.

> Cuando la tierra enlosaba
> de la noche el manto oscuro,
> dejó las fraguas Vulcano,
> 192 y a su alcoba se retrujo,
>
> a lo que a dormir llamamos
> los que somos algo rudos,
> de la vida intermisión,
> 196 del dios Morfeo tributo.
>
> Ya que la noche enfaldaba
> la cola al monjil de luto,
> huyendo del dios cochero,
> 200 de sus tinieblas verdugo,
>
> Bronte y sus dos compañeros,
> tres oficiales machuchos,
> ayudantes de Vulcano
> 204 ojinones y membrudos,
>
> dieron voces al maestro,
> que lo dispertó el retumbo
> de las fugas que formaban
> 208 los martillos campanudos.
>
> Salió del lecho y vistióse
> micer Cornelio Castrucho,

cuyos pies de copla estaban
212   de sílabas diminutos.

En un tronco de alcornoque
tropezó, terrible augurio,
y mirando la escalera,
216   llegó al suelo en cuatro tumbos.

When the dark cloak of night spread around the earth, Vulcan left the forge and retired to his bedroom to sleep—what those of us who are somewhat simple call an intermission from life, a tribute from the god Morpheus. Now that Night was gathering up the skirts of her mourning dress, fleeing from the coach-driver god (Apollo), executioner of her darkness, Bronte and his two companions, three skilled assistants, odd-eyed and muscular, cried out to their master Vulcan, for the ringing of the fugues created by the resonant hammers woke him up. Mister Cornelius Castrato, whose poetic feet didn't scan properly, got out of bed and got dressed. He tripped up on the trunk of a cork oak, a terrible omen, and looking at the stairs he ended up on the floor after four big bangs.

When Vulcan places the net around the marriage bed, he does not feign departure for Lemnos. Instead, he retires to his room and goes to sleep, as a Classically inspired personification of Night shrouds the world in darkness. Sleep is presented periphrastically as both an intermission from life and a form of tribute to Morpheus, the god of sleep. However, the use of erudite circumlocution, a device heavily employed by *culto* poets, is prefaced by the deflatory suggestion that such techniques are particular to *los que [son] algo rudos* (194), *rudo* denoting 'el hombre de ruýn ingenio y tardo' (*Cov.*). The image in 197–200 of Night hurriedly gathering up her skirts and fleeing from *el dios cochero* is absurd. *Coches* were often associated with illicit sexual encounters involving prostitutes: the chariot of the sun, driven by *el verdugo de las tinieblas* (200), is metamorphosed into a carriage full of women of ill repute.

When *tres oficiales machuchos* (202), 'three skilled Cyclopes', wake their master with the sound of their work, it is not Vulcan who arises but *micer Cornelio Castrucho*. With this mock-heroic title, Polo sums up the character of Vulcan. The word *micer*, related to the French *monsieur* and the Italian *messer*, is both a title given to men of great eminence and another name for the male sexual organ. *Cornelio* (*Corn-*) implies the horns of cuckoldry, whilst *Castrucho* carries connotations of castration. The name, which is ideally suited to the archetypal cuckold, is perhaps inspired by both the title of Lope's play *El rufián castrucho* (c.1598), which deals with relationships between soldiers and prostitutes, and the figure of Cornelio, the man rejected by Leonisa in favour of Ricardo at the end of Cervantes's 'El amante liberal'. Lines 211–12 compare Vulcan's feet to poetic lines that do not scan. *Cov.* makes sense of the basic meaning of *pies de copla* (211), defining *copla* as 'cierto verso castellano, que llamamos redondillas, *quasi copula*, porque va copulando y juntando unos pies con otros para medida y unos consonantes con otros para las cadencias'. Just as a line of poetry that has either too many or too few syllables is *poetically* deficient, Vulcan's deformed, asymmetrical, feet are held to be *physically* deficient; *diminuto* corresponds to that which is 'defectuoso y falto de lo que debía tener para su cabal perfección' (*Aut.*). Thus, Polo finds an innovative way of alluding to the tradition of Vulcan's lame leg. The linguistic humour of the very ignoble noble name is compounded by the ensuing visual comedy of the lame blacksmith tripping on the roots of a cork oak and crashing down the stairs. The *alcornoque* (213) is chosen to enhance the linguistic comedy based on the image of horns (*-corno-*).

> **Marte, que acechando estaba,**
> **puesto en vela como grullo,**
> **oyó un suspiro, que Venus**
> 220 **le despachaba por nuncio.**
>
> **Bajó por la chimenea,**
> **transformado en avechucho**
> **y el lado ocupó de Venus,**
> 224 **de marido sustituto.**
>
> **Ya cuando Marte empezaba**
> **las jerigonzas del gusto,**
> **sin encanto de hechiceros**
> 228 **se vio ligado y compulso.**

Mars, who was lying in wait, placed on watch like a crane, heard a sigh, for Venus was employing him as a bearer of news. He flew down the chimney, transformed into some ugly little bird, and took his place next to Venus, as a substitute for her husband. As soon as Mars started uttering his amorous mumbo-jumbo he found himself tied up and bound, though sorcerers' spells had nothing to do with it.

Even when Mars is with Venus, his Classical authority is undermined through extensive use of *germanía*. In the first quatrain (217–20), we see Mars on nightwatch, *puesto en vela como grullo* (218). The *grulla*, 'crane', is a bird associated with sentry duty: 'De noche, mientras duermen, y de día, en tanto que pazen, tienen sus centinelas que las avisan si viene gente; es término rústico' (*Cov.*). Fittingly, *grullo* is thus a slang word for an 'alguacil' (Chamorro 2002: 466). Humorously, Mars is also presented as a *nuncio* (220), both a bearer of news and a diplomatic representative of the Pope: 'el embaxador que Su Santidad embía a la Corte de algún rey o príncipe, para que assista en ella, y es persona de grande autoridad y veneración' (*Cov.*; compare p.125 above). Of course, Mars is no papal ambassador, 'de grande autoridad y veneración', but a self-deceiving underworld figure, instructed by Venus to keep watch on her husband's movements. In order to take up his place as a substitute husband, Mars flies down the chimney, having been transformed into an *avechucho*, both an 'ave de mal talle, que no es conocida ni se le sabe nombrar' (*Cov.*) and a 'rufián [o] personaje de mala catadura' (Chamorro 2002: 119).

Polo's persistent attack on the modes of expression employed by Góngora and his less illustrious followers is completed when he describes Mars's sweet nothings as *las jerigonzas del gusto* (226). While *jerigonza* denotes both 'la melopea rogativa de los ciegos' (this is one of the first things that Lázaro learns from his first master, the *ciego*, in the 1554 tale *Lazarillo de Tormes*) and 'jerga de germanía usada por rufianes y valentones' (Alonso 1976: 456–57), it had also come to be associated with a derogatory approach to the poetry of Góngora. In his 'Receta para hacer soledades en un día', Quevedo launches an explicit attack on Góngora (and on doctors): 'Quien quisiere ser culto en sólo un día, | la jeri (aprenderá) gonza siguiente: | *fulgores, arrogar, joven, presiente,* | *candor, construye, métrica armonía*' (Q.825: 1–4). By placing the future verb 'aprenderá' in the middle of the noun 'jerigonza', Quevedo mocks Góngora's tendency to use radical hyperbaton, a rhetorical device involving the disjunction of expected word order. The fact that Quevedo associates *jerigonza* with Góngora is confirmed in the poem 'Este que, en negra tumba, rodeado': 'Éste a la jerigonza quitó el nombre, | pues después que escribió cíclopemente, | la llama jerigóngora la gente' (Q.840: 17–19). As soon as Mars begins to utter his sweet nothings, the lovers find themselves ensnared in Vulcan's trap, *sin encanto de hechiceros* (227). Though it is stated that sorcery and witchcraft have nothing to do with Vulcan's device, it is left unclear, as in both the *Odyssey* and the *Metamorphoses*, how precisely the trap works. A brief glance at contemporary prints, etchings, or woodcuts of this scene, such as those found in vernacular translations of the *Metamorphoses*, confirms that no one quite knew how Vulcan's net operated once erected around the marriage bed. Three complete Spanish translations of Ovid's text appeared before 1590: a prose version by Jorge de Bustamante (c.1540), and two verse translations by Antonio Pérez Sigler (1580) and Pedro Sánchez de Viana (1589). Such works often included illustrations, either at the beginning of each book or inserted into the middle of the text at appropriate points in the narrative. For example, the 1595 Antwerp edition of Bustamante's translation features illustrations based on a set of prints by the Nuremberg engraver Virgil Solis. In the centre of the image that deals with the story of Mars, Venus, and Vulcan, the smith-god is shown about to throw the *nudos ciegos* directly over the lovers, who are lying naked in each other's arms on the left, while their Olympian peers gossip and point through an opening top-right.

Venus dice: '¡Que me aprietan!'
y él dice: 'Yo me escabullo.'

Prueban a desenredarse,
232 mas ninguno de ellos supo.

En su magna conjunción,
de su mismo ardor combustos,
en orbes de red quedaron
236 los dos planetas conjuntos.

Salió el sol con luz escoba,
barriendo sombras y nublos,
según versistas lo mienten
240 en sus cantos o rebuznos;

y enhilando un sutil rayo
por el ojo de un rasguño
que él hizo en una ventana
244 con las uñas de sus cursos,

entró, y vio los dos amantes
hechos al vivo un dibujo
de aquel signo que a sus potros
248 sirve de establo por junio.

Venus says 'I'm being squashed' and he says 'I'm off'. They try to untangle themselves, but neither of them could do so. In their great conjunction, consumed in their own passion, the two conjoined planets were left stranded in the spheres of the net. Out came the sun with his brush of light, sweeping away shadows and patches of darkness, or at least that's how poor poets would have it in their songs and brayings; and by threading a subtle ray through the tiny hole of a scratch that he made in a window with the nails of his daily journeys, he entered, and saw the two lovers acting out a sketch of the sign of the zodiac that serves as a stable for his colts in June (i.e. Cancer).

When Venus is ensnared in Vulcan's net, she exclaims: '¡*Que me aprietan!*' (229). Alonso draws our attention to one possible meaning of the verb *apretar*: an *apretada* is defined as 'la mujer que no siendo virgen pasa por ello por haberse reducido el coño con *apretaduras*. Se aplica, sobre todo, a las prostitutas jóvenes y que se venden varias veces por vírgenes antes de dedicarse abiertamente a la prostitución' (1976: 55). Perhaps this exclamation is an oblique reference to Venus's (previous) status as an *apretada*. The term was most commonly applied to canny prostitutes-in-the-making who wanted to sell their virginity on numerous occasions before dedicating themselves openly to the art of prostitution (compare p. 149, above). Mars's exclamation, '*Yo me escabullo*', shows him to be a cowardly figure accustomed to fleeing from responsibility and justice. Both Mars and Venus are powerless to free themselves from the net. Lines 233–36 draw a parallel between the love-making (and imprisonment) of the gods and the conjunction of the planets

Mars and Venus; we see the humorous use of astrological terms, such as *conjunción* and *orbes*, to describe the lovers' naked embrace, a phenomenon that is not in the least celestial. The allusion to the moment when Mars moves into the astrological sphere of Venus, as captured in Francisco de Aldana's c.1565 sonnet 'Marte en aspecto de Cáncer' (2000: 233–34), may be intended as a further, ironic, nod in the direction of Neoplatonist interpretations of the myth of Mars, Venus, and Vulcan. Significantly, both Mars and Venus are outside their customary spheres, stranded *en orbes de red* (235).

Lines 237–48 recount the moment when Apollo learns of the lovers' affair. First, the sun-god comes out with his *luz escoba | barriendo sombras y nublos* (237–38). This is, at least, typical of what *versistas*, here one assumes poor, or perhaps *culto*, poets, would say in their writings, or *cantos*, which are derogatively labelled *rebuznos*, 'brayings'. The penultimate quatrain of the above section represents an elaborate allusion to the all-seeing power of Apollo: 'videt hic deus omnia primus' (*Metamorphoses*, IV.172), 'this god sees all things first' (1984 : I.191). A fine ray of light passes through a tiny hole made in a window by the *uñas de sus cursos* (244), 'the nails of his daily journeys'. Polo appears to be playing with the phrase *sol con uñas*, which is used 'quando viene entrevelado con algunas nuvezicas ralas que las asimilan y comparan a uñas' (*Cov.*). In this way, (the chariot of) the sun, drawn daily across the sky by Apollo's *potros*, 'colts', may be said to have the *uñas* required to scratch (or tap) at the lovers' window. When Apollo enters the room and catches sight of the lovers, he sees them *hechos al vivo un dibujo | de aquel signo que a sus potros | sirve de establo por junio* (246–48). As *Cov.* explains, *dibuxo* 'valdrá delineación de pintura escura sin colores'. Thus, Mars and Venus are said to represent a real-life enactment, or illustration, of a black and white outline drawing of an astrological symbol associated with the month of June. As *Cov.* makes clear, 'En este mes reyna el signo Cáncer'. This is not an invitation to picture the crab; the fact that we are dealing with a *dibujo* points the reader in the direction of a more primitive symbol for the sign of Cancer. In order fully to understand this conceit, the reader must know that the *dibujo* in question is: ♋. In lines of remarkable conceptual density, Polo forces the reader to work through a chain of associations and to establish the links between June and Cancer, between Cancer and a particular *dibujo*, and between the symbol ♋ and a very specific sexual act.

> Dio al punto a Vulcano el soplo,
> que estaba en lugar de puño
> echando cachas de cuerno
> 252 al puñal de un hombre zurdo.
>
> Tomó el martillo, furioso,
> y aunque zompo y barrigudo
> embistió con la escalera,
> 256 sin ser capa, echando bufos.

> Subió el primer escalón,
> mas no pasó del segundo;
> que como cojo y pesado
> 260 de cabeza, se detuvo.
>
> En culta voz de becerro,
> porque en la humana no pudo,
> llamó a los dioses que bajen
> 264 a vengar su agravio injusto.

He immediately tipped off Vulcan, who was in his workplace, fixing handles made of horn to the hilt of a left-handed man. Enraged, Vulcan grabbed his hammer and, despite being clumsy and potbellied, charged at the stairs, snorting like a bull, even though there wasn't a cape in sight. He climbed up the first step but got no further than the second for being lame and top-heavy he came to a halt. In the culto voice of a little ox, for he couldn't in his human one, he called to the gods to come down and avenge this unjust insult.

When the *soplón* Apollo informs Vulcan of the entrapment of the lovers, we come to one of the most important episodes of the Classical myth. However, Polo concentrates not on the moment of exchange between Apollo and Vulcan but on the subsequent reaction of the blacksmith. Whereas Cueva's Vulcan drops his hammer on receiving the news of his wife's infidelity (Vulcan's rather theatrical response to Apollo's message is described in lines 417–32 of Cueva's poem), and Velázquez's is depicted with his fist clenched firmly around his tools (*La Fragua de Vulcano*), Polo's Vulcan seizes the hammer and, as if he were in the bullring, charges at the stairs, *echando bufos*; associated with 'el toro, el buey, y el búfalo', *bufo* is '[lo mismo que *bufido*], el acto de bufar en los animales, el soplo, o el resoplido dado con furor y con ira' (*Aut.*). As Vulcan is already aware of the affair, and because he has already forged the net and caught the lovers, the focus here is on the physical and linguistic comedy of the smith's desperate attempt to avenge such a slight on his honour.

Polo stresses the fact that Vulcan is a cuckold, associating him with both *cachas de cuerno*, 'los cabos de los cuchillos, por hazerse de pedaços de cuernos con que los guarnecen' (*Cov.*), and animals equipped with horns, both bulls and young oxen. The image of Venus's husband *embisti[endo] con la escalera* (255) develops the link between Vulcan and a bull that is introduced in the adjectival expression of oneiric fantasy *jarameño y corajudo* (170). The references to the (absence of the) bullfighter's cape and the noises made by an enraged bull serve to develop this parallel further. As a four-legged animal, who is *pesado de cabeza* (259–60), owing to the ever-growing horns of his cuckoldry, Vulcan is unable to climb the stairs. Vulcan is no raging bull; he is a lame, clumsy, pot-bellied dimwit whose comic charge is brought to a very sudden halt. As in the *Odyssey* (VIII. 306–20),

Vulcan calls out to the gods of Olympus; however, this time he does so *en culta voz de becerro* (261), as Polo incorporates another oblique attack on *culto* poets.

> Luego que la oreja el bramo
> oyó de los dioses sumos,
> rompiendo golfos de estrellas,
> 268   descendieron a pie enjuto.
>
> Halláronlos jadeando,
> por salir de aquel tabuco,
> y aunque de sudor aguados,
> 272   estaban en cueros puros:
>
> Venus, desgreñado el moño,
> desrizado su apatusco,
> y medrosa de otra espina,
> 276   dos argentados pantuflos;
>
> Marte, con un tocador
> y escarpines que se puso,
> teniendo un francés catarro
> 280   con dolores de Acapulco.
>
> Y porque el rumor no fuese
> despertador de tumultos,
> unos renuncian zapatos
> 284   y otros repudian coturnos.

When the ear of the great gods caught the bellow, breaking through oceans of stars, they came down dry-shod. They found them panting, struggling to get out of that tiny space, and although they were covered in buckets of sweat, they were stark naked. Venus's hair was all dishevelled, her attire all undone, and fearful of another (porcupine) spine, she wore two silvered slippers. Mars was wearing a night-cap and some bedsocks that he'd put on, suffering from a French catarrh and pains from Acapulco. And so that the gossip didn't give rise to great commotion, some of them took off their shoes and others gave up their footwear.

When the gods of Olympus respond to Vulcan's *bramo* (265), a noise associated with 'fieras, como el toro' (*Cov.*), they are greeted by the spectacle described in 269–80. As noted above, it is this scene that is most frequently portrayed in illustrated editions of the *Metamorphoses*. It is also alluded to in Góngora's 1585 parody 'Ensíllenme el asno rucio' (GR.18: 17–28). Incorporated into the list of elements requested by Galayo is a mock breastplate decorated with an image of the lovers' entrapment: 'aquella patena en cuadro | donde de latón se ofrecen | la madre del virotero | y aquel Dios que calza arneses, | tan en pelota y tan juntos | que en nudos ciegos los tienen, | al uno redes y brazos, | y al otro brazos y redes, | cuyas figuras en torno | acompañan y guarnecen | ramos de nogal y espigas, | y por letra: *Pan y nueces.*' In Polo's poem, Mars and Venus are engaged in a desperate struggle to free themselves from the net: *aunque de sudor aguados | estaban en cueros puros* (271–72), 'although they were covered in buckets of sweat, they were stark naked'. As noted in relation to Quevedo's 'Los borrachos', *sudor* frequently refers to the pains associated with syphilis (see above, pp. 142–43). Lines 271–72 also suggest that Mars and Venus might be drunk, for 'se dice de los borrachos que al emborracharse parecen cueros llenos de vino' (Alonso 1976: 249 ; see also above, p. 144); the juxtaposition of *de sudor aguados* and *en cueros puros* alludes to the watering down of wine, a much criticized practice associated with contemporary innkeepers (see above, pp. 140).

Four lines are dedicated to the description of each god and to what they are wearing on their heads and feet (273–80). Venus is totally dishevelled, *desgreñado el moño, | desrizado su apatusco* (273–74). On her feet she has *dos argentados pantuflos* (276) to protect her from another *espina*. The word *espina/o* incorporates a range of meanings, including the spine of a porcupine, the male sexual organ, and, in *germanía*, 'el hospital para prostitutas enfermas de enfermedades venéreas' (Alonso 1976: 339; Chamorro 2002: 384–85). There are at least two possible interpretations of the Gongorine *argentados*. First, it suggests that Venus is so scared of a return to a correctional institution for prostitutes that she has wet herself. Venus may already have paid several visits to one of the institutions established to combat the vice of prostitution in the seventeenth century (Hsu 2002: 70). Góngora's ballad 'Noble desengaño' (1584) offers a similar use of the verb *argentar* (lines 57–64, see above pp. 35). While *argentar*, which means 'platear' or 'guarnecer con plata', specifically comes to refer to the process in Andalusia of applying a thin metallic layer or shine to the surface of leather shoes, both Góngora and Polo employ the verb to describe, in an inappropriately high register, the process by which the lover's black shoes and Venus's slippers are decorated with a coating of urine. Second, her slippers may be described as *argentados* if they have been covered with a layer of *argento vivo*, or mercury, in order to protect her from syphilis. Either way, the subversion of the *culto* meaning of this Latinate word offers a prime example of the way in which highly erudite words are incorporated into the grotesque lexicon of contemporary slang.

Unsurprisingly, Mars fares no better than Venus. He is dressed in an entirely incongruous and unflattering manner, sporting *un tocador* (277), a 'night-cap' and not a fine military helmet, on his head and some strange bedsocks on his feet; this image of Mars is reminiscent of the description at the end of chapter VI of *El Buscón* of Pablos hiding from the *Justicia* 'echado en la cama con un tocador' (Quevedo 2001: 160). Having paid for sex, Mars appears to have received rather more than he quite literally bargained for: he has contracted *un francés catarro* and *dolores de Acapulco* (279–80).

Catarro is 'la distilación que cae de la cabeça a la garganta y al pecho' (*Cov.*). 'French catarrh' must, therefore, be syphilis, the famous *mal francés* whose origins were associated with the discovery and conquest of Mexico (hence *dolores de Acapulco,* 280). The unusual placing of the adjective *francés* before the noun *catarro*, in part dictated by the need to make the line scan as an octosyllable, may be ridiculous (compare Cervantes's 'manchego horizonte', cited earlier, which certainly is), but it also serves to underline the unpleasantness of Mars's plight. If only he had heeded the advice given by Quevedo in 'A la Corte vas, Perico' (above, Chapter 7). The final quatrain (281–84) prepares us for a series of veiled attacks on the other gods of Olympus. In order to guard against the danger of their gossip getting out of hand, *rumor* denoting 'lo que se dize, no en público, pero se esparce secretamente en el pueblo' (*Cov.*), the gods and goddesses take off their shoes, *zapatos* (283) and *coturnos* (284). *Coturnos* were large cork platform shoes worn by actors, often when playing the roles of gods, in Greco-Roman tragedy. The fact that the gods of Olympus make a habit of wearing such shoes suggests that they are nothing more than pretend gods acting out parts. When they take off their *coturnos* and step down from their high platforms (physical and moral), their true nature is revealed.

> Sonó al punto, en risa envuelto,
> entre los sacros alumnos,
> como en corro de poetas,
> 288   un murmurador susurro.
>
> Juno, que del matrimonio
> ostenta celosa el yugo,
> mal contenta lo miraba,
> 292   haciendo varios discursos.
>
> Palas, cuya flor estaba
> recogida en su capullo,
> los mira, haciendo en sus ojos
> 296   mil melindrosos repulgos.
>
> Dïana, que estaba hecha
> a pisar bosques incultos,
> donde de virgen silvestre
> 300   guardaba los estatutos,
>
> viéndolos tan descompuestos,
> a su memoria redujo
> de Acteón la vista osada,
> 304   de Susana el rigor justo,
>
> cuando desnuda en la fuente,
> vio por cuartos y por puntos

> de su claustro virginal
> 308 los lunares más reclusos.
>
> '¡Miren, y ¡qué desvergüenza!',
> dijo con un rostro turbio,
> y en él la mano miraba
> 312 por los dedos al descuido.

Straightaway, as if they were a circle of poets, a murmuring whisper broke out amongst the sacred pupils, who were seized by a fit of laughter. Juno, who jealously parades the yoke of marriage, looks on not at all pleased, offering various judgements. Pallas Athene, whose flower was hidden away in its bud, watches them, making with her eyes thousands of prudish airs and graces. For Diana, who was born to step foot in uncultivated woods, where she kept the statutes of virgins in the forests, seeing them in such a dishevelled state reminded her of the just rigour of Susanna and the daring glance of Actaeon, when bit by bit he caught sight of the most hidden blemishes of her virginal senate bathing naked in the fountain. 'Look, how shameful!' she said with a perturbed expression, with her hand over her face, watching nonchalantly through her fingers.

Following Homeric and Ovidian tradition, the gods, or *sacros alumnos* (286), burst into hysterical laughter. They are compared to a *corro de poetas* (287), who are, one must assume, of the *culto* persuasion, as *corro* denotes 'junta o reunión de maleantes de todo tipo' (Alonso 1976: 232). As in Cueva's 'Los amores de Marte y Venus', the female gods bear witness to the shaming of their peers. In the Spanish Golden Age, Juno, Pallas Athene, and Diana are no longer in possession of the modesty that kept their Homeric counterparts at home. Juno is displeased by what she sees; the spectacle no doubt reminds her of her husband Jupiter's penchant for high-profile affairs often involving some form of transformation on his part (into a bull, a swan, a shower of gold, and so on). Pallas Athene is one of the three virgin goddesses of Olympus, thus her sexual *flor* (293) is still *recogida en su capullo* (294). As *Cov.* puts it (*s.v. capullo*), 'las rosas dezimos estar en capullos, quando no se han abierto del todo'. Affecting daintiness in response to the disagreeable sight of the lovers in the net, Pallas responds with *mil melindrosos repulgos* (296); *repulgo* denotes 'la... torcedura asida con hilo o seda, pespunte o vaynilla' (*Cov.*), while the phrase *repulgar la boca* means 'plegar los labios, formando un género de hocico u doblez en ellos' (*Aut.*).

Diana, chaste goddess of the hunt, is reminded of the mythological figure of Actaeon (303) and the Biblical figure of Susanna (304), two subjects popular in Renaissance and Baroque history painting (see, for example, Titian's *Diana and Actaeon* (c.1556), in the National Gallery of Scotland, and Tintoretto's *Susanna and the Elders* (c.1555), which is in the Kunsthistorisches Museum in Vienna). When Actaeon happened upon Diana and her nymphs as they bathed naked in a clearing in the woods, he was turned into a stag by Diana and torn apart by his own hounds. In the Apocrypha, Susanna, the wife of Joachim, was propositioned by some elders, wrongly sentenced to death for alleged sexual misconduct, and then acquitted. Though the reference to Susanna is not developed, 305–08 develop the allusion to the tale of Actaeon, who saw *por cuartos y por puntos* (306) the *lunares más reclusos* (308) of Diana's *claustro virginal* (307). The phrase *por cuartos y por puntos*, which suggests that Actaeon sees them bit by bit, may also refer to the buttocks and sexual organs of Diana's nymphs, for while *cuartos* denote the 'parte trasera de la mujer' (Chamorro 2002: 285), a *mujer de punto* is a prostitute; here, *punto* being 'signo distintivo entre unos maleantes y otros; lo que hace que unos sean considerados más que otros. Generalmente cuando se dice que alguien es de punto, se quiere significar que es de importancia' (Alonso 1976: 641). Diana's chaste followers are transformed into a bunch of prostitutes. *Claustro virginal* is doubly ironic, for, in Salamanca, *claustro* represents 'el lugar donde se juntan los doctores y maestros de la Universidad, rector y consiliarios y donde se toman los votos para las cátedras y se regulan' (*Cov.*). Diana comments on the shame associated with the spectacle (309). Nevertheless, she takes it all in whilst pretending to cover her face with her hands (311–12).

> **Momo, el fisgón de los dioses,**
> **haciendo un gesto a Vertumno,**
> **por festejar maldiciente**
> 316 **tan soberano concurso,**
>
> **dio tres silbos a Vulcano**
> **que estaba como un lechuzo,**
> **contemplando en un rincón**
> 320 **sus presentes infortunios.**
>
> **Ignorando el nombre propio,**
> **llamaba al bicorne búho,**
> **como a animal de carreta,**
> 324 **ya Naranjo, ya Aceituno.**

Momus, the joker of the gods, gesturing to Vertumnus to celebrate with his foul mouth such a sovereign gathering, whistled to Vulcan three times, who was like an owl, contemplating his present misfortunes in a corner. Unaware of Vulcan's actual name, he called the two-horned guy a tewit-tewoo, just as you'd call a cart animal now Orange-Tree and now Olive-Tree.

In a change from the Homeric and Ovidian original, the male figure who comments on the spectacle is not Mercury but Momus, the god of mockery, and, thus, someone who is *maldiciente* (315). The lovers, or perhaps all the gods, are described as *tan soberano concurso* (316), 'such a sovereign gathering'. It is hard to imagine a more inappropriate label for this group of immoral, degenerate, and self-serving individuals. Whereas Mercury had implied that he would give anything to be in Mars's shoes, Momus, *el fisgón de los dioses* (313), concentrates on highlighting the misfortune suffered by Vulcan. Though *Cov.* suggests that *fisgón* describes 'el que dissimuladamente haze burla de otros', Momus openly mocks Vulcan. Gesturing to Vertumnus, the shape-shifter god of the seasons, plant growth, and fruit trees, Momus *dio tres silbos a Vulcano* (317), mimicking the noise made by an owl. Vulcan is *bicorne* (322), 'two-horned', on account of the horns of his cuckoldry and he is labelled *búho* in a play on the word *lechuzo*, not because the owl is a symbol of wisdom but on account of its association with both ill omens and social recluses. Appropriately, Vulcan is *arrinconado*; 'Dezimos estarse al rincón y arrinconado y arrinconarse, por retirarse y esconderse' (*Cov.*). In the final two lines of the above section, it is suggested that calling Vulcan a *búho* is equivalent to calling an *animal de carreta,* | *ya Naranjo, ya Aceituno* (323–24). It is unclear to me precisely what Polo intends us to understand in these lines. Perhaps it is a further play on the fact that Vulcan is literally *pesado de cabeza* (259–60); just as either a beast of burden or a fruit tree in season may be weighed down by its full load, the same may be said of Vulcan with his enormous shoots. The last three lines might also be translated thus: '[Momus] called out to the two-horned tewit-tewoo, as if he were a cart animal, "Go on, Orange-Tree", "Go on, Olive-Tree"'. In this case, Momus calls out to the cuckold, driving him on as if Vulcan were a slow-witted beast of burden.

> Él, corriendo como un toro,
> quisiera ser de un saúco,
> si no pendiente espantajo,
> 328 cabrahígo de su fruto.
>
> Sueltos de la red los presos,
> cubrieron sus miembros rucios,
> Venus con baquero verde,
> 332 Marte con ropón lobuno.
>
> Condénanle por sentencia,
> con un falso y un pronuncio,
> a que sirva de atambor
> 336 en las islas del Maluco.
>
> Y a Venus a que se vaya
> sin coche y sin moño a Burgos,
> donde, sin gustar la carne,
> 340 tenga tres meses de ayuno.

Running around like a bull, he would want to be, if not a scarecrow dangling in an elder, then the means by which the tree's fruit comes to maturity. Once free from the net, the prisoners covered their fair bits and pieces, Venus with a dirty green smock, Mars with thick grey cloth. By way of sentence, they

condemn him, in the presence of an executioner and a stand-in nuncio, to
serve as a kettledrum in the Spice Islands, and her to go to Burgos stripped of
her carriage and hairbun, where, without enjoying the pleasure of any meat,
she should go on an empty stomach for three months.

A detailed analysis of the first quatrain of this section demonstrates the complexity of Polo's verse. Line 325 makes explicit the parallel that has already
been established between Vulcan and a bull. By now, the blacksmith's
dreams of being an agile and strong fighting bull lie in tatters. The only link
that can be drawn between the smith-god and a bull relates, as we have
seen, to their respective horns. The rest of the quatrain develops a multi-
faceted conceit of remarkable complexity, based on this simple point of
comparison. At first, one is struck by the presence of the rhetorical formula
'*si no a, b*' so characteristic of the poetry of Góngora (see Alonso 1955). On
closer examination, we see that Polo develops the full range of semantic
possibilities associated with the words *saúco* (326), *pendiente espantajo*
(327), *cabrahígo*, and *fruto* (328). The *pendiente espantajo* is literally something that is hung in the elder to scare birds away. As *Cov.* explains an
espantajo is 'El trapo o figura de trapos que ponen en los árboles para espan-
tar los páxaros; tales son algunos hombres puestos en dignidades, que al
principio, como no los conocen, les tienen respeto, y después (como tratados
no hallan en ellos sustancia) los tienen en poco, como hazen los tordos a los
espantajos que les ponen en las higueras'. In line with Polo's development
of the slang connotations of ornithological terms, based on the words *cuervo*
(133), *grullo* (217), and *avechucho* (221), it is tempting to imagine Vulcan
as a comical scarecrow hanging in the *saúco*, an 'arbusto *capri*foliáceo', in
order to frighten off his wife's possible suitors, who are busy trying to eat
the fruit that is hanging from the tree (that is, trying to have sex with
Venus). However, this rather light-hearted image of the *pendiente espantajo*
is replaced by something more sinister if we consider that, according to
popular pious legend, Judas Iscariot hanged himself from the branches of a
saúco; *Fraile cuco, aceite de saúco. Fraile cuco, lámpara de saúco*: 'que el
tal fraile esté hecho lámpara de saúco, esto es, colgado de un saúco, como
lámpara, a la manera de Judas' (Correas 1967: 342). The image of hanging
is completed if we consider that the phrase *hacer fruto* means the same as
ahorcar (Alonso 1976: 371). The Gongorine '*si no a, b*' throws light onto
the *cabrahígo*, a word derived from the Latin *caprificus*. As *Cov.* explains,
the *cabrahígo* is a 'género de higuera silvestre, cuya fruta no llega a
madurar, pero es medio para que las higueras maduren, por quanto cría unos
mosquitos que, no hallando en su propio madre sustento, se van a las
higueras cultivadas y frutíferas, y picando los higos por los ombligos, los
horadan y gastan el humor aguoso que tienen, y aviendo abierto camino y
entrada al ayre y al sol, son medio para que vengan a madurar'. Thus, the
cabrahígo relies upon a third party in order to reach full maturity. Though
Vulcan would like to be the one having sex with his own wife, Polo appears

to be alluding to the smith's impotence and to the tendency for other men to impregnate her.

Things do not get much better for the lovers when they are freed from the net. Venus is dressed in a *baquero verde*, ironically appropriate given that this is the thick cotton cloth associated with criminals on their way from prison to the gallows (Alonso 1976: 95) and that green is the colour of lust. Mars is given a *ropón lobuno*, an item of clothing associated, through its adjectival qualifier, with picaresque thieves and drunkards. Lines 333–40 comment on the lovers' respective sentences, passed in the presence of a *falso*, 'verdugo' (Chamorro 2002: 396), and a *pronuncio*, a substitute ambassador standing in for the disgraced warrior-god, who had been described earlier as Venus's *nuncio* (220). For his misdemeanours, Mars is sent to the Spice Islands to serve as an *atambor* (335), both a kettledrum (presumably on account of the size of his potbelly) and the individual who plays such a drum (a lowly military station); the word *atambor* may also denote the technique used by traders of drawing attention to a particular customer in the hope that they would feel shamed into buying more than they needed; *treta del atambor* being 'artimaña de hoteleros o vendedores que consiste en atraer la atención de varias personas sobre una que está sola con el fin de que coaccionada por la vergüenza, para no pasar por avara, compre o encargue más de lo que necesita o pensaba comprar' (Alonso 1976: 74).

Venus is shipped off to Burgos, a centre of morally upright living, *sin coche y sin moño* (338), the former, as we have seen, associated with prostitutes as a stage for amorous encounters, the latter, like *guardainfantes*, *chapines*, and *enaguas*, characteristic of women of ill repute. In Chapter V of Alonso de Castillo Solórzano's 1632 picaresque novel *La niña de los embustes Teresa de Manzanares*, Teresa explains how the making and selling of *moños* (elaborate hairpieces that allow women obsessed with the latest fashions to style their hair in a very short space of time) enables her to move up in the world. She builds up a large client-base: 'No se vaciaba la casa de mujeres de todos estados, unas, peladas de enfermedades; otras, calvas de naturaleza; otras, con canas de muchos años; todas venían con buenos deseos de enmendar sus defetos, y porque se les supliesen, no reparaban en cualquier dinero que les pedía' (Zamora Vicente 1974–76: III. 171). Thus, Polo's Venus is denied the use of both the latest fashion accessory (which would allow her to pose as a lady) and the means of concealing the hair-loss occasioned by diseases contracted in the line of duty. She is sentenced to *tres meses en ayuno* (340), 'on an empty stomach'. She is banned from eating meat or, in other words, from practising as a prostitute or brothel madame, a far cry from the restitution of her divine status effected by the Three Graces in the *Odyssey*. *Tres meses de ayuno* also represent a period of religious penitence (based on abstinence from certain foods), a period in which Venus would be expected to cleanse her spirit, learn to suppress the desires of the flesh, and start the process of seeking union with the one true

God. However, as is the case with Tirso's Marta, any show of piety from Polo's Venus will, one must assume, be nothing more than a front.

> **Y a Vulcano, por paciente,**
> **le dejaron por indulto**
> **que de maridos de cachas**
> 344   **fuese abogado absoluto.**
>
> **Con esto, dioses y diosas**
> **al cielo hicieron recurso,**
> **ellas en forma de urracas,**
> 348   **y ellos como abejorrucos.**
>
> **Vulcano, que iba esparciendo**
> **olor de secretos flujos,**
> **no quiso salir de casa**
> 352   **sin guantes de calambuco;**
>
> **y por cubrir de sus sienes**
> **ciertos renuevos talludos**
> **dicen que fue el inventor**
> 356   **de las guedejas y tufos.**

On account of his patience, they pardoned Vulcan, allowing him to be the absolute judge of cuckolded husbands. With this, the gods and goddesses went back up to heaven, the latter as a group of magpies and the former as bee-eaters. Vulcan, who was going around scattering the smell of secret discharges, did not want to leave home without perfumed gloves, and to cover up some mature shoots that had grown from his temples, it is said that he was the inventor of ringlets and quiffs.

The final sentence is reserved for Vulcan. As a reward for his patience, one of the qualities of the 'marido resignado', he is made the *abogado absoluto* (344) of *maridos de cachas* (343), or cuckolded husbands. As an *abogado*, 'el letrado que defiende o acusa a alguno en juizio' (*Cov.*), Vulcan will be responsible for determining whether or not other individuals are cuckolds. Once the sentences have been passed, the gods and goddesses return to Olympus, the former leaving *como abejorrucos* (348) whilst the latter leave *en forma de urracas* (347). The *abejorruco*, or *abejaruco*, is a 'pájaro hermoso, y vistoso por los varios colores de su pluma, el cual se come las abejas, y destruye los colmenares, y tiene la particularidad de volar igualmente hacia delante, o hacia atrás... Metaphóricamente se dice de un hombre no conocido, entremetido, y de mala catadura' (*Aut.*). The bee-eater, *Merops apiaster*, is remarkable for its brilliant colours, but, more significantly, it is also communal and known for its song. The *(h)urraca* 'imita la voz humana como el papagayo', and the phrase *hablar más que una hurraca* is a 'phrase familiar para exagerar lo mucho que habla una persona:

y especialmente se dice de las mujeres (*Aut.*). The gods of Olympus are seen not as a group of majestic divinities but as a band of malicious, low-life gossips. In Quevedo's *La hora de todos y la Fortuna con seso*, the gods are presented in similar vein when Fortune criticizes Jupiter for a multitude of sins: 'que has hecho otras cien mil picardías y locuras, y que todos esos y esas que están contigo han sido avechuchos, urracas y grajos, cosas que no se dirán de mí' (Quevedo 1987: 157).

In the poem's final two quatrains, Polo fires a couple of parting shots at Vulcan. First, Venus's husband is reluctant to leave home without *guantes de calambuco* (352). These 'perfumed gloves', a symbol of affected sophistication, are designed to hide the smell of *secretos flujos*; presumably Vulcan is trying to mask either the odours associated with the adulterers' lovemaking or the fact that the coward has soiled himself. In the final quatrain, it is stated that, in order to cover up *ciertos renuevos talludos* (355), the 'mature shoots' that have been growing from his temples, the blacksmith invented *las guedejas y tufos* (366), two contemporary hairstyles banned in the 1630s (*guedejas* possibly being sported by the figure of Apollo in Velázquez's *La Fragua de Vulcano*). The poem draws to a close with yet another example of Polo's insistent wordplay, for here *tufos* denote not only 'soberbia, vanidad, o entonamiento' (*Aut.*) but also the 'pleasant aromas' associated with *guantes de calambuco*. A final reference to Sancho Panza's portrayal of Dulcinea offers an example of this third meaning of *tufo(s)* (though, as we know, this time Sancho is lying to his master about even having been to see Dulcinea). When, in I. XXXI, Don Quixote questions his squire about the delivery of a love-letter to Dulcinea, he asks Sancho about how she smelt close-up: 'cuando llegaste junto a ella, ¿no sentiste un olor sabeo, una fragancia aromática y un no sé qué de bueno, que yo no acierto a dalle nombre? Digo, ¿un túho o tufo como si estuvieras en la tienda de algún curioso guantero?' Needless to say, Sancho's response comically undermines his master's suggestion, for he experienced nothing of the sort: 'sentí un olorcillo algo hombruno, y debía de ser que ella, con el mucho ejercicio, estaba sudada y algo correosa' (Cervantes 2005: I. 393).

* * * * *

It is easy to dismiss Polo's mythological burlesques as derivative imitations of Góngora's ballads on the tales of Hero and Leander and Pyramus and Thisbe, but it is Quevedo with whom Polo has the most in common. 'A Vulcano, Venus y Marte' displays many characteristics and stylistic features typical of Quevedo's satirical poetry and prose. Polo employs the language of contemporary slang, or *germanía*, as a mode of artistic expression and exploits the range of meanings and registers associated with individual words. Like Quevedo, he develops elaborate conceits based on intricate and complex wordplay, levels of literal and metaphorical meaning, and allusions to contemporary norms. Both show a concern for conceptual complexity and mental gymnastics in the search for the most striking *conceptos*. Polo also demonstrates the ability to establish humorous associations between seemingly disparate objects based upon a particular aspect, quality, or defect. He takes aim at common targets to denounce contemporary social ill-doing and vice. Such targets include the narcissistic and the hypocritical; professionals such as lawyers, prison warders, innkeepers, and merchants; *culto* poets and their obscure writings; cuckolds, neighbours, and cowards; the venereal and the syphilitic; the ugly and the physically deformed; and, perhaps most prominently, women, prostitution, and sexual commerce. While Quevedo's vitriolic satire may have been replaced by a subtler brand of wit, the subjects of Polo's humorous asides are very much the same.

Like Quevedo, Polo shows an irreverent attitude to the gods of Antiquity: the idealising façade erected around the gods in the Renaissance is exposed as a sham, as the pagan gods are shown to be every bit as corrupt and as susceptible to sinful ways as their human counterparts. The insistence on graphic sexual and scatological innuendo is intended to be humorous but it is also designed to promote discomfort and disconcertion, encouraging the reader to see through the *burlas* to the domain of *veras*. The gods of Olympus are exposed as embodiments not of heroic virtue but of human moral weakness. Polo revels in the base, the ugly, and the incongruous, bringing together the worlds of the pagan gods and picaresque prostitution. Whereas, in the sixteenth century, the myth of Mars and Venus is often employed to symbolize the harmony produced by the conjunction of love and war, here the balance between male and female is upset. The Neoplatonic idylls of Botticelli's *Venus and Mars* (c.1483) and Aldana's 'Marte en aspecto de Cáncer' could not be further away: an ugly, pompous, and self-deceiving *Miles Gloriosus* (Mars) has to pay a professional swindler (Venus) for sex. Venus displays many of the qualities or characteristics ascribed to women by the century's two most famous misogynists, Quevedo and Gracián. Like Quevedo in satirical mode, Polo suggests that women are interested in men only because of their money and, in doing so, hints at the moral corruption of contemporary society by insinuating that all relationships between men and women are based upon sex and monetary exchange. The end product of the conjunction of Mars and Venus is no longer peace and harmony, but bathos and wit.

The gods of Olympus are presented as practitioners of *culto* forms of discourse: Mars and Venus are *unánimes en lo culto* (94); Vulcan calls out to the gods *en culta voz de becerro* (261); and the gods of Olympus are portrayed as a gathering of *culto* poets (287). It is entirely appropriate that the pagan gods, who are false gods, should employ such modes of parlance; *culto* language is morally obfuscatory, for it prettifies and idealizes iniquity, most prominently here the deadly sins of Greed and Lust. By associating *cultismos*, or *jerigonza*, with a series of Classical gods whose authority is undermined, Polo attacks servile imitators of Góngora and proponents of *culto* discourse. However, like both Lope and Quevedo, Polo verbalizes his apparent hatred of the modes of expression associated with Góngora and his followers, whilst simultaneously engaging in many of the stylistic practices most characteristic of *culto* poetry. Despite the prevalence of anti-*culteranista* comments and jokes, 'A Vulcano, Venus y Marte' offers numerous examples of linguistic and rhetorical devices that we have come to associate with the high *culto* style. The use of complex metaphor, metonymy, periphrasis, hyperbole, hyperbaton, *bimembración*, erudite Classical allusion, and Latinate neologism does not in itself make a poet *culto*, for such devices are the very building blocks of poetry. However, while in many cases Polo may employ the above devices in order to parody the works of servile imitators of Góngora, the frequency with which he turns to such devices in 'A Vulcano, Venus y Marte' confirms that there is a significant amount of overlap between *culteranismo* and *conceptismo*. As ever, there is a fine line between imitation and parody; whatever a poet may profess in his theoretical utterances, his practical efforts will always reveal the impossibility of ever separating the two.

WORKS CITED

Abrams, Meyer H. 1993. *A glossary of literary terms*. 6th edn. New York & London: Harcourt Brace Jovanovich.

Alarcos García, Emilio. 1942. *El dinero en las obras de Quevedo: Discurso de apertura, curso 1942–43*. Valladolid: Universidad de Valladolid.

Aldana, Francisco de. 2000. *Poesías castellanas completas*. Ed. José Lara Garrido. Letras Hispánicas 223. Madrid: Cátedra.

Alín, José María (ed.). 1991. *Cancionero tradicional*. Clásicos Castalia 190. Madrid: Castalia.

Alonso, Dámaso. 1935. *La lengua poética de Góngora*. Anejos de la *Revista de Filología Española* 20. Madrid: S. Aguirre.

——. 1955. *Estudios y ensayos gongorinos*. Biblioteca Románica Hispánica: Estudios y Ensayos 18. Madrid: Gredos.

——. 1962. *Romance de Angélica y Medoro: Estudio-comentario*. Madrid: Acies.

——. 1985 [1961]. *Góngora y el 'Polifemo'*. 7th edn. 3 vols. Biblioteca Románica Hispánica VI. 17. Madrid: Gredos.

Alonso Hernández, José Luis. 1976. *Léxico del marginalismo del Siglo de Oro*. Acta Salmanticensia: Filosofía y Letras 99. Salamanca: Universidad de Salamanca.

Alpers, Paul J. 1996. *What is pastoral?* Chicago IL & London: University of Chicago Press.

Alvar Ezquerra, Alfredo. 1989. *El nacimiento de una capital europea: Madrid entre 1561 y 1606*. Madrid: Turner & Ayuntamiento de Madrid.

Alzieu, Pierre, Robert Jammes, & Yvan Lissorgues (eds). 1975. *Floresta de poesías eróticas del Siglo de Oro, con su vocabulario al cabo por el orden del a.b.c.* Toulouse-le-Mirail: France-Ibérie Recherche.

Amelang, James S. 2005. 'Mourning becomes eclectic: Ritual lament and the problem of continuity', *Past and Present* (Oxford) 187: 3–31.

Arellano Ayuso, Ignacio. 1984. *Poesía satírico burlesca de Quevedo: Estudio y anotación filológica de los sonetos*. Pamplona: Ediciones Universidad de Navarra.

——. 1997. 'Notas sobre el refrán y la fórmula coloquial en la poesía burlesca de Quevedo', *La Perinola, Revista de Investigación Quevediana* (Pamplona) 1: 15–38.

——. 2002. *Un minibestiario de Quevedo*. Pliego Volandero del GRISO 1. Pamplona: Grupo de Investigación Siglo de Oro de la Universidad de Navarra.

Ariosto, Ludovico. 1975–77. *Orlando furioso* [1516–32]. Tr. Barbara Reynolds. 2 vols. Penguin Classics. Harmondsworth : Penguin.

Armistead, Samuel G., Antonio Sánchez Romeralo, & Diego Catalán (eds).

1979. *El romancero hoy: II Coloquio Internacional, University of Califor-nia at Davis.* 3 vols. Romancero y Poesía Oral 2–4. Madrid: Cátedra & Seminario Menéndez Pidal.

Armstrong, David. *Horace.* 1989. Hermes Books. New Haven: Yale University Press.

Artigas Ferrando, Miguel. 1925. *Don Luis de Góngora y Argote: Biografía y estudio crítico.* Madrid : Tip. de la Revista de Archivos.

Asenjo Barbieri, Francisco. 1890. *Cancionero musical español de los siglos XV y XVI.* Madrid: Montemar.

Asensio. Eugenio. 1965. *Itinerario del entremés: Desde Lope de Rueda a Quiñones de Benavente, con cinco entremeses de D. Francisco de Que-vedo.* Biblioteca Románica Hispánica II. 82. Madrid: Gredos.

Aubrun, Charles. 1975. *Mélanges offerts à Charles Vincent Aubrun.* Ed. Haïm Vidal Sephiha. 2 vols. Paris : Éditions Hispaniques.

Aut. = Diccionario de autoridades. 1979 [1726–39]. *Diccionario de la lengua castellana, en que se explica el verdadero sentido de las voces, su natura-leza y calidad, con las phrases o modos de hablar, los proverbios y refranes, y otras cosas convenientes al uso de la lengua.* 6 vols. Madrid: Francisco del Hierro for La Real Academia Española. Facsimile repr. 3 vols. Madrid: Gredos.

Barbeito, Isabel (ed.). 1991. *Cárceles y mujeres en el siglo XVII:* Magdalena de San Gerónimo, *Razón y forma de la Galera*; Teresa Valle de la Cerda, *Proceso inquisitorial de san Plácido.* Biblioteca de Escritoras 21. Madrid: Castalia & Instituto de la Mujer.

Benedict, St, *of Monte Cassino.* 1976. *The Rule of St Benedict.* Tr. Justin McCann. Spiritual Masters. London: Sheed & Ward.

Blecua, José Manuel (ed.). 1945. *Cancionero de 1628: Edición y estudio del Cancionero 250–2 de la Biblioteca Universitaria de Zaragoza.* Anejos de la *Revista de Filología Española* 33. Madrid: CSIC, Patronato 'Menéndez y Pelayo', Instituto 'Antonio de Nebrija'.

Bocángel y Unzueta, Gabriel. 1985. *La lira de las musas* [1637]. Ed. Trevor J. Dadson. Letras Hispánicas 226. Madrid: Cátedra.

Borelius, Aron. 1960. 'En torno a *Los borrachos*', in Gallego y Burín 1960: I. 245–49.

Borges, Jorge Luis. 1974. *Obras completas 1923–1972.* Ed. Carlos V. Frías. Buenos Aires: Emecé.

Boscán, Juan. 1999. *Obra completa.* Ed. Carlos Clavería. Letras Hispánicas 453. Madrid: Cátedra.

Boyd, Stephen (ed.). 2005. *A companion to Cervantes' 'Novelas ejemplares'.* Támesis A 218. Woodbridge: Tamesis.

Brown, Jonathan. 1998. *Painting in Spain 1500–1700.* Pelican History of Art. New Haven & London: Yale University Press.

—— & Carmen Garrido Pérez. 1998. *Velázquez: The technique of genius.* New Haven & London: Yale University Press.

Cacho Casal, Marta. 2007a. '"La memoria en el pincel, la fama en la pluma": Fuentes literarias en el *Libro de retratos* de Francisco Pacheco', *Bulletin Hispanique* (Bordeaux) 109: 47–96.

Cacho Casal, Rodrigo. 2004. 'Difusión y cronología de la poesía burlesca de

Quevedo: Una revisión', *Revista de Literatura* (Madrid) 132: 409–29.

——. 2007b. 'El ingenio del arte: Introducción a la poesía burlesca del Siglo de Oro', *Criticón* (Toulouse) 100 (=*La poesía burlesca del Siglo de Oro: Problemas y nuevas perspectivas*, ed. Alain Bègue & Jesús Ponce Cárdenas): 9–26.

Calderón de la Barca, Pedro. 1636. *Primera parte de comedias*. Madrid: María de Quiñones. Facsimile repr., ed. Don W. Cruickshank & John E. Varey. Farnborough: Gregg International, in association with Támesis Books Ltd.

——. 1981. *El alcalde de Zalamea*. Ed. José María Díez Borque. Clásicos Castalia 82. Madrid: Castalia.

——. 1982. *Entremeses, jácaras y mojigangas*. Ed. Evangelina Rodríguez & Antonio Tordera. Clásicos Castalia 116. Madrid: Castalia.

——. 1985. *El mágico prodigioso*. Ed. Bruce W. Wardropper. Letras Hispánicas 217. Madrid: Cátedra.

Candelas Colodrón, Miguel Ángel. 2004. 'Quevedo y el *Diccionario de autoridades*', in Schwartz 2004: 69–89.

Carbajo Isla, María F. 1987. *La población de la villa de Madrid: Desde finales del siglo XVI hasta mediados del siglo XIX*. Economía y Demografía. Madrid: Siglo XXI de España.

Carr, Dawson W., with Xavier Bray, John H. Elliott, Larry Keith, & Javier Portús. 2006. *Velázquez*. London: National Gallery Company & Yale University Press.

Carrasco, Raphaël. 1994a. 'Lazare sur le trottoir, ou ce que ne dit pas le roman picaresque', in Carrasco 1994b: 91–109.

—— (ed.). 1994b. *La prostitution en Espagne: De l'époque des Rois Catholiques à la IIe République*. Annales Littéraires de l'Université de Besançon 526: Centre de Recherches sur l'Espagne Moderne 2. Paris: Les Belles Lettres.

Carreño, Antonio. 1979. *El romancero lírico de Lope de Vega*. Biblioteca Románica Hispánica: Ensayos y Estudios 285. Madrid: Gredos.

Castillo Solórzano, Alonso de. 1985. *Las harpías en Madrid* [1631]. Ed. Pablo Jauralde Pou. Clásicos Castalia 139. Madrid: Castalia.

Catalán, Diego. 1969. *Siete siglos de romancero: Historia y poesía*. Biblioteca Románica Hispánica II.134. Madrid: Gredos.

——. 1997–98. *Arte poética del romancero oral*. Lingüística y Teoría Literaria. Madrid: Siglo XXI de España.

—— & Álvaro Galmés de Fuentes. 1950. 'La vida de un romance en el espacio y en el tiempo', 2nd edn in Catalán & Galmés 1954: 143–280.

—— & —— (eds). 1954. *Cómo vive un romance: Dos ensayos sobre tradicionalidad*. Anejos de la *Revista de Filología Española* 60. Madrid: CSIC.

Cernuda, Luis. 1993–95. *Obras completas*. Ed. Derek Harris & Luis Maristany. 3 vols. Madrid: Siruela.

Cervantes, Miguel de. 1986. *Novelas ejemplares* [1613]. Ed. Harry Sieber. 2 vols. Letras Hispánicas 105–06. Madrid: Cátedra.

——. 1995. *La Galatea* [1585]. Ed. Francisco López Estrada & María Teresa López García-Bedoy. Letras Hispánicas 389. Madrid: Cátedra.

——. 2005. *Don Quijote de la Mancha: Edición del Instituto Cervantes*

1605–2005. Ed. Francisco Rico, with Joaquín Forradellas. Prologue Fernando Lázaro Carreter. 2 vols. Barcelona: Galaxia Gutenberg, Círculo de Lectores, & Centro para la Edición de los Clásicos Españoles.

Chamorro Fernández, María Inés. 2002. *Tesoro de villanos: Diccionario de germanía, lengua de jacarandina: Rufos, mandiles, galloferos, viltrotonas, zurrapas, carcaveras, murcios, floraineros y otras gentes de la carda*. Barcelona: Herder.

——. 2005. *Léxico del naipe del Siglo de Oro: Juegos, gaiteros, gansos, abrazadores, andarríos, floreos, fullerías, fulleros, guiñones, maullones, modorros, pandilladores, saladores, voltarios y ayudantes en las casas de tablaje*. Estudios Históricos La Olmeda: Colección Mínima Historia. Gijón: Trea.

Cherry, Peter. 1996. 'Artistic training and the Painters' Guild in Seville', in Clarke 1996: 67–75.

Clarke, Michael (ed.). 1996. *Velázquez in Seville*. Edinburgh: National Gallery Scotland.

Close, Anthony J. 2000. *Cervantes and the comic mind of his age*. Cambridge: Cambridge University Press.

Codoñer, Carmen. 1982. 'La ejemplificación de Juvenal en Quevedo', in Concha 1982: 139–51.

Coleman, Robert (ed.). 1977. *Vergil: Eclogues*. Cambridge Greek and Latin Classics. Cambridge: Cambridge University Press.

Concha, Víctor G. de la (ed.). 1982. *Homenaje a Quevedo: Actas de la II Academia Literaria Renacentista, Universidad de Salamanca 10, 11 y 12 de diciembre 1980*. Biblioteca Académica 2. Salamanca: Caja de Ahorros y Monte de Piedad de Salamanca.

Corominas, Joan with José A. Pascual. 1980–91. *Diccionario crítico etimológico castellano e hispánico de la lengua castellana*. 6 vols. Biblioteca Románica Hispánica V. 7. Madrid: Gredos.

Correas, Gonzalo. 1967. *Vocabulario de refranes y frases proverbiales* [1627]. Ed. Louis Combet. Bordeaux: Institut d'Études Ibériques et Ibéroaméricaines de l'Université de Bordeaux.

Cov. = Covarrubias Horozco, Sebastián. 2006 [1611]. *Tesoro de la lengua castellana o española: Edición integral e ilustrada*. Ed. Ignacio Arellano & Rafael Zafra, with Christoph Strosetski & Marc Vitse. Biblioteca Áurea Hispánica 21. Madrid: Universidad de Navarra, Iberomericana-Vervuert, Real Academia Española, & Centro para la Edición de los Clásicos Españoles.

Crosby, James O. (ed.). 2005. *Nuevas cartas de la última prisión de Quevedo*. Támesis B 47. Woodbridge: Tamesis.

Curtius, Ernst R. 1953. *European literature and the Latin Middle Ages*. Tr. Willard R. Trask. London: Routledge & Kegan Paul.

Deleito y Piñuela, José. 1942. *Sólo Madrid es Corte: La capital de dos mundos bajo Felipe IV, el recinto de la villa, la fisonomía urbana, las márgenes del Manzanares, organización municipal, servicios públicos, la vida madrileña*. Prologue Gabriel Maura Gamazo. Madrid: Espasa-Calpe.

——. 2005. *La mala vida en la España de Felipe IV*. Prologue Julián San Valero Aparisi. Libro de Bolsillo: Humanidades, Historia H 4235. Madrid:

Alianza.

Delicado, Francisco. 1994. *La Lozana andaluza* [1528]. Ed. Claude Allaigre. 2nd edn. Letras Hispánicas 212. Madrid: Cátedra.

Devoto, Daniel. 1972. *Introducción al estudio de Don Juan Manuel y en particular de 'El Conde Lucanor': Una bibliografía*. Madrid: Castalia.

Díaz, Lorenzo. 1992. *Madrid: Tabernas, botillerías y cafés, 1476–1991*. Madrid: Espasa-Calpe.

Díaz Roig, Mercedes (ed.). 1985. *El romancero viejo*. Letras Hispánicas 52. Madrid: Cátedra.

Don Juan Manuel. 1969. *El conde Luncanor* [1335]. Ed. José Manuel Blecua. Clásicos Castalia 9. Madrid: Castalia.

Dopico Black, Georgina. 2001. 'Public bodies, private parts: The virgins and Magdalens of Magdalena de San Gerónimo', *Journal of Spanish Cultural Studies* (Abingdon) 2/i: 81–96.

Dryden, John (tr.). 1944. *The works of Virgil, translated by John Dryden*. The World's Classics 37. London: Humphrey Milford for Oxford University Press, 1944.

Duque de Estrada, Diego. 1982. *Comentarios del desengaño de sí mismo: Vida del mismo autor* [1607?–45]. Ed. Henry Ettinghausen. Clásicos Castalia 109. Madrid: Castalia.

Durán, Agustín. 1859–61. *Romancero general, o Colección de romances castellanos anterior al siglo XVIII*. 2 vols. Biblioteca de Autores Españoles 10, 16. Madrid: M. de Ribadeneira.

Edwards, Gwynne. 1972. 'On Góngora's "Angélica y Medoro"', in Shergold 1972: 73–94.

Eliot, Simon, Andrew Nash, & Ian Willison (eds). 2007. *Literary cultures and the material book*. The British Library Studies in the History of the Book. London: The British Library.

Elliott, John H. 1986. *The Count-Duke of Olivares: The statesman in an age of decline*. New Haven CT & London: Yale University Press.

——. 1989a. 'Quevedo and the Count-Duke of Olivares', in Elliott 1989b: 189–209.

——. 1989b. *Spain and its world 1500–1700*. New Haven CT: Yale University Press.

——. 2006. 'Appearance and reality in the Spain of Velázquez', in Carr *et al.* 2006: 10–23.

Eslava Galán, Juan. 1991. *Verdugos y torturadores*. Historia de la España Sorprendente. Madrid: Temas de Hoy.

Fernández de Avellaneda, Alonso. 1971. *El ingenioso hidalgo don Quijote de la Mancha, que contiene su tercera salida y es la quinta parte de sus aventuras* [1614]. Ed. Fernando García Salinero. Clásicos Castalia 41. Madrid: Castalia.

Forster, Leonard. 1969. *The icy fire: Five studies in European Petrarchism*. Cambridge: Cambridge University Press.

Frenk, Margit (ed.). 2004. *Lírica española de tipo popular*. Letras Hispánicas 60. 13th edn. Madrid: Cátedra.

Fucilla, Joseph G. 1960. *Estudios sobre el petrarquismo en España*. Anejos de la *Revista de Filología Española* 72. Madrid: CSIC, Instituto 'Miguel de Cervantes'.

Gallego y Burín, Antonio (ed.). 1960. *Varia Velazqueña: Homenaje a Veláz-quez en el III centenario de su muerte*. 2 vols. Madrid: Ministerio de Educación Nacional, Dirección General de Bellas Artes.

García, Carlos. 1977. *La desordenada codicia de los bienes agenos* [1619]. Ed. Giulio Massano. Studia Humanitatis. Madrid: José Porrúa Turanzas.

García Valdés, Celsa Carmen (ed.). 2005. *Entremesistas y entremeses barrocos*. Letras Hispánicas 573. Madrid: Cátedra.

Garcilaso de la Vega. 1981. *Obras completas, con comentario*. Ed. Elias L. Rivers. Madrid: Castalia.

——. 1995. *Obra poética y textos en prosa*. Ed. Bienvenido Morros Mestres. Biblioteca Clásica 27. Barcelona: Crítica.

Gardner, Helen. 1959. *The business of criticism*. Oxford: Oxford University Press.

Garvin, Mario. 2007. *Scripta manent: Hacia una edición crítica del romancero impreso (siglo XVI)*. Forum Iberoamericanum: Acta Coloniensia 4. Frankfurt am Main: Vervuert & Madrid: Iberoamericana.

Góngora y Argote, Luis de. 1976. *Sonetos completos*. Ed. Biruté Ciplijauskaité. Clásicos Castalia 1. Madrid: Castalia.

——. 1980. *Letrillas*. Ed. Robert Jammes. Clásicos Castalia 101. Madrid: Castalia.

——. 1991. *Obras de Don Luis de Góngora (manuscrito Chacón): Homenaje a Dámaso Alonso*. Introduction Dámaso Alonso. Prologue Pere Gimferrer. 3 vols. Biblioteca de los Clásicos 3. Madrid: Real Academia Española & Ronda: Caja de Ahorros de Ronda.

——. 1998. *Romances*. Ed. Antonio Carreira Vélez. 4 vols. Nueva Caja Negra 25: Romances 1–4. Barcelona: Quaderns Crema.

——. 2000a. *Romances*. Ed. Antonio Carreño. Letras Hispánicas 160. 5th edn. Madrid: Cátedra.

——. 2000b. *Obras completas*. Ed. Antonio Carreira Vélez. 2 vols. Biblioteca Castro. Madrid: Fundación José Antonio de Castro.

González Palencia, Ángel (ed.). 1932. *La Junta de Reformación: Documentos procedentes del Archivo Histórico Nacional y del General de Simancas*. Colección de Documentos Inéditos para la Historia de España y de sus Indias 5. Madrid & Valladolid: Archivo Histórico Español.

—— (ed.). 1947. *Romancero general (1600, 1604, 1605)*. 2 vols. Clásicos Españoles 3–4. Madrid: CSIC.

Gordon, Alan M. & Evelyn Rugg (eds). 1980. *Actas del sexto congreso internacional de hispanistas celebrado en Toronto del 22 al 26 de agosto de 1977*. Toronto: Department of Spanish and Portuguese, University of Toronto, for La Asociación Internacional de Hispanistas.

Gracián, Baltasar SJ. 1969. *Arte y agudeza del ingenio* [1642]. 2 vols. Ed. Evaristo Correa Calderón. Clásicos Castalia 14–15. Madrid: Castalia.

——. 1984. *El criticón* [1651]. Ed. Santos Alonso. Letras Hispánicas 122. Madrid: Cátedra.

Grant, Helen F. 1973. 'The world upside down', in Jones 1973: 103–35.

Graves, Robert (ed.). 1957. *English and Scottish ballads*. Poetry Bookshelf. London: Heinemann.

Griffin, Clive. 2007. 'Literary consequences of the peripheral nature of Spanish printing in the sixteenth century', in Eliot *et al.* 2007: 207–14.

Guevara, Antonio de OSF. 1984. *Menosprecio de corte y alabanza de aldea. Arte de marear* [1539]. Ed. Asunción Rallo Gruss. Letras Hispánicas 213. Madrid: Cátedra.

Halperin, David M. 1983. *Before pastoral: Theocritus and the ancient tradition of bucolic poetry*. New Haven & London: Yale University Press.

Harris, Enriqueta. 1982. *Velázquez*. Oxford: Phaidon.

Hayes, Francis C. 1939. 'The use of proverbs as titles and motives in the *Siglo de Oro* drama: Tirso de Molina', *Hispanic Review* (Philadelphia PA) 7: 310–23.

Hernández Alonso, César & Beatriz Sanz Alonso. 1999. *Germanía y sociedad en los Siglos de Oro: La cárcel de Sevilla*. Serie Lingüística y Filología 38. Valladolid : Universidad de Valladolid.

—— & ——. 2002. *Diccionario de germanía*. Biblioteca Románica Hispánica V. 24. Madrid: Gredos.

Hollings, Michael. 1977. *Living priesthood*. Great Wakering: Mayhew-McCrimmon.

Horace. 1733. *Oeuvres d'Horace en latin et en françois, avec des remarques critiques et historiques*. Ed. André Dacier. 5th edn. 4 vols. Hamburg & London: Vanderhoeck.

——. 1929. *Satires, Epistles, Ars Poetica*. Tr. H. Rushton Fairclough. The Loeb Classical Library. Cambridge MA: Harvard University Press & London: Heinemann.

Hsu, Carmen Y. 2002. *Courtesans in the literature of the Spanish Golden Age*. Prologue Francisco Márquez Villanueva. Teatro del Siglo de Oro: Estudios de Literatura 71. Kassel: Reichenberger.

Huarte Echenique, Amalio. 1930. 'El Mesón del Toro', *Revista de la Biblioteca, Archivo y Museo* (Madrid) 7/xxv: 81–83.

Iffland, James. 1978–82. *Quevedo and the grotesque*. 2 vols. Támesis A 69, A 92. London: Tamesis Books Ltd.

Ignacio de Loyola, San. 1963. *Obras completas*. Ed. Ignacio Iparraguirre SJ. Madrid: Biblioteca de Autores Cristianos.

Infantes, Víctor (ed.). 1982. *Dança general de la Muerte (siglo XV–1520)*. Visor Literario 127. Madrid: Visor.

Jammes, Robert. 1967. *Études sur l'oeuvre poétique de Don Luis de Góngora y Argote*. Bibliothèque de l'École des Hautes Études Hispaniques 40. Bordeaux: Institut d'Études Ibériques et Ibéro-Américaines de l'Université de Bordeaux.

Jauralde Pou, Pablo (ed.). 1974. *Cancionero de obras de burlas provocantes a risa, basado en la edición original, Valencia 1519, con las composiciones suprimidas del Cancionero general de Hernando del Castillo, y las adiciones y advertencias de Luis de Usoz y Río, Londres 1841–43*. Prologue Juan Alfredo Bellón Cazabán. Colección Manifiesto 3: Serie Clásicos 1. Madrid: Akal.

——. 1998a. *Francisco de Quevedo (1580–1645)*. Prologue Alonso Zamora Vicente. Nueva Biblioteca de Erudición y Crítica 15. Madrid: Castalia.

——. 1998b. 'El Madrid de Quevedo', *Edad de Oro* (Madrid) 17: 59–95.

Jones, Royston O. 1966. *Poems of Gongora*. Cambridge: Cambridge University Press.

—— (ed.). 1973. *Studies in Spanish literature of the Golden Age presented to Edward M. Wilson*. Támesis A 30. London: Tamesis Books Ltd.

Joseph, Bertram L. 1971. *Shakespeare's Eden: The Commonwealth of England, 1588–1629*. History and Literature. London: Blandford Press.

Jump, John D. 1972. *Burlesque*. Critical Idiom 22. London: Methuen.

Juvenal. 2004. *Juvenal and Persius*. Ed. & tr. Susanna Morton Braund. Loeb Classical Library. Cambridge MA & London: Harvard University Press.

Lara Garrido, José. 1983. 'El motivo de las ruinas en la poesía española de los siglos XVI y XVII (funciones de un paradigma nacional: Sagunto)', *Analecta Malacitana* (Málaga) 6/ii: 223–77.

Lee, Rensselaer W. 1977. *Names on trees: Ariosto into art*. Princeton Essays on the Arts 3. Princeton NJ: Princeton University Press.

León, *Fray* Luis de OSA. 1998. *Poesías completas: Obras propias en castellano y latín y traducciones e imitaciones latinas, griegas, bíblico-hebreas y romances*. Ed. Cristóbal Cuevas García. Nueva Biblioteca de Erudición y Crítica 14. Madrid: Castalia.

Liñán y Verdugo, Antonio (attr.). 1980. *Guía y avisos de forasteros que vienen a la Corte* [1620]. Ed. Edisons Simons. Biblioteca de la Literatura y el Pensamiento Hispánicos H 41. Madrid: Editora Nacional.

Lleó Cañal, Vicente. 1996. 'The cultivated elite of Velázquez's Seville', in Clarke 1996: 23–27.

López Grigera, Luisa. 1975. 'La silva *El pincel* de Quevedo', in Romanós *et al.* 1975: 221–42.

López de Mendoza, Íñigo, *Marqués de Santillana*. 2003. *Poesías completas*. Ed. Maxim P.A.M. Kerkhof & Ángel Gómez Moreno. Clásicos Castalia 270. Madrid: Castalia.

López-Rey, José. 1963. *Velázquez: A catalogue raisonné of his oeuvre, with an introductory study*. London: Faber & Faber.

Luna, Juan de. 1988. *Segunda parte de la vida de Lazarillo de Tormes, sacadas de la corónicas antiguas de Toledo* [1555]. Ed. Pedro M. Piñero. Letras Hispánicas 282. Madrid: Cátedra.

Lyle, Emily B. (ed.). 1976. *Ballad studies*. The Folklore Society Mistletoe Studies. Totowa NJ: Rowan & Littlefield.

Macintyre, Alasdair C. 1967. *A short history of ethics: A history of moral philosophy from the Homeric age to the twentieth century*. London: Routledge & Kegan Paul.

Manero Sorolla, María Pilar. 1987. *Introducción al estudio del petrarquismo en España*. Estudios de Literatura Española y Comparada. Barcelona: Promociones y Publicaciones Universitarias.

Maravall, José Antonio. 1986. *Culture of the Baroque: Analysis of a historical structure*. Tr. Terry Cochran. Foreword Wlad Godzich & Nicholas Spadaccini. Theory and History of Literature 25. Manchester: Manchester University Press.

Menéndez Pidal, Ramón. 1920. 'Sobre geografía folklórica: Ensayo de un método', *Revista de Filología Española* (Madrid) 7: 229–338. 2nd edn in Catalán & Galmés (1954: 1–141) and in Menéndez Pidal (1973: 217–323).

——. 1940a. 'Lope de Vega, *El arte nuevo* y la nueva autobiografía:Virtud y nobleza, arte y naturaleza', in Menéndez Pidal 1940b: 69–143.

——. 1940b. *De Cervantes y Lope de Vega*. Colección Austral 120. 6th edn. Madrid: Espasa-Calpe.

——. 1953. *Romancero hispánico (hispano-portugués, americano y sefardí): Teoría e historia*. 2 vols. Madrid: Espasa-Calpe.

—— (ed.). 1954–56. *Cantar de Mio Cid*. 3rd edn. 3 vols. Obras Completas de R. Menéndez Pidal III–V. Madrid: Espasa-Calpe.

—— (ed.). 1963. *Flor nueva de romances viejos*. Colección Austral 100. 14th edn. Buenos Aires: Espasa-Calpe.

——. 1973. *Estudios sobre el romancero*. Ed. Diego Catalán. Obras Completas de R. Menéndez Pidal XI. Madrid: Espasa-Calpe.

Michael, Ian D.L. 2000. '*Celestina* and the Great Pox', in Michael & Pattison 2000: 103–38.

——. 2005. 'Constructing and reconstructing the canon: The problem of medieval Iberian literature', in Taylor & West 2005: 252–71.

—— & David G. Pattison (eds). 2000. *Context, meaning, and reception of 'Celestina': A fifth centenary symposium*. Glasgow: Carfax, Taylor & Francis & University of Glasgow.

Milton, John. 1971. *Complete Shorter Poems*. Ed. John Carey. London: Longman.

Molina Molina, Ángel Luis. 1998. *Mujeres públicas, mujeres secretas: La prostitución y su mundo (siglos XIII–XVII)*. Colección Historia y Patrimonio 2. Murcia: Editorial KR.

Moncada, Sancho de. 1974. *Restauración política de España* [1619]. Ed. Jean Vilar. Clásicos del Pensamiento Económico Español 1. Madrid: Instituto de Estudios Fiscales & Ministerio de Hacienda.

Montemayor, Jorge de. 1996. *Los siete libros de la Diana* [1559?]. Ed. Julián Arribas. Támesis B 41. London: Tamesis.

Morel d'Arleux, Antonia. 1994. 'Regimientos y cofradías del *pecado mortal* en los siglos XVI y XVII', in Carrasco 1994b: 111–35.

Nieto Ballester, Emilio. 2002. '*Maroto, Manotera, Salmerón*: Aportaciones de toponimia española a propósito de la expresión de loma', *Revista de Filología Española* (Madrid) 82: 295–317.

Noble Wood, Oliver J. 2007. 'Mars recontextualized in the Golden Age of Spain: Psychological and aesthetic readings of Velázquez's *Marte*', in Torres 2007: 139–55.

Nygard, Holder Olof. 1976. 'Popular ballad and medieval romance', in Lyle 1976: 1–19.

O'Donoghue, Bernard. 1982. *The Courtly Love tradition*. Literature in Context. Manchester: Manchester University Press.

Orso, Steven N. 1993. *Velázquez, Los Borrachos, and painting at the Court of Philip IV*. Cambridge: Cambridge University Press.

Ovid. 1595. *Las transformaciones de Ovidio en lengua española*. Tr. Jorge de Bustamante. Illustrations Virgil Solis. Antwerp: Pedro Bellero.

——. 1984. *Metamorphoses*. Tr. Frank Justus Miller. 2 vols. Loeb Classical Library 42–43. 2nd edn. Cambridge MA: Harvard University Press.

Pacheco, Francisco. 1990. *Arte de la pintura* [1649]. Ed. Bonaventura Bassegoda i Hugas. Arte: Grandes Temas. Madrid: Cátedra.

Pavur, Claude SJ (ed. & tr.). 2005. *The Ratio Studiorum: The official plan for Jesuit education.* St Louis MO: Institute of Jesuit Sources.

Pedraza Jiménez, Felipe B. 2003. *El universo poético de Lope de Vega.* Arcadia de las Letras 16. Madrid: Laberinto.

Pellicer de Tovar, José. 2002–03. *Avisos: 17 de mayo de 1639–29 de noviembre de 1644.* Ed. Jean-Claude Chevalier & Lucien Clare. 2 vols. Paris: Éditions Hispaniques.

Petrarca, Francesco. 1964. *Canzionere.* Ed. Gianfranco Contini & Daniele Ponchiroli. Nouva Universale Einaudi 41. Turin: Einaudi.

Piñero, Pedro M. & Virtudes Atero (eds). 1987. *Romancero de la tradición moderna.* Seville: Fundación Machado & Texto e Imagen.

Plata Parga, Fernando. 1997. *Ocho poemas satíricos de Quevedo: Estudios bibliográfico y textual, edición crítica y anotación filológica.* Anejos de *La Perinola, Revista de Investigación Quevediana* 1. Pamplona: Ediciones Universidad de Navarra.

Plautus. 1969. *Plautus.* Tr. Paul Nixon [1916–38]. 5 vols. Loeb Classical Library. London: William Heineman Ltd & Cambridge MA: Harvard University Press.

Pliny the Elder. 1936–62. *Natural History.* Tr. H. Rackham *et al.* 10 vols. Loeb Classical Library. London: William Heineman Ltd & Cambridge MA: Harvard University Press.

Ponce Cárdenas, Jesús. 2007. 'De burlas y enfermedades barrocas: La sífilis en la obra poética de Anastasio Pantaleón de Ribera y Miguel Colodrero de Villalobos', *Criticón* (Toulouse) 100 (= *La poesía burlesca del Siglo de Oro: Problemas y nuevas perspectivas*, ed. Alain Bègue & Jesús Ponce Cárdenas): 115–42.

Porteman, Karel. 2000. 'The use of the visual in Classical Jesuit teaching and education', *Paedagogica Historica: International Journal of the History of Education* (Ghent) ns 36: 179–96.

Pring-Mill, Robert D.F. 1968. 'Some techniques of representation in the *Sueños* and the *Criticón*', *Bulletin of Hispanic Studies* (Liverpool) 45: 270–84.

Pym, Richard J. (ed.). 2006. *Rhetoric and reality in Early Modern Spain.* Támesis A 227. London: Tamesis.

Quevedo y Villegas, Francisco de. 1699. *Obras de don Francisco de Quevedo y Villegas, Señor de la Villa de Torre de Juan-Abad.* Ed. Pedro Aldrete Quevedo y Villegas. 3 vols. Antwerp: Henri & Cornelis Verdussen.

——. 1876–77. *Obras de don Francisco de Quevedo y Villegas.* Ed. Aureliano Fernández-Guerra y Orbe. 3 vols. Biblioteca de Autores Españoles 23, 48, 69. Madrid: M. Rivadeneyra.

——. 1932. *Obras completas.* Ed. Luis Astrana Marín. 2 vols. Madrid: Aguilar.

——. 1961. *Obras completas.* Ed. Felicidad Buendía. 5th edn. 2 vols. Madrid: Aguilar.

——. 1969a. *An anthology of Quevedo's poetry.* Ed. Reece M. Price. Spanish Texts. Manchester: Manchester University Press.

——. 1969b. *La cuna y la sepultura para el conocimiento propio y desengaño de las cosas agenas* [1634]. Ed. Luisa López Grigera. Anejos del *Boletín de la Real Academia Española* 20. Madrid: Real Academia Española.

——. 1969–81. *Obra poética.* Ed. José Manuel Blecua. 4 vols. Madrid: Castalia.

——. 1972. *Sueños y discursos de verdades descubridoras de abusos, vicios y engaños de todos los oficios y estados del mundo* [1631]. Ed. Felipe C.R. Maldonado. Clásicos Castalia 50. Madrid: Castalia.

——. 1981. *Poesía varia.* Ed. James O. Crosby. Letras Hispánicas 134. Madrid: Cátedra.

——. 1987. *La hora de todos y la Fortuna con seso* [1650]. Ed. Jean Bourg, Pierre Dupont, & Pierre Geneste. Letras Hispánicas 276. Madrid: Cátedra.

——. 1990. *Historia de la vida del Buscón* [1626]. Ed. Pablo Jauralde Pou. Clásicos Castalia 177. Madrid: Castalia.

——. 1991. *Los sueños. Versiones impresas: Sueños y discursos. Juguetes de la niñez. Desvelos soñolientos.* Ed. Ignacio Arellano Ayuso. Letras Hispánicas 335. Madrid: Cátedra.

——. 1993. *Sueños y discursos.* Ed. James O. Crosby. 2 vols. Nueva Biblioteca de Erudición y Crítica 6. Madrid: Castalia.

——. 1998a. *El chitón de las tarabillas: Obra del Licenciado Todo lo Sabe* [1630]. Ed. Manuel Urí Martín. Clásicos Castalia 243. Madrid: Castalia.

——. 1998b. *Un Heráclito cristiano, Canta sola a Lisi, y otros poemas.* Ed. Lía Schwartz Lerner & Ignacio Arellano. Biblioteca Clásica Crítica 62. Barcelona: Crítica.

——. 2003–. *Obras completas en prosa.* Ed. Alfonso Rey *et al.* 3 vols (to date). Nueva Biblioteca de Erudición y Crítica 24. Madrid: Castalia.

Rawlings, Helen. 2006. '*Arbitrismo* and the early seventeenth-century Spanish Church: The theory and practice of anti-clericalist philosophy', in Pym 2006: 26–40.

Redondo, Augustin (ed.). 1979. *L'humanisme dans les lettres espagnoles: XIXe Colloque International d'Études Humanistes, Tours, 5–17 juillet 1976. De Pétrarque à Descartes.* Paris: Librarie Philosophique J. Vrin.

——. 1983. 'Del personaje de Aldonza Lorenzo al de Dulcinea del Toboso: Algunos aspectos de la invención cervantina', *Anales Cervantinos* (Madrid) 21: 9–22. Repr. in Redondo 1997: 231–49.

——. 1997. *Otra manera de leer el Quijote: Historia, tradiciones culturales y literatura.* Madrid: Castalia.

Ringrose, David R. 1983. *Madrid and the Spanish economy, 1560–1850.* Berkeley CA: University of California Press.

Rioyo, Javier. 2003. *La vida golfa: Historia de las casas de lenocinio, holganza y malvivir.* 2nd edn. Madrid: Aguilar.

Rivers, Isabel. 1994. *Classical and Christian ideas in English Renaissance poetry: A students' guide.* 2nd edn. London & New York: Routledge.

Rodríguez, Evangelina & Antonio Tordera. 1983. *Calderón y la obra corta dramática del siglo XVII.* Támesis A 91. London: Tamesis Books Ltd.

Rodríguez-Moñino, Antonio R. 1968. *Construcción crítica y realidad histórica en la poesía española de los siglos XVI y XVII.* 2nd edn. Madrid: Castalia.

Rojas, Fernando de. 1991. *Celestina: Comedia o tragicomedia de Calisto y Melibea.* Ed. Peter Russell. Clásicos Castalia 191. 2nd edn. Madrid: Castalia.

Romancero general. 1604. *Romancero general en que se contienen todos los romances que andan impressos, ahora nuevamente añadido y enmendado*. Madrid: Juan de la Cuesta for Francisco López.

Romanós, Melchora *et al.* (eds). 1975. *Homenaje al Instituto de Filología y Literaturas Hispánicas 'Dr. Amado Alonso' en su cincuentenario 1923–1973*. Buenos Aires: Universidad de Buenos Aires.

Ruiz, Juan, *Arcipreste de Hita*. 1989. *Libro de buen amor*. Ed. Gerald B. Gybbon-Monypenny. Clásicos Castalia 161. Madrid: Castalia.

Ruiz de Alarcón, Juan. 1999. *La verdad sospechosa*. Ed. José Montero Reguera. Clásicos Castalia 250. Madrid: Castalia.

Ruiz Pérez, Pedro & Klaus Wagner (eds). 2001. *La cultura en Andalucía: Vida, memoria y escritura en torno a 1600*. Estepa: Ayuntamiento de Estepa.

Russell, Peter E. 1969. '*Don Quixote* as a funny book', *Modern Language Review* (London) 64: 312–25. Repr., tr. Alejandro Pérez, as 'Don Quijote y la risa a carcajadas', in Russell 1978: 407–40.

——. 1978. *Temas de 'La Celestina' y otros estudios*. Letras e Ideas. Barcelona: Ariel.

Saavedra Fajardo, Diego de. 1967. *República literaria* [1655]. Ed. John Dowling. Biblioteca Anaya 79. Salamanca: Anaya.

Salas Barbadillo, Alonso J. de. 1983. *La hija de Celestina y La ingeniosa Elena* [1619]. Ed. José Fradejas Lebrero. Clásicos Madrileños 2. Madrid: Instituto de Estudios Madrileños.

Salomon, Noël. 1965. *Recherches sur le thème paysan dans la 'comedia' au temps de Lope de Vega*. Bibliothèque de l'École des Hautes Études Hispaniques 31. Bordeaux: Institut d'Études Ibériques et Ibéro-Américaines de l'Université de Bordeaux.

Sánchez Jiménez, Antonio. 2006. *Lope pintado por sí mismo: Mito e imagen del autor en la poesía de Lope de Vega Carpio*. Támesis A 229. Woodbridge: Tamesis.

Schama, Simon. 1999. *Rembrandt's eyes*. London: Allen Lane.

Schwartz Lerner, Lía. 2002. 'Velázquez and two poets of the Baroque: Luis de Góngora and Francisco de Quevedo', in Stratton-Pruitt 2002: 130–48, 217–23.

—— (ed.). 2004. *Studies in honor of James O. Crosby*. Hispanic Monographs: Homenajes 23. Newark DE: Juan de la Cuesta.

Screech, Michael A. 1997. *Laughter at the foot of the Cross*. London: Allen Lane.

Shergold, Norman D. 1967. *A history of the Spanish stage from medieval times until the end of the seventeenth century*. Oxford: Clarendon.

—— (ed.). 1972. *Studies of the Spanish and Portuguese ballad*. Támesis A 26. London: Tamesis.

Sliwa, Krzysztof (ed.). 2005. *Cartas, documentos y escrituras de Francisco Gómez de Quevedo y Villegas (1580–1645), Caballero de la Orden de Santiago, Señor de la Torre de Juan Abad, y sus parientes*. Anejos de *La Perinola, Revista de Investigación Quevediana* 16. Pamplona: Ediciones Universidad de Navarra.

Smith, Colin C. 1973. 'Serranas de Cuenca', in Jones 1973: 283–95.

——— (ed.). 1996. *Spanish ballads*. 2nd edn. London: Bristol Classical Press.

Smith, Paul J. 1991. *Quevedo, 'El Buscón'*. Critical Guides to Spanish Texts 51. London: Grant & Cutler, in association with Tamesis Books.

Sobejano, Gonzalo (ed.). 1978. *Francisco de Quevedo*. El Escritor y la Crítica: Persiles 108. Madrid: Taurus.

Stanyhurst, Richard (ed. & tr.). 1583. *The first foure bookes of Virgil's Aeneis, translated into Engl. heroicall verse by R. Stanyhurst. With other poëticll deuises thereto annexed*. London: H. Bynneman.

Stratton-Pruitt, Suzanne L. (ed.). 2002. *The Cambridge companion to Velázquez*. Cambridge: Cambridge University Press.

Suárez de Figueroa, Cristóbal. 1621. *Varias noticias importantes a la humana comunicación*. Madrid: Thomas Junte.

Sumption, Jonathan. 1975. *Pilgrimage: An image of medieval religion*. London: Faber.

Tato Puigcerver, José J. 2000–01. 'Una nota sobre Quevedo, Copérnico y Galileo', *Espéculo: Revista de Estudios Literarios* 16 [digital journal at <http://www.ucm.es/info/especulo>].

Taylor, Barry & Geoffrey West (eds). 2005. *Historicist essays on Hispano-medieval narrative in memory of Roger M. Walker*. Publications of the Modern Humanities Research Association 16. Leeds: Maney.

Tellechea, José Ignacio. 1979. 'Bible et théologie en *langue vulgaire*: Discussion à propos du *Cathéchisme* de Carranza', in Redondo 1979: 219–31.

Terry, Arthur (ed.). 1965–68. *An anthology of Spanish poetry, 1500–1700*. 2 vols. Commonwealth and International Library. Oxford: Pergamon.

———. 1993. *Seventeenth-century Spanish poetry: The power of artifice*. Cambridge: Cambridge University Press.

Theocritus. 1579. *Idyllia & Epigrammata*. Geneva: H. Stephanus II.

———. 1604. *Theocriti, Moschi, Bionis, Simmii quae extant*. Heidelberg: H. Commelianus.

———. 2002. *Idylls*. Tr. Anthony Verity. Ed. Richard Hunter. Oxford: Oxford University Press.

Thomas Aquinas, St. 1961–65. *Summa theologica*. 5 vols. BAC 77, 80, 81, 83, 87. Madrid: Biblioteca de Autores Cristianos.

Thompson, Colin P. 2005. '*Eutrapelia* and exemplarity in the *Novelas ejemplares*', in Boyd 2005: 261–82.

Thompson, Peter E. 2006. *The triumphant Juan Rana: A gay actor in the Spanish Golden Age*. Toronto: University of Toronto.

Torres, Isabel (ed.). 2007. *Rewriting classical mythology in the Hispanic Baroque*. Támesis A 233. Woodbridge: Tamesis Books Ltd.

Trueblood, Alan S. 1974. *Experience and artistic expression in Lope de Vega: The making of 'La Dorotea'*. Cambridge MA: Harvard University Press.

Truman, Ronald W. 1999. *Spanish treatises on government, society, and religion in the time of Philip II: The 'De regimine principum' and associated traditions*. Brill's Studies in Intellectual History 95. Leiden: Brill.

Vaíllo, Carlos. 1982. 'El mundo al revés en la poesía satírica de Quevedo', *Cuadernos Hispanoamericanos* (Madrid) 127/ccclxxx: 364–93.

Varga, Suzanne. 2002. *Lope de Vega*. Paris: Fayard.

Vega Carpio, Lope Félix de. 1872a. 'Introducción a la justa poética de San

Isidro en las fiestas de su beatificación' [1621], in Vega 1872b: 144–47.

——. 1872b. *Colección escogida de obras no dramáticas de Fray Lope Félix de Vega Carpio*. Ed. Cayetano Rosell. Biblioteca de Autores Españoles 38. Madrid: Rivadeneyra.

——. 1925–26. *Poesías líricas*. Ed. José F. Montesinos. 2 vols. Clásicos Castellanos 68, 75. Madrid: La Lectura.

——. 1969. *Obras poéticas: Rimas, Rimas sacras, La Filomena, La Circe, Rimas humanas y divinas del licenciado Tomé de Burguillos*. Ed. José Manuel Blecua. Clásicos Planeta. Barcelona: Planeta.

——. 1982. *Lírica*. Ed. José Manuel Blecua. Clásicos Castalia 104. Madrid: Castalia.

——. 1983. *La gatomaquia* [1634]. Ed. Celina Sabor de Cortázar. Clásicos Castalia 131. Madrid: Castalia.

——. 1984. *Fuente Ovejuna* [1612–14]. Ed. Juan María Marín. Letras Hispánicas 137. 5th edn. Madrid: Cátedra.

——. 2000. *El acero de Madrid* [1607–09]. Ed. Stefano Arata. Clásicos Castalia 256. Madrid: Castalia.

Vilar, Jean. 1975. 'Judas selon Quevedo; *Despensero, ministro, arbitrista*', in Aubrun 1975: II. 385–97. Revised as Vilar 1978.

——. 1978. 'Judás según Quevedo (un tema para una biografía)', in Sobejano 1978: 106–19. Revised version of Vilar 1975. Tr. Gonzalo Sobejano.

Virgil. 1999. *Eclogues, Georgics, Aeneid 1–6*. Tr. H. Rushton Fairclough & G.P. Goold. Loeb Classical Library 63. Cambridge MA: Harvard University Press.

Vranich, Stanko B. 1980. 'La evolución de la poesía de las ruinas en la literatura española de los siglos XVI y XVII', in Gordon & Rugg 1980: 765–67.

Wagner, Klaus. 2001. 'Viajeros por Andalucía entre dos siglos', in Ruiz Pérez & Wagner 2001: 33–47.

Whinnom, Keith. 1967. *Spanish literary historiography: Three forms of distortion*. Exeter: University of Exeter.

White, Terence H. 1984. *The book of beasts, being a translation from a Latin bestiary of the twelfth century*. Sovereign. Gloucester: Alan Sutton.

Wilson, Edward M. 1953. 'On Góngora's *Angélica y Medoro*', *Bulletin of Hispanic Studies* (Liverpool) 30: 85–94.

Wittkower, Rudolf & Irma Blumenthal Jaffe (eds). 1972. *Baroque art: The Jesuit contribution*. New York: Fordham University Press.

Wright, Roger M. 1991. *Spanish ballads*. Critical Guides to Spanish Texts 52. London: Grant & Cutler Ltd, in association with Tamesis Books.

——. 1994. *Early Ibero-romance: Twenty-one studies on language and texts from the Iberian Peninsula between the Roman Empire and the thirteenth century*. Juan de la Cuesta Hispanic Monographs: Estudios Lingüísticos 5. Newark DE: Juan de la Cuesta.

Yates, Frances. 1966. *The art of memory*. London: Routledge & Kegan Paul.

Zabaleta, Juan de. 1983. *El día de fiesta por la mañana y por la tarde* [1654–60]. Ed. Cristóbal Cuevas García. Clásicos Castalia 130. Madrid: Castalia.

Zamora Vicente, Vicente (ed.). 1974–76. *Novela picaresca española*. 3 vols. Clásicos Hispánicos Noguer. Barcelona: Noguer.

INDEX OF WORDS AND PHRASES

INDEX OF FIRST LINES

INDEX OF POEM TITLES

INDEX

An asterisk (*) marks a cross-reference to another entry. The following abbreviations are used:

¹ (²)	1st (2nd) half of	(g)fa.	(grand)father of
auth.	author of	fl.	flourished
(a)bp	(arch)bishop of	k.	king of
b.	born (in)	ma.	married
bro.	brother of	(g)mo.	(grand)mother of
c.	circa	prov.	province of
comm.	commentator (on)	pseud.	pseudonym of
d.	died (in)	r.	reigned
(g)da.	(grand-)daughter of	(g)s.	(grand)son of, *saeculum*
ed.	editor, edition	tr.	translator (of)